T0386113

CALLIMACHUS

II

LCL 129

CALLIMACHUS

HECALE · HYMNS
EPIGRAMS

EDITED AND TRANSLATED BY
DEE L. CLAYMAN

HARVARD UNIVERSITY PRESS
CAMBRIDGE, MASSACHUSETTS
LONDON, ENGLAND
2022

Library of Congress Control Number 2022904856
CIP data available from the Library of Congress

ISBN 978-0-674-99733-2

*Composed in ZephGreek and ZephText by
Technologies 'N Typography, Merrimac, Massachusetts.
Printed on acid-free paper and bound by
Maple Press, York, Pennsylvania*

CONTENTS

HECALE

INTRODUCTION

INTRODUCTION TO THE *HECALE*

The *Hecale* is extant only in fragments, but its plot is summarized in the *Diegeseis* (*Dieg.* 10.18–11.7): Theseus arrived unexpectedly at the home of his father, Aegeus, king of Athens. His stepmother, Medea, tried to poison him, but he escaped from his father's house and set out to overcome a monstrous bull that was ravaging the countryside around Marathon. When a torrential rainstorm broke out, he sought refuge in the home of an impoverished old woman named Hecale, who received him hospitably. The next morning he dispatched the bull, then returned to find that she had died. Since he was unable to repay her in person, he established a deme in her name and a holy precinct in honor of Zeus Hecaleius in return for her hospitality. A few more details are added in Plutarch's biography (*Thes.* 14.1–3): Theseus captured the bull alive, drove it through the city, then sacrificed it to Delphinian Apollo. Plutarch also confirms the story of Hecale's hospitality and the honors she received from the townspeople, who used to assemble and sacrifice the Hecalesia[1] to Zeus Hecalus (Plutarch's spelling) while calling her by the pet name of Hecaline. Two important episodes gleaned from the frag-

[1] An annual feast in her honor.

ments, but not included in these summaries, are the dinner and conversation that Theseus enjoyed in Hecale's cottage and a discussion between two birds, one of which, a long-lived crow, gives an account of the birth of Ericthonius and the foundation of Athens.

ATTIC ROOTS

Though Plutarch cites the Atthidographer Philochorus (*BNJ* 328 F 109) as his source, it is likely that some details in his account, such as the nicknames that Hecale gave Theseus and the entertainment she offered him, derive indirectly from Callimachus' poem.[2] Callimachus himself looked to the Atthidographers for material, as we learn from Antigonus of Carystus.[3] He says that Amelesagoras (*BNJ* 330 F 1) was Callimachus' source for the birds' discourse on the mythical foundation of Athens (*Hec.* 70–74). The poem is filled with rare Attic names for objects that the poet also mined from these sources and others, especially Attic comedy.[4] They give it a patina of antiquity, authenticity, and charm that characterize Callimachus' style generally.

Comedy and tragedy were the hallmark genres of Athens, and Callimachus also invokes the latter, especially in the character and the circumstances of old Hecale. She

[2] Plutarch never cites Callimachus by name and probably found the information in commentaries or summaries.

[3] *Hist. mir. coll.* 12. A cruder version credited to the *Hecale* is found in the Homeric scholia (Schol. ad Hom. *Il.* 2.547); see Hollis, 227.

[4] E.g., ἀσκάντης, "a couch" (*Hec.* 29, from Ar. *Nub.* 633); for others, see Hollis, 9.

once was wealthy and blessed by two excellent sons, but now lives alone in abject poverty (*Hec.* 40–41, 48). The details of her life are revealed to Theseus in a nightlong conversation (*Hec.* 40), which would invoke tragic pity for her abasement and fear for Theseus' life as he prepares to confront the bull.[5] Hecale's status as a tragic heroine is also suggested by the way she expresses her anger at the bandit Cercyon who apparently killed one of her sons:

> . . . I would stab him in his shameless eyes with a pointed stake, and if it were right I would eat him raw. (*Hec.* 49.14–15)

Here she recalls Euripides' Hecuba, who blinded Polymestor after she learned that he had murdered her youngest son (Eur. *Hec.* 1132–71).[6] Both Sophocles and Euripides wrote tragedies entitled *Aegeus* that treated aspects of Theseus' story and may also have contributed to Callimachus' shaping of his tale.[7]

GENRE AND LITERARY FEATURES

Though the estimated length of the *Hecale* is about that of a tragedy or a comedy (1,200–1,800 lines),[8] both its

---

[5] Gutzwiller 2012, 238.

[6] Hutchinson 1988, 58–59. Epic characters also express their anger as a desire to eat their enemies raw (e.g., Hom. *Il.* 4.34–36, 22.346–47, 24.212–14, where the speaker is Hecuba).

[7] Acosta-Hughes and Stephens 2012, 198. Euripides' *Aegeus* apparently treated the scene in Troezen where Aegeus recognizes Theseus as his son; and Sophocles, the subduing of the Marathonian bull.

[8] Hollis, Appendix II.

meter, a finely wrought dactylic hexameter,[9] and its structure, a continuous narrative with direct speeches, are characteristic not of tragedy, but of epic. The generic label usually applied to it is *epyllion*, i.e., "little epic." Though there has been a long scholarly discussion about the status of this term, there is no dispute that Callimachus, some of his contemporaries, and a number of their successors mastered the form without naming it.[10]

The *Hecale* itself is clear about its epic affiliation. The first line,

> An Attic woman[11] once lived on the high grounds (*gounōi*) of Erechtheus[12]

is a clear reference to Homer's Ariadne, "whom Theseus once brought to the high grounds (*gounon*) of Athens" (*Od*. 11.323). This is the only time that Theseus is mentioned anywhere in Homer, and his encounter with the half-man, half-bull Minotaur—a central element in Ariadne's story—seems foreshadowed in his capture of the Marathonian bull. *Gounos* also provides a link to a Hesiodic passage (*Theog.* 53–54) in which Mnemosyne gives birth to the Muses in Pieria, where she rules over the high

---

[9] For metrical analysis, see Hollis, 15–23.

[10] See Gutzwiller 1981 and 2012. The length and the literary qualities of epic were issues even among ancient critics. This is evident from a scholium to the end of Callimachus' *Hymn to Apollo* (Schol. ad Call. *Hymn.* 2.106): "[Here] he blames those who mocked him because he was not able to write a long poem, and from this he was forced to write the *Hecale*."

[11] Hecale.

[12] A legendary early king of Athens.

6

grounds (*gounoisin*) of Eleuther. Though Callimachus' short epic lacks the formal salutation to the Muses that is traditional in Homer and Hesiod, this subtle allusion to both epic predecessors in the poem's first line serves a similar purpose in establishing the poem's generic affiliation.

Callimachus' engagement with Homeric language is evident in almost every line of the poem. This can take the form of creating new verses by restitching parts of Homer's (e.g., *Hec.* 74.22, which is constructed from the first four feet of *Od.* 15.494 and the last four of *Od.* 12.407).[13] It is also evident in Callimachus' use of words that appear only once in Homer (i.e., hapax legomena)[14] and new formations with analogies in Homer.[15] Callimachus also borrows from Homer on a larger scale. For example, Hecale's gracious reception of Theseus in her threadbare cottage is linked thematically to Odysseus' visit to the rustic hut of his swineherd Eumaeus (*Od.* 14). And Hecale's washing of Theseus' feet (*Hec.* 34) looks back to the Homeric episode in which Eurycleia, Odysseus' ancient nurse, washes his (*Od.* 19.386–94).[16] Other themes, such as the conversation between the birds recounting the foundation of Athens (*Hec.* 70–74), have roots in folklore and fable.

---

[13] Two feet overlap in the center. See Cameron (1995, 441), who offers additional examples.

[14] E.g., ἀπηλοίησε (*Il.* 4.522; *Hec.* 69.1); μέλδοντες (*Il.* 21.363; *Hec.* 127), etc.

[15] E.g., πολυπτώξ, "of many hares" (*Hec.* 84), after πολυτρήρωνα, "of many doves" (*Il.* 2.502); for other examples, see Hollis, 13.

[16] Hollis, 170–71.

CALLIMACHUS

METAMEANINGS

It is also possible to read the *Hecale* as an expression of Callimachus' literary agenda. Its impoverished, abject heroine and the dinner she prepares of simple roots gathered from the forest can be construed as a metaphor for the "thin" or "slender" style that he promotes in the Prologue of the *Aetia*, his epigrams (e.g., *Epig.* 6), and the conclusion of his *Hymn to Apollo*.[17] The *Hecale*'s brevity relative to other epics as well as the rarity and artistic arrangement of its diction seem to illustrate Callimachus' more abstract expressions of his stylistic ideals.

A historical context has also been proposed.[18] We do not know exactly when the *Hecale* was written, but its celebration of Athens and Theseus, its local hero, can also be read as an expression of Callimachus' lifelong support of the Ptolemaic political agenda. From about 287 BC until the end of the Chremonidean War in 262, during the reign of Ptolemy Philadelphus, Alexandria and Athens were closely allied against the interests of Macedon and its ruler Antigonus Gonatus. The relationship between Athens and Alexandria apparently had the support of Philadelphus' sister/wife, Arsinoe II, for whom Callimachus wrote poems to celebrate her marriage, her apotheosis, and more.[19] There is also some evidence that around 247 BC Callimachus himself traveled to Athens, where a contribution to an emergency fund was made in his

17 Gutzwiller 2012, 241–42.

18 Acosta-Hughes and Stephens 2012, 196–97.

19 On the significance of Arsinoe's name in the decree of Chremonides (*SIG*³ 4334–35), see Carney 2013, 92–93.

name.[20] The evidence is not conclusive, but it does suggest an association with Athens that could provide a historical context for the *Hecale* and the Athenian sections of the *Aetia*.

THE DATE OF THE *HECALE*

There are no specific indications of the *Hecale*'s date, but links with Callimachus' *Iamb* 4 suggest that it was not among his last poems. Both poems feature a pair of chattering birds (*Ia.* 194.61–93; *Hec.* 70–74) who talk of Cecrops' role in the foundation of Athens (*Ia.* 194.66–68; *Hec.* 70), and both present Theseus eating pickled olives (*Ia.* 194.77; *Hec.* 36). Since Theseus is a central character in the *Hecale* and olives are a key component of Hecale's hospitality, it seems likely that the *Hecale* was written before the *Iamb*, which includes these items in a list of arguments for the olive's precedence over a laurel tree. *Iamb* 4 cannot be attached to a specific date, but *Iamb* 1 is set before the wall of the Great Serapeum (*Ia.* 191.9).[21] This was built by Ptolemy III, whose reign began in 246 BC. Since Callimachus' thirteen *Iambi* are a tightly organized ensemble, it is likely that *Iamb* 4 belongs to the same period, and the *Hecale* was composed at an earlier date.

THE AFTERLIFE OF THE *HECALE*

Though the *Hecale* is extant only in fragments, it is still possible to demonstrate that it was read and appreci-

[20] Oliver 2002, 6.
[21] See Clayman 2014, 160–62.

ated for centuries afterward. Hollis (pp. 388–91) has compiled a complete index of literary allusions and imitations beginning with Callimachus' contemporaries Apollonius of Rhodes, Lycophron, and Eratosthenes.[22] By the first century BC its influence was apparent at Rome through a reference in Lucretius, who borrows from it an explanation of why crows avoid the Acropolis (*DRN* 6.749–55; *Hec.* 73–74) and three in Cicero (fr. 6.73 Büchner; *Tusc.* 4.50; *Att.* 8.5.1), the last of which quotes a whole verse (*Hec.* 165) without attribution because he was confident Atticus would recognize it. The *Hecale*'s greatest impact came in the first century AD, when it formed the basis of two important episodes in Ovid's *Metamorphoses*. These include the story of the daughters of Cecrops (*Met.* 2.531–68), including a conversation between a crow and a raven whose plumage changed from white to black, and the tale of Baucis and Philemon (*Met.* 8.626–724), which features a scene of rustic hospitality featuring many verbal echoes of the *Hecale*.[23] After Ovid, Petronius parodies Theseus' visit to Hecale in his own account of Encolpius' visit to Oenothea, another old woman living in poverty (*Sat.* 135–36). His allusion is signaled by a near translation of the *Hecale*'s first line and a reference to its last.

Callimachus' rare diction caught the attention not only of poets but also of scholars. In the first centuries BC and AD, Theon of Alexandria began writing commentaries on

[22] Hollis (p. 26) assumes that the *Hecale* predates the *Argonautica* and the *Alexandra* but acknowledges that the order could be reversed.

[23] According to Hollis (p. 350), the echoes are so numerous that the Latin approaches a translation.

Hellenistic poets, including Callimachus, which preserved scholarship from the earlier Hellenistic period and passed it along to his successors, including Salustius, who wrote the first known commentary on the *Hecale*. Additionally, Didymus Chalcenterus made use of much Callimachean material in his commentary on Pindar.[24]

Though Callimachus was widely popular in the first century AD, interest in him among literary authors seems to wane by the second. Copies of the *Hecale* were still in circulation (in fact, all of the extant papyri with fragments of the poem date from the second to the seventh centuries), but more and more it is grammarians and lexicographers who transmit his rare forms and usages.[25] Among their most impressive works are the *Etymologicum Genuinum* (9th c.),[26] and its descendants: the *Etymologicum Magnum* (12th c.), the *Etymologicum Gudianum* (11th c.), and the *Etymologicum Symeonis* (12th c.).[27] Most important for the *Hecale* is the *Suda* (10th c.), which was enriched with the work of earlier scholars, including Salustius' commentary on the *Hecale* (perhaps 4th c.).

The last known complete copy of the *Hecale* was read and admired by Michael Choniates, Bishop of Athens, but

[24] Pontani 2011, 107–11.

[25] Among them were Apollonius Dyscolus (2nd c.), Gregorius of Nazianzus (4th c.), Hesychius of Alexandria (5th–6th c.), Stephanus of Byzantium (early 6th c.), and Georgius Choeroboscus (8th–9th c.).

[26] Hollis, 51–53. There are two copies extant, both incomplete: cod. A (Vaticanus gr. 1818) and cod. B (Laur. S. Marci 304). Neither has been published in full.

[27] See Dickey 2007, 91–92, with information on published editions.

was apparently lost in 1205 when the city was razed during the Fourth Crusade.[28] What remains today are fragments, mostly small, from the aforementioned sources.

CONSTITUTION OF THE TEXT

The process of salvaging the text began in the fifteenth century when Angelus Politianus collected some testimonia and a few fragments of the text, which he published as Chapter 24 in the first book of his *Miscellanea* in 1489.[29] A few more fragments were attached to early editions of the *Hymns* before a breakthrough by Bentley, who collected and edited twenty-six fragments of the *Hecale* published in Graevius' omnibus edition of Callimachus in 1697. No more significant progress was made until the nineteenth century, when August Naeke (1833–1837)[30] and Alphons Hecker (1842) identified many more citations in Byzantine lexica. Hecker's work with the *Suda* led to the formulation of what is now called "Hecker's law," the *Regula Heckeriana*, which states that a hexameter quotation in the *Suda* not ascribed to another author or work and not found elsewhere must be from the *Hecale*.[31] Given the size of the great *Suda* and the variety of its contents, it seems unlikely that the "law" could hold without exception, yet papyri published many years after Hecker have

---

[28] Pontani 2011, 114–17.

[29] Pfeiffer vol. 2, xliii.

[30] Naeke's work first appeared in articles in *RhM* 2–5 (1833–1837) that were later published together in *Opuscula* ii (1845).

[31] Hecker 1842, 133. Though Hecker believed that the *Suda* quotes the *Hecale* directly, Reitzenstein (1890/1, 13–17) noted that its source was more likely the commentary of Salustius.

confirmed its value as a heuristic tool to a remarkable extent.[32]

Though skeptical of the "law," Otto Schneider (1873) was able to benefit from Hecker's work for his own *Callimachea*, as did Ida Kapp, who produced the first standalone edition of the *Hecale* in 1915.[33] She was the first to increase the number of fragments with evidence from papyri including *P.Oxy.* 853 (fr. 154 K. = *Hec.* 85) and the Vienna Tablet, *T.Vindob.* (fr. 58 K. = *Hec.* 69.1–16; fr. 60 K. = *Hec.* 70.1–14; fr. 62 K. = *Hec.* 73.5–14; fr. 64 K. = *Hec.* 74.14–28). To Kapp's contribution, Pfeiffer added a significant number of additional fragments from papyri and the Byzantine *etymologica* in his landmark edition of 1949–1953, which is enhanced with copious notes and a full apparatus. The most recent critical edition is the second edition of Hollis (2009), which builds on Pfeiffer and adds still more fragments from Byzantine sources, especially the *Suda*, as well as a commentary and a prose translation in English.

CODICES

Et. Gen.	*Etymologicum Genuinum*
A	Vaticanus gr. 1818, 10th c.
B	Laurentianus S. Marci 304, 10th c.

[32] Hecker 1842, 133. See Hollis (pp. 41–44) for cautions in the application of this "law" and confirmation of it in the papyri.

[33] Ida Kapp,, *Callimachi Hecalae Fragmenta* (Berlin, 1915). This was her dissertation directed by U. von Wilamowitz and H. Diels. It contains 16 testimonia and 154 fragments. In Pfeiffer's edition, her fragment numbers are printed with Schneider's in brackets after his own.

Et. Mag.	*Etymologicum Magnum*
D	Dorvillianus Bodl. xi.1.1.2 15th c. (?)
M	Marcianus gr. 530, 13th c.
P	Parisinus gr. 2654, ann. 1273
R	Hauniensis reg. 414, 15th c.
Et. Sym.	*Etymologicum Symeonis*
F	Vindobonensis phil. gr. 131, 13th c.
V	Vossianus gr. 20, 13th c.
Et. Gud.	*Etymologicum Gudianum*
C	Vindobonensis philos. gr. 23, 12th c.
D	Vaticanus Barberinus gr. 70, 11th c.
O	Vaticanus Palatinus gr. 244, 15th c.
W	Guelferbytanus (Wolfenbüttel) gr. 29–30, ann. 1298
Z	Parisinus suppl. gr. 172, 13th c.
Suda	
A	Parisini gr. 2625 and 2626, 13th and 14th c.
F	Laurentianus 55.1, ann. 1422
V	Vossianus, fol. 2, 12th c.
S	Vaticanus gr. 1296, ann. 1205
G	Parisinus gr. 2623, 15th c.
I	Angelicanus 75, 15th c.
T	Vaticanus gr. 881, ann. 1434
M	Marcianus gr. 448, 13th c.

CATALOG OF PAPYRI

The end of the nineteenth century and the beginning of the twentieth ushered in the golden age of papyrus discovery, and Rudolph Pfeiffer integrated into his authoritative edition six that contain some text or information about the *Hecale*. Since then selected papyri have been reedited and new fragments added both in the *Supplementum Hellenisticum* (1983) and in Hollis' *Hecale* (2nd ed., 2009).

The list of papyri below follows the numbering and order of Mertens-Pack[3], the online database of the Centre de documentation de papyrologie littéraire (CEDOPAL) at the Université de Liège, which provides additional information and bibliography.[34] Each entry begins with the inventory number assigned by Mertens-Pack[3] followed by the series name in standard abbreviations; the numbers in *SH*, Hollis[2], and Pfeiffer, where relevant; its estimated date; and the passages in the *Hecale* that it supplies.

00186.000: *P.Oxy.* 2258 (+ *P.Oxy.* 30, pp. 91–92; *SH* 290–91). Pap. 2 Hollis, 37 Pf. 6th–7th c. AD. *Argumentum Hecalae*, *Hec.* 5, 6, 96, 97.

00201.000: *PSI* 133 (+ *P.Oxy.* 2168 + *P.Berol.* inv. 11629a–b + *P.Berol.* inv. 13417a–b; *SH* 285). Pap. 5 Hollis, 32 Pf. 4th–5th c. AD. *Hec.* 40, 42.

00211.000: *P.Mil.Vogl.* 18 (*P.Cair.* inv. JE 67340) + *P.Mil.Vogl.* inv. 28b + *P.Mil.Vogl.* inv. 1006). Pap. 1 Hollis, 8 Pf. 1st–2nd c. AD. *Dieg.* in *Hec.* 1.

00226.000: *P.Oxy.* 2216 + pp. 145–46. Pap. 3 Hollis, 30 Pf. 3rd c. AD. *Hec.* 17, 18.3–18, 20–23.

00227.000: *T.Vindob.* inv. G HT 6 (*SH* 288.1–43A) = *P.Rain.* VI. Pap. 8 Hollis, 36 Pf. 4th–5th c. AD. *Hec.* 69.1–14, 70, 73, 74.14–28.

00227.010: *P.Oxy.* inv. 112/87 (b). Not in Hollis or Pfeiffer. N. Gonis, in Bastianini and Casanova 2006, 29–30. *Hec.* 69.

---

[34] Further information about the papyri can also be found in Pfeiffer vol. 2, ix–xxvi; Hollis, 48–51; *SH* 122–135; Lehnus 2011, 23–38; Asper 2004, 537–39.

00227.100 (prev. 00231.000 Pack²): *P.Oxy.* 2398 (*SH* 288.43B–69). Pap. 9 Hollis, not in Pfeiffer. 2nd c. AD. *Hec.* 74.1–17.

00227.200: (prev. 00232.000 Pack²): *P.Oxy.* 2437 (*SH* 288.43B–47). Pap. 10 Hollis, not in Pfeiffer. 2nd c. AD. *Hecale* 74.1–6.

00228.000: *P.Oxy.* 2217 (*SH* 288.44–58). Pap. 11 Hollis, 33 Pf. 4th c. AD. *Hec.* 74.3–17.

00229.000: *P.Oxy.* 2376 (*SH* 287.1–10 [col. I], 17–26 [col. II]). Pap. 7 Hollis, not in Pfeiffer. 2nd c. AD. *Hec.* 48 and 49.7–16.

00230.000: *P.Oxy.* 2377 (*SH* 286, 287.11–30). Pap. 6 Hollis, not in Pfeiffer. 3rd–4th c. AD. *Hec.* 47 and 49.

00230.100: *P.Oxy.* 2529 (*SH* 282–83). Pap. 4 Hollis, not in Pfeiffer. 3rd–4th c. AD. *Hec.* 27, 36, and likely 37.

00230.200: *P.Oxy.* 2823 (*SH* 280). Not in Hollis or Pfeiffer. 2nd c. AD. Perhaps *Hec.* 4.

THIS EDITION

The text below is based on Hollis' second edition (2009), which in turn depends on Pfeiffer's (1949–1953). Hollis follows Pfeiffer in ordering the fragments first following the narrative offered by the *Diegeseis*.[35] After these are fragments that cannot be associated with the story line that are first grouped by subject matter (e.g., *res Atticae*, pottery, etc.), and where the subject is not clear, arranged in alphabetical order of their sources.

In both Pfeiffer and Hollis, one can find a fuller ap-

---

[35] Hollis, 46–48.

paratus and more detailed notes than are offered below. Hollis' edition is particularly rich in literary references, from which I have selected only the most salient. My text follows his with only a few small changes, and I use his fragment numbers. Those of Pfeiffer and the *Supplementum Hellenisticum*, where relevant, follow in parentheses.

BIBLIOGRAPHY

CRITICAL STUDIES

Barigazzi, Adelmo. "Sull' Ecale di Callimaco." *Hermes* 82 (1954): 308–30.

———. "Il dolore materno di Ecale (*P.Oxy.* 2376 e 2377)." *Hermes* 86 (1958): 453–71.

Benedetto, Giovanni. "Callimachus and the Atthidographers." In *Brill's Companion to Callimachus*, edited by Benjamin Acosta-Hughes and Susan Stephens, 349–83. Leiden: Brill, 2011.

Gutzwiller, Kathryn. *Studies in the Hellenistic Epyllion*. Meisenheim am Glan: Hain, 1981.

———. "The *Hecale* and Hellenistic Conceptions of Short Hexameter Narratives." In *Brill's Companion to Greek and Latin Epyllion and Its Reception*, edited by Manuel Baumbach and Silvio Bär, 221–44. Leiden: Brill, 2012.

Hollis, Adrian. "Attica in Hellenistic Poetry." *ZPE* 93 (1992): 1–15.

Livrea, Enrico. "The Tempest in Callimachus' *Hecale*." *CQ* 42 (1992): 147–51.

McNelis, Charles. "Mourning Glory: Callimachus' *Hecale* and Heroic Honors." *Materiali e discussioni per l'analisi dei testi classici* 50 (2003): 155–61.

Pontani, Filippomaria. "Callimachus Cited." In *Brill's*

Companion to Callimahus, edited by Benjamin Acosta-Hughes and Susan Stephens, 93–117. Leiden: Brill, 2011.

Reinsch-Werner, Hannelore. *Callimachus Hesiodicus, die Rezeption der Hesiodischen Dichtung durch Kallimachos von Kyrene.* Berlin: Mielke, 1976.

Reitzenstein, Richard. "Inedita Poetarum Graecorum Fragmenta." *Index Lectionum* in *Academia Rostochiensi* (1890/1): 1–18.

Rengakos, Antonios. "Aristarchus and the Hellenistic Poets." *Seminari Romani di Cultura Greca* 3 (2000): 325–35.

Zanker, Graham. *Realism in Alexandrian Poetry: A Literature and Its Audience.* London: Croom Helm, 1987.

———. "The Concept and the Use of Genre-Marking in Hellenistic Epic and Fine Art." In *Genre in Hellenistic Poetry*, edited by Annette Harder et al., 225–38. Groningen: Forsten, 1998.

ΕΚΑΛΗ

DIEGESIS HECALAE

Dieg. 10.18–11.7

Ἀκταίη τις ἔναιεν Ἐρεχθέος ἔν ποτε γουνῷ

Θησεὺς φυγὼν τὴν ἐκ Μηδείης ἐπιβουλὴν διὰ πάσης ἦν φυλακῆς τῷ πατρὶ Αἰγεῖ, ἅτ᾽ αἰφνίδιον ἀνακομισθὲν ἐκ Τροιζῆνος μειράκιον αὐτῷ οὐ προσδοκήσαντι. βουλόμενος δ᾽ ἐπὶ τὸν λυμαινόμενον τὰ περὶ Μαραθῶνα ταῦρον ἐξελθεῖν ὅπως χειρώσαιτο, καὶ εἰργόμενος, κρύφα τῆς οἰκίας ἐξελθὼν περὶ ἑσπέραν ἀπῆρεν.[1] αἰφνίδιον δὲ ὑετοῦ ῥαγέντος κατ᾽ ἐσχατιὰν οἰκίδιον θεασάμενος Ἑκάλης τινὸς πρεσβύτιδος ἐνταῦθα ἐξενοδοκήθη. πρὸς δὲ τὴν ἔω ἀναστὰς ἐξῄει ἐπὶ τὴν χώραν, χειρωσάμενος δὲ τὸν ταῦρον ἐπανῄει ὡς τὴν Ἑκάλην· αἰφνίδιον δὲ ταύτην εὑρὼν τεθνηκυῖαν ἐπιστε[νάξ]ας ὡς ἐψευσμένος τῆς προσδοκίας, ὃ ἐφ[....]εν[2] μετὰ θάνατον εἰς ἀμοιβὴν τῆς ξενίας

---

[1] ἀπῆρεν Norsa-Vitelli: απηρετ *P.Med.* 18
[2] ἐφ[ρόνησ]εν suppl. Pfeiffer: ἐφ[ήμισ]εν Norsa-Vitelli

HECALE

NARRATIVE OF THE *HECALE*

Diegeseis

An Attic woman[1] once lived on the high grounds of
Erechtheus.

After he escaped the treachery of Medea, Theseus was
under heavy guard by his father Aegeus who had not ex-
pected him to return suddenly from Troezen.[2] He wished
to set out against the bull that was wreaking havoc around
Marathon[3] and subdue it. Since he was prevented from
doing so, he secretly left the house around evening and set
out. Suddenly a heavy rainstorm broke out and he saw the
little house at the foot of a hill of a certain old woman
named Hecale, where he was received as a guest. Toward
dawn he went out to the place and after he subdued
the bull he returned to Hecale. When he found that she
had unexpectedly died he sighed because he had been
cheated of his expectation and repaid her after death for

---

[1] Hecale. This is the first line of the poem.   [2] Town on the
eastern Peloponnese and birthplace of Theseus.   [3] Town in
the northeast of Attica and later the site of a famous victory over
the Persians (490 BC).

ταὐτῃ³ παρασχέσθαι, τοῦτο [ἐπετέλεσεν δ[ῆ]μον συν-
στησάμενος ὃν ἀπ᾽ αὐτῆς ὠνόμα[σ]εν, καὶ τέμενος
ἱδρύσατο Ἑκαλείου Δι[ό]ς.

³ ταὐ pap.: αὐτῇ Norsa-Vitelli

ARGUMENTUM HECALAE

P.Oxy. 2258A verso, fr. 9 a–d

```
              .   .   .   .
            ]ην χωρ[    ]να
          ]ενοσηνυ[
     .   .   ] πεφευ[    .    .    .   .
        ]..ντ..λ[]..[                    ].[
5      ]ν ἐκπέμπε[         ]ουκ[
     ]νης κρύβδ.[              ].ηεπ[
     ὑε]τοῦ κα[τ]αρραγέντοσ[        .   .
     νυκτὸς ἐ]πιλαμβανούσης[
        ο]ἶκον Ἑκάλης· τ[           .
10        ].[        ].[
              .   .   .
```

FRAGMENTA 1–83 IN ORDINE HOLLIS

1 (230 Pf.) *P.Med.* 18; *Dieg.* 10.19

Ἀκταίη τις ἔναιεν Ἐρεχθέος ἔν ποτε γουνῷ

her hospitality. He brought it about that a deme was established which he named for her, and founded the holy precinct of Zeus Hecaleius.

PLOT OF THE *HECALE*

Oxyrhynchus papyrus

. . . .

[1] place . . . [3] he fled . . . [5] he sent out . . . [6] secretly . . . [7] a rainstorm breaking out . . . [8] night falling . . . [9] the house of Hecale

FRAGMENTS 1–83 HOLLIS

1 (230 Pf.) *Diegeseis*

An Attic woman[1] once lived on the high grounds of Erechtheus.[2]

[1] Hecale. She is not named here in the first line of the poem, and it is not clear from the fragments when the poet first revealed her identity. [2] A legendary early king of Athens associated with Poseidon, whose temple on the Acropolis is called the Erechtheion. To live on the high grounds of Erechtheus is to live near Athens. Hecale probably lived on Mt. Brilessus, between Athens and the plain of Marathon (cf. *Hec.* 169 below).

2 (231 Pf.) Schol. ΕΓLh ad Ar. *Ach.* 127a (p. 26 Wilson)

τοὺς δὲ ξενίζειν οὐδέποτ᾽ ἴσχει γ᾽ ἡ θύρα· ἐπὶ τῶν
πολλοὺς ξένους ὑποδεχομένων· μέμνηται . . . καὶ
Καλλ. ἐν Ἑκάλῃ·

τίον[1] δέ ἑ πάντες ὁδῖται

ἦρα φιλοξενίης· ἔχε γὰρ[2] τέγος[3] ἀκλήιστον

[1] τίον Pfeiffer: τῖον Schol. ad Ar.   [2] ἔχε γὰρ Suda, Et.
Gud.: ἔσχε γὰρ ΑΟ 2: ἔσχ᾽ ἐς γῆν Schol. E.: ἔσχε σιγῆς
Schol. Γ   [3] τέγος Schol. Γ: τέλος Schol. E.: τεῖχος Suda

3 (364 Pf.[1]) *Suda* π 1967

πολύθρονον· πολυφάρμακον.

πολύθρονον

[1] *Hec.* trib. Schol.; *Hec.* Adler; *Medea* Pfeiffer

4 (232 Pf.[1]) *Et. Gen.* AB s.v. θυοσκόος

θυοσκόος· ὁ ἱερεύς, ὁ μάντις, ὁ ἀπὸ τῶν θυομένων
κοῶν, ὅ ἐστι νοῶν, τὸ μέλλον. Καλλ.,

ἡ δ᾽ ἐκόησεν

τοὔνεκεν Αἰγέος ἔσκεν

[1] *Hec.* trib. Reitzenstein 1891/2, 4

2 (231 Pf.) Scholia to Aristophanes, *Acharnians*

The door was never closed for entertaining guests: of
those entertaining many guests; and it recalls . . . also Cal-
limachus in the *Hecale*,

> All the travelers honored her
> on account of her hospitality: for she kept an open
> house.

3 (364 Pf.) *Suda*

polythronon: of many drugs.

> of many poisons[1]

[1] Of Medea, who tried in vain to poison her stepson Theseus.

4 (232 Pf.) *Etymologicum Genuinum*

thuoskoos: the priest; the seer who perceives the future
from the sacrifices is the one who knows it. Callimachus,

> but she realized
> that he was Aegeus' son[1]

[1] The subject is Medea, who recognized Theseus' identity
before his father, Aegeus, did.

5 (Add. vol. 1, p. 506 Pf.[1]) *P.Oxy.* 2258A fr. 11 verso, scholia marginalia

```
        .   .
    ].φ.[.]..[
    ]ωνεπανω[
    Σκί]ρου² δὲ ὁ Αἰ[γεὺς³
    Παν]δίονος
    ἀκολ]ουθησα̣[⁴
        ]νονμ.[
        ]παρδα[
    .    .    .    .
```

[1] *Hec.* trib. Lobel   [2] Suppl. Pfeiffer
[3] Suppl. Lobel   [4] Suppl. Lobel

6 (Add. vol. 1, p. 507 Pf.) *P. Oxy.* 2258A fr. 11 recto

```
      .   .
    ].οο....[
    ]φοσουκ[
    ]        [
    ] . αιερε.[
     ]ωσδ̣ .[
       ].. [
```

5 (Add. vol. 1, p. 506 Pf.) Oxyrhynchus papyrus (marginal scholia)

Is Aegeus the son of Pandion or Sciros?[1]

[1] The question about Aegeus' parenthood may be Callimachus' or the scholiast's. On Pandion and Sciros, see Apollod. *Bibl.* 3.15.5; Paus. 1.5.4, 1.39.4. On Aegeus' legitimacy, see Plut. *Thes.* 13.

6 (Add. vol. 1, p. 507 Pf.) Oxyrhynchus papyrus

Two lines of text are followed by two lines of scholia. There are no recognizable words.

7 (233 Pf.[1]) Anon. *De barbarismo et soloecismo* (*Anec. Gr.* vol. 3, p. 239 Boissonade)

σολοικισμὸς γίνεται . . . περὶ ἐγκλίσεις, ὡς παρὰ Καλλ.

    ἴσχε τέκος, μὴ πῖθι

[1] *Hec.* trib. Hecker

8 (234 Pf.[1]) *Suda* π 527

παρὲκ νόον· ἀντὶ τοῦ παρ' ἐλπιδα,

    παρὲκ νόον εἰλήλουθας

[1] *Hec.* trib. Kapp, fr. 80

9 (235 Pf.) Schol. ad Lyc. *Alex.* 494 (Tzetz. cod. s[4])

ἐκ κοίλης πέτρας· ὁ Αἰγεὺς ὑπὸ κοίλην πέτραν ἔθετο ξίφος καὶ ὑποδήματα ὥς φησι Πλούταρχος (*Thes.* 3), καὶ Καλλ. λέγων,

    ἐν γάρ μιν[1] Τροιζῆνι[2] κολουραίη[3] ὑπὸ πέτρη
    θῆκε σὺν ἀρπίδεσσιν

[1] ἐν γάρ μιν *Et. Gen.* A, Schol. ad Lyc. *Alex.* 1322: ἔργα δέ μιν Schol. ad Lyc. *Alex.* 494 et cod. Pal. 18 (γ2), Schol. 1322
[2] Τροιζῆνι Schol. ad Lyc. *Alex.* 494: τρυζῆνι *Et. Gen.* A
[3] κολουραίη Schol. ad Lyc. *Alex.* 1322: κολλουραίη *Et. Gen.* A

7 (233 Pf.) Anonymous, *On Barbarism and Solecism*

It is a solecism concerning the mood, as in Callimachus,

> Stop, son! Do not drink![1]

[1] Aegeus prevents Theseus from drinking the poison offered by his stepmother, Medea (Plut. *Thes.* 12; Schol. ad Hom. *Il.* 11.741).

8 (234 Pf.) *Suda*

parek noon: "beyond expectation" instead of "against hope,"

> you have come beyond expectation[1]

[1] Aegeus to his son Theseus.

9 (235 Pf.) Scholia to Lycophron, *Alexandra*

from the hollow rock: Aegeus placed a sword under a hollow rock and sandals, as Plutarch says (*Thes.* 3) and Callimachus says,

> in Troezen[1] he placed it with the sandals
> under a hollow rock[2]

[1] City in Argolis where Aethra gave birth to Theseus.
[2] Aegeus left tokens of recognition for his son, a sword and some sandals.

CALLIMACHUS

10 (236.1–2 Pf.[1]) Schol. AT ad Hom. *Il.* 5.99 (vol. 2, p. 18 Erbse)

θώρηκος γύαλον· ὅτι τὸ ὅλον κύτος τοῦ θώρακος γύαλον διὰ τὴν κοιλότητα λέγει, οὐ μέρος ὡρισμένον τοῦ θώρακος. τὸ γυαλὸν ὅταν ἐπίθετον ᾖ ὀξύνεται·

> εὖτ᾽ ἂν ὁ παῖς ἀπὸ μὲν γυαλὸν λίθον
>   ἀγκάσσασθαι[2]
> ἄρκιος ᾖ χείρεσσιν, ἑλὼν[3] Αἰδήψιον[4] ἆορ

[1] Coniunxit Hecker, *Philol.* 4 (1849): 479   [2] ἀγκάσσασθαι corr. Hecker: ἀγκάσασθαι Schol. ad Eust., *Suda*
[3] ἑλὼν Steph.: ἑλὼν δ᾽ Schneider: ἑλεῖν δ᾽ Wilamowitz
[4] Steph. Byz. s.v. Αἰδηψός· πόλις Εὐβοίας . . . ἦν δὲ καὶ σιδηρᾶ καὶ χαλκᾶ μέταλλα κατὰ Εὔβοιαν . . . Καλλ.

11 (236.3 Pf.[1]) *Suda* ε 3703

εὐρώς· ὑγρότης σεσηπυῖα· Καλλ.,

> πέδιλα, τὰ μὴ πύσε νήχυτος εὐρώς

[1] *Hec.* trib. Naeke, 87

12 (237 Pf.[1]) Schol. MNAB ad Eur. *Hipp.* 11

ἁγνοῦ Πιτθέως· ἦν δὲ ὁ Πιτθεὺς σοφὸς καὶ χρησμολόγος καὶ ἱερὸς θεοῖς, ὃς καὶ ἔλυσε τὸν χρησμὸν τῷ Αἰγεῖ καὶ τὴν θυγατέρα ἔδωκεν, εἰδὼς τῇ σοφίᾳ οἷος ἔσται ὁ τεχθησόμενος. παρ᾽ αὐτῷ δὲ ὁ Θησεὺς ἐπαιδεύετο, ὡς Καλλ.

[1] *Hec.* trib. Blomfield

30

10 (236.1–2 Pf.) Scholia to Homer, *Iliad*

hollow shield: he says that the whole body of the corselet is "hollow" (*gualon*) on account of its concavity, no portion of the corselet is divided. When *gualon* is an adjective it has an acute accent, such as,

> When the boy is strong enough to lift it with his hands from the hollow rock, then taking the sword made in Aedepsus[1]

[1] Aegeus' instructions to Aethra. Aedepsus was a town in Euboea known for its metalwork (cf. Steph. Byz. α 118 Billerbeck, quoted opposite).

11 (236.3 Pf.) *Suda*

eurōs: moldering dampness. Callimachus,

> sandals, which the damp mold did not rot

12 (237 Pf.) Scholia to Euripides, *Hippolytus*

Of holy Pittheus: Pittheus[1] was a wise expounder of oracles, sanctified by the gods, who explained the oracle to Aegeus and gave him his daughter, knowing in his wisdom that he would be able to father [a son]. And in his house Theseus was brought up, as Callimachus says.[2]

[1] Theseus' maternal grandfather. He also appears as an expounder of oracles in *Iamb* 5 (*Ia.* 195.33).   [2] No text of the *Hecale* is quoted directly.

CALLIMACHUS

13 (345 Pf.[1]) *Suda* λ 441

λῆμα· ἀξία καὶ ἀνδρεία. φρόνημα, κέρδος,

   τοιοῦτον γὰρ ὁ παῖς ὅδε[2] λῆμα φαείνει

[1] *Hec.* trib. Maas   [2] Dactylum deesse inter ὅδε et λῆμα
coniecit Wendel, *Gnomon* 15 (1939): 43 ("vix recte" Hollis).

14 (361 Pf.[1]) *Suda* π 1167

περίθριξ· ὁ ἀπὸ γενετῆς πλόκαμος, ὁ μηδέπω καρείς,

   ἔτι πλοκάμοιο περίθριξ

[1] *Hec.* trib. Naeke, 160

15 (281 Pf.[1]) *Et. Gen.* AB s.v. ἐγκυτί

ἐγκυτί· ἐν χρῷ, ἐπίρρημα,. Καλλ.,

   τὺ δ᾽ ἐγκυτὶ τέκνον ἐκέρσω

[1] *Hec.* trib. Naeke, 159

16 (283 Pf.[1]) *Suda* ε 800

ἔλλερα ἔργα· φόνια, χαλεπά, κακά.

   ἵν᾽ ἔλλερα ἔργα[2] τέλεσκεν

[1] *Hec.* trib. Naeke, 166   [2] ἔργα *Suda*: πολλὰ *Et. Gen.*
A¹¹B: πολλὰ τέλεσκεν ἔργα coni. Reitzenstein

13 (345 Pf.) *Suda*

lēma: dignity and courage; high spirits; ambition. As

    the boy[1] radiates such courage

  [1] Theseus.

14 (361 Pf.) *Suda*

perithrix: the lock of hair from birth, which has not yet been shorn,

      still the first growth of hair

15 (281 Pf.) *Etymologicum Genuinum*

enkuti: on the skin, an adverb. Callimachus,

  you were shorn close to the skin, child[1]

  [1] Naeke conjectured that the verse refers to Theseus' haircut.

16 (283 Pf.) *Suda*

evil deeds: deadly, grievous, bad.

  where it[1] accomplished evil deeds

  [1] Probably the Marathonian bull.

17 (238.1–14 Pf. + *SH* 281) *P.Oxy.* 2216 fr. 1 recto, 1–14

. . . .

```
          ].....μεν..φ...[
          ]κέλευε δὲ μήποτ᾽ ἐλέγξα[ι
          ]νε. η δ᾽ ὑπὸ πάντας ἀέθλου[s
   ,τῷ <ῥα>, πάτερ, μεθίει με· σόον δέ κεν α,ὖ,θι δέχοιο¹
5                 ]δ....´..εχ..ά...[
          ].αρὴν κεκύθεσθε κ.[
          ] ...[.].´..νε.[
          ]ε δ᾽ ἦν τόδε χειραεσα[
          ]τας ἀκὴν ἔχε· τῆι δε.[
10        ]ν.ου αἰσυμνῆτις[
   †ῆ τ᾽ ἄκρησθ† ἵ,να Γλαυκώπιον ἵζε,ι
          ]εν ἀεὶ περὶ πότνια γα[
          ]s ὅθι πτολέμοιό μ᾽ ἐπ.[
              ].[ ]´[
```

. . . . .

¹ *SH* 281 = Ammon. *De diff. verb.* 89 (p. 23 Nickau) τὸ μὲν αὖθις ἐστὶ τὸ πάλιν ἢ μετὰ ταῦτα, τὸ δ᾽ αὖθι <τὸ> αὐτόθι. κακῶς οὖν Καλλίμαχός φησι, "αὖθι τὸ δ᾽ ἐκδύοιμι" (fr. 1.35 Pf.), ἀντὶ τοῦ μετὰ ταῦτα, καὶ [τῇ Ἑκάλῃ] "τῶ—δέξοιο" ἀντὶ τοῦ πάλιν

18 (238.15–32 Pf.) *Suda* ε 1180; 3–18, *P.Oxy.* 2216 fr. 1 verso, 1–16

,ὄφρα μὲν οὖν ἔνδιος ἔην ἔτι, θέρμετο δὲ χθών,

17 (238.1–14 Pf. + *SH* 281) Oxyrhynchus papyrus

[2] she[1] ordered me never to ask questions, [3] but [to persevere] under all the labors. [4] Father, let me go and you would welcome me back again safe . . . [6] conceal it . . . [9] be silent . . . [10] the Queen [11] who on the peak presides over the Glaucopion,[2] [12] . . . the goddess who always [cares] for the land [13] . . . where me from the war

---

[1] Athena, in the words of Theseus, who is summarizing the orders she gave him. He is likely asking Aegeus for permission to confront the bull.   [2] Either a mountain in Attica (Lycabettus), or the Acropolis of Athens, or the temple of Athena on the Acropolis.

18 (238.15–32 Pf.) *Suda*; Oxyrhynchus papyrus

As long as it was midday, and the earth was warm, the brilliant sky was clearer than glass . . . and nowhere even

τόφρα δ᾿ ἔην ὑάλοιο φαάντερος οὐρανὸς ἦνοψ,
οὐδέ ποθ‿ι,[1] κν‿ηκὶς ὑπεφαίνετο, πέπτατο δ᾿ αἰθήρ
ἀν[ν]έφελος·[2] σ[

5 μητέρι δ᾿ ὁππ[ότε[3]
   δειελὸν[4] αἰτίζ‿ουσιν, ἄγουσι δὲ χεῖρας ἀπ᾿ ἔργου,
   τῆμος ἄρ᾿ ἐξ‿.[.]...[
   πρῶτον ὑπὲρ Πά[ρνηθος,] ‿ἐπιπρὸ δὲ μᾶσσον ἐπ᾿
       ἄκρου
   Αἰγαλέως θυμόε‿ντος, ἄγων μέγαν ὑετόν, ἔστη·
10 τῷ δ᾿ ἐπ[ὶ] διπλόον‿[
   τρηχέος Ὑμηττ[οῖο
   ἀστεροπαὶ[ι] σελάγι[ζον
   ‿ἱ[ο]ν ὅτε κλονέ‿[
   Αὐσόν[ι]ον κ‿ατ‿ὰ π[όντον
15 ἡ δ᾿ ἀπὸ Μηρισοῖο θ‿ι‿οὴ βορέαο κατάϊξ
   εἰσέπεσεν νεφέλ[ησιν
   ...[..]ν ὅθ[
       ]ερ‿.[

¹ ποθι suppl. Lobel: ποθ᾿ ἡ Suda cod. A: ποθι cett.

² ἀν[ν]έφελος suppl. Lobel: ἔφελος pap.   ³ μητέρι δ᾿
ὁππ[ότε suppl. Lobel: τέριδ᾿ pap.   ⁴ δείελον schol. V ad
Hom. Od. 17.599 et Suda δ 306: διὲλον pap., ι ε post δ supra
lineam additis: δειελίην Eust.

19 (319 Pf.¹) Suda α 4704

ἀχλύς· σκότος, ὁμίχλη, ζόφος, ἀμβλυωπία, ʻκαὶ-
ἀχλύσαντοςʼ ἀντὶ τοῦ σκοτισθέντος.

     καὶ ἠέρος ἀχλύσαντος

a pale vapor showed itself, but the upper air stretched out
[4] cloudlessly. But at the time when [girls] ask their
mother [6] for supper and take their hands from their
work, then first [the storm] stood over Parnes,[1] and on-
ward with greater force from the peak [9] of thyme-
covered Aegaleus,[2] bringing a great downpour. And twice
as much [11] from rough Hymettus.[3] Lightning flashed
such as when the [bolts] clash on the Ausonian Sea,[4] and
the swift squall of Boreas[5] from Merisus[6] [16] fell on the
clouds.

[1] Highest mountain in Attica, with an altar to Zeus Rain-
bringer (Paus. 1.32.1–2).   [2] Mountain range in Attica be-
tween Parnes and Salamis.   [3] Mountain in Attica east of
Athens known for its honey (Paus. 1.32.1).   [4] The part of
the Mediterranean Sea between Sicily and Crete (Strabo 2.5.20).
[5] The North Wind.   [6] Mountain in Thrace north of Greece
(Plin. *HN* 4.50).

19 (319 Pf.) *Suda*

achlus: darkness, fog, gloom, dim sightedness, and instead
of *skotisthentos*,

> the misty [sky] grew dark.

---

[1] *Hec*. trib. Hecker, 105

20 (238a Pf.) *P.Oxy.* 2216 fr. 2 recto

```
      .    .    .
  ·  ].,[ ].....[
]μεν ἐνισπ[
      ].[
 .         .    .
```

21 (238b Pf.) *P.Oxy.* 2216 fr. 2 verso

```
      .
    ].[
    ]ίω.[    ]βν[
   ]κ[.].[..].πεθ.[
      .    .    .
```

22 (238c Pf.) *P.Oxy.* 2216 fr. 3 recto

```
  .    .    .
 ].σον...[
  ]δεν.[
  .    .    .
```

23 (238d Pf.) *P.Oxy.* 2216 fr. 3 verso

```
      .    .
   ]γενοιτο[
   ]μοιαη[
      .    .
```

20 (238a Pf.) Oxyrhynchus papyrus

21 (238b Pf.) Oxyrhynchus papyrus

22 (238c Pf.) Oxyrhynchus papyrus

23 (238d Pf.) Oxyrhynchus papyrus

24 (311 Pf.[1]) *Suda* α 663

ἀήσυρον· τὸ λεπτόν, τὸ μετέωρον καὶ κοῦφον, τὸ ἐλα-
φρόν, παρὰ τὸ ἀέρι σύρεσθαι. ἐπὶ ὀρνέων,

ἀήσυρον <—>[2] γόνυ κάμψοι

[1] *Hec.* trib. Hecker, 111   [2] Lacuna ind. Meineke 1843,
168, suppl. ὄν: ὡς Bergk: ἐν West

25 (269 Pf.) Hdn. Περὶ ὀνομάτων (*AO* vol. 3, p. 230.31
Cramer) et ap. Choerob. in Theod. (*Gramm. Gr.* vol. 4.1,
p. 158.1 Hilgard)

μύκης, μύκου καὶ μύκητος· τοῦτο . . . διάφορα σημαί-
νει· σημαίνει γὰρ καὶ τὰ καρβώνια τὰ ἐπικείμενα τοῖς
λύχνοις, ὡς παρὰ Καλλ. ἐν τῇ Ἑκαλῃ,

ὁππότε[1] λύχνου
δαιομένου πυρόεντες ἄδην[2] ἐγένοντο μύκητες

[1] ὁππότε Choerob. in Theod.: ὥς ποτε *AO*: var. lect. Schol.
ad Arat. *Phaen.*   [2] ἄδην Choerob. cod. P: ἄρδην Choerob.
cod. NC

26 (525 Pf.[1]) *Et. Gen.* AB s.v. ἐλαχύς

ἐλαχύς· ὁ μικρός. Καλλ.,

ἐλαχὺν δόμον

[1] *Hec.* trib. Schneider, fr. 349

24 (311 Pf.) *Suda*

aēsyron: slight, in midair and light, nimble, to be drawn through the air. In respect to birds,

> it would bend its slight knee

25 (269 Pf.) Herodian, *On Words*

mykes, *mykou*, and *myketos* (mushroom): This is a metaphor. It is the charcoal lying on lamps as in Callimachus' *Hecale*,

> when smoldering wicks from the burning lamp were formed continuously[1]

[1] A portent of rain.

26 (525 Pf.) *Etymologicum Genuinum*

elachus: small. Callimachus,

> a small house[1]

[1] Perhaps Hecale's. Hollis suggests that this may be Theseus' first sight of it.

CALLIMACHUS

27 (*SH* 282[1]) *P.Oxy.* 2529 recto

. . .
]πεκλινεν[
]ὑπ᾽ ἀρπῖδα[
]άδα τὴν αγ[
]μο.φαέεσ[
. . .

[1] *Hec.* trib. Lobel

28 (239 Pf.[1]) *Et. Gen.* AB s.v. διερός

διερός· ὁ ὑγρός. Καλλ.

διερὴν δ᾽ ἀπεσείσατο λαίφην

[1] *Hec.* trib. Schneider, fr. 245

29 (240 Pf.[1]) *Et. Gen.* AB s.v. ἀσκάντης

ἀσκάντης· κλινίδιον εὐτελές, ὅ καὶ ὑπὸ τῶν Ἀττικῶν σκίμπους ὀνομάζεται. Καλλ.

τὸν μὲν ἐπ᾽ ἀσκάντην[2] κάθισεν

[1] *Hec.* trib. Salustius
[2] ἀσκάντην E. Schwartz ap. Reitzenstein, 1890/1, 14: ἀσκάνταν *Et. Gen.* A: ἀσκάντα *Et. Gen.* B

27 (*SH* 282) Oxyrhynchus papyrus

it tilted on its foundation.[1] . . . shining

[1] Perhaps of Hecale's decrepit house.

28 (239 Pf.) *Etymologicum Genuinum*

dieros: wet. Callimachus,

he shook off his wet cloak[1]

[1] Theseus seeking refuge at Hecale's cottage during the storm.

29 (240 Pf.) *Etymologicum Genuinum*

askantes: a cheap small couch which the Athenians call a hammock. Callimachus,

she sat him down on the couch

30 (241 Pf.[1]) *Suda* αι 158

αἰθύξασα· κινήσασα.

αὐτόθεν ἐξ εὐνῆς ὀλίγον ῥάκος αἰθύξασα

[1] *Hec.* trib. Hecker, 112

31 (242 Pf.) *Et. Gr. Par.* s.v. καλοστρόφοι (*AO* vol. 3, p. 53.17 Cramer)

. . . κᾶλον δὲ τὸ ξύλον εἴρηται, ἀφ᾽ οὗ καὶ καλόπους, Καλλ. Ἑκάλη,

παλαίθετα κᾶλα καθήρει

32 (243 Pf.[1]) *Suda* δ 56

δανά· τὰ ξηρὰ ξύλα. τὸ δᾶ μακρόν. Καλλ.,

δανὰ ξύλα . . . κεάσαι . . .[2]

[1] *Hec.* trib. Kapp, fr. 17   [2] Hom. *Od.* 15.322 ξύλα δανὰ κεάσσαι

33 (244 Pf.[1]) *Suda* κ 2684

κυμαίνει· ταράσσει. καὶ ἐπὶ τοῦ ζέειν,

αἶψα δὲ κυμαίνουσαν ἀπαίνυτο χυτρίδα κοίλην

[1] *Hec.* trib. Ruhnken

30 (241 Pf.) *Suda*

aithuxasa: she put in motion.

> at once she shook out a small rag from the bed

31 (242 Pf.) *Etymologicum Graecum Parisinum*

. . . wood is called *kalon*, and from this, *kalopous*. Callimachus in the *Hecale*,

> she took down some wood that she had put up
>> long ago

32 (243 Pf.) *Suda*

dāna: dry wood. The alpha is long. Callimachus,

> to split the dry wood

33 (244 Pf.) *Suda*

kumainei: it is agitated. Also on the boil,

> quickly she took off the boiling hollow pot

CALLIMACHUS

34 (246 Pf.[1]) *Suda* κ 1289

κελέβη· κόγξη, ἢ λεκάνη, ἢ τοιοῦτον σκεῦος, ἐν ᾧ
δυνατὸν νίψασθαι πόδας,

> ἐκ δ' ἔχεεν κελέβην, μετὰ δ' αὖ κερὰς ἠφύσατ'
> ἄλλο

[1] *Hec.* trib. Meineke 1843, 168 et Hecker, 112

35 (251 Pf.[1]) *Et. Gen.* AB s.v. σιπύη

σιπύη· σημαίνει τὴν ἀρτοθήκην, Καλλ.,

> ἐκ δ' ἄρτους σιπύηθεν ἅλις κατέθηκεν ἑλοῦσα
> οἵους βωνίτῃσιν[2] ἐνικρύπτουσι γυναῖκες

[1] Duos versus coniunxit Naeke, 145.   [2] Cf. *Et. Gen.* AB
s.v. βωνίτης· σημαίνει τὸν βουκόλον, Καλλ.

36–37 (*SH* 283; *inc.* 334, 248 Pf.[1]) *P.Oxy.* 2529 verso

```
                       .   .   .
                    ].νικ.. [ ].[
εἰκαίην² τῆς οὐδὲν ἀπέβρασ.ε³ φαῦλον .ἀλετρίς⁴
                    ]ο.οἶσε δελαι[
γεργέριμον⁵ πίτυρίν τε καὶ. ἦν ἀπεθήκ.ατο λευκήν
εἰν ἁλὶ νήχεσθαι φθινοπ.ωρ.ίδ.α [
          .   .   .   .   .   .
```

46

34 (246 Pf.) *Suda*

kelebē: vessel, pot, or some such object in which it was
possible to wash feet.

> she poured out the tub and drew another draft,
>   lukewarm

35 (251 Pf.) *Etymologicum Genuinum*

sipyē: it means pantry, Callimachus,

> taking them from the breadbasket, she served abun-
> dant loaves such as women hide in the ashes for
> herdsmen

36–37 (*SH* 283; *inc.* 334, 248 Pf.) Oxyrhynchus papyrus

> rustic [flour] from which the mill-worker sifted out noth-
> ing coarse . . . she brought . . . the tree-ripened olive, the
> bran olive, and the light colored one she put up to swim
> in brine

---

[1] Fragm. coniungenda sugg. Hollis, ZPE 89 (1991): 25–26.
[2] Cf. *Suda* ει 66 εἰκαία· ὀλίγη, ὡς ἔτυχεν Καλλ.
[3] Cf. *Suda* α 3259 ἀποβράσματα· τὰ πίτυρα παρὰ Καλλ.
[4] Fr. 37 Hollis   [5] *Suda* γ 187 γεργέριμον· τὴν ἐν τῷ δένδρῳ πεπανθεῖσαν ἐλαίαν

38 (249 Pf.) Plin. *HN* 26.82

eadem vis *crethmo* ab Hippocrate (*Nat. mul.* 2) admodum
laudato; est autem inter eas quae eduntur silvestrium her-
barum—hanc certe apud Callimachum adponit rustica illa
Hecale—speciesque elatinae hortensiae;

κρῆθμος (aut κρῆθμον)

Cf. Schol. ad Nic. *Ther.* 909a (p. 311 Crugnola) πολλάκι κρῆθ-
μον . . . ἀμέργεο· ἤτοι λάχανόν ἐστι. καὶ γὰρ μέμνηται
αὐτοῦ καὶ Καλλ. ἐν τῇ Ἑκάλῃ.

39 (250 Pf.) Plin. *HN* 22.88

estur et soncos—ut quem Theseo apud Callim. adponat
Hecale—uterque, albus et niger; lactucae similes ambo.

σόγχος

40 (*SH* 285.1–6; 253.1–6 Pf.) *PSI* 133 recto, 1–6

```
       ].ς Μαραθῶνα κατέρχομαι ὄφρακ......
       ].δε καθηγήτειρα κελεύθου
        ]ηκας ἅ μ᾽ εἴρεο καὶ σύ [γε] μαῖα
        ]ι τι ποθὴ σέο τυτθὸν ἀκοῦσαι
5             ] χρηῢσ ἐρημαίη ἔνι ναίεις
                     ].ι γενέθλη
```

38 (249 Pf.) Pliny the Elder, *Natural History*

crēthmos, praised much by Hippocrates, has the same property. It is, moreover, among the edible herbs of the forest—certainly in Callimachus the rustic Hecale serves it—and a species of garden elatine.

crēthmos (or *crēthmon*)

39 (250 Pf.) Pliny the Elder, *Natural History*

and sow thistle is eaten—which in Callimachus Hecale serves to Theseus—both the white and the black types; both are similar to lettuce.

sow thistle

40 (*SH* 285.1–6; 253.1–6 Pf.) Papyrus fragment

I[1] am going down to Marathon[2] in order to . . . with [Pallas] the guide of my journey. [3] What you asked of me, Mother, you [now know]. [4] But I wish to hear a little from you. [Why] do you, an old woman, live in a desolate place? [And what is your] family?

[1] Theseus is speaking.   [2] A plain in northeast Attica. Hecale's cottage was probably on Mt. Brilessus, above it.

CALLIMACHUS

41 (254 Pf.) *Et Gen.* AB s.v. λιπερνήτης καὶ λιπερνῆτις θηλυκόν

λιπερνήτης καὶ λιπερνῆτις[1] θηλυκόν· σημαίνει ἡ λέξις τὸν ἐνδεᾶ καὶ πτωχόν, οἷον,

οὐ γάρ μοι πενίη πατρώιος, οὐδ᾽ ἀπὸ πάππων
εἰμὶ λιπερνῆτις· βάλε μοι, βάλε τὸ τρίτον εἴη

[1] λιπερνῆτις *Et. Gen.* A, *Suda*: λιπερνήτης *Et. Gen.* B: λιπερνίτης *Et. Sym.*

42 (SH 285.7–12 = 253 + 255 Pf.) *PSI* 133 verso

δινομένην[1] ὑπὸ[2] βουσὶν ἐμὴν ˾ἐφύλασσον ἅλωα·[3]
τὸν δ᾽ ἀπ᾽ Ἀφιδνάων ἵπποι φ[έρον[4]
εἴκελον, οἵ τ᾽ εἶεν Διὸς υἱέε[ς
μέμνημαι καλὴν μὲν α[
5 ἄλ˾λ˾ικα χρυσείῃσιν ἐεργομˌένην ἐνετῆσιν,[5]
ἔργον ἀˌραˌχνάωˌν ˌ.ˌ].´... [6]

[1] δινομένην *Et. Gen.* AB: δεινομένην pap., Choerob. cod. V, *Et. Sym.*: testes alii alia   [2] υπο pap., ὑπὸ *Suda*: περὶ Choerob.   [3] Fr. 255 Pf. = Choerob. in Theod. (*Gramm. Gr.* vol. 4.1, p. 249.32 Hilgard)   [4] φ[έρον suppl. Vitelli: δνάων pap.   [5] *Suda* α 1224 ἐνετή. Hapax legomenon, *Il.* 14.180.
[6] *Suda* α 3750 ἀράχνη· θηλυκῶς τὸ ὕφασμα . . . Καλλ.

50

41 (254 Pf.) *Etymologicum Genuinum*

lipernētēs, and the feminine *lipernētis*: the word means impoverished and beggarly, such as,

> My poverty is not ancestral, nor from my father's side am I a pauper. I wish, I wish I had a third [of my former possessions]!

42 (*SH* 285.7–12 = 253 + 255 Pf.) Papyrus fragment

they[1] guarded my threshing floor circled by the oxen. [2] Horses brought him[2] from Aphidnae[3] [3] like those who are sons of Zeus. [4] And I recall the beautiful cloak [5] closed with golden brooches, [6] the work of spiders

[1] Or, "I guarded my threshing floor."   [2] Perhaps Theseus' father (Aegeus), or Hecale's late husband.   [3] An Attic deme.

CALLIMACHUS

43 (293 Pf.) Schol. ad Ap. Rhod. 3.1226

Αἰήτης περὶ μὲν στήθεσσιν ἕεστο θώρηκα στάδιον·
ὅτι οὐκ ἦν ἁλυσιδωτός, ἀλλὰ σταδιαῖος· ἀπὸ τῆς
στάσεως ἐσχημάτισται. τινὲς δὲ στάδιον τὸν εὐπαγῆ,
ὃν καὶ ὁ Καλλ. λέγει,

στάδιον[1] δ' ὑφέεστο χιτῶνα

[1] Suda σ 981 στάδιον· . . . καὶ "στάδιος χιτών," ὁ ποδήρης,
ὁ τέλειος· παρὰ Καλλ. ἐν Ἑκάλῃ

44 (376 Pf.[1]) Suda φ 558

φόβη· κόμη, θρίξ,

ὅς τε φόβῃσι
ξανθοτάταις ἐκόμα

[1] Hec. trib. Hecker, 107

45 (274 Pf.[1]) Suda α 3981

ἁρμοῖ που· ἀρτίως, νεωστί. οὕτω που Καλλ. ἐν Ἑκάλῃ,

ἁρμοῖ που κἀκείνῳ ἐπέτρεχεν ἁβρὸς[2] ἴουλος
ἄνθει ἑλιχρύσῳ ἐναλίγκιος[3]

[1] Hec. trib. Hecker, 108   [2] ἐπέτρεχεν ἁβρὸς Suda: ἐπέ-
τρεχε λεπτὸς Et. Gen. AB s.v. ἁρμοῖ   [3] Suda ε 874 ἑλίχρυ-
σος· τὸ τοῦ κισσοῦ ἄνθος

43 (293 Pf.) Scholia to Apollonius of Rhodes, *Argonautica*

Aeëtes wore around his chest a rigid breast-plate: that was not chain mail, but plated armor. It took its form from the plate. Some say the plate was solid, which Callimachus says,

> and under it he wore a stiff[1] tunic

[1] *Suda* σ 981 Adler . . . reaching to the feet, full-sized.

44 (376 Pf.) *Suda*

phobē: lock, hair.

> who had
> the yellowest hair

45 (274 Pf.) *Suda*

harmoi pou: lately, just now, as Callimachus somewhere in the *Hecale*,

> recently perhaps soft down spread on that boy
> like the flower Helichryse[1]

[1] *Suda* ε 874 identifies Helichryse as the flower of ivy, but this seems to be an error based on a misreading of Theoc. *Id*. 1.30 (Hutton, *Suda online*).

46 (304 Pf.[1]) Schol. Laur. ad Soph. *OC* 314

κρατὶ δ' ἡλιοστερής κυνῆ πρόσωπα Θεσσαλίς νιν
ἀμπέχει· καὶ γὰρ περισσοὶ ἦσαν οἱ Θεσσαλικοὶ πῖ-
λοι, ὡς καὶ Καλλ.,

> ἀμφὶ δέ οἱ κεφαλῆ νέον Αἱμονίηθεν
> μεμβλωκὸς πίλημα περίτροχον ἄλκαρ ἔκειτο
> εἴδεος[2] ἐνδίοιο

[1] *Hec*. trib. L. Valckenaer, *Theocriti decem Eidyllia Latinis
pleraque numeris* . . . (Leiden, 1773), 344 (ad Theoc. *Id.* 15)
[2] εἴδεος ab v. 1 ad v. 3 in Hollis removit Toup: ἴδεος Naeke

47 (*SH* 286 *inc.* 639, 327 Pf.) *P.Oxy* 2377 recto

```
                . . .
            ]λ.ων.[
            ].... λοκα[
          ]εν ὃς καὶ μο[
          ].ιν Ὀρνείδαο κ[
5         ].λης ἐπὶ νηὸς ο.[
    ἵππους, καιτάεντος .ἀπ' Εὐρώταο κομίσσαι[1]
          ]..κῦμα κ.[
          ]εια..ν ὁθιδ[
          ]..αἰθυίης[2] γὰρ .ὑπὸ πτερύγεσσιν ἔλυσ-
10  πείσ,ματα τῆς μήτ' αὐτ[
    μ]ήθ' ὅτις ἄμμι βεβουλ[
    ..].... ιηι κακονο.τ..[
    ..].ν.[....]..[.]..[.]..[.].β[
```

46 (304 Pf.) Laurentian Scholia to Sophocles, *Oedipus at Colonus*

on her head, a Thessalian hat, a sunscreen, protected her face: Thessalian felt hats were remarkable, and also Callimachus,

> on his head sat a circular hat newly arrived from Haemonia,[1] a defense against the heat of midday

[1] Thessaly.

47 (*SH* 286 *inc.* 639, 327 Pf.) Oxyrhynchus papyrus

and who to me . . . the son of Orneus[1] . . . on a ship . . . [6] to bring horses from mint-filled Eurotas[2] . . . a wave . . . under the wings of the shearwater[3] [10] they let loose the stern cables . . . neither I myself . . . [11] nor whoever

[1] Peteus (the son of Orneus), an enemy of Aegeus (Paus. 10.35.8). Peteus' son Menestheus was an opponent of Theseus (Plut. *Thes.* 32). Perhaps Peteus sent Hecale's husband to Sparta to bring back some horses, and he perished in a shipwreck (*SH* 127). [2] River in Sparta. [3] An omen of storms at sea (Arat. *Phaen.* 918–19).

---

[1] Fr. 639 Pf. = Schol. HMQR ad Hom. *Od.* 4.1 κοίλην Λακε-δαίμονα κητώεσσαν [2] Fr. 327 Pf. = *Suda* αι 155 αἴθυια· . . . καὶ ἡ θαλαττία ὄρνις

ἀν]θρώποις ὅτε νῆα· τ[
15 μ͵έσσον ἐπεὶ ναύταις[³
..].μεν ἐγὼ π[
....]κεναντ[
...].χιδας.[
.....]ων ὀ.[
...].οι βασιλ[

.   .   .   .   .

³ Fr. 629 Pf. = Schol. bT ad Hom. Il. 15.628 τυτθὸν γὰρ ὑπὲκ
θανάτοιο φέρονται· τὸ τυχὸν γὰρ ἀπέχουσι τοῦ θανάτου

48 (SH 287.1–10 inc. 337, 366, 247, 284 Pf.) P.Oxy. 2376
col. I

.   .   .   .   .

τὼ μὲν ἐγὼ θαλέεσσιν ἀνέτρε͵φον¹ οὐδέ τις οὕτως
γε]νέθλην
ῥυδὸ͵ν ἀφινύονται·²
]ετονη.. ϛ·
5   τινθαλέοισι κατικμήναι͵ντο λοετροῖς³
͵ανε παῖδε φερούσῃ·
τώ μοι ἀναδραμέτην ἅτε κερ͵κίδες,⁴ αἵτε χαράδρης
π]ουλὺ δὲ μήκει
]ον [ἡ]έξαντο
10] ἐπεμαίετο παισίν·

.   .   .   .   .

56

wishes us [well][4] . . . for men when a ship . . . [15] since for sailors between[5] . . . [16] and I [20] . . . kings

[4] Conventionally followed by "May I never experience such a thing" (Hollis, 193).   [5] For sailors there is only a thin plank between life and death (Schol. bT ad Hom. *Il.* 15.628, quoted opposite; cf. Diog. Laert. 1.103; Arat. *Phaen.* 299).

48 (*SH* 287.1–10 *inc.* 337, 366, 247, 284 Pf.) Oxyrhynchus papyrus

and I fed the two on delicacies nor did anyone in this way . . . family . . . are very rich . . . [5] that they might bathe in warm water . . . carrying the two boys . . . [7] My two shot up like aspens which by a stream . . . they grew to a great height [10] . . . [death?] grasped the children

---

[1] Fr. 337 Pf. = *Suda* θ 12 θαλέεσσιν· τρυφαῖς, θάλλειν ποιούσαις

[2] Fr. 366 Pf. = *Suda* ρ 283 ῥύδην· . . . λέγεται καὶ ῥυδόν

[3] Fr. 247 Pf. = *Suda* τ 641 Τινθαλέοισι· χλιαροῖς, θερμοῖς

[4] *Et. Mag.* p. 506 s.v. κερκίς· . . . καὶ εἶδος φυτοῦ

49 (*SH* 287.11–30 *inc.* 350, 294, 368 Pf.) *P.Oxy.* 2377 verso + 2376 col. II

]ε̣ν̣εστερ̣.[

ἠρνεόμην θανάτοιο πάλ̣,αι καλέοντ̣ος ἀκοῦσαι
μὴ μετὰ δὴν¹ ἵνα καὶ σοὶ ἐ̣,πιρρήξαιμι χ̣ι̣τῶνα;

]μασεφιλησ[

5   ].̣δ' ἀπο μέτρα[

]άσκονταλε̣[

πειο.[   ] ελπιδεση̣.[

Κέρκ[νον-   πα]λαίσμασι πε[

φθει.[   ]αστεος, ὅς ῥ' ἔφυγεν μέν

10   Ἀρκ̣αδίην, ἡμῖν δὲ κακὸς ̣, παρενάσσα̣το γείτων²

μη̣.[   ]λαι χέρες α̣.[

τεκ[   ].̣ισεμονοικ[

τουπ[   ]ρε̣.εμαπαν[

αὐτη [   ] ζώοντος ἀναι̣δέσι̣ν̣, ἐμπήξαι̣μι

15   σκώλου̣ις ὀφθαλμοῖσι καί̣,, εἰ θέμις, ὠμὰ

π̣ασαίμην³

ειδουο[   ]ε̣[.̣]ος ἐστινο̣.̣[

] ληεσε[

]̣νσαντα[

].̣τοδα.̣[..

20   ].̣τελ.̣.[

¹ Fr. 350 Pf. = *Suda* μ 863 μή· τὸ ἀπαγορευτικόν· ἀντὶ τοῦ οὐ κεῖται παρὰ Καλλιμάχῳ   ² Fr. 294 Pf. = Schol. vet. ad Ar. *Nub.* 508a (p. 114 Holwerda)

HECALE

49 (*SH* 287.11–30 *inc.* 350, 294, 368 Pf.) Oxyrhynchus papyrus

Did I refuse long ago to hear death calling [3] so that afterward I would tear my tunic for you too? . . . [7] hopes . . . Cercyon[1] . . . by wrestling . . . [10] he fled Arcadia, evil for us, a bad neighbor . . . his hands . . . [12] my house . . . [14] I would stab him in his shameless eyes with a pointed stake, and if it were right I would eat him raw.

[1] A mythical king of Eleusis who challenged passersby to a wrestling match and killed them when they lost. He was ultimately beaten by Theseus and dispatched in turn.

---

[3] Fr. 368 Pf. = *Suda* σ 686 σκῶλος· εἶδος ἀκάνθης, ἢ σκάν-δαλον· "τοῦ μὲν ἐγὼ ζώοντος ἀναιδέσιν ἐμπήξαιμι σκώλους ὀφθαλμοῖσι, καί, εἰ θέμις, ὠμὰ πασαίμην."

50 (367 Pf.[1]) *Suda* σ 175

σέβας· τιμή, ἔκπληξις. παρὰ δὲ Καλλ. τὸ Θαῦμα.

τόδ᾽ ἔχω σέβας

[1] *Hec.* trib. Naeke, 160

51 (300 Pf.) Schol. HQ ad Hom. *Od.* 14.199

ἐκ μὲν Κρητάων· ἀπὸ τοῦ Κρῆται. καὶ τὰς Ἀθήνας
γὰρ ποτὲ ἑνικῶς, ποτὲ πληθυντικῶς ὀνομάζει. τοῦτο
δὲ ζηλώσας ὁ Καλλ. τὸν Κολωνὸν Θηλυκῶς καὶ πλη-
θυντικῶς εἶπεν,

ἔκ με[1] Κολωνάων τις ὁμέστιον ἤγαγε δαίμων[2]
τῶν ἑτέρων

[1] ἐκ με corr. Porson et Buttmann: ἐκ μὲν HQ   [2] δαίμων
coniecit Naeke, 127: δήμου HQ

52 (272 Pf.[1]) *Et. Gen.* AB s.v. ἀμπρόν

ἀμπρόν· σχοινίον τι· καὶ ἀμπρεύειν δὲ τὸ ἕλκειν.
Καλλ.,

ἄνδρες[2] †ἐλαιοί[3] Δεκελειόθεν ἀμπρεύοντες

[1] *Hec.* trib. Schneider, fr. 234   [2] ἄνδρες *Et. Gen.* AB
ἀμπρόν: ἄνδρ᾽ *Et. Gen.* A s.v. ἀμπρεῦω, *Et. Mag.*   [3] ἐλαιοί
vel -οὶ codd.: ἐλαιολόγοι Diels ap. Kapp, fr. 85: δείλαιοι Pf.:
ἐλαιηρούς Barber

50 (367 Pf.) *Suda*

sebas: honor, consternation, but astonishment in Callimachus,

> I am in awe at this

51 (300 Pf.) Scholia to Homer, *Odyssey*

from Crete (pl.): i.e., from Crete (sing.). Just as at one time Athens was spoken of in the singular and at another, in the plural. Callimachus, imitating this, designates Colona as a singular and a plural,

> some evil spirit[1] led me from the other Colonae[2]
> to be a housemate

[1] On another *daimon* leading to inexplicable behavior in Callimachus, see *Iamb* 1 (*Ia.* 191.63).   [2] An Attic deme.

52 (272 Pf.) *Etymologicum Genuinum*

ampron: a rope; and the verb *ampeuein*, to haul. Callimachus,

> men carting . . . from Decelea[1]

[1] An Attic deme.

53 (275 Pf.[1]) *Et. Gen.* AB s.v. ἄστηνος

ἄστηνος· ὁ δυστυχὴς καὶ πένης. Καλλ.,

πάσχομεν ἄστηνοι· τὰ μὲν οἴκοθε[2] πάντα
δέδασται[3]

[1] *Hec*. trib. Kapp, fr. 120   [2] οἴκοθε Pfeiffer: οἴκοθεν *Et. Gen.* AB   [3] δέδασται Schneider, fr. 476: λέλασται *Et. Gen.* B: λέλασθαι *Et. Gen.* A

54 (329 Pf.[1]) *Suda* ε 777

ἐλέγχομεν· ἀντὶ τοῦ κακολογοῦμεν,

νυκτὶ δ᾽ ὅλῃ βασιλῆας ἐλέγχομεν

[1] *Hec*. trib. Hecker, 112

55 (290 Pf.[1]) Hesychius s.v. γηφάγοι

γηφάγοι· πένητες, ἄποροι ὡς τὰς ἐκ γῆς βοτάνας σιτιζόμενοι, τροφῆς ἀμοιροῦντες, Καλλ. ἐν Ἑκάλῃ,

γηφάγοι

[1] *Hec*. trib. Naeke, 107

56 (365 Pf.[1]) *Suda* π 3076

ποίην· πόαν, βοτάνην. καὶ ποιηφάγον, τὴν σταφυλο-

[1] *Hec*. trib. Adler

53 (275 Pf.) *Etymologicum Genuinum*

astēnos: the one who is unfortunate and impoverished.
Callimachus,

> we wretches suffer; everything at home has been
> given away

54 (329 Pf.) *Suda*

elenchomen: instead of "speak ill of,"

> the whole night we gripe about the kings[1]

[1] A parallel might be Hesiod's railing against unjust kings (Pf. vol. 1, 288).

55 (290 Pf.) Hesychius

gēphagoi: poor men, without means such as those feeding on weeds from the earth, having no portion of food. Callimachus in the *Hecale*,

> eating from the earth

56 (365 Pf.) *Suda*

poiēn: [also] *poan*, a plant. And *poēphagon* (grass-eating),

λόγον· ἢ τὴν τοὺς ἀστάχυας ὄπισθεν τῶν θεριζόντων σωρεύουσαν,

ποιηφάγον

57 (313 Pf.[1]) *Suda* α 1429

ἁλυκόν· δριμύ,

ἁλυκὸν δέ οἱ ἔκπεσε δάκρυ

[1] *Hec.* trib. Naeke, 239 et Hecker, 123

58 (310 Pf.[1]) *Suda* α 633

ἀείπλανα· πεπλανημένα, φλύαρα, πλήρη φλυαρίας,

ἀείπλανα χείλεα γρηός

[1] *Hec.* trib. Ruhnken; cf. Hecker, 112

59 (296 Pf.[1]) Schol. NAB ad Eur. *Hipp.* 979

ὁ Σκείρων ἦν ἐν Μεγάροις τύραννος ἄξενος ὃν τῇ χελώνῃ ἔρριψεν ὁ Θησεύς. Σκειρωνίδες δὲ πέτραι καλοῦνται ἀπὸ Σκείρωνος τοῦ τὴν χελώνην τρέφοντος, οὗ μέμνηται Καλλ.

[1] *Hec.* trib. Naeke, 176

Cf. *Et. Gen.* AB s.v. Σκείρων· ὄνομα λῃστοῦ, πολλῆς φθορᾶς ὧν αἴτιος, καὶ γὰρ τοὺς παρερχομένους ἔρριπτεν ἐπάνω τῆς χελώνης· ἡ δὲ δεχομένη ἤσθιεν αὐτούς. γράφεται δὲ διὰ τῆς εἶ διφθόγγου ἀπὸ ἱστορίας ... Καὶ γὰρ Καλλιμάχου γε-

as in she the grape-gatherer, or she who heaps the ears of
corn behind the harvesters,

> eating grass

57 (313 Pf.) *Suda*

halukon: salty, bitter,

> a salty tear fell from her[1]

[1] Adapted from Homer (*Il*.2.266, *Od*. 16.16).

58 (310 Pf.) *Suda*

aeiplana: ever-wandering, wandering, nonsense, full of
nonsense,

> the ever-wandering lips of a crone

59 (296 Pf.) Scholia to Euripides, *Hippolytus*

Sceiron was an inhospitable king in Megara whom The-
seus threw down at Chelone (the place of the tortoise).
The rocks are called those of Sceiron from Sceiron's feed-
ing the tortoise, as Callimachus recalls.[1]

[1] Theseus' killing of the notorious outlaw Sceiron took place
before his arrival in Marathon. It appears from this and the fol-
lowing fragments that Callimachus treated the incident in the
early part of the *Hecale*. Alternatively, Theseus may have told the
story himself to Hecale. On Callimachus' unusual orthography
(viz., Scīron), see the passage from the *Etymologicum Genuinum*
quoted opposite.

γραφότος αὐτὸ τοῦ ῑ, Ἀριστοφάνης ὁ γραμματικὸς προσ-
έθηκε τὸ ε̄.

CALLIMACHUS

60 (245 Pf.[1]) *Suda* χ 607

χύτλα· ὑδρέλαιον. καὶ χυτλάζειν, τὸ μιγνύναι, καὶ δι-
αχεῖν. χύτλα λέγεται κυρίως τὸ ὑγροῦ ἔτι ἀπὸ ὕδατος
ὄντος τοῦ σώματος ἀλείψασθαι.

>   φράσον δέ μοι, εἰς ὅ τι τεῦχος
> χεύωμαι[2] ποσὶ χύτλα καὶ ὁππόθεν

[1] *Hec*. trib. Schneider, fr. 66   [2] χεύωμαι corr. Stephanus:
χεύομαι codd. aut χεύε F

61 (306 Pf.) Steph. Byz. ι 11 Billerbeck s.v. Ἰαπις

Ἰαπίς· χαράδρα Ἀττικὴ εἰς Μέγαρα ἀπάγουσα, ὡς
Καλλ. Ἑκάλῃ.

62 (328 Pf.[1]) *Suda* ε 10

ἔαρ· λέγεται καὶ τὸ αἷμα διὰ τὸ ἐν τῷ ἔαρι πλεονάζειν.

>   ἧχι κονίστραι
> ἄξεινοι λύθρῳ τε καὶ εἴαρι πεπλήθασι

[1] *Hec*. trib. Ruhnken

60 (245 Pf.) *Suda*

chutla: water mixed with oil. Also the verb *chutlazein*, to anoint after a bath, and to mix and pour. *Chutla* is used precisely of anointing [with oil] when the body is still damp from the water.

> Tell me, into what basin
> should I pour the water and oil for your feet and from
> where[1]

[1] Theseus, talking to Sceiron, who made travelers wash his feet and then threw them over a cliff into the sea (Hollis, *CR* 15 [1965]: 259–60).

61 (306 Pf.) Stephanus of Byzantium

Iapis: an Attic stream flowing toward Megara, as Callimachus in the *Hecale*.[1]

[1] Naeke (p. 182) conjectured that after defeating Sceiron, Theseus went along the Iapis to Cercyon.

62 (328 Pf.) *Suda*

eär: it also means blood because blood increases in the spring.

> where the unwelcoming
> wrestling arenas are filled with gore and blood[1]

[1] Naeke (p. 184) suggests that the fragment describes Cercyon's wrestling floor.

CALLIMACHUS

63 (256 Pf.[1]) *Suda* κ 1811

κλισία· ἡ σκηνή. λαμβάνεται δὲ καὶ ἐπὶ κλίνης,

    λέξομαι ἐν μυχάτῳ· κλισίη δέ μοί ἐστιν ἑτοίμη

[1] *Hec.* trib. Hecker, 94, 117

64 (257 Pf.[1]) *Suda* μ 45

μαθών· ἰδών . . . καὶ αὖθις,

    ὡς ἔμαθεν κἀκεῖνον ἀνιστάμενον

[1] *Hec.* trib. Schneider, fr. 44

65 (292 Pf.[1]) Schol. ad Ap. Rhod. 4.972

ἀργύρεον χαῖον· χαῖόν ἐστι καμπύλη βακτηρία, ᾗ οἱ
ποιμένες χρῶνται . . . Καλλ.,

    ἔπρεπέ τοι προέχουσα κάρης εὐρεῖα καλύπτρη,
    ποιμενικὸν πίλημα, καὶ ἐν χερὶ χαῖον †ἔχουσα[2]

[1] *Hec.* trib. L. Valckenaer, *Theocriti decem Eidyllia Latinis pleraque numeris* . . . (Leiden, 1773), 344 (ad Theoc. *Id.* 15)
[2] Corruptum, Pfeiffer (vol. 2, 120)

66 (355 Pf.[1]) *Suda* ο 131

ὀκχή· στήριγμα, βάσταγμα,

                    γέντο δ᾽ ἐρείκης
σκηπάνιον <   > ὃ δὴ πέλε γήραος ὀκχή

63 (256 Pf.) *Suda*

klisia: a tent. It is used also for a bed,

  I will sleep within. A cot is ready for me[1]

  [1] Hecale may be speaking here of her own bed.

64 (257 Pf.) *Suda*

mathōn: having learned, having seen . . . ,

  when she learned that he too had arisen

65 (292 Pf.) Scholia to Apollonius of Rhodes, *Argonautica*

argureon chaion: it is the curved staff that shepherds use
. . . Callimachus,

  wide headgear projecting forward from your head
    suited you,
  a shepherd's felt hat, and in your hand a staff[1]

  [1] The poet apostrophizes his heroine.

66 (355 Pf.) *Suda*

okchē: support, prop, burden,

                    she grasped her staff
  of heath . . . which was the support of old age

---

  [1] *Hec.* trib. Hemsterhuys in Ernesti, *Call.*, 439; Naeke, 111

CALLIMACHUS

67 (358 Pf.[1]) *Suda* ε 3064

ἐρωήσας· ἀντὶ τοῦ μειώσας, κατάξας, Καλλίμαχος,

θηρὸς ἐρωήσας[2] ὀλοὸν κέρας

[1] *Hec.* trib. Buttmann, Naeke, 253   [2] θηρὸς ἐρωήσας
Sylburg: ἐρωήσας θηρὸς *Et. Mag.* s.v. ἐρωή

68 (259 Pf.[1]) Schol. ad Ap. Rhod. 1.1162

ὁ τούσγε . . . ἐφέλκετο κάρτεϊ χειρῶν Ἡρακλέης·
πρὸς τὴν πάντων αὐτῶν ἀργίαν καὶ τὴν τοῦ κύματος
ὑπερβολὴν τὸ "ἐφέλκετο" πρὸς πλείονα εἶπεν ἔμφα-
σιν· ὅπερ καὶ Καλλ. ἐπὶ τοῦ ταύρου ἡττηθέντος φη-
σίν,

ὁ μὲν εἷλκεν, ὁ δ᾽ εἵπετο νωθρὸς ὁδίτης

[1] *Hec.* trib. Buttmann, Naeke, 253–54

69 (*SH* 288.1–15; 260.1–15 Pf.) *P.Rain.* 6 (Tabula Vindo-
bonensis) col. I

οἰόκερως· ἕτερον γὰρ ἀπηλοίησε[1] κορύνη.
ὡς ἴδον, ὧ[ς] ἅμα πάντες ὑπέτρεσαν, οὐδέ τις ἔτλη
ἄνδρα μέγαν καὶ θῆρα πελώριον ἄντα ἰδέσθαι,
μέσφ᾽ ὅτε δὴ Θησεύς φιν ἀπόπροθι μακρὸν ἄϋσε·
5 "μίμνετε θαρσήεντες, ἐμῷ δέ τις Αἰγέι πατρί

[1] Hapax legomenon, *Il.* 4.522

70

HECALE

67 (258 Pf.) *Suda*

erōēsas: the opposite of diminished, forced down, as Callimachus,

> he forced down the deadly horn of the beast[1]

[1] Theseus subdues the Marathonian bull by grasping its horn.

68 (259 Pf.) Scholia to Apollonius of Rhodes, *Argonautica*

He dragged them with the strength of his hands, Heracles: considering the exhaustion of all [the Argonauts] and the power of the wave, he [Apollonius] said "dragged" for greater emphasis, which Callimachus says about the defeated bull,

> one dragged and the other followed, an indisposed
>   traveler

69 (*SH* 288.1–15; 260.1–15 Pf.) Vienna Tablet

single-horned, for he crushed[1] the other with his club.[2] When they saw [them],[3] at once they all trembled, nor did anyone dare to look at the great man and the mighty beast, until Theseus shouted loudly to them from a distance, [5] "Stay with confidence, and let someone, who is the

[1] Homeric hapax legomenon (*Il.* 4.522).   [2] Theseus had taken the club from Periphetes (Plut. *Thes.* 8).

[3] Modeled on *Il.* 14.294. Alternatively, "When they saw, how they trembled . . ."

71

νεύμενος ὅς τ᾽ ὤκιστος ἐς ἄστυρον² ἀγγελιώτης
ὧδ᾽ ἐνέποι—πολέων κεν ἀναψύξειε μεριμνέων—
'Θησεὺς οὐχ ἑκὰς οὗτος, ἀπ᾽ εὐύδρου Μαραθῶνος
ζωὸν ἄγων τὸν ταῦρον.'" ὁ μὲν φάτο, τοὶ δ᾽ ἀΐοντες
10 πάντες "ἰὴ παιῆον" ἀνέκλαγον, αὖθι δὲ μίμνον.
οὐχὶ νότος τόσσην γε χύσιν κατεχεύατο φύλλων,
οὐ βορέης οὐδ᾽ αὐτὸς ὅτ᾽ ἔπλετο φυλλοχόος μ‹ε›ίς,
ὅσσα τότ᾽ ἀγρῶσται περί τ᾽ ἀμφί τε Θησέϊ βάλλον,
οἵ μιν ἐκυκλώσα]ντο περισταδόν, αἱ δὲ γυναῖκες
15 ⌊στόρνησιν³ ἀνέστεφον⌋

² Suda a 4272 ἄστυρον· πόλιν. Καλλίμαχος
³ Suda σ 1145 στόρνησι· ζώναις

Inter frr. 69 et 70 versus fere 22 desunt.

70 (*SH* 288.16–29; 260.16–29 Pf.) *P.Rain.* 6 (Tabula Vin-
dobonensis) col. II

καί ῥ᾽ ὅτ᾽ ἐπ.[.]ιθυσσ.....ε......]νεκ.τοι
Οὐρανίδαι.α.οιε....π.ρ....επαλλας
τῆς μὲν ἐγὼ δην......δρ..........ι.
5 μέσφ᾽ ὅτε Κεκροπίδ[η]σιν επ...... κατολ.αν

swiftest messenger, go to the city and say to my father Aegeus,[4] for he would relieve him of many anxieties, 'Theseus here is not far off, but is bringing the bull alive from well-watered Marathon.'" He spoke, and all of them [10] when they heard cried out "Hië Paeëon,"[5] and remained in place. The south wind does not pour down so great a flood of leaves, nor the north wind, not even when it is the very month of leaf-fall, as those which the farm workers cast around Theseus.[6] They circled him on every side, and the women [15] wreathed him with their belts.[7]

[4] Theseus' concern that his father hear the good news as soon as possible contrasts with the tradition that he caused the old man's suicide by forgetting to signal his success in slaying the Minotaur, by raising a white sail, as they had agreed when he set out to Crete (Catull. 64.207–50).   [5] A ritual triumphant cry mostly associated with cults of Apollo. Callimachus describes its origin in his *Hymn to Apollo* (*Hymn* 2.97–104), when the infant Apollo kills the serpent at Delphi. It appears without reference to Apollo when the Greeks sing the *paeëon* in Homer to celebrate the death of Hector (*Il.* 22.391).   [6] The *phyllobolia* was a ritual commonly used to honor athletic victors by pelting them with leaves (e.g., Pind. *Pyth.* 9.123–24). It was first performed for Theseus to celebrate his killing of the Minotaur (*Suda* π 1054).

[7] Garlanding with belts is connected with the *phyllobolia* in Eratosthenes (*FGH* 241 F 14).

About 22 verses are missing between fragments 69–70.

70 (*SH* 288.16–29; 260.16–29 Pf.) Vienna Tablet

and . . . the gods . . . Pallas, of whom I long ago . . . [5] until the time when . . . to the daughters of Cecrops[1]

[1] Cecrops, half man and half snake, was a mythical king of Athens.

λάθριον ἄρρητον, γενεῇ δ᾽ ὅθεν οὔτε νιν ἔγνων
οὔτ᾽ ἐδάην, φ.......ωγαγιουσε....υται
οἰωνούς, ὡς δῆθεν ὑφ᾽ Ἡφαίστῳ τέκεν Γαῖα.
τουτάκι δ᾽ ἡ μὲν ἑῆς ἔρυμα χθονὸς ὄφρα βάλοιτο,
10 τήν ῥα νέον ψήφῳ τε Διὸς δυοκαίδεκά τ᾽ ἄλλων
ἀθανάτων ὄφιός τε κατέλλαβε μαρτυρίῃσιν,
Πελλήνην ἐφίκανεν Ἀχαιΐδα· τόφρα δὲ κοῦραι
αἱ φυλακοὶ κακὸν ἔργον ἐπεφράσσαντο τελέσσαι,
κ.ιστη....[.].....ακαδ......ανεισαι

Inter frr. 70 et 73 versus fere 22 desunt. Frr. 71 et prob. 72 in eo
numero sunt.

. . . hidden, unspeakable, in birth from where he[2] came neither did I know [7] nor did I learn . . . primordial [8] birds . . . how long ago Earth bore them to Hephaestus. Then [Pallas] came to Achaean Pellene[3] so that she could set down a safeguard[4] for her land [10] which she had recently gained by the vote of Zeus and twelve other immortals with the testimonies of the snake.[5] Then the guardian girls[6] plotted to do an evil deed

[2] Erichthonius. Schol. AD ad Hom. *Il.* 2.547: Erichthonius was born from Hephaestus. He pursued Athena out of love . . . and ejaculated on the leg of the goddess. After wiping it off with wool, she threw their offspring into the earth. From this the child was called Erichthonius, because he was delivered from the wool and from the earth. Callimachus tells the story in the *Hecale*.

[3] On difficulties with Athena's itinerary, see H. Lloyd-Jones, *HSCP* 72 (1968): 137–40.

[4] Lycabettus Hill (cf. *Hec.* 71).

[5] The dispute was between Athena and Poseidon for possession of Attica. The snake is Cecrops, who proved that it was Athena who first produced the olive (*Ia.* 194.66–80).

[6] The three daughters of Cecrops were Aglaurus, Pandrosus, and Herse. Athena gave them the infant Erichthonius in a basket with instructions not to open it. They disobeyed the goddess, and when it was discovered, they committed suicide by jumping from the Acropolis. Sources differ as to which of the girls took part in the plot and how they were punished. The Atthidographer Amelesagoras is thought to be Callimachus' source. His treatment included the story of how the crow brought the bad news to Athena.

About 22 verses are missing between fragments 70 and 73. Among them are fragments 71 and probably 72, below.

71 (*SH* 289; 261 Pf.[1]) *Et. Gen.* AB s.v. ἄστυρον

ἄστυρον· τὸ ἄστυ. Καλλ.,

> ἣ μὲν ἀερτάζουσα μέγα τρύφος Ὑψιζώρου
> ἄστυρον εἰσανέβαινεν, ἐγὼ δ᾽ ἤντησα Λυκείου
> καλὸν ἀεὶ λιπόωντα κατὰ δρόμον Ἀπόλλωνος[2]

[1] Duo fragmenta coniunxit Kapp, fr. 61.   [2] Schol. Laur.
ad Soph. *OT* 919 πρός σ᾽ ὦ Λύκει᾽ Ἄπολλον· Λύκειον γυμνά-
σιόν ἐστιν Ἀθήνησιν ἔνθα Ἀπόλλων τιμᾶται· καὶ Καλλ.

72 (374 Pf.[1]) *Suda* υ 488

ὑποδράξ· . . . τουτέστιν ὠχριάσασα καὶ ὑποβλεψα-
μένη διὰ τὴν ὀργήν,

> ἣ δὲ πελιδνωθεῖσα καὶ ὄμμασι[2] λοξὸν ὑποδράξ
> ὀσσομένη

[1] *Hec.* trib. Hecker, 118   [2] ὄμμασι *Suda*: ὄθμασι Pfeiffer

73 (*SH* 288.30–43A; 260.30–43 Pf.) *P.Rain.* 6 (Tabula
Vindobonensis) col. III

5 . . . . ν . σ
. . . . ουναι δὲ παραπ . . . . κορῶναι
δ . . . . ου γὰρ ἔγωγε τεόν ποτε πότνια θυμόν
. . . . πολλὰ παραίσια μήπο[τ]᾽ ἐλαφροί

71 (*SH* 289; 261 Pf.) *Etymologicum Genuinum*

astyron: a city. Callimachus,

> She[1] entered the city carrying high a huge hunk of
> Mt. Hypsizorus,[2] and I met her at the lovely colon-
> nade[3] of the beautiful and always radiant Lycean
> Apollo[4]

[1] Athena. The first-person narrator appears to be the crow,
who is bringing Athena the bad news that the daughters of Ce-
crops have exposed Erichthonius.   [2] A mountain in Thrace.
She would throw it down to earth in Athens to create Lycabettus
Hill.   [3] The gymnasium of Lycean Apollo (cf. Schol. Laur.
ad Soph. *OT* 919, quoted opposite), where Aristotle taught.
    [4] Because it was well oiled by the wrestlers.

72 (374 Pf.) *Suda*

hypodrax: askance . . . she became pale and looked askance
on account of her anger,

> she grew pale with anger and looking with her eyes
> askance from under her brows

73 (*SH* 288.30–43A; 260.30–43 Pf.) Vienna Tablet

crows . . . I would not ever . . . your anger, queen [8] . . .
many things of ill omen never lighthearted [9] . . . birds,

.......οἰωνοί, τότε δ᾽ ὤφελον ε.........
10 .υτω.[..].τερην μὲ[ν] ἀπε...εν......
ἡμετερ[..] ἐκλειν.ε....λλ.ε.οι
μηδ[έ] ποτ᾽ ἐκ θυμοῖο· βαρὺς χόλος αἰέν Ἀθήνης.
αὐτὰρ ἐγὼ τυτθὸς παρέῃ[ν] γόνο[ς.].δ[.]... γάρ
ἤδη μοι γενεὴ π...δε.[..]εν.....
15   ]...ε.

Inter frr. 73 et 74 versus fere 22 desunt.

74 (SH 288.43B–69; 260.44–69, inc. 346, 351 Pf.) P.Rain.
6 (Tabula Vindobonensis) col. IV + P.Oxy. 2398, 2437,
2217

γαστέρι μ.οῦνον ἔ.χοιμι κ.ακῆς ἀλκτήρια λιμοῦ[1]
.]δουμεχ[......]έχειδο[
ἀ]λλ᾽ Ἑκάλ[η..].ε λιτὸν ἐδ.[
....ακ[......]νον παγ.[
5 καὶ κ.ρῖμν.ον. κυκεῶνος ἀπ.οστάξαντος ἔραζε·[2]
..].μης[....]. οὔτις ἐπέσσεται[
....]θων[...]ν[ι] κακάγγελον· εἴθε γὰρ [εἴης
κεῖ]νον ἔτι] ζώουσα κατὰ χρόνον, ὄφρα τ[....]ης
Θρ.ιαὶ τὴν. γρῆϋ.ν. ἐπιπνείουσι κορών.ην.[3]
10 ναὶ μὰ τ.όν.—οὐ γὰρ [π]ῳ πάντ᾽ ἤματα—ναὶ .μ.ὰ τὸ
         ῥικνὸν
σῦφαρ ἐμόν,[4] ναὶ το.ῦτ.ο τὸ δένδ.ρ.εον αὖον ἐόν
         περ—
οὐκ ἤδη ῥυμόν τε κ[α]ὶ ἄξονα κανάξαντες
ἠέλιοι δυ[σ]μέων εἴσω πόδα πάντες ἔχουσι,

then I ought . . . [12] not ever from anger. Always heavy is the wrath of Athena. [13] But I was a small fledgling. Now I am in my [eighth] generation[1]

[1] Crows were said to live nine generations of men (Hes. fr. 304.1–2 M.-W.; Arat. *Phaen.* 1022). Here she is voicing her regret for being the bearer of bad news long ago.

Between fragments 73 and 74 nearly 22 verses are missing.

74 (*SH* 288.43B–69; 260.44–69, *inc.* 346, 351 Pf.) Vienna Tablet; Oxyrhynchus papyrus

May I have only a defense against evil hunger for my belly . . . but Hecale . . . simple [5] . . . and barley meal from a potion[1] that dripped on the ground . . . . . . messenger of evil. I wish that you were still alive at that time, so that . . . how the Thriai[2] inspired the old crow. [10] Yes by—not yet in all time—yes by my wrinkled hide, yes by this tree, though it is withered—not yet have all the suns after breaking their pole and axles put a foot in the west, but

[1] The potion, or posset, usually contained barley and a liquid like wine, honey, or water. [2] The nymphs of Parnassus who nursed Apollo (*Hymn. Hom. Herm.* 4.552–66) and taught him prophecy. Apollo later gave their power to Hermes.

[1] *Suda* λ 556 λιμός [2] Schol. ad Lyc. *Alex.* 607 κρίμνόν· ἐστι μὲν καὶ γένος κριθῆς, νῦν δὲ τὸ ἀπόσταγμα τοῦ κυκεῶνος, ὡς καὶ Καλλ. [3] Hdn. (*AO* vol. 4, 337.29 Cramer) = Schneider, fr. 325 [4] *Suda* σ 1694 σύφαρ· τὸ δέρμα ἡ ἀνθρωπῆ. ναὶ μά τὸ ῥικνὸν σύφαρ ἐμόν . . . Καλλίμαχος ἐν Ἑκάλῃ

δ]‹ε›ίελος ἀλλ' ἢ νὺξ ἢ ἔνδιος ἢ ἔσετ' ἠώς,
15 εὖτε κόραξ, ὅς νῦν γε καὶ ἂν κύκνοισιν ἐρίζοι
καὶ γάλακι χροιὴν καὶ κύματος ἄκρῳ ἀώτῳ,
κυάνεον φὴ πίσσαν ἐπὶ πτερὸν οὐλοὸν ἕξει,
ἀγγελίης ἐπίχειρα, τά οἵ ποτε Φοῖβος ὀπάσσει
ὁππότε κεν Φλεγύαο Κορωνίδος ἀμφὶ θυγατρός
20 Ἰσχύϊ πληξίππῳ σπομένης μιαρόν τι πύθηται."
τὴν μὲν ἄρ' ὣς φαμένην ὕπνος λάβε, τὴν δ'
        ἀΐουσαν.
καδδραθέτην δ' οὐ πολλὸν ἐπὶ χρόν[ο]ν, αἶψα γὰρ
        ἦλθεν
στιβήεις ἄγχαυρος, ὅτ' οὐκέτι χεῖρες ἔπαγροι
φιλητέων· ἤδη γὰρ ἑωθινὰ λύχνα[5] φαείνει,
25 ἀείδει καί πού τις ἀνὴρ ὑδατηγὸς ἱμαῖον,[6]
ἔγρει καί τιν' ἔχοντα παρὰ πλόον[7] οἰκίον ἄξων
τετριγὼς ὑπ' ἄμαξαν, ἀνιάζουσι δὲ πυκνοί
....ωοι χαλκῆες ἐνανόμενοι.........

[5] Et. Mag p. 572.22 λύχνα· ὡς παρὰ Καλλ. (fr. 255
Schneider)   [6] Suda ι 343 ἱμαῖον ᾆσμα· τὸ ἐπὶ τῇ ἀντλή-
σει λεγόμενον: παρὰ τὸ ἱμᾶν. οἱ δὲ τὸ μυλωθρικόν . . . Καλ-
λίμαχος Ἑκάλη   [7] Schol. ad Ap. Rhod. 3.1150 περιπλο-
μένας· παριούσας, ἐπεὶ καὶ πλόος λέγεται ἡ ὁδός. Καλλ. (fr.
278 Schneider)

there will be an evening, or a night, or a midday, or dawn
[15] when the raven who now rivals the swans and milk in
color and the bloom at the peak of the wave,[3] will be black
as pitch on its ill-omened wing, the reward that Apollo will
give him when he hears something ugly about Coronis the
daughter of Phlegyas [20] running off with Ischys the
charioteer."[4] And sleep overcame the one who was speak-
ing and the one hearing and the two slept, but not for a
long time, for at once it was frosty daybreak, when the
hands of thieves no longer search out prey, but already the
morning lamps are glowing, [25] and somewhere a man
drawing water sings a well-song, and an axle creaking un-
der a wagon rouses someone whose house is by the high-
way, and many people annoy the smiths by asking for kin-
dling.

[3] *Hymn* 2.112.   [4] Coronis, daughter of Phlegyas, was
pregnant by Apollo when she took up with the charioteer Ischys.
When Apollo was informed of this by the raven, he either asked
his sister Artemis to kill her or killed her himself. Hermes saved
the child, Asclepius, brought up by the Centaur Chiron, who
taught him the healing arts (Hes. fr. 60 M.-W. = Schol. ad Pind.
Pyth. 3.52b; Apollod. *Bibl*. 3.10.3).

CALLIMACHUS

75 (267 Pf.[1]) Sophron (*Gramm. Gr.* vol. 4.2, p. 396 Hilgard)

γίνεό· . . . ὁ Καλλ. λέγει.

γίνεό[2] μοι τέκταινα βίου δαμάτειρά τε λιμοῦ

[1] *Hec.* trib. Schneidewin (fr. 290 Schneider)
[2] γίνεο Sophron cod. G: γίναιο Choerob. cod. NC: γείνεο Sophron cod. H

76 (271 Pf.[1]) *Et. Gen.* AB s.v. ἀμορμεύεσκεν

ἀμορμεύεσκεν· συνῳδοιπόρει, οἷον,

σὺν δ᾽ ἡμῖν ὁ πελαργὸς ἀμορβεύεσκεν ἀλοίτης

[1] *Hec.* trib. Blomfield

77 (326 Pf.) *Suda* αι 137

αἴθ᾽ . . . ὀρχήσασθαι· ἐπειδὴ τὴν γλαῦκα ὅταν λάβωσι τά παιδία περιάγουσιν: ἡ δὲ μὴ βλέπουσα δι᾽ ἡμέρας ὥσπερ ὀρχεῖται. ἢ ὅταν πληγῇ τελευτῶσα στρέφεται ὥσπερ ὀρχουμένη. Καλλίμαχος ἐν Ἑκάλῃ λέγει περὶ αὐτῆς.

αἴθ᾽ ὄφελες θανέειν †ἢ πανύστατον†[1] ὀρχήσασθαι

[1] πανύστατον *Suda* codd.: πανύχιον cod. recens C: ἢ πάννυχον Naeke: ἢ ὕστατον Bentley: θνήσκουσα πανύστατον Lloyd-Jones

75 (267 Pf.) Sophron

gineo: . . . Callimachus says,

> be the author of my livelihood and conqueror of my
>> hunger[1]

[1] Possibly the crow addressing Hecale (Hollis, 258).

76 (271 Pf.) *Etymologicum Genuinum*

amormeuesken: he used to travel together with, such as,

> the stork, that avenger, used to accompany us[1]

[1] Perhaps the crow. Storks had a reputation as upholders of
justice (Schol. ad Ar. *Av.* 1353).

77 (326 Pf.) *Suda*

aith' . . . *orchēsasthai*: when they take her children they
lead the owl around, and being blind during the day she
dances as it were; or when she is dying after a beating it is
as if she dances. Callimachus says this about her in the
Hecale,

> I wish you had died or danced[1]

[1] The speaker is not clear; perhaps the crow.

CALLIMACHUS

78 (371 Pf.[1]) *Suda* ν 43

ὕδδειν ἔοικε. καὶ ὑδέοιμι, ἀντὶ τοῦ ὑμνοῖμι,

    Αἴθρην τὴν εὔτεκνον ἐπ᾿[2] ἀγρομένης ὑδέοιμι

[1] *Hec.* trib. Toup (*Emend. in Suid.* vol. 2, 291) et Ruhnken
(*Epist. ad Ernest.*, p. 21 Tittmann)   [2] ἐπ᾿ *Suda* codd.: ἐν
Bernhardy, Wilamowitz

79 (262 Pf.[1]) *Et. Gen.* AB s.v. ἠρία

ἠρία· διάφορος τόνος διάφορον ποιεῖ σημαινόμενον.
ἐὰν μὲν προπαροξυτόνως, σημαίνει τὰ ἔρια κατὰ ἔκ-
τασιν, ἐὰν δὲ παροξυτόνως ἠρία, σημαίνει τοὺς τά-
φους παρὰ τὴν ἔραν τὴν γῆν . . . καὶ Καλλ.

        τίνος ἠρίον ἵστατε[2] τοῦτο;

[1] *Hec.* trib. Naeke, 268–69   [2] ἵστατε corr. Bentley:
ἵσταται *Et. Gen.* AB, *Et. Mag.*

80 (263 Pf.) *Suda* ε 1990

ἐπαύλια· . . . ἐπαύλιον δὲ μονή. περὶ Ἑκάλης θανού-
σης,

           ἴθι, πρηεῖα γυναικῶν,
    τὴν ὁδόν, ἣν ἀνίαι θυμαλγέες[1] οὐ περόωσι.[2]
    ⟨   ⟩ πολλάκι σεῖο,
    μαῖα, ⟨   ⟩ φιλοξείνοιο καλιῆς[3]
5   μνησόμεθα· ξυνὸν γὰρ ἐπαύλιον ἔσκεν ἅπασιν

HECALE

78 (371 Pf.) *Suda*

(*h*)*yddein eoike* (it is like to chant); and "I would chant"
instead of "I would sing."

> may I sing of Aethra,[1] who has a noble son, among
> the gathered women

[1] Theseus' mother.

79 (262 Pf.) *Etymologicum Genuinum*

ēria: a different accent gives it a different meaning. If it
has an acute on the antepenult it means "wool" with the
lengthing of the short syllable. If the acute is on the penult,
it means "tombs" along the wide earth . . . and Callima-
chus,

> whose tomb are you building?[1]

[1] Hecale's. The speaker is probably Theseus.

80 (263 Pf.) *Suda*

epaulia: . . . the singular is *epaulion* (hut). Concerning
Hecale after she has died,

> go, gentle woman,
> along the road which heart-grieving sorrows do not
> traverse
> ⟨ ⟩ often,
> good mother, ⟨ ⟩ we will remember your
> hospitable cottage, for it was a retreat open to all

---

[1] θυμαλγέες *Suda*: θυμοφθόροι cett.   [2] περόωσι *Et.
Mag.*: περέοσι *Suda* cod. A: περῶσι *Suda* GIVM   [3] Sic
distrib. vers. 3–4 Maas, alii in unum versum redigerunt.

85

CALLIMACHUS

81 (342 Pf.) *Suda* κ 2260

κωμῆται· καὶ οἱ γείτονες· κώμη γάρ ἡ γειτονία. Καλ-
λίμαχος Ἑκάλῃ,

                              τοῦτο γὰρ αὐτήν[1]
κωμῆται κάλεον περιηγέες[2]

    [1] αὐτήν Hemsterhuys, Ruhnken: αὐτῆς *Suda* cod. A: αὐτῃ
GVM: αὐτοί F   [2] περιηγέες Toup: περιαγέες codd.

82 (T 36 Pf.; T 15a Hollis; cf. *SH* 284 et 252 Pf.[1]) Michael
Choniates (vol. 1, p. 157.11 Lambros)

καὶ οὕτω τι φιλοφρονηθῆναι ἥδιον ὡς ἀεὶ μεμνῆσθαι
τῆς ὀλίγης τραπέζης ἐκείνης καὶ αὐχμηρᾶς, καὶ μὴ
ἂν ἄλλην οὕτω ποτὲ τερπνοτέραν λογίσασθαι.

    [1] *Hec.* trib. comm. Salustii Hecker, 112

83 (264 Pf.; T 14 Hollis) Michael Choniates, *Theano* 337
(vol. 2, p. 386 Lambros)

εἰ δὲ γρηὶ πενιχρῇ, τὴν Ἑκάλην καλέεσκον,
Θησεὺς ὦφλε χάριν ξενίης ὀλίγης τε μιῆς τε
καί ἑ θανοῦσαν ἐνὶ μνήμῃ θέτο οὐ θνησκούσῃ
—οὐ γὰρ ἔην νήκουστα ἐτήσια δεῖπν᾽ Ἑκάλεια

81 (342 Pf.) *Suda*

cōmētae (villagers): neighbors; a village is a neighborhood.
Callimachus in the *Hecale*,

> for this is what
> the neighboring countrymen used to call her

82 (T 36 Pf.; T 15a Hollis; cf. *SH* 284 et 252 Pf.) Michael
Choniates

and nothing sweeter is more welcome, as always, to recall
than that woman's small and dusty table,[1] and not to think
that anything ever was more pleasant

[1] A commentary entry that apparently includes a few words
from a speech of Theseus about Hecale's generous but impover-
ished hospitality.

83 (264 Pf.; T 14 Hollis) Michael Choniates, *Theano*

If to the poor old woman whom they used to call Hecale
Theseus owed a debt of gratitude for her meager hospital-
ity, after her death he established an undying memorial—
the famous annual dinner called the Hecaleia.[1]

[1] Not mentioned in any other source.

84 (266 Pf.) Choerob. in Theod. (*Gramm. Gr.* vol. 4.1, p. 187.2 Hilgard)

πᾶν γὰρ ὄνομα μονοσύλλαβον ἐν τῇ συνθέσει ἀνα-
βιβάζει τὸν τόνον . . . χωρὶς τοῦ πτώξ πολυπτώξ,
"πολυπτῶκές τε Μελαιναί." τὸ δὲ Μελαιναὶ τόπος . . .
τῆς Ἀττικῆς, πολυπτῶκες δὲ οἱονεὶ αἱ ἔχουσαι πολ-
λοὺς λαγωούς· τοῦτο γὰρ τὴν ὀξεῖαν τάσιν ἐφύλαξε
τοῦ ἁπλοῦ.

πολυπτῶκές τε Μελαιναί

85 (305 Pf.) *P.Oxy.* 853 col. X, 7–8 (Schol. ad Thuc. 2.15.4; Schol. RV ad Ar. *Ran.* 216)

ἐν Λίμναισιν· . . . Λίμναι δὲ χωρίον τῆς Ἀττικῆς, ἐν
ᾧ Διονύσου ἱερόν. Καλλ. ἐν Ἑκάλῃ,

οὐδὲ Διωνύ[σῳ Μελαναίγ]ιδι, τόν [πο]τ᾽ Ἐλευθήρ
εἵ[σατο, ͺΛιμναίῳ δὲ χͺοροστάδας ἦγον ἑͺορτάς

86 (321 Pf.[1]) *Suda* γ 46

Γαμβρὸς Ἐρεχθῆος· ὁ Βορρᾶς. τὴν γάρ Ὠρείθυιαν
θυγατέρα αὐτοῦ ἔγημεν, ἐξ ἧς τίκτεται Ζήτης καὶ Κά-
λαϊς.

γαμβρὸς Ἐρεχθῆος

[1] *Hec.* trib. Hecker, 111

84 (266 Pf.) Choeroboscus

Every monosyllabic noun throws back its accent in synthesis except *ptōx*, *polyptōx* (hare, many-hared) as in "many-hared Melaenae." Melaenae is a place in Attica that has many hares. This word retains the acute accent of the simple form (*ptōx*).

> Melaenae[1] with many hares

1 Attic deme on the border of Boeotia.

85 (305 Pf.) Oxyrhynchus papyrus (Scholia to Thucydides and to Aristophanes, *Frogs*)

en Limnaisin: . . . Limnae is a place in Attica where there was a festival for Dionysus. Callimachus in the *Hecale*,

> he introduced a festival with choral dances for Dionysus of Limnae,[1] not the one for Dionysus of the black goatskin which Eleuther once established

1 In the marshes.

86 (321 Pf.) *Suda*

gambros Erechthēus: Borras.[1] He married Erechtheus' daughter Oreithuia from whom were born Zetes and Calaïs.

> the son-in-law of Erechtheus

1 Also Boreas, the North Wind, who abducted Orithyia either from the Areopagus, or from the banks of the river Ilysseus, or from Mt. Brilessus in Attica.

CALLIMACHUS

87 (338 Pf.[1]) *Suda* θ 308

Θείας ἀμνάμων· ὁ Βορέας ὁ ἄνεμος. ἀμνάμων δὲ
ἀπόγονος. ὡς γάρ Ἡσίοδος λέγει, τῆς Θείας
ἀπόγονοι οἱ ἄνεμοι.

Θείας ἀμνάμων[2]

[1] *Hec*. trib. Pfeiffer   [2] In *Aet*. 110.44 ordine inverso.

88 (308 Pf.) Steph. Byz. τ 191 Billerbeck s.v. Τρινεμεῖς

Τρινεμεῖς· δῆμος τῆς Κεκροπίδος φυλῆς. Διόδωρος[1]
καὶ Δίδυμος[2] Τρινεμεῖς ἀναγράφουσι τὸν δῆμον,
Καλλ. Ἑκάλῃ Τρινέμειαν.

Τρινέμεια[3]

[1] *BNJ* 372 F 24   [2] M. Schmidt, *Didymi Chalcenteri
grammatici Alexandrini fragmenta quae supersunt omnia* (1854),
352   [3] Aut Τρινέμειαν

89 (349 Pf.[1]) *Suda* μ 177

Μαραθών· τόπος Ἀθήνησιν. ἀπὸ Μαράθου, υἱοῦ
Ἀπόλλωνος. τοῦτον Καλλίμαχος ἐννότιον λέγει, του-
τέστιν ἔνυδρον. καὶ "Μαραθώνιον ἔργον."

[1] *Hec*. trib. Hecker, 187

87 (338 Pf.) *Suda*

Theias amnamōn: descendant of Theia, Boreas the wind. Descendant means offspring. As Hesiod says, the winds are the children of Theia.

a descendant of Theia[1]

[1] Boreas. Eos, whose mother was Theia, gave birth to the winds (Hes. *Theog.* 371–80).

88 (308 Pf.) Stephanus of Byzantium

Trinemeis: the deme of the tribe of Cecropis. Diodorus and Didymos call the deme Trinemeis, Callimachus in the *Hecale*, Trinemeia.

Trinemeia

89 (349 Pf.) *Suda*

Marathon: a place in Athens; from Marathos, son of Apollo. Callimachus says it is damp, that is watery and [speaks of] the "Marathonian labor."[1]

[1] Perhaps Theseus' slaying of the bull (Hecker, 107), but Pfeiffer cautions that the phrase usually refers to the famous battle of Marathon (Paus. 10.10.1).

CALLIMACHUS

90 (288 Pf.¹) *Et. Gud.* (p. 304.1 Sturz) s.v. κατακᾶσα

κατακᾶσα· ἡ κατωφερὴς καὶ πόρνη. Καλλ.,

> Σκύλλα γυνὴ κατακᾶσα καὶ οὐ ψύθος οὔνομ'
> ἔχουσα
> πορφυρέην ἤμησε κρέκα²

¹ Coniunxit duo fragmenta et *Hec.* trib. Naeke, 61–62.
² *Suda* κ 2365 κρέκα· τὴν τρίχα. πορφυρέην ἤμησε κρέκα.
ἀντὶ τοῦ ἔκοψε.

91 (297 Pf.) Schol. Arethae ad Euseb. *Praep. evang.*
4.16.2 (p. 155b in marg. cod. Paris 451)

ἐν δὲ τῇ νῦν Σαλαμῖνι, πρότερον δὲ Κορωνείαι ὀνομα-
ζομένῃ· οὐ τὴν πρὸς ταῖς Ἀθήναις Σαλαμῖνα λέγει.
αὕτη γὰρ Κούλουρις¹ πάλαι ἐλέγετο, ὡς καὶ Καλλ. ὁ
Κυρηναῖος ἐν τῇ Ἑκάλῃ φησίν.

¹ Κούλουρις Schol.: Κόλουρις Hollis

92 (341 Pf.) *Suda* κ 2240

Κωλιάς· ναός ἐστι τῆς Ἀφροδίτης, οὕτω καλούμενος,
ἀπὸ τοῦ συμβεβηκότος τὴν προσηγορίαν λαβὼν . . .
ὅθεν ὁ τόπος Κωλιὰς ἐκλήθη. μέμνηται καὶ Καλλ. ἐν
Ἑκάλῃ.

> Κωλιάδος κεραμῆες

90 (288 Pf.) *Etymologicum Gudianum*

katakāsa: a lewd woman and prostitute. Callimachus,

the woman Scylla, a whore who has a name that is no
lie,[1]
sheared the purple lock[2]

[1] Callimachus suggests that the name Scylla is derived from
skylax, "bitch" (Hom. *Od.* 12.86–87). [2] Scylla was the
daughter of Nisus, king of Megara. Nisus had a purple lock of hair,
which was the key to his life and his kingdom. His daughter be-
trayed him by cutting off the lock out of love for Minos of Crete,
who was invading the land. When the truth came out, she leaped
off a cliff before her father could catch her, and both were turned
into sea birds ([Hyg.] *Fab.* 198, 242).

91 (297 Pf.) Scholia of Arethas to Eusebius, *Preparation
for the Gospel*

In what is now Salamis, previously named Coroneia: He
is not speaking of Salamis near Athens. This was called
Coulouris long ago, as Callimachus of Cyrene says in the
Hecale.

92 (341 Pf.) *Suda*

Colias: there is a temple of Aphrodite which takes its name
from something that happened . . . and from this the place
is called Colias. Callimachus recalls it in the *Hecale.*

the potters of Colias[1]

[1] A district of Attica where Aphrodite had a temple. The exact
location was disputed even in antiquity (Paus. 1.1.5).

93 (268 Pf.[1]) *Suda* υ 48

ὗδος· τὸ ὕδωρ. ἡ δοτικὴ "ὕδει."

  ἔστιν ὗδος καὶ γαῖα καὶ ὀπτήτειρα κάμινος

[1] *Hec.* trib. Hecker, 105

94 (344 Pf.[1]) *Suda* λ 149

λάτρον· ὁ μισθός. λατρεία γὰρ δουλεία ἐπὶ μισθῷ.

  λάτριν ἄγειν παλίνορσον ἀεικέα τῷ κεραμῇ

[1] *Hec.* trib. Hecker, 105

95 (307 Pf.) Steph. Byz. λ 111 Billerbeck s.v. Λύρκειον

Λύρκειον· ὄρος Ἄργους. Καλλ. Ἑκάλῃ. τὸ τοπικὸν,

  Λυρκήιον ὕδωρ[1]

[1] Cf. Pf. vol. 1, 281.

96 (*SH* 290 *inc.* 279 Pf.) *P.Oxy.* 2258 recto

                ].πτ[
         ].. [].νμε[
  αὐτίκα Κενθίππην[1] τε, πολύκριμν‚όν[2] τε Πρόσυμναν
                ]στο[
5   ]οστ‚[
         .   .   .   .   .

93 (268 Pf.) *Suda*

hydos: water. The dative is *hydei*.

there is water and earth and a baking oven[1]

[1] Either the basic elements of civilization or clay and a kiln for the use of potters.

94 (344 Pf.) *Suda*

latron: a fee. *Latreia* is service for a wage.

to bring again a shameful wage for the potter

95 (307 Pf.) Stephanus of Byzantium

Lyrceion: an Argive mountain. Callimachus, in the *Hecale*. A commonplace,

the water of Lyrceium

96 (*SH* 290 *inc.* 279 Pf.) Oxyrhynchus papyrus

at once Centhippe[1] and Prosymna[2] rich in barley

[1] A place in Argos.   [2] Location of the Argive temple of Hera (Paus. 2.17.2).

---

[1] *Et. Gen.* AB s.v. Κενθίππη· τόπος Ἄργους. Καλλ.
[2] πολυκριμνον pap.: πολύκρημνον *Et. Gen.* AB

97 (*SH* 291[1]) *P.Oxy.* 2258 verso

```
         .
        ].[
     ]....ν[
    ]ιφυλαττε[²
    ]καιδ[
       ]ου̣.δ[
       ]μ̣ εμ̣[
      .    .    .
```

¹ *Hec.* trib. Hollis; Lobel, marginalia   ² Forma Attica

98 (280 Pf.) *Et. Gen.* AB s.v. δόναξ

δόναξ· ὁ κάλαμος. Καλλ.

> καὶ δόνακι πλήθοντα¹ λιπὼν ῥόον Ἀστερίωνος

¹ πλήθοντα *Et. Gen.* A: πλήθουσιν *Et. Gen.* B

99 (278 Pf.) *Et. Gen.* AB s.v. δανάκης

δανάκης· τοῦτο νομίσματός ἐστιν ὄνομα βαρβαρικοῦ, πλέον ὀβολοῦ, ὃ τοῖς νεκροῖς ἐν τοῖς στόμασιν ἐτίθεσαν. Καλλ.,

> τοὔνεκα καὶ νέκυες πορθμήιον οὔτι φέρονται
> μούνῃ ἐνὶ πτολίων, ὅ τε τέθμιον οἰσέμεν ἄλλους
> δανοῖς ἐν στομάτεσσι †νεὼς Ἀχερουσίας
> ἐπίβαθρον δανάκης†

97 (*SH* 291) Oxyrhynchus papyrus

keep guard!

98 (280 Pf.) *Etymologicum Genuinum*

donax: a reed. Callimachus,

and leaving the stream of Asterion[1] full of reeds

[1] A river near the Heraeon of Argos (Paus 2.17.2) where it is close to Prosymna (cf. *Hec.* 96).

99 (278 Pf.) *Etymologicum Genuinum*

danakēs: this is the name of a foreign coin larger than the obol which they placed in the mouths of the dead. Callimachus,

Therefore in this city[1] alone the dead do not carry the ferryman's fee which is customary for others to carry in their dry mouths.

[1] Perhaps Hermione in the Argolid (Strabo 8.6.12), either because the distance to Hades was so short from there or the fee was remitted because the inhabitants had told Demeter that Pluto had carried off her daughter (Apollod. *Bibl.* 1.5.1).

100 (285 Pf.[1]) *Suda* κ 1843

Κλύμενος· οὕτω λέγεται ὁ Ἅιδης· ἢ ὅτι πάντας προ-
σκαλεῖται εἰς ἑαυτόν, ἢ ὁ ὑπὸ πάντων ἀκουόμενος,

Δηώ τε Κλυμένου τε πολυξείνοιο δάμαρτα

[1] *Hec.* trib. Pfeiffer e comment. Salustius

101 (339 Pf.[1]) *Suda* κ 1733

Κλεωναίου χάρωνος· τοῦ χαροποῦ λέοντος.

Κλεωναίοιο[2] χάρωνος

[1] *Hec.* trib. Pfeiffer   [2] Κλεωναίοιο corr. Meineke 1843,
85: Κλεωναίου *Suda* codd.: Κλεωναῖοι ὁ χάρωνος Steph. Byz.
(RV): Κλεωναῖος (Ald); cf. Billerbeck vol. 3, 88–89

102 (277 Pf.[1]) *Et. Gen.* A s.v. γέγειος

γέγειος· ὁ ἀρχαῖος. καὶ γέγειαι. εἴρηται παρ᾽ Ἑκα-
ταίῳ (*BNJ* 1 F 362) καὶ Καλλιμάχῳ (*Fr. Inc. Sed.* 510),

βόες[2] ᾗχι γέγειαι
ἄνθεα μήκωνός τε καὶ ἤνοπα πυρὸν ἔδουσι

[1] *Hec.* trib. Reitzenstein 1890–91, 113   [2] *Suda* γ 90 γέ-
γειαι βόες· αἱ ἀρχαῖαι

HECALE

100 (285 Pf.) *Suda*

clymenos: Hades is called Clymenus either because he calls everyone to himself or because he is heard by all,

Deo[1] and the wife of Clymenus,[2] receiver of many

[1] Demeter (*Hymn* 6.17)   [2] Hades (Paus. 2.35.9), whose wife was Demeter's daughter Persephone.

101 (339 Pf.) *Suda*

Kleōnaiou charōnos: of a fierce lion.

of the bright-eyed one[1] of Cleonae[2]

[1] The lion.   [2] Village near Nemea (*Aet.* 54c.37) in the northeastern Peloponnese, where the Nemean lion was killed by Heracles.

102 (277 Pf.) *Etymologicum Genuinum*

gegeios: ancient. And *gegeiai*. [The word] is used by Hecataeus (*BNJ* 1 F 362) and Callimachus (*Fr. Inc. Sed.* 510)

where ancient cattle
eat poppy flowers and gleaming wheat

CALLIMACHUS

103 (302 Pf.[1]) Schol. BDPTU ad Pind. *Nem.* 1.3

Ὀρτυγία, δέμνιον Ἀρτέμιδος· ἔχοι δ' ἂν οὐ φαύλως
δέμνιον Ἀρτέμιδος λέγεσθαι τὴν Ὀρτυγίαν, οἷον ἐν-
διαίτημα καὶ διατριβήν· ἱερὰν γὰρ τὴν πᾶσαν νῆσον
Φερσεφόνης εἶναι· ὅτι δὲ ἡ αὐτή ἐστι τῇ Ἀτέμιδι,
Καλλ. ἐν Ἑκάλῃ,

> οἴ νυ καὶ Ἀπόλλωνα παναρκέος Ἡελίοιο
> χῶρι[2] διατμήγουσι καὶ εὔποδα Δηωίνην
> Ἀρτέμιδος

[1] *Hec.* trib. Naeke, 45
[2] χῶρι corr. Bentley: χωρίον cod. B: χωρὶ cod. rec. U

104 (273 Pf.[1]) *Et. Gen.* B s.v. ἀγαυγή [sic]

ἀγαυγή. . . παρὰ τὸ αὐγή· οἷον,

> Ἀπόλλωνος ἀπαυγή[2]

[1] *Hec.* trib. Pfeiffer [2] ἀπαυγή corr. Hecker: ἀγαυγή
Et. Gen. B

105 (265 Pf.[1]) Choerob. in Theod. (*Gramm. Gr.* vol. 4.2,
p. 114.8 Hilgard)

ἐληλύθειν γὰρ ὁ ὑπερσυντελικὸς διὰ τοῦ ε̄· ὅθεν ἀνα-
λογώτερόν φασι παρὰ Καλλ.,

> ὅθεν ἠληλούθειν[2]

[1] *Hec.* trib. Pfeiffer [2] ἠληλούθειν Choerob. codd. VO:
ἐληλούθειν codd. C: εἰληλούθειν *Suda* ει 115

103 (302 Pf.) Scholia to Pindar, *Nemean Odes*

Ortygia, demnion Artemidos: it is not wrong to call Orty-
gia the bed of Artemis, that is, a dwelling place and retreat.
The whole island is sacred to Persephone. That she is the
same as Artemis, Callimachus says in the *Hecale*,

> those who distinguish Apollo from Helius, who
> shines on all, and the well-shod Deoine from Arte-
> mis[1]

[1] Deoine is Demeter's daughter, sometimes conflated with
Artemis (Diana). These lines appear to frame a debate about gods
assimilated to others. It is not clear whether the discussion was in
the *Hecale* or whether it was a concern only to the scholiast.

104 (273 Pf.) *Etymologicum Genuinum*

agaugē: . . . derived from *augē* (light), such as

> the gleam of Apollo

105 (265 Pf.) Choeroboscus

ēlēlythein is pluperfect on account of the long *e*. By anal-
ogy from this he says in Callimachus,

> whence I had come

106 (270 Pf.[1]) *Suda* α 1430

ἀλυκρά· χλιαρά,

γέντο δ᾽ ἀλυκρά

[1] *Hec.* trib. Hecker, 113

107 (276 Pf.[1]) *Suda* α 4255

ἄστρια (sic)· οἱ ἀστράγαλοι. παρὰ Καλλ.,

δέκα δ᾽ ἄστριας[2] αἴνυτο[3] λάτρον

[1] *Hec.* trib. Kapp, fr. 121   [2] ἄστριας *Et. Gen.*: ἄστρια *Suda* α 4255   [3] αἴνυτο codd.: prob. ἄρνυτο Pfeiffer

108 (343 Pf.[1]) *Suda* κ 2515

κτείς· τὸ ἐφήβαιον, καὶ τὸ τῶν τριχῶν κάλλυντρον. Καλλίμαχος,

οὐδ᾽ οἷσιν ἐπὶ κτενὸς ἔσκον ἔθειραι

[1] *Hec.* trib. Kapp, fr. 136

109 (282 Pf.[1]) *Et. Gud.* (p. 409.13 De Stefani) s.v. εἰδυλίς

εἰδυλίς· ἐπιστήμων, εἰδυῖα· Καλλ.,

ὀκκόσον[2] ὀφθαλμοὶ γὰρ ἀπευθέες, ὅσσον ἀκουή
εἰδυλίς

[1] *Hec.* trib. Naeke, *Opuscula* vol. 1, 71   [2] ὀκκόσον corr. Naeke: καὶ κόσσον cod. Gud.

106 (270 Pf.) *Suda*

alykra: warm,

      they became warm

107 (276 Pf.) *Suda*

astria: knucklebones. In Callimachus,

      he took ten knucklebones[1] as a fee

  [1] A paltry sum.

108 (343 Pf.) *Suda*

kteis: pubis and a styling implement for hair. Callimachus,

      not for them was there hair on the pubis

109 (282 Pf.) *Etymologicum Gudianum*

eidylis: understanding, knowing; Callimachus,

    the eyes are ignorant, as much the ears are knowing[1]

  [1] On the relative virtues of the senses, cf. Hdt. 1.8.

110 (286 Pf.[1]) *Et. Gen.* s.v. λάκτιν

λάκτιν· σημαίνει ἡ λέξις τὴν σκυτάλην, τορύνην. Καλλ.,

αὖτις ἀπαιτίζουσαν ἐὴν εὐεργέα[2] λάκτιν

[1] *Hec.* trib. Toup in Naeke, 140   [2] εὐεργέα *Suda* λ 71: εὐεργέτα *Et. Gen.* A: εὐαργέα *Suda* cod. F

111 (287 Pf.[1]) *Et. Gen.* A s.v. φαρῶ

φαρῶ· τὸ ἀροτριῶ. Καλλ.,

ἢ ἄφαρον φαρόωσι, μέλει δέ φιν ὄμπνιον ἔργον

[1] *Hec.* trib. Hecker, 90

112 (289 Pf.[1]) *Et. Gen.* AB s.v. σιπαλός

σιπαλός· ὁ εἰδεχθὴς καὶ ἄμορφος·

ἀλλὰ σὺ μὲν σιπαλός τε καὶ ὀφθαλμοῖσιν
ἔφηλος

[1] *Hec.* trib. Pfeiffer

113 (291 Pf.) Olymp. in Arist. *Mete.* 1.6.343a20

αὕτη γὰρ διὰ τὸ οἰκεῖον μέγεθος ἔσθ' ὅτε πλεῖον ἀπέχουσα τοῦ ἡλίου κατὰ πλάτος ἐν μιᾷ ἡμέρᾳ καὶ ἑῴα καὶ ἑσπερία γίνεται. ὅθεν φησὶν ὁ ἐξηγητὴς καὶ μόνον κατ' ἐξαίρετον ἑῷον καὶ ἑσπέριον λέγεσθαι τὸν

110 (286 Pf.) *Etymologicum Genuinum*

laktin: the word means a ladle, a stirrer. Callimachus,

again demanding back her well-made ladle

111 (287 Pf.) *Etymologicum Genuinum*

pharō: to plow. Callimachus,

or they plow fallow land, and raising corn is their
business

112 (289 Pf.) *Etymologicum Genuinum*

sipalos: the ugly and misshapen one,

but you are ugly and there are white specks in your
eyes

113 (291 Pf.) Olympiodorus in Aristotle, *Meteorologica*

[Aphrodite] is in her great house when farthest from the
sun in latitude she appears in the morning and evening of
the same day. From this the commentator says that excep-
tionally only the star of Aphrodite is called both the morn-

τῆς Ἀφροδίτης ἀστέρα διὰ τὸ δύνασθαι ἐν μιᾷ ἡμέρᾳ
καὶ ἑῷον καὶ ἑσπέριον φαίνεσθαι. ὅτι γὰρ αὐτός ἐστι
καὶ ἑῷος καὶ ἑσπέριος, δηλοῖ καὶ Καλλ. λέγων ἐν
Ἑκάλῃ,

> ἡνίκα μὲν γὰρ †φαίνεται τοῖς ἀνθρώποις ταῦτα†[1]
> αὐτοὶ μὲν φιλέουσ᾽, αὐτοὶ δέ τε πεφρίκασιν,
> ἑσπέριον φιλέουσιν, ἀτὰρ στυγέουσιν ἑῷον

[1] Ex Olymp. paraphrasi, Hecker, 130 et Naeke, 140.

114 (295 Pf.[1]) *Suda* ι 550

ἵπνια· τά ἀποκαθάρματα τοῦ ἰπνοῦ, τοῦ λεγομένου
φούρνου. ἢ τά πρὸς τὴν κάμινον ἐπιτήδεια καύσιμα.
λέγει δὲ τὴν κόπρον τῶν ζῴων Καλλίμαχος,

> σὺν δ᾽ ἄμυδις φορυτόν τε καὶ ἵπνια λύματ᾽
> ἄειρεν[2]

[1] *Hec.* trib. Meineke 1861, 146   [2] ἄειρεν *Suda* ι 550:
ἀείρας *Suda* φ 623

115 (298 Pf.[1]) Schol. ad Greg. Naz. *Or.* 4.113

καὶ γέλωτα ἐν δακρύοις ποιηταὶ γινώσκουσιν· Καλλι-
μάχειον τοιοῦτο φέρεται,

> ἐπεὶ θεὸς οὐδὲ γελάσσαι[2]
> ἀκλαυτὶ[3] μερόπεσσιν ὀιζυροῖσιν ἔδωκεν

ing and evening star because it is able in one day to appear
in the morning and evening. That it is both the morning
and evening [star] is clear from Callimachus, who says in
the *Hecale*,

> When that star appears to men, the same people
> love it and the same hate it, they love the evening
> star but they hate the morning star.[1]

[1] Said perhaps of lovers or of laborers. Cf. Catull. 62.34–35;
[Verg.] *Ciris* 352.

114 (295 Pf.) *Suda*

ipnia: what is cleaned off a stove, a furnace. The fuel nec-
essary for burning. Callimachus says it is the dung of ani-
mals,

> She gathered together the rubbish and the filth from
> the dunghill[1]

[1] Apparently Hecale or someone else is firing up a stove.

115 (298 Pf.) Scholia to Gregory of Nazianzus, *Orations*

and the poets perceive laughter in tears: this Callimachean
quotation expresses it,

> since the god does not give
> to miserable mortals laughter without tears

---

[1] *Hec.* trib. Naeke, 155 et Hecker, 124   [2] γελᾶσσαι Schol.
ad Greg. Naz.: γέλασεν Schol. T ad Hom. *Il.* 6.484   [3] ἀκλαυτί
schol. Hom.: ἀκλαυστί Schol. Greg.

CALLIMACHUS

116 (299 Pf.¹) Schol. A ad Hom. *Il.* 1.98b²

ἑλικώπιδα· μελανόφθαλμον, ἀφ' οὗ εὐπρεπῆ· ὡς
"ὕδωρ μέλαν Αἰσήποιο" (*Il.* 2.825) καὶ Καλλ.,

Αἴσηπον ἔχεις, ἑλικώτατον ὕδωρ,
Νηπείης ἥ τ' ἄργος, ἀοίδιμος Ἀδρήστεια²

¹ Fragmenta coniunxit Naeke, 265   ² Cf. Schol. ad Ap.
Rhod. 1.1116 καὶ πεδίον Νηπήιον· πεδίον Νηπείας ἔστι περὶ
Κύζικον. μνημονεύει δὲ αὐτοῦ καὶ Καλλ. ἐν Ἑκάλῃ.

117 (301 Pf.) Schol. vulg. ad Hom. *Od.* 22.299

οἶστρος· ὁ οἶστρος ἀπογεννᾶται ἐκ τῶν ἐν τοῖς ποτα-
μοῖς πλατέων ζωαρίων . . . ὁ δὲ μύωψ ἐκ τῶν ξύλων
ἀπογεννᾶται. καὶ Καλλ. περὶ τοῦ μύωπος,

βουσόον ὅν τε μύωπα βοῶν καλέουσιν ἀμορβοί

118 (303 Pf.¹) Schol. Laur. ad Soph. *Tr.* 7

ὄκνον· εἰ δὲ γράφεται ὄτλον, τὴν ταλαιπωρίαν ἢ τὸ
μεμορημένον καὶ πεπρωμένον· Καλλ.,

κενεὸν πόνον ὀτλήσοντες

¹ *Hec.* trib. Pfeiffer

116 (299 Pf.) Scholia to Homer, *Iliad*

(*h*)*elikōpida*: black-eyed, from which it is acceptable, as
"the black water of Aesepus" (*Il.* 2.825) and Callimachus,

> you have Aesepus,[1] the blackest[2] water,
> and the plain of Nepeia, O Adrasteia,[3] worthy of
> song[4]

[1] In the Homeric catalogue of ships, the river Aesepus (*Il.*
2.825) is listed near the town of Adrasteia (*Il.* 2.828).   [2] An-
other option is "eddying" (*Suda* ε 854).   [3] Nemesis, i.e., the
goddess of retribution.   [4] According to the scholia on Apollo-
nius of Rhodes, *Argonautica* (quoted opposite), the plain of Ne-
peia is near Cyzicus, according to Callimachus in the *Hecale*.

117 (301 Pf.) Scholia to Homer, *Odyssey*

oestrus: the gadfly is generated from the flats of rivers . . .
but the horsefly [*myōps*] from wood. And Callimachus
says about the horsefly,

> [the horsefly][1] that drives oxen mad, which herdsmen
> call the goad of cattle[2]

[1] Probably in the previous line (R. F. Thomas, *HSCP* 86
[1982]: 83n11).   [2] Callimachus follows Aesch. *Suppl.* 308
and was followed in turn by Ap. Rhod. 3.276–77.

118 (303 Pf.) Laurentian Scholia to Sophocles, *Trojan
Women*

oknon: if it is written *otlon*, the hard labor which is des-
tined and allotted; Callimachus,

> about to endure pointless labor

119 (309 dub. Pf.[1]) *Suda* α 248

ἄγκος· ὑψηλὸς τοῦ ὄρους τόπος.

ποσσὶ δ' ἀνελθεῖν[2]
ἄγκος ἐς ὑψικάρηνον ἐδίζετο· πᾶσα δ' ἀπορρώξ[3]
πέτρη ἔην ὑπένερθε καὶ ἄμβασις οὔ νύ τις ἦεν

[1] *Hec.* trib. Hecker, 122; coniunxit Bergk   [2] ποσσὶ δ'
ἀνελθεῖν corr. Toup, Valckenaer: ποσὶ δ' αὖ ἐλθεῖν codd. *Suda*
[3] *Suda* α 3508 ἀπορρῶγας· ἐξοχὰς ἀπεσχισμένας . . . καὶ
ἀπορρώξ, ἀπόσπασμα ὄρους

120 (312 Pf.[1]) *Suda* α 907

ἄκμηνος· ἄγευστος.

    ἄκμηνον δόρποιο

[1] *Hec.* trib. Hecker, 125

121 (314 Pf.[1]) *Suda* α 1592

ἀμιθρῆσαι· μετρῆσαι, ἀριθμῆσαι, παρά Καλλιμάχῳ.

     ἀμιθρῆσαι

[1] *Hec.* trib. Pfeiffer

119 (309 dub. Pf.) *Suda*

agkos: a high place on a mountain,

> and he could not determine how to go up on foot
> into the high-topped mountain glen; all the rocks
> below were sheer and there was no way up

120 (312 Pf.) *Suda*

akmēnos: fasting,

> without supper[1]

[1] Cf. Hom. *Il.* 19.163.

121 (314 Pf.) *Suda*

amithrēsai: to measure, to count, in Callimachus,

> to count

122 (315 Pf.[1]) *Suda* α 3622

ἀπ᾽ οὔατος ἄγγελος ἔλθοι· **παρά Καλλιμάχῳ.** τουτέ-
στι δύσφημος, μὴ ἄξιος τοῦ μὴ ἀκουσθῆναι.

ἀπούατος[2] ἄγγελος ἔλθοι

[1] *Hec.* trib. Hecker, 97   [2] ἀπούατος Schneider, fr. 301:
ἀπ᾽ οὔατος *Suda*

123 (316 Pf.[1]) *Suda* α 4208

ἀσπαστοί· ἄσμενοι, θεοειδεῖς. παρὰ δὲ Καλλιμάχῳ
"ἀσπαστύς," "ἀσπαστύος," τουτέστι προσηγορία φι-
λία.

ἀσπαστύς aut ἀσπαστύος

[1] *Hec.* trib. Naeke, 154

124 (317 Pf.[1]) *Suda* α 4216

ἀσταγὲς ὕδωρ· τὸ πολυσταγές.

ἀσταγὲς ὕδωρ

[1] *Hec.* trib. Hecker, p. 109

125 (318 Pf.[1]) *Suda* α 4645

ἀφραστύες· ἀσυνεσίαι.

σχέτλιαι ἀνθρώπων ἀφραστύες

[1] *Hec.* trib. Ruhnken

122 (315 Pf.) *Suda*

ap' ouatos angelos elthoi: in Callimachus. Of ill-omen, not worthy of being heard.

> an ill-omened messenger may come[1]

[1] Perhaps said by the crow or Aegeus reporting on Theseus' encounter with the Marathonian Bull.

123 (316 Pf.) *Suda*

aspastoi: welcome, godlike. In Callimachus (with different spellings) this is a friendly greeting.

> Welcome

124 (317 Pf.) *Suda*

astages (h)ydōr: a gusher.

> spouting water[1]

[1] Perhaps about the rainstorm that sent Theseus to Hecale's cottage.

125 (318 Pf.) *Suda*

afrastues: follies.

> the cruel oversights of men

126 (320 Pf.[1]) *Suda* β 225

βέβυστο· ἐπεπλήρωτο.

βέβυστο δὲ πᾶσα χόλοιο

[1] *Hec.* trib. Hecker, 118

127 (322 Pf.[1]) *Suda* γ155

γέντα· τά μέλη . . . Καλλίμαχος.

γέντα βοῶν μέλδοντες[2]

[1] *Hec.* trib. Kapp, fr. 125   [2] Hapax legomenon, *Il.* 21.363

128 (323 Pf.[1]) *Suda* γ 363

γοερόν· θρηνῶδες, λυπηρόν, κατανυκτικόν. καὶ,

γοεροῖο γόοιο[2]

[1] *Hec.* trib. Kapp, fr. 126   [2] γοεροῖο γόοιο *Suda* codd.
GITVM: γοεροῖς γόοις AF

129 (324 Pf.[1]) *Suda* δ 164

δέδοιμι ⟨sic⟩· οἰκοδομοίην.

οἰκίον εὖτε δέμοιμι[2]

[1] *Hec.* trib. Hecker, 119   [2] δέμοιμι corr. Stephanus: δέ-
δοιμι *Suda*

126 (320 Pf.) *Suda*
bebysto: to be filled up.

      she was filled with rage

127 (322 Pf.) *Suda*
genta: limbs . . . Callimachus,
  cooking the flesh of oxen

128 (323 Pf.) *Suda*
goeron: mournful, painful, pricking at heart, and
              of mournful wailing

129 (324 Pf.) *Suda*
dedoimi: I might build a house,
  when I might build a house

130 (330 Pf.[1]) *Suda* ε 861

ἐλινύειν· στραγγεύειν.[2] διατρίβοντας ἢ ἐγχρονίζοντας. καὶ . . . ἀντὶ τοῦ τὴν δυστυχίαν παύσειεν,

> πότμον ἐλινύσειεν

[1] *Hec.* trib. Hecker, 108   [2] στραγγεύειν Toup: στρατεύειν *Suda*

131 (325 Pf.[1]) *Suda* δ 1566

δύη· ἡ κακοπάθεια, ἡ δυστυχία . . . Καλλίμαχος,

> δύην ἀπόθεστον[2] ἀλάλκοι

[1] *Hec.* trib. Naeke, 251   [2] ἀπόθεστον corr. Porson: ἀπόθ᾽ ἐστ᾽ *Suda* cod. A: ἀπόθ εστ᾽ GIM: ἀπόθεσθ᾽ V: ἀπόθετ᾽ F

132 (331 Pf.[1]) *Suda* φ 667

φώρια· λαθραῖα, λῃστήρια· ἢ κλοπιμαῖα πράγματα,

> ἐπήλυσιν ὄφρ᾽ ἀλέοιτο
> φώριον

[1] *Hec.* trib. Hecker, 93

133 (332 Pf.[1]) *Suda* ε 2251

ἐπιβρίσῃσιν ὀδόντας· παρ᾽ ὅσον οἱ θυμούμενοι τρίζουσι τούς ὀδόντας.

> ἐπιπρίσῃσιν[2] ὀδόντας

116

130 (330 Pf.) *Suda*

elinuein (to rest): to be idle, wasting time, delaying. And
. . . instead of putting an end to misfortune,

    may destiny be sent on vacation

131 (325 Pf.) *Suda*

duē: misery, misfortune . . . Callimachus,

       he might ward off despised misery

132 (331 Pf.) *Suda*

phōria: stolen things, secreted away; things acquired by
theft,

       in order to avoid an attack by robbers

133 (332 Pf.) *Suda*

epibrisēsin odontas: as angry people gnash their teeth.

        gnashing of teeth

---

[1] *Hec.* trib. Pfeiffer   [2] ἐπιπρίσῃσιν Meineke 1823, 278:
ἐπιβρίσῃσιν Suda

134 (333 Pf.[1]) *Suda* ε 2389

ἐπικλινές· ἐπιρρεπὲς εἰς κακόν. ἐπικλινές ἐστι τάλαντον. Καλλίμαχος.

ἐπικλινές ἐστι τάλαντον

[1] *Hec.* trib. Kapp, fr. 132

135 (335 Pf.[1]) *Suda* η 128

ἠέρος ὄγμοι· αἱ ὁδοί, οἱ τόποι.

ἠέρος ὄγμοι

[1] *Hec.* trib. Adler

136 (336 Pf.[1]) *Suda* ι 330

ἰλυοῖσι· ταῖς καταδύσεσιν.

ἑρπετὰ δ' ἰλυοῖσιν ἐνέκρυφεν[2]

[1] *Hec.* trib. Hecker, 109
[2] ἐνέκρυφεν Suda cod. V: ἐνέκρυφθεν

137 (340 Pf.[1]) *Suda* κ 1917

κοκκύαι· αἱ πρόγονοι.

†ἀφ' ὑμέων†[2] κοκύησι καθημένη ἀρχαίησι

[1] *Hec.* trib. Hecker, 122   [2] ἀφ' ὑμέων Suda: ἀμφ' ὑμέων Schneider

134 (333 Pf.) *Suda*

epiklines: inclining toward evil. Callimachus,

  the balance is tipped

135 (335 Pf.) *Suda*

ēeros ogmoi (misty tracks): roads, places.

  misty tracks

136 (336 Pf.) *Suda*

iluoisi (lairs): dens.

  creeping things hid in their lairs[1]

  [1] A sign of a coming storm.

137 (340 Pf.) *Suda*

kokkuai: the ancestors.

  sitting on ancient ancestors[1]

  [1] Perhaps a bird perched on a tomb.

119

138 (347 Pf.[1]) *Suda* λ 594

λίποιμι· καταλείψαιμι.

    λίποιμι

[1] *Hec*. trib. Pfeiffer

139 (348 Pf.[1]) *Suda* μ 114

μαλκίστατον· ψυχρότατον.

    τόδε μοι μαλκίστατον ἦμαρ

[1] *Hec*. trib. Naeke, 239

140 (352 Pf.[1]) *Suda* ν 551

Νωνακρίνη· λέγεται ἡ Καλλιστώ.

    Νωνακρίνη

[1] *Hec*. trib. Adler

141 (353 Pf.[1]) *Suda* ν 562

νωσάμενος· νοήσας, γνούς. παρά Καλλιμάχῳ,

    νωσάμενος

[1] *Hec*. trib. Hecker, 91

138 (347 Pf.) *Suda*

lipoimi: I would leave behind.

> I might forsake

139 (348 Pf.) *Suda*

malkistaton (the coldest): most freezing.

> this day is the coldest for me

140 (352 Pf.) *Suda*

nōnakrinē: it means Callisto.

> Lady of Nonacris[1]

[1] The nymph Callisto (*Aet*. 17.9–10). Nonacris is an area in Arcadia.

141 (353 Pf.) *Suda*

nōsamenos: having thought, having known. In Callimachus,

> after considering

CALLIMACHUS

142 (354 Pf.[1]) *Suda* μ 555

μεμβλώκατον· . . . ἀντὶ τοῦ μετ' ἐπιμελείας ἐγένετο.

μέμβλετό μοι

[1] *Hec.* trib. Pfeiffer

143 (356 Pf.[1]) *Suda* o 131

ὀκχή· στήριγμα, βάσταγμα . . . καὶ ὀκχήσασθαι, ἐπικαθεσθῆναι.

ὀκχήσασθαι

[1] *Hec.* trib. Pfeiffer

144 (357 Pf.[1]) *Suda* o 304

ὄμπνιον ὕδωρ· τὸ τρόφιμον, καὶ πολύ.

ὄμπνιον ὕδωρ

[1] *Hec.* trib. Hecker, 90

145 (348 Pf.[1]) *Suda* π 730

πὰρ πόδα· εὐθύς, παραυτίκα.

εἰ δὲ Δίκη σε[2]
πὰρ πόδα μὴ τιμωρὸς ἐτείσατο, δὶς τόσον αὖτις
ἔσσεται, ἐν πλεόνεσσι παλίντροπος,

[1] *Hec.* trib. Hecker, 122   [2] δὲ Δίκη σε transp. Küster: δέ σε Δίκη *Suda* cod. GVM: δέ τε δίκη A: ἐς δὲ δίκη V

122

142 (354 Pf.) *Suda*

memblōkaton (care): . . . instead of "attention was paid."

> it [or he] was of concern to me

143 (356 Pf.) *Suda*

okchē: a support, foundation . . . and to be supported, to sit on.

> to lean on

144 (357 Pf.) *Suda*

ompnion (h)*udōr*: nourishing and plentiful.

> abundant water

145 (348 Pf.) *Suda*

parpoda: at once, immediately.

> If Dike the avenger has not punished you immediately, it will be two times as much hereafter, returning among the dead,[1]

1 Literally, "the many" (*Epig.* 4).

146 (359 Pf.[1]) *Suda* π 747

πασσαγίην· πανοπλίαν.

   εἷλε δὲ πασσαγίην, τόδε δ' ἔννεπεν

  [1] *Hec*. trib. Naeke, 237

147 (360 Pf.[1]) *Suda* π 1094

περιδέξιος· ὁ καὶ τῇ ἀριστερᾷ ἐργαζόμενος . . . περι-
δέξιος καὶ ὁ σοφός . . . παρὰ Καλλιμάχῳ.

    οἷος ἐκεῖνος ἀεὶ περιδέξιος ἥρως

  [1] *Hec*. trib. Hecker, 99

148 (362 Pf.[1]) *Suda* π 1248

περιπηχύναντες· περιπλεξάμενοι. παρὰ Καλλιμάχῳ.

      περιπηχύναντες

  [1] *Hec*. trib. Naeke, 169

149 (363 Pf.[1]) *Suda* π 1638

πίσεα· οἱ κάθυγροι τόποι.

       καὶ ἀγλαὰ πίσεα γαίης
βόσκεο

  [1] *Hec*. trib. Hecker, 108

146 (359 Pf.) *Suda*

passagiēn: a suit of armor.

   and he took up his armor and spoke thus

147 (360 Pf.) *Suda*

peridexios: one working also with his left hand . . . ambi-dextrous and wise . . . in Callimachus.

      such as that ever skillful hero

148 (362 Pf.) *Suda*

peripēchynantes: having embraced. In Callimachus.

            after embracing

149 (363 Pf.) *Suda*

pisea: wetlands.

   And you[1] pastured on the splendid meadows of the earth

   [1] Addressed to the Marathonian bull.

150 (369 Pf.[1]) *Suda* τ 357

τερπνιστόν· ἐπιτερπέστερον, προσφιλέστερον

  τέρπνιστον

[1] *Hec.* trib. Schol. in Call. Adler

151 (372 Pf.[1]) *Suda* υ 41

ὑδέουσιν· ᾄδουσι, λέγουσιν.

  ὑδέουσιν

[1] *Hec.* trib. Pfeiffer

152 (373 Pf.[1]) *Suda* υ 97

ὑληωροί· οἷς τὰ διὰ τῆς ὕλης ἔργα ἐν φροντίδι ἐστί.
λέγει δὲ τοὺς φύλακας †τοῦ ὄρους†.

  ὑληωροί

[1] *Hec.* trib. Schol. in Call. Adler

153 (375 Pf.[1]) *Suda* υ 523

ὑπόκρηνον· ὑπὸ τὴν κεφαλήν.

       θῆκε δὲ λᾶαν
σκληρὸν ὑπόκρηνον

[1] *Hec.* trib. Hecker, 117

150 (369 Pf.) *Suda*

terpniston: rather enjoyable, very well disposed

      most pleasant

151 (372 Pf.) *Suda*

(h)ydeousin: they sing, they tell of.

      they sing

152 (373 Pf.) *Suda*

(h)yleōroi: those for whom working in the woods is a duty.
He says that they are guardians of the mountain.

      woodsmen

153 (375 Pf.) *Suda*

(h)ypokrenon: under the head.

               he placed a hard
   stone under his head

154 (377 Pf.[1]) *Suda* ψ 113

ψίω· . . . καὶ ψισθεῖεν . . . τραφεῖεν διά ψιχῶν

ψισθεῖεν

[1] *Hec.* trib. Schol. in Call. Adler

155 (245 Pf.[1]) *Suda* χ 608

χυτλώσαιντο· ἀλείψαιντο.

χυτλώσαιντο

[1] *Hec.* trib. Pfeiffer

FRAGMENTA INCERTA

156 (495 Pf.[1]) Didym. *Ad Dem.* 13.32; *P.Berol.* 9780 col. XIV, 34 (Berl. Klass. Texte vol. 1, p. 69)

κ[αὶ] ἔστιν ὁ λόγος τὰ νῦν τῷ Δη[μ]οσθένε[ι π]ερ[ὶ] τῆς Μεγαρικῆς Ὀργάδ[ος], ἧς καὶ Καλλίμαχός που μνημονεύων φησ[ί]·

Νισαίης ἀγλῖθες ἀπ᾽ Ὀργάδος

[1] *Hec.* trib. Wilamowitz, ed. pr.

HECALE

154 (377 Pf.) *Suda*

psiō: . . . and *psistheien* . . . they might be nourished on
gruel

> they might be fed with gruel

155 (245 Pf.) *Suda*

chytlōsainto: they might be anointed.

> they might be anointed

FRAGMENTS OF DOUBTFUL
ATTRIBUTION OR LOCATION

156 (495 Pf.) Didymus, *On Demosthenes*; Berlin papyrus

There is a story relevant to these current matters in De-
mosthenes about the sacred land of Megara. Callimachus,
recalling it somewhere, says,

> heads of garlic[1] from the sacred field of Nisaea[2]

[1] Perhaps among the olives offered to Theseus (*Hec.* 36, 38–
39; cf. Hollis, 125).   [2] The port city of Megara.

157 (585 Pf.[1]) Plin. *HN* 25.167

erigeron a nostris vocatur senecio. . . . nomen hoc Graeci
dederunt, quia vere canescit. caput eius numerosa dividi-
tur lanugine, qualis est spinae, inter divisuras exeunte,
quare Callimachus eam acanthida appellavit, alii pappum.
nec deinde Graecis de ea constat.

Ἀκανθίς[2]

[1] *Hec.* trib. Naeke, 138   [2] vel Ἀκανθίδα

158 (682 Pf.[1]) Schol. Laur. ad Soph. *OC* 510

δεινὸν μὲν τὸ πάλαι κείμενον ἤδη κακόν, ὦ ξεῖν', ἐπε-
γείρειν· τῆς Ἰσμήνης ἀποστάσης ὁ χορὸς ἐρωτᾷ τὸν
Οἰδίποδα καί φησι· τὸ ἐπεγείρειν μὲν καὶ ἀνακινεῖν
τὰ πάλαι συμβάντα δυσχερές, ὅμως δὲ μαθεῖν ἐπι-
θυμῶ τὴν αἰτίαν τῆς πηρώσεως· καὶ ἔστι παθητικά.
Καλλ.,

τί δάκρυον εὗδον ἐγείρεις;

[1] *Hec.* trib. Naeke, 156

HECALE

157 (585 Pf.) Pliny the Elder, *Natural History*

We call Erigeron *senecio* ... The Greeks gave it this name because in the spring it becomes white. Its head is divided by numerous hairs like those of a thorn, coming out from between the sections, which is why Callimachus called it *acanthis*, but others call it *pappus*. Beyond this, the Greeks do not agree about this plant.

acanthis[1]

[1] It could be one of the herbs served to Theseus by Hecale (*Hec.* 38–39; cf. Naeke, 138).

158 (682 Pf.) Laurentian Scholia to Sophocles, *Oedipus at Colonus*

It is a terrible thing to rouse up an evil that is long laid to rest, O stranger: After Ismene has departed the chorus asks Oedipus and says, to rouse and stir up things that happened long ago is difficult. Nonetheless I am eager to hear the cause of your blindness; and it is moving. Callimachus,

Why do you rouse a sleeping tear?[1]

[1] Naeke (p. 156) suggests that this fragment belongs with Hecale's response to Theseus' request to hear the cause of her impoverishment (*Hec.* 40), and Hollis (pp. 125, 320) links it directly to *Hec.* 41.

159 (619 Pf.[1]) Schol.[2] ad Dion. Thrax (*Gramm. Gr.* vol. 3, p. 430.29.31 Hilgard)

τὸ εἴθε καὶ τὸ ἀβάλε ἐκ παραλλήλου κεῖται . . . τὸ ἀβάλε παρὰ Καλλ., ἔνθα φησίν,

ἀβάλε[2] μηδ᾽ ἀβόλησα[3]

[1] *Hec.* trib. Pfeiffer   [2] ἀβάλε Schol.[2]: ἀβάλλε Schol.[1]
[3] ἀβόλησα Schol.[1]: ἀμβόλησα Schol.[2]

160 (370 dub. Pf.[1]) *Suda* οι 35

οἶδμα· κῦμα, ἢ πέλαγος,

καὶ ἄγριον οἶδμα θαλάσσης

[1] *Hec.* trib. Hollis, 321

161 (591 Pf.[1]) Schol. M ad Aesch. *Cho.* 438

ἔπειτ᾽ ἐγὼ νοσφίσας ὀλοίμαν· ἐκ τούτου εἴρηται τὸ . . . Καλλιμάχου,

τεθναίην ὅτ᾽ ἐκεῖνον ἀποπνεύσαντα πυθοίμην

[1] *Hec.* trib. Hecker, 120

159 (619 Pf.) Scholia to Dionysius Thrax

eithe (would that) and *abale* (would that) are parallel . . .
abale [appears] in Callimachus where he says,

> I wish that I had not met

160 (370 dub. Pf.) *Suda*

oidma: swell, wave or the sea,

> a savage swell of the sea

161 (591 Pf.) Scholia to Aeschylus, *Libation Bearers*

then may I die after I have deprived her of life: from this
comes the saying . . . of Callimachus,

> may I die when I have learned that that man has
> breathed his last[1]

---

[1] Perhaps Hecale speaking of Cercyon, who killed one of her
sons.

162 (721 Pf.[1]) *Et. Gud.* (p. 104.21 De Stefani) s.v. Ἀμα-
ζών

Ἀμαζών· ὄνομα ἔθνους . . . καὶ ἀμαζόνες· οἱ πένητες,
οἱ μᾶζαν μὴ ἔχοντες ἤτοι τροφήν.

ἵν' ἀμαζόνες ἄνδρες ἔασιν

[1] *Hec.* trib. Theod. περὶ τῆς κλίσεως

163 (489 Pf.[1]) Choerob. in Theod. (*Gramm. Gr.* vol. 4.1,
p. 401.34 Hilgard)

καὶ πάλιν ἐστὶν ἐπιτηδέες καὶ κατὰ κρᾶσιν ἐπιτηδεῖς.
καὶ βιοπλανέες καὶ κατὰ κρᾶσιν βιοπλανεῖς, καὶ λοι-
πὸν κατὰ ἀποβολὴν τοῦ ῑ γίνεται ἐπιτηδές καὶ βιο-
πλανές· ὡς παρὰ Καλλ.,

φοιτῶσιν οἷοί τε[2] βιοπλανὲς ἀγρὸν ἀπ' ἀγροῦ

[1] *Hec.* trib. Buttmann, 43   [2] οἷοί τε Naeke: οἵ τε Choerob.

164 (513 Pf.[1]) *Et. Gen.* AB s.v. γραίδιον

γραίδιον· . . . ἔστι γραῦις, γραύιδος, γραύιδι [*Et.
Mag.*]· παρὰ Καλλ.,

γραύιδι

[1] *Hec.* trib. Schneider, fr. 326

162 (721 Pf.) *Etymologicum Gudianum*

Amazōn: an ethnic name . . . and *amazones*; the poor, those not having bread or nourishment.

> where the men are Amazons (without bread)

163 (489 Pf.) Choeroboscus

And again there is *epitēdees* and by the process of *crāsis* (combining vowels) it becomes *epitēdeis*. And also by *crāsis*, *bioplanees* becomes *bioplaneis*; and then by dropping the iota they become *epitēdes* and *bioplanes*; as in Callimachus,

> like nomads who roam from land to land

164 (513 Pf.) *Etymologicum Genuinum*

graidion (little old lady): . . . it is *grauis* (old lady) *grauidos*, *grauidi* [*Et. Mag.*]: in Callimachus,

> to the old lady

CALLIMACHUS

165 (732 Pf.[1]) Cic. *Att.* 157.1

nam quod ad te non scripseram, postea audivi a tertio
miliario tum eum isse πολλὰ . . . θυμήναντα multa, in-
quam, mala cum dixisset.

> πολλὰ μάτην κεράεσσιν ἐς ἠέρα θυμήναντα

[1] *Hec.* trib. Scaliger. Cf. M. Haupt, *Opuscula* (1875–76),
vol. 2, 81.

166 (756 Pf.[1]) *Et. Gen.* AB s.v. μύρσος

μύρσος· . . . Μύρσος πλεκτόν τί ἐστιν ἀγγεῖον ἐξ
ἄγνου πλεκόμενον λύγων· παλαιφαμένης δέ, τῆς πά-
λαι τετμημένης ἄγνου.

> μύρσον ἐς ὠτώεντα παλαιφαμένης ἄγνοιο

[1] *Hec.* trib. Meineke 1847, vol. 2.1, 6

167 (519 Pf.[1]) *Et. Mag.* (p. 268.10 Lasserre-Livadaras)
s.v. διάκτορος

διάκτορος· . . ἢ ὁ διάγων τὰς ψυχάς· τοῦ γὰρ Ἑρμοῦ
ἐπίθετον· παρὰ δὲ τοῖς ἄλλοις ποιηταῖς ἁπλῶς ἐπὶ τοῦ
διακόνου τίθεται. Καλλ. ἐπὶ γλαυκὸς τὸ ἐπίθετον,

> ἀλλὰ θεῆς ἥτις με διάκτορον ἔλλαχε Παλλάς

[1] *Hec.* trib. Meineke 1861, 145

136

165 (732 Pf.) Cicero, *Letters to Atticus*

For what I had not written to you I heard afterward that when he was three miles from Rome not only "was he . . . raging," but he also cursed a lot.

> raging much in vain with its horns in the air[1]

[1] Perhaps of the bull as Theseus engages it. Cicero does not state the source of the quote, which suggests that it was well known to his correspondent Atticus. Catullus apparently imitates this line in his description of Theseus' encounter with the Minotaur (Catull. 64.110–11), and Cicero demonstrates knowledge of this part of the poem elsewhere (Cic. *Tusc.* 4.50).

166 (756 Pf.) *Etymologicum Genuinum*

myrsos: . . . a basket, a receptacle woven from twigs of the chaste-tree; *palaifamenēs* means that the tree was cut long ago.

> into a basket with handles from the legendary chaste-tree[1]

[1] Pfeiffer (vol. 1, 476) connects this verse to the story of Erichthonius hidden by Athena in a basket (*Hec.* 70).

167 (519 Pf.) *Etymologicum Magnum*

diaktoros (messenger): . . or the one accompanying the soul; an epithet of Hermes; in other poets it is used simply for "attendant." In Callimachus, an epithet for the owl,

> but, of the goddess Pallas who obtained me as her messenger[1]

[1] Spoken by the owl, who took this role after the crow fell out of favor by bringing bad news to Athena.

168 (608 Pf.[1]) Schol. VM (Ald.) ad Ar. *Av.* 261

κικκαβαῦ· τὰς γλαύκας οὕτω φωνεῖν λέγουσιν, ὅθεν κικαβᾶς αὐτὰς λέγουσιν. ἔστι δὲ ἱερὰ τῆς Ἀθηνᾶς . . . ὡς Καλλ.,

κάρτ᾽ ἀγαθὴ κικυμωίς

[1] *Hec.* trib. Kapp, fr. 67

169 (552 Pf.[1]) Gal. *De praesag. ex puls.* 3.16 (vol. 9, p. 368 Kühn)

ὁ μὲν τρόπος τῆς τοιαύτης χρήσεως ὀνομάζεται μεταφορά . . . καθ᾽ οἵαν ὁμοιότητα καὶ πόδες εἴρηνται καὶ κορυφαὶ καὶ λαγόνες ὄρους . . . ὡς ἐπὶ τοῦ ὄρους τοῦ Βριλησσοῦ Καλλ. εἴρηκε,

Βριλησσοῦ λαγόνεσσιν ὁμούριον ἐκτίσσαντο

[1] *Hec.* trib. Naeke, 225

170 (704 Pf.[1]) Steph.Byz. s.v. Ἁλιμοῦς

Ἁλιμοῦς· δῆμος τῆς Λεοντίδος φυλῆς. Καλλ. δὲ πόλιν ἡγεῖται.

Ἁλιμοῦς[2]

[1] *Hec.* trib. Hecker, *Commentatio critica de anthologia Graeca* (Leiden 1843), 197   [2] vel Ἁλιμοῦντα, Pf. vol. 456

HECALE

168 (608 Pf.) Scholia to Aristophanes, *Birds*

kikkabau (screech!): In this way, they say, owls speak.
From this they call the birds themselves *kikkabas*. It is
sacred to Athena . . . as Callimachus,

> an owl of very good omen

169 (552 Pf.) Galen, *On Prognoses from the Pulse*

The manner of such a usage is called metaphor and based
on . . . such a likeness: mountains are said to have feet and
heads and flanks . . . in this way Callimachus spoke of the
flanks of Mt. Brilessos,

> They founded a . . . bordering on the flanks of Mt.
> Brilessus[1]

[1] Hecale apparently lived on Mt. Brilessus (Pentelicus), and
this perhaps refers to the foundation of the holy precinct and/or
the deme named for her at the conclusion of the poem (Hollis,
326).

170 (704 Pf.) Stephanus of Byzantium

(*H*)*alimous*: a deme of the tribe of Leontis.[1] Callimachus
calls it a city.

> Halimous

[1] One of the twelve tribes (*phylae*) of Attica; named for Leos,
a son of Orpheus, who sacrificed his three daughters at the orders
of the Oracle of Delphi (Paus. 1.5.2).

CALLIMACHUS

171 (680 Pf.[1]) Schol. Laur. ad Soph. *OC* 3

τίς τὸν πλανήτην Οἰδίπουν· . . . δύναται . . . καὶ τοῖς
ἄνω συνάπτεσθαι τοῦ τίς μὴ πυσματικῶς κειμένου,
ἀλλ᾽ ἀντὶ τοῦ ἤ ἄρθρου, ὥστε τῷ "πόλιν" συντετάχθαι
καὶ τὸν λόγον ἔχειν οὕτως, "τίνας χώρους ἀφίγμεθα
ἢ τίνων ἀνδρῶν πόλιν, ἢ τὸν πλανήτην Οἰδίπουν δέ-
ξεται"; ὅτι δὲ τὸ τίς ἀντὶ ἄρθρου χρῶνται, Καλλ. φη-
σιν οὕτως,

> ὑπεὶρ ἅλα κεῖνος ἐνάσθη,
> Ἀλκαθόου τίς ἄπυστος

[1] *Hec.* vel *Galat.* trib. Pfeiffer

172 (611 Pf.[1]) Schol. PM ad Clem. Alex. *Protr.* 2.20.1
(vol. 1, p. 303.25 Stählin)

ἀλωμένη γὰρ ἡ Δηὼ κατὰ ζήτησιν τῆς Θυγατρὸς τῆς
Κόρης περὶ τὸν Ἐλευσῖνα . . . ἀποκάμνει καὶ φρέατι
ἐπικαθίζει λυπουμένη· τὸ φρέαρ Καλλίχορον οἱ πα-
λαιοὶ ὀνομάζουσιν. Καλλ. φησιν,

> Καλλιχόρῳ ἐπὶ φρητὶ καθέζεο παιδὸς ἄπυστος[2]

[1] *Hec.* trib. dubiter Hollis   [2] ἄπυστος corr. Naeke, 11:
ἄπαυστος Schol. PM

171 (680 Pf.) Laurentian Scholia to Sophocles, *Oedipus at Colonus*

who will receive the wanderer Oedipus: It is possible for *tis*, when it is not being used interrogatively, to be connected to preceding [words], but in the place of the article, so that [in this case] it is joined with "city" [in the preceding verse] and has this sense, "We have arrived at what places or the city of what men, which will receive Oedipus the wanderer?" That they use *tis* instead of an article, [is proved by] Callimachus who says,

> whoever is ignorant of Alcathous,[1]
> that one has lived beyond the sea

[1] Likely the founder of Megara (Thgn. 773–74).

172 (611 Pf.) Scholia to Clement of Alexandria, *Protrepticus*

Wandering about Eleusis in the search for her daughter Kore, Deo . . . grew weary and sat at a well grieving; the ancients call the well Callichorus. Callimachus says,

> you sat at the well Callichorus not knowing about
> your child[1]

[1] Addressed to Demeter. Callichorus was at Eleusis, Demeter's cult center and the place where Theseus killed Hecale's nemesis Cercyon (*Hec.* 49.8).

173 (490 Pf.[1]) Choerob. (?) Περὶ Ποσότητος, exc. ex Hdn. Περὶ Ὀρθογραφίας (*AO* vol. 2, p. 286.9 Cramer)

οἶον γραῦς γράϊος καὶ γρήϊος παρα Καλλ. . . . τουτέστι γραός.

γρήϊον εἶδος ἔχουσα

[1] *Hec*. trib. Pfeiffer

174 (705 Pf.[1]) Steph. Byz. s.v. Ἅλυκος

Ἅλυκος· πόλις Πελοποννήσου· Καλλ.,

εἰς Ἀσίνην Ἅλυκόν τε καὶ ἂμ πόλιν Ἑρμιονήων

[1] *Hec*. trib. Naeke, 208; *Aet.*, Hecker, 78

175 (684 Pf.[1]) Schol. ad Stat. *Theb.* 4.44–47

quaeque pavet longa spumantem valle Charadron Neris· Neris montis nomen Argivi, ut ait Callimachus.

Νηρίς.

[1] *Hec*. trib. Naeke, 174

176 (687 Pf.[1]) Schol. K ad Theoc. *Id.* 6.39

ἔπτυσα κόλπον· τὸ νεμεσητὸν ἐκτρεπόμενοι ποιοῦσι τοῦτο, καὶ μάλιστα αἱ γυναῖκες. Καλλ.,

δαίμων, τῇ κόλποισιν ἐνιπτύουσι[2] γυναῖκες

[1] *Hec*. trib. Hecker, 121   [2] ἐνιπτύουσι Hecker: ἐπιπτύουσι cod. K

173 (490 Pf.) Choeroboscus (?), *On Quantity*, taken from Herodian, *On Orthography*

like *graus*, *graïos* and *grēïos* in Callimachus . . . that is to say *graos* (old woman).

> having the appearance of an old woman[1]

[1] During the search for Persephone, Demeter disguised herself as an old woman (*Hymn. Hom. Dem.* 2.101). The fragment probably does not refer to Hecale herself.

174 (705 Pf.) Stephanus of Byzantium

Alycus: a city of the Peloponnese; Callimachus,

> Into Asine, Alycus, and up to the city of the
> Hermioneans[1]

[1] Three towns of the Peloponnese.

175 (684 Pf.) Scholia to Statius, *Thebaid*

and Neris which quakes at the Charadros foaming down its long valley; Neris, the name of an Argive mountain, as Callimachus says.[1]

> Neris

[1] The reference stops here without the quotation from Callimachus.

176 (687 Pf.) Scholia to Theocritus, *Idylls*

she spat into her bosom; they do this to avert retribution, and especially women [do it]. Callimachus,

> The goddess[1] for whom women spit into their bosom

[1] Nemesis, to avoid retribution for arrogance.

177 (527a Pf.[1]) *Et. Gen.* AB s.v. ἐχῖνος

ἐχῖνος· χερσαῖον ζῶιον . . . ἐχῖνος δὲ καὶ ἡ γαστήρ,
ὥς φησι Καλλ.,

> ὅν τε[2] μάλιστα βοῶν ποθέουσιν ἐχῖνοι

[1] *Hec.* trib. Schneider, 489   [2] ὅν τε *Et. Gen.* B.: οὔτε *Et.*
Gen. A

178 (725 Pf.[1]) Zenod. *De voc. an.*

ὠρυγὴ κυρίως λέγεται ἡ τῶν λύκων φωνή, καὶ ὠρύε-
σθαι . . . παρὰ Καλλ,

> καὶ ὡς λύκος ὠρυοίμην

[1] *Hec.* trib. Pfeiffer

179 (741 Pf.[1]) *Et. Gen* AB s.v. ἀρρηφόροι καὶ ἀρρη-
φορία

ἀρρηφόροι καὶ ἀρρηφορία· ἑορτὴ ἐπιτελουμένη τῇ
Ἀθηνᾷ ἐν Σκιροφοριῶνι μηνί· λέγεται δὲ καὶ διὰ τοῦ
ε ἐρρηφορία, παρὰ τὸ τὰ ἄρρητα ἢ μυστήρια φέρειν,
ἢ ἐὰν διὰ τοῦ ε̄, παρὰ τὴν Ἕρσην τὴν Κέκροπος θυ-
γατέρα ἐρσηφορία· ταύτῃ γὰρ ἦγον τὴν ἑορτήν. οὕτω
Σαλούστιος.

Ἐρσηφορία

[1] *Hec.* trib. Reitzenstein 1890/1, 15

HECALE

177 (527a Pf.) *Etymologicum Genuinum*

echinos (stomach): in reference to a land animal . . . the abdomen or stomach, as Callimachus says,

> which the stomachs of oxen especially crave

178 (725 Pf.) Zenodotus, *On the Sounds of Animals*

ōrygē (howl) he says correctly is the voice of wolves, and *ōryesthai* (to howl) . . . in Callimachus,

> and I could howl like a wolf

179 (741 Pf.) *Etymologicum Genuinum*

arrēphoroi and *arrēphoria*: a festival celebrated at Athens in the month of Skriophorion. It is also written with an *e*, *errēphoria*, derived from the carrying of *arrēta* (things not to be divulged) and *mystēria* (secret implements), or if with an *e* (the Ersephoria), from Herse the daughter of Cecrops.[1] They held a festival for her according to Salustius.

> The Ersephoria[2]

[1] Cf. *Hec.* 70 on the daughters of Cecrops.
[2] Also Hersephoria. For Salustius' commentary on the *Hecale*, see Introduction.

HYMNS

INTRODUCTION

GREEK HYMNS

Hymns are songs of praise, entreaty, or thanksgiving sung to deities and sometime humans, undoubtedly one of the oldest forms of song in the Greek tradition.[1] They are found in literary sources, on papyri, and in inscriptions, but performance was of the essence, since a god who does not hear a hymn cannot be expected to respond to it. Hymns usually include an invocation naming the god, lists of attributes, sometimes narratives, such as a birth story or an epiphany, and they conclude with a salutation and/or prayer. They can be of any length and were often accompanied by music and/or dance. There is evidence of large-scale choral presentations and competitions at the great cult centers of Delos and Delphi, as well as at Athens, and local cult sites, common throughout the Greek world, could offer venues for more modest performances. Many of the hymns would be traditional, but some of the greatest Greek poets, including Simonides, Pindar, and Bacchylides, produced newly composed hymns for special occasions. An example is Pindar's *Paean* 6, written for the Theoxenia in Delphi.

[1] Furley and Bremer 2001, 1–40.

THE *HOMERIC HYMNS*

The earliest hymns that have reached us though the medieval manuscript tradition are the *Homeric Hymns*. This is a collection of thirty-three hymns in dactylic hexameters addressed to various deities, which range in length from 3 (*Hymn. Hom.* 13 for Demeter) to 580 lines (*Hymn. Hom.* 4 for Hermes). Most date between 700 and 500 BC, but some are later.[2] The first reference to them in antiquity is found in Thucydides (3.104.5), who includes a quotation from the *Homeric Hymn to Apollo* that he calls a *prooemion* (prelude). This suggests that it was sung by rhapsodes as the first part of a performance of epic poetry,[3] and several hymns that conclude with sign-offs serving as transitions to a following poem appear to corroborate this.[4] The six longer hymns seem to modern critics, at least, to be too long for an introductory role, and Thucydides is clear that the *Homeric Hymn to Apollo* was performed in a competition that took place in a festival environment that included choral singing. His citation also suggests that hymns of the Homeric type were already understood as a distinct genre by the fifth century BC. They were certainly known to Callimachus, whose own hymns contain many references to them.

[2] The *Homeric Hymn to Ares* (*Hymn. Hom.* 8) is considered to be especially late (perhaps 5th c. AD).

[3] Early evidence for this practice is found in Pindar (*Nem.* 2.1–5).

[4] E.g., *Hymn. Hom.* 2.495, 3.546, 4.580, 5.293, etc.

CALLIMACHUS' *HYMNS*

The *Hymns* and sixty-three epigrams are the only poems of Callimachus that have come down to us from antiquity almost intact. There are six hymns in all, with a total of 1,083 lines of verse. Five are in dactylic hexameters, (*Hymns* 1–4, and 6) like the *Homeric Hymns*, and four are in Homer's epic-Ionic dialect (*Hymns* 1–4), but one is composed in elegiac couplets (*Hymn* 5), and two in literary Doric (*Hymns* 5–6). This kind of arrangement, which begins with a traditional combination of meter and dialect, then gives way to more creative combinations, is reminiscent of Callimachus' *Iambi*, and indicates that the *Hymns* were also organized as a collection by the poet himself.[5] Suggestive patterning of subject and theme further supports this view. *Hymns* 1 and 2 are for male deities, 5 and 6 for females; 3 and 4, the two longest, are devoted to a brother/sister pair, Artemis and Apollo, whose father Zeus introduces the collection. *Hymns* 1 and 6, the first and the last, focus on another brother/sister pair, Zeus and Demeter. The fraternal pairs at both ends and at the exact center point to the Ptolemies, whose habit of incest began with Ptolemy II; his marriage to his sister Arsinoe II is celebrated by Callimachus elsewhere (*Var.* 392). It was imitated by their immediate successors, Ptolemy III and Berenice II, who are called brother and sister

---

[5] On Callimachus' *Iambi* as a collection, see Clayman 1980, 48–51; Kerkhecker 1999, 282–87. On Callimachus' *Hymns* as a collection, see Morrison 2007, 105–6, with bibliography at 105n16.

in official documents, but were in fact only cousins.[6] The presence of the Ptolemies is felt elsewhere in Callimachus' *Hymns*, as in *Hymn* 2 to Apollo, where "my king" is associated with the founding of Cyrene (*Hymn* 2.26–27),[7] and in *Hymn* 1 a clear equation is made between Zeus, king of the gods, and "our ruler" (*Hymn* 1.84–85), though precisely which Ptolemies the poet had in mind is controversial. The most direct reference is found in *Hymn* 4 to Delos, where an unborn Apollo prophesies the birth of Ptolemy II on Cos and foresees his "victory" over the Galatians (*Hymn* 4.162–90).

Callimachus was a court poet who wrote for the Ptolemies elsewhere, so it is not surprising to find them in hymns that ostensibly praise deities. The slippage between human and divine was deliberately cultivated by the Ptolemies, who were honored in their own ruler cults and shared temples with Egyptian gods. They were also portrayed in art and coinage with attributes traditionally associated with Greek gods, notably Dionysus and Heracles for the kings, and Aphrodite and Isis for the queens.[8] Though Callimachus could not be expected to write a Greek hymn to Isis, it is possible to find evidence in his *Hymns* of Egyptian culture, particularly the ideology of

[6] Callimachus refers to their notional siblinghood in both the "Victoria Berenices" (*Aet*. 54.2) and the "Lock of Berenice" (*Aet*. 100d; Catull. 66.22).

[7] Cyrene was the birthplace of Berenice II, wife of Ptolemy III, but the identity of "my king" is still debated.

[8] Interestingly, Callimachus dedicated none of his six hymns to these particular gods. Heracles has a minor role in the *Hymn to Artemis* (*Hymn* 3.144–61), and Dionysus is briefly mentioned in the *Hymn to Demeter* (*Hymn* 6.70–71), but Aphrodite is ignored altogether.

Egyptian kingship.[9] An example is Zeus' birth in Arcadia as it is described in the first hymn, where it causes the life-bringing rivers to inundate a previously dry land (*Hymn* 1.17–41). This can be equated with the birth of the god Horus, the prototype of all pharaohs, and the annual flooding of the Nile.[10] Likewise, Apollo's prophesying from his mother's womb in the *Hymn to Delos* (*Hymn* 4.162–95) has parallels in an Egyptian hymn to Osiris.[11]

Callimachus' work on the *Pinakes* made him especially sensitive to the rules of genre, some of which he probably invented himself, and the *Homeric Hymns* are always in the background of his own. For the most part, he follows their example in language, dialect, and meter, though he defines his own work against them in creative ways. There are examples of how he goes about this below and in the notes. He also looks back to other predecessors, especially Hesiod and Pindar. A large portion of his vocabulary in the *Hymns* comes directly from known epic-Ionic sources, and most of the rest can be found in previous or contemporary Greek poetry, though he also coins new words and creates some of his own variants.[12] As a metrician he is less creative, but more consistent, in following metrical conventions than Homer himself.

Though hymns by nature require performance, there have been questions about whether Callimachus' *Hymns* were ever performed, and whether the poet had a genuine

[9] Pioneering work in the identification of the Egyptian contribution to Callimachus' poetics was done by Koenen 1993; Selden 1998; and Stephens 2003.

[10] Stephens 2003, 96–99.

[11] Stephens 2003, 120.

[12] Lapp, 1965, 155–72.

religious sensibility or treated the gods as essentially literary figures. The first issue is complicated by the mimetic hymns (*Hymns* 2, 5, and 6), where the narrator, perhaps the poet himself, seems to be an active participant in a ritual for the god. S/he speaks in the first person describing events as they unfold and gives directions to other participants. Legrand showed long ago that it was not possible to coordinate these elaborate re-creations of ritual with actual ones, but left open the possibility that Callimachus' three narrative hymns could have been performed at festivals.[13] Even this concession has been widely rejected, and most readers today agree that the *Hymns* were intended only for secular consumption, which could include performance at a symposium, at a private reading, or no performance at all.[14] This view is based on no evidence except the texts themselves, and the way that their literary qualities and the poet's playful attitude fail to fulfill the expectations of modern religious sensibilities. It may be shortsighted, and comparisons of the *Hymns* with religious purity regulations, oracles, and especially inscribed hymns suggest promising ways to move the discussion forward.[15]

Hymn I to Zeus

The hymn begins with a rhetorical question: Is there a better subject of song at libations for Zeus than the god himself? (1–3). The hymn's dramatic setting, then, appears

[13] Legrand 1901.

[14] An exception is Cameron 1995, 63–67.

[15] E.g., Petrovic 2011. See also Hunter 1992 on the challenges of interpreting mythic narrative in Hellenistic poetry.

HYMNS

to be a symposium where the proceedings typically began
and concluded with a libation to Zeus (Ath. 15.692f–93c).
A second question follows in the form of a priamel offering
a choice between two accounts of the god's birth, Cretan
or Arcadian (4–7). This has a parallel in the *Homeric
Hymn to Dionysus*, which also begins with alternative
birth stories (1–7). Since it is likely that the *Dionysus* came
first in the collection of *Homeric Hymns* known to Callim-
achus, the choice of birth stories suggests that he is an-
nouncing the *Hymn to Zeus* as the first in his own collec-
tion of hymns.[16]

Callimachus expresses the agony of having to choose
between the two accounts (5) in the words of Antagoras
of Rhodes (fr. 1.1 Powell) from a *Hymn to Eros* expressing
doubt about that god's parentage.[17] There is no real doubt
in Callimachus' hymn, where the decision to begin with
the Arcadian birth story is settled by a voice quoting Epi-
menides of Crete (B1 DK): "Cretans are always liars" (8).
Epimenides was a poet of theogonies, who claimed that
he slept for many years in the cave of Dictean Zeus, where
he dreamed of meeting the goddesses Truth and Justice.
His verse recalls, in turn, a passage on poetic lying and
truth-telling in Hesiod (*Theog.* 26–28), to which Callima-
chus returns later in the hymn. Ironically, the choice be-

[16] On the *Homeric Hymn to Dionysus* and Callimachus' *Hymn
to Zeus*, see Hunter and Fuhrer 2002. Another model for Callim-
achus' priamel may be the beginning of the fragmentary first
hymn of Pindar (fr. 29 S.-M.). If this was addressed to Zeus, as
has long been believed, it would be a particularly compelling par-
allel, but the addressee may be Apollo (D'Alessio 2009, 129–48).

[17] On Antagoras' association with the Academic school and
the philosophical implications of Callimachus' quotation, see
Cuypers 2004.

tween birth stories turns out to be no choice at all. Though Callimachus begins his tale in Arcadia (10–32), baby Zeus is soon handed over to the nymph Neda, who carries him to Crete, where the Corybantes, Dictean Meliae, and the goat Adrasteia play their traditional roles as guardians of his infancy (33–53).

Zeus matures quickly and swiftly accomplishes everything he set out to do (54–56).

> That is why your siblings, though older, did not think it too much that you have heaven as your allotted home. The ancient bards were not altogether truthful. They said that homes were distributed to the three sons of Cronus by lot, yet who but a fool would draw lots for Olympus and Hades? (58–63)

Here Callimachus rejects Homer, who describes how Zeus and his two brothers, Poseidon and Hades, received their realms by lot (*Il.* 15.187–92), in favor of Hesiod (*Theog.* 881–85), who claims that the other gods invited Zeus to become their king. Most readers connect these verses with lines in which Callimachus equates Zeus with "our ruler" (84–85), and see in them a reference to a Ptolemy's accession to power. This is usually understood to be Ptolemy II, which dates the poem to 285/4 BC, when Ptolemy II became his father's co-regent and the opposition had not yet become apparent.[18]

With Zeus on the throne, the hymn turns to his power, and specifically to his patronage of kings (72–89). This

---

[18] Clauss 1986. Alternatively, Carrière (1969) argues for Ptolemy I, and the circumstances surrounding the accession of Ptolemy III also suit Callimachus' language.

recalls the brief hymn to Zeus that introduces Hesiod's *Works and Days* (*Op.* 1–10), and Callimachus underlines the Hesiodic connection with a direct quotation (*Theog.* 96) claiming that kings are from Zeus (78). Zeus' care for kings is illustrated by one who is particularly blessed and wealthy, "our ruler" (85), the unspecified Ptolemy, who by evening accomplishes the greatest things he thinks of in the morning, and the lesser, as soon as he thinks of them (86–87). It is this king assimilated to Zeus himself who receives the poet's final salute and request for financial aid (90–95).

Hymn II to Apollo

The *Hymn to Apollo* is the first "mimetic" hymn, that is, it re-creates a highly dramatic ritual performance. The first words are the voice of a participant-narrator excitedly pointing to signs of the god's approach: Apollo's laurel branch and shrine tremble, the Delian palm nods, swans sing, and the bolts of the door push back by themselves (1–7). The expectation of Apollo's epiphany creates dramatic tension throughout the poem that will not be resolved until the conclusion, when the god himself appears and speaks (105–13). The narrator is addressing a chorus of young men whom he urges to begin their song and dance (8–15), while an audience is asked to listen to the song in silence (17–21), and then to shout Apollo's ritual cry, *Hie Paieon* (25). "Apollo will honor the chorus that sings according to his heart" (28), and it would be an error to resist him. "Whoever fights with the Blessed Ones would fight with my king. Whoever fights with my king would fight even with Apollo" (26–27). There is no consensus concerning the identity of the king who is here associated with the god, though the scholiast plausibly names Ptolemy III.[19] If this is correct, the poem would be dated after 246 BC, when he ascended the throne.

The body of the hymn is devoted to Apollo's traditional powers and accouterments, some associated with the construction of his cult center at Delos (57–64) and some with his shrine at Delphi (97–104). This division reflects the *Homeric Hymn to Apollo*, which has distinct Delian and Pythian parts. In Callimachus' hymn the two are separated by a much longer narrative on the settlement of Cyrene and the establishment there of the cult of Carneian Apollo (65–96). Callimachus relies here on Pindar's fifth Pythian ode for the last Battiad king, Archesilaus IV (*Pyth.* 5.54–93), and his ninth for Telesicrates of Cyrene (*Pyth.* 9.1–8). The latter describes the courtship of Apollo and the lion-slaying nymph Cyrene. Callimachus moves the scene to the site of Cyrene itself, where the couple, now married, look down with pleasure at the choruses of dancing men and women as they celebrate the first Carneian festival (85–96). It is hard to resist seeing this set piece as an homage to the royal couple, Berenice II, who was born in Cyrene, and Ptolemy III. Alternatively, Cyrenean Callimachus may be expressing his patriotism or even writing for

---

[19] In addition to identifying "my king" as Ptolemy III Euergetes, the scholiast explains that Callimachus honored him because the king was *philologos*: "a lover of literature." Some believe that the adjective better fits Ptolemy II, and another candidate is Magas, who was king of Cyrene until his death circa 250 BC. On these options, see Cameron 1995, 408.

a festival there, but this is more likely an example of the poet using his Cyrenean birth as a way to assert his own special relationship to the queen.[20]

The poem concludes with a personal appearance by the god himself, who kicks away Envy and Blame and asserts the superiority of Callimachus' aesthetics in an oracular statement that speaks metaphorically of poetry as water. Ocean and the great Assyrian River filled with refuse are contrasted with pure droplets that bees carry to Demeter from a holy fountain (105–12). The precise meaning of these terms and the relationship of these verses, often called the hymn's *sphragis* (seal), to the rest of the poem has been long debated.[21] It can be plausibly read as an endorsement of short poems over long ones, clarity over bombast, and pure sources over polluted ones. It may be connected to the rest of the poem by reference to the *Homeric Hymn to Apollo*, whose narrator speaks glowingly of his own talents at the conclusion of the Delian section, where he directs the chorus to say, if asked, that he is the "sweetest of singers" (*Hymn. Hom. Ap.* 3.165–78).[22] At the end of his own hymn, Callimachus likewise argues for the superiority of his art, but now in the voice of Apollo himself.

[20] Clayman 2014, 24–26.

[21] A review of the most influential interpretations is in Cheshire 2008, 354–55n2.

[22] Hunter and Furher 2002, 150–52. A complementary approach is taken by Petrovic (2011, 270–75), who stresses the connection between the pure, unpolluted poetry of the conclusion of the poem with the call at the beginning for those who are ritually impure to depart from the ritual.

CALLIMACHUS

Hymn III to Artemis

There is no long Homeric hymn to Artemis, though Callimachus knew the short ones (*Hymn. Hom.* 9, 27). It seems right, then, that he would begin, "Artemis we hymn, for it is no small matter for singers to forget her," and that this poem is the second-longest of Callimachus' hymns. Scholars used to complain about its lack of organization, but Bing and Uhrmeister demonstrate that it follows a logical plan that sets out the goddess' development from early childhood to her full maturity as the subject of myth and recipient of cult.[23] She is introduced as a baby sitting on the lap of her father, Zeus, where she asks for the accouterments and honors that were traditionally assigned to her: virginity, more titles even than Apollo, a quiver and bow, a short chiton for hunting, and a chorus of nymphs (6–25). The scene was inspired by a passage in Homer (*Il.* 21.468–513), where Hera seizes Artemis' weapons and beats her with them until she has to be rescued in tears by her mother, Leto, and led to her father's lap for consolation. In Callimachus' hymn, baby Artemis is only paying her father a casual visit. Zeus is charmed by her precociousness and exclaims, as if in answer to Homer, "When goddesses bear such children to me I care little about the jealousy of angry Hera" (29–31). He gives her everything she asks for and more.

In the absence of a major Homeric hymn to Artemis, Callimachus looks back to the long, complex *Homeric Hymn* for her brother, Apollo. That poem begins with Apollo's arrival on Olympus, where all the gods rise to

[23] Bing and Uhrmeister 1994.

greet him, his mother, Leto, takes his quiver and bow, and his father, Zeus, offers a toast (*Hymn. Hom. Ap.* 3.1–13). When Artemis arrives at Olympus in her own hymn, it is Hermes who takes her armor, and Apollo receives her catch from the hunt, or at least he used to until ravenous Heracles joined the Olympic party (138–57). This is Apollo's only appearance in his sister's Callimachean hymn, and it balances her small part in his, where she supplies him with the horns of goats, which he uses to build his famous altar at Delos (*Hymn* 2.60–63).[24]

The *Hymn to Artemis* also looks back to Callimachus' own *Hymn to Apollo* and ahead to his *Hymn to Delos*.[25] A clue to the importance of the latter comes at the beginning of Artemis' hymn, where she says,

> I will live on the mountains and visit the cities of men only when women suffering from sharp birth pains call for help. For these the fates assigned me from my very birth to bring aid, since my mother when she gave birth to me and carried me did not suffer, but took me from her own womb without pain. (20–25)

This is a pointed contrast to the *Hymn to Delos*, which is structured around the pregnant Leto's long, painful search for a place to give birth to Apollo. Among other parallels, the conclusions of the two hymns stand out. In Artemis' hymn, her temple at Ephesus is built by the Amazons, who

[24] For these and other similarities between the *Homeric Hymn to Apollo* and Callimachus' *Hymn to Artemis*, see Hunter and Furher 2002, 161–62.

[25] A summary of the main points of contact is in Stephens, 107.

establish her rites there by dancing around her image (*Hymn* 3.237–47). At Delos, Apollo's festival begins when Theseus leads a chorus of dancing men, and the other islands circle Delos itself (*Hymn* 4.300–315). Artemis, then, is flanked by her brother on both sides, and the many interconnections between these three hymns provide a strong indication that Callimachus himself organized the collection.

There is no explicit connection between the *Hymn to Artemis* and the Ptolemies, but its finale at Ephesus perhaps points to Arsinoe II, whose first husband, Lysimachus, king of Thrace, controlled the city in his lifetime and renamed it Arsinoea (Strabo 14.1.21).[26] There is no evidence that Arsinoe took charge of the city as she did others, but she was there when her husband was killed on the plain of Corupedium in 281 BC, when he was defending his holdings in Asia Minor against Seleucus. Arsinoe managed to escape, perhaps in disguise (Polyaenus, *Strat.* 8.57). The city was not under Ptolemaic control again until after her death, but her association with it could have remained as a point of pride.

Hymn IV to Delos

The *Hymn to Delos* is the longest of Callimachus' six hymns and perhaps the liveliest. It follows Apollo's mother, Leto, in her last stages of pregnancy as she travels throughout the Greek mainland and the islands searching for a place to give birth to the god while Hera rages and her minions threaten. The landscape itself flees from her in

---

[26] Carney 2013, 36–37, 47–48.

fear for its very existence until the fetus itself speaks twice from her womb, first to refuse a birth at Thebes because that will be the home of Niobe, who boasted that her children were better than Leto's (88–98), and again to give his mother directions to the wandering island, which will be called Delos, where he will be born (190–95). The *Homeric Hymn to Apollo* has the same storyline in its first, Delian section, but in a condensed form.[27] Callimachus follows his Homeric model in its general structure, meter, and diction, but his narrative is greatly expanded and animated, even comic. He is as interested in Delos itself as he is in Apollo, and this unexpected focus has been traced to Pindar's *Paeans* (5.35–48, 7b.42–51 S.-M.) and to his first *Hymn* (fr. 33c–d S.-M.).[28]

Apollo's second speech from his mother's womb (162–95) begins at the exact center of the poem and contains the only specific, identifiable references in the *Hymns* to Callimachus' Ptolemaic patrons. It begins with an injunction not to bear him on the island of Cos because "to her is owed by the Fates some other god, the highest lineage of the Saviors." This is Ptolemy II Philadelphus, born on Cos in 309/8 BC, whose parents, Ptolemy I and Berenice I, had the cult title *Sōtēres*, or "Saviors."[29] The god also predicts Ptolemy's victory in a war with the Galatians, the "later-born Titans" who will attack Delphi (171–87). Here

---

[27] *Hymn. Hom. Ap.*: the search for a birthplace, 3.30–48; Leto's request to Delos, 3.49–60; Delos' quick agreement, 3.61–82.

[28] Perhaps, fittingly, a hymn to Apollo (D'Alessio 2009). On Callimachus' and Pindar's Delos, see Bing 2008, 91–143.

[29] The date and the place of his birth are confirmed by the Parian Marble (*BNJ* 239 B 19).

the oracular fetus is referring to an episode in Philadelphus' reign when he sent four thousand Celtic mercenaries to their deaths. They had been hired in about 275 BC to assist in defending Alexandria against an invasion by Ptolemy's half brother Magas of Cyrene and had revolted when Magas had to return unexpectedly to Libya. The poet magnifies the importance of this episode by conflating it with an earlier Celtic invasion of Delphi in 279 BC that Callimachus likely described in his now lost *Galateia*.[30] Then, it was said, the god defended his shrine by sending a storm to destroy the invaders.[31] The suggestion seems to be that Ptolemy and Apollo have much in common. The remainder of the poem celebrates Apollo's birth on Delos and the foundation of his cult there, in parallel with the *Hymn to Artemis*.

Hymn V to Athena (The Bath of Pallas)

The *Hymn to Athena* is the second of Callimachus' mimetic hymns. It begins with the words of the narrator, who is organizing a ritual bath for a statue of Athena that is about to emerge from her temple in a procession to the river Inachus. The scene and the ritual, which features Diomedes' shield as well as the Palladium, are clearly Argive. Though there is no evidence of such a rite in Argos itself, there are parallels for the ritual bathing of statues in other Greek cities, so the dramatic setting is plausible. Other ritual details are described, and then to fill the time

[30] *Var.* 378–79. See Fraser 1972, vol. 2b, 925n352.

[31] Thanksgiving for the miracle is recorded in a decree of Cos (*SIG.*[3] 398).

while the party waits for the goddess to appear, the narrator tells the story of Teiresias, who was blinded by the goddess when he accidently saw her bathing with his mother, the nymph Chariclo. It is a cautionary tale meant to warn men against gazing on the goddess during her ritual bath. This suggests that the narrator is also female and that the story has a sexual undercurrent. Teiresias is punished for his intrusion but also compensated with the gifts of prophecy and an intellect that will live on after death. The hymn concludes with Athena's arrival and a prayer for the well-being of Argos.

The *Hymn to Athena* is unique for its elegiac meter and shares its Doric dialect with the *Hymn to Demeter* that follows. While no satisfactory explanation has been found for the meter, the dialect suits its Argive setting.[32] Both dialect and setting point to the self-presentation of the Ptolemies, who claimed an association with Peloponnesian Argos by virtue of their descent from Heracles.[33] The events surrounding that hero's vanquishing of the Nemean Lion occupy most of Callimachus' "Victoria Berenices," the first episode in Book 3 of the *Aetia*, written in honor of Berenice II, who was a victor at the Nemean games. As the *aition* begins, Callimachus traces the trajectory of the news of the queen's triumph "from the land of Danaus . . . to the island of Helen" (*Aet.* 54.4–6), that is,

[32] Elegiac meter was associated with lament and was widely used in epigrams on grave steles. The anguished speech of Chariclo as she witnessed her son's blinding perhaps determined the hymn's meter.

[33] As Ptolemy III asserts in the opening lines of the Adoulis inscription (*OGIS* 54).

from Argos to Egypt. Berenice's four-horse chariot team won the prize sometime after her marriage to Ptolemy III in 246 BC, and this event may be connected to Athena's devotion to her own horses described at the beginning of the hymn. After her battle with the giants, Athena first groomed her horses and only afterward cleaned her own filthy armor (5–12).

Hymn VI to Demeter

The *Hymn to Demeter*, the last of the collection, forms a pair with the *Hymn to Athena* to balance the hymns to Zeus and Apollo that open it. Both are mimetic hymns in which a narrator seems to be organizing a religious procession. In both, the procession pauses for a mythical narrative recounting how the goddess punished a young man who violated her sacred space. In both cases the nature of the violation is sexual, though not explicitly so. Both return to sacred rituals in their conclusions, and end traditionally in brief prayers. There are many other similarities in addition to these in theme, structure, language, and dialect.[34]

Although Callimachus' hymns to Apollo and Delos cannot be appreciated without reference to the *Homeric Hymn to Apollo*, his *Hymn to Demeter* seems to dismiss its Homeric counterpart. "No, let us not mention what brought a tear to Deo" (17), the narrator says after only eight lines describing her wanderings in search of her abducted daughter, as opposed to the *Homeric Hymn*, where they occupy most of the long narrative. The Homeric account of the journey avoids specific place-names, but Cal-

---

34 Other similarities are discussed in Hopkinson, 13–17.

limachus' account names three: "the black men," which points to Africa; the Garden of the Hesperides, which Apollonius locates in the Cyrenaica; and the river Achelous, which is in Aetolia. The last two were of more than a little interest to Berenice II, who was born in Cyrene, and her husband, Ptolemy III, who formed an alliance with the Aetolian league in 229/8 BC.[35]

The misguided young man in Callimachus' Demeter is Erysichthon, a king's son who intrudes into the goddess's sacred grove and recklessly takes his ax to a tree, killing the resident nymph. The goddess is livid and sends Nicippe to reason with him. Nicippe is her public priestess who does not appear in traditional versions of the story. Her name, which means "she who is victorious with horses," seems to point to Berenice II, whose teams won victories at Nemea and Olympia, and whose own name means "she who brings victory."[36]

When the Homeric Demeter expresses her anger at the universe, the whole world is plunged into famine, but in Callimachus' hymn only the miscreant Erysichthon becomes cursed with an implacable hunger. His compulsive consumption of the royal household and his parents' de-

[35] The League honored the Ptolemies with life-sized statue groups in Thermos and Delphi (IG IX.1², 1.56, 1.202). See Huss 2001, 356.

[36] Callimachus' "Victoria Berenices" (*Aet.* 54–60j) celebrates her Nemean victory, and Hyginus (*Poet. astr.* 2.24) confirms her Olympic victory. The epigrammatist Posidippus (3rd c. BC) wrote a group of eighteen *Hippika* celebrating chariot victories that includes five for certain and probably two more for Ptolemies. Among these are Berenice I, Berenice II, and Arsinoe II; see Clayman 2012.

spair and embarrassment at his behavior turns the hymn into a kind of farce that would be at home in iambic poetry or comedy. At its conclusion, the poet/narrator asks the goddess that he not have friends who are hateful to her, that is, like Erysichthon, and the procession, which opened the hymn, continues to its conclusion.

HISTORY AND CONSTITUTION
OF THE TEXT

Although direct evidence is lacking, it seems likely that the *Hymns* were organized as a collection by the poet himself.[37] References in Propertius, Tibullus, Virgil, Ovid, Heliodorus, and Nonnus attest to their popularity in the Hellenistic and Roman periods, though we do not know by whom they were copied and edited. The *Hymns* were also included in ancient editions of Callimachus' collected works along with the *Hecale*, *Aetia*, *Iambi*, and more. [38]

The oldest texts survive only as small fragments of papyri copied between the first century BC and the seventh century AD and found in Egypt. Their modern discovery and editing began at the end of the nineteenth century and is still in progress. The first to use the papyri systematically in improving the text of the *Hymns* was Rudolph Pfeiffer in 1953. He lists ten that contain some text or information about the *Hymns*, and eight more papyri have been published since then. The list that follows uses the numbering and order of Mertens-Pack[3], the online data-

---

[37] Stephens, 12–14.
[38] Bulloch, 80–81; Stephens, 39.

base of the Centre du documentation de papyrologie lit-
téraire (CEDOPAL) at the Université de Liège, which
provides additional information and bibliography for each
papyrus.[39] Each entry below begins with the inventory
number assigned by Mertens-Pack[3], followed by the series
name in standard abbreviations, the number assigned by
Pfeiffer if he knew the document, its date, and the rele-
vant passages in the *Hymns*.

00185.010: *PSI* 15.1477 (*PSI* inv. 2409). Not in Pfeiffer.
2nd c. AD. *Hymn* 1.32–41.

00186.000: *P.Oxy.* 2258 (+ *P.Oxy.* 30, pp. 91–92).
Pap. 37 Pf. 5th–6th c. AD. *Hymn* 1.53–60, 76–83;
2.1–18, 24–40; 3.2–4, 12–14, 28–29, 36–39; 4.130–
34, 158–62, 169–74, 196–99, 232–35, 240–45, 260–
63, 268–73, 282–83, 308–9; 6.125–34.

00187.000: *P.Ant.* 1.20. Pap. 44 Pf. 4th–5th c. AD.
Scholia to *Hymn* 2.38–76; 3.37–94.

00188.000: *P.Mil.Vogl.* 2.42 (*P.Mil.Vogl.* inv. 174).
Pap. 38 Pf. 1st c. BC. *Hymn* 3.1–6, 16, 22–54.

00188.100: *P.Oxy.* 3328. Not in Pfeiffer. 2nd c. AD.
Glossary to *Hymn* 3.2–6, 10–12.

00188.200: *PLG* Carlini 3 (*P.Genav.* inv. 209). Not in
Pfeiffer. 4th–5th c. AD. *Hymn* 3.31–61, 62–92.

00189.000: *P.Cair.* inv. 47993b. Pap. 39 Pf. 1st c. AD.
Hymn 3.46–54, 78–84 with scholia.

00189.100: *P.Fay.Coles* 5. Not in Pfeiffer. 2nd c. AD.
Hymn 3.67–80.

[39] Additional information about the papyri can be found in
Pfeiffer vol. 2, li–liv; Lehnus 2011, 23–28; Stephens, 43–46;
Asper, 540–41.

00190.000: *P.Amh*. 2.20. Pap. 43 Pf. 4th c. AD. Scholia
to *Hymn* 3.107–63, 172–78.

00190.100: *P.Ant*. 3.179. Not in Pfeiffer. 4th–5th c. AD.
Hymn 3.162–65, 189–92; 6.10–12, 37–39 with mar-
ginal glosses.

191.000: *P.Oxy*. 2225. Pap. 42 Pf. 2nd c. AD. *Hymn*
4.11–25, 38–40, 68–75, 81–92, 102–10, 141–46,
156–81, 186–205, 209–18, 230–43.

00192.000: *Bodl.Libr.* inv. Ms.Gr.cl.f.109(P). Pap. 45
Pf. 5th–6th c. *Hymn* 4.53–69, 80–98 with marginalia.

00193.000: *PLG* Carlini 12 (*P.Alex*. inv. 5). Pap. 40 Pf.
1st c. AD. *Hymn* 4.84–94.

00193.010: *P.Montserrat* inv. 145. Not in Pfeiffer. 2nd
c. AD. *Hymn* 4.138–48.

00193.020: *P.Montserrat* inv. 198. Not in Pfeiffer. 1st
c. AD. *Hymn* 4.199–206.

00193.030: *BKT* 9.73 (*P.Berol*. inv. 21170). Not in Pfeif-
fer. 5th c. AD. *Hymn* 4.271–88, 307–20.

00194.000: *P.Oxy*. 2226. Pap. 41. Pf. 2nd c. AD. *Hymn*
6.32–37, 41–43, 54–63, 79–117, 138.

00211.000: *P.Mil.Vogl*. 1.18 (*P.Cair*. inv. JE 67340) +
P.Mil.Vogl. inv. 28b + *P.Mil.Vogl*. inv. 1006. Pap. 8
Pf. 1st–2nd c. AD. *Diegeseis* including summaries of
Hymns 1 and 2.

The papyri contain only short passages, often truncated,
and sometimes as little as a single word. If we had to rely
on them exclusively for our knowledge of the text, as is the
case with most of Callimachus' poems, we would know
very little about the *Hymns*. Evidence in a variety of tes-
timonia, including scholia on other ancient authors and
citations in lexica, indicate that Callimachus' works were

read until the fall of Byzantium in the thirteenth century.[40] At that time most of Callimachus was lost, and this would have been the fate of the *Hymns* as well, had not an unnamed editor decided to include them together with some scholia in a collection along with the *Homeric Hymns*, the *Hymns* of Proclus, the *Orphic Hymns*, and the *Orphic Argonautica*. Johannes Aurispa carried a copy of it, probably in the form of a paper codex, from Constantinople to Italy in 1423. It is from this manuscript, no longer extant, that the twenty-four known manuscripts of the *Hymns* descend.[41]

The first editor to collate some of the manuscripts was J. A. Ernesti for his edition of 1761, but the modern history of the text begins with Wilamowitz, who systematically collated a larger number of manuscripts and attempted a reconstruction of the archetype, Ψ.[42] He had great faith in Ψ, which thoroughly informs his text. It was Smiley, though, whose new collations demonstrated that all of the manuscripts available to us descend from four hyperarchetypes that had been copied from Ψ. This is proved by shared lacunae at *Hymn* 4.177[a]–78 and 4.200–201 that can be traced to damage in a common ancestor. Also several shared areas of corruption that are not always

[40] Michael Choniates (d. 1220), archbishop of Athens, is the last person known to have a copy in his possession.

[41] This number includes two that can no longer be consulted: T (destroyed in a fire in 1904), and R (now lost).

[42] Wilamowitz published four editions: 1882, 1897, 1907, and 1925. His third edition is based on a thorough re-collation of the manuscripts, while the fourth makes only a limited number of small improvements in the text.

exactly the same in each manuscript suggest that Ψ deteriorated over the years. Smiley's work laid the groundwork for Pfeiffer's careful reassessment based on his own collations that established the modern text of the *Hymns*. Pfeiffer's stemma, modified slightly by Bulloch, is now universally accepted.[43]

SIGLA

The extant manuscripts are grouped into four families, designated α, β, (ε), and ζ. Each is labeled by a standard siglum for easy identification in the apparatus criticus. The information on the manuscripts below depends on Smiley, Pfeiffer, and Bulloch; the arrangement follows Stephens.[44]

α[45]

F	Milan, Ambrosianus 120 (B 98 sup.), 15th c. (1420–1428). In the hand of Georgius Chrysococces, Constantinople.
At	Athos, Vatopedi cod. Gr. 671, 15th c.
I	Vaticanus gr. 1379, 1496. Copied by Georgius Moschus.
G	Vienna, Austrian National Library, Phil. Gr. 318. 15th c.
H	Leiden, Vossianus 59. Late 15th–early 16th c.

[43] Pf. vol. 2, lxxxiii; Smiley 1920–21; Bulloch, 66. The corrected stemma is reproduced in Stephens, 41.

[44] Stephens, 41–43.

[45] Smiley 1921a; Pfeiffer vol. 2, lvi–lxiii.

HYMNS

Λ   Florence, Laurentianus suppl. 440, late 15th–
         early 16th c. Copied by Georgius Moschus.
Anon.   Anonymous Bernensis. Marginalia in the edi-
Bern.   tion of Vasconsan, Paris, 1549, including text
         from a different source and conjectures.

$$\beta^{46}$$

E   Paris, Bibliothèque nationale gr. 2763. 15th c.,
         with marginal scholia.
e   Milan, Ambrosianus 734. 15th c.

$$(\epsilon)^{47}$$

$$\gamma^{48}$$

Π   Paris, Bibliothèque nationale gr. suppl. 1095.
         15th c. Page containing *Hymn* 3.66–145 lost.
[D]   Florence, Laurentianus 32.45. 15th c. Text of
         Callimachus removed.
La.   Ianus Lascaris, ed., *Callimachi Cyrenaei hymni*,
         probably published between 1494 and 1498.
         Editio princeps.
Pol.   Angelo Poliziano, ed., *Angeli Politiani Miscella-
         nea centuriae primae ad Laurentium Medi-
         cem.* Florence, 1498. Editio princeps of
         Hymn 5.

[46] Smiley 1920c, 112–22; Pfeiffer vol. 2, lxii–lxv.
[47] Pfeiffer vol. 2, lxxx.
[48] Smiley 1920c, 105–12; Pfeiffer vol. 2, lxv–lxviii.

δ^{49}

S	Madrid, Biblioteca Nacional gr. 4562 (= N 24), 1464. With conjectures by Lascaris added after 1489.
Q	Modena, Estensis 164. 15th c. Copied with comments by Georgius Valla.
q	Ambrosianus 11 (A 63 sup.). Ca. 1509. Copied from Q.

ζ^{50}

A	Vatican, gr. 1691.
K	Vatican, Urbinas gr. 145. 15th c. Copy of A partly in the hand of Georgius of Crete.
C	Venice, Marcianus 480. 15th c. Hymns copied by Georgius of Crete ca. 1468.
B	Vatican, gr. 36. 15th c. Copy of C by Georgius of Crete.

Lost manuscripts[51]

N	Basis of Robortelli's *Locorum variorum annotationes*, 1543, and his *Hymni*, Venice, 1555.
O	Basis of Stephanus' *Poetae Graeci principes heroici carminia et alii nonnulli*. Paris, 1566.
R	Matritensis codex gr. 122. 15th c. Collated by

---

[49] Smiley 1920b; Pfeiffer vol. 2, lxviii–lxx.
[50] Smiley 1920a, 6–15; 1921b; Pfeiffer vol. 2, lxx–lxxii.
[51] Smiley 1920a, 4–5; Pfeiffer vol. 2, lxxiv.

Smiley in the Biblioteca Nacional, Madrid,
but now lost.

T   Taurinensis, Biblioteca Nazionale B.v.26. 16th c.
Lost in a fire in 1904.

Very Late Copies (codices recentissimi)[52]

THIS EDITION

The Greek text of this edition is based on Pfeiffer's, en-
riched by papyri published since 1953 and the judgment
of later editors, especially Williams, Bulloch, and Asper.
The notes on the text do not constitute a full apparatus,
but give the reader additional information about textual
difficulties and variants that affect the meaning. They also
point to places where papyri correct the textual tradition,
and to a few places where the reconstructed archtype Ψ
has a better reading than the much earlier papyri. I have
not flagged the many points where my text differs from
Mair's.

THE CITATION OF
CALLIMACHUS' *HYMNS*

Callimachus' *Hymns* have both names and numbers. They
are designated by both name and number in the Introduc-
tions, e.g., *Hymn to Artemis* (*Hymn* 3), but in the notes

---

[52] Pf. vol. 2, lxxii–lxxiv.

and in references embedded in the Introductions they are cited only by number (e.g., *Hymn* 3.126). The *Homeric Hymns* are cited by name and number in the Introductions, e.g., *Homeric Hymn to Aphrodite* (*Hymn. Hom.* 5), and in the notes by abbreviated title and number, e.g., *Hymn. Hom. Aphr.* 6.9.

BIBLIOGRAPHY

CRITICAL STUDIES

Acosta-Hughes, Benjamin, and Christophe Cusset. "Callimaque face aux hymnes homériques." In *Hymnes de la grèce antique. Approches littéraires et historiques: Actes du colloque international de Lyon, 19–21 juin 2008*, edited by Richard Bouchon et al., 123–33. Lyon: Maison de l'Orient et de la Méditerranée-Jean Pouilloux, ca. 2012.

Bing, Peter, and Volker Uhrmeister. "The Unity of Callimachus' *Hymn to Artemis*." *JHS* 114 (1994): 19–34.

Carrière, Jean. "Philadelphe ou Sotèr? À propos d'un hymne de Callimaque." *Studii Clasice* 11 (1969): 85–93.

Cheshire, Keyne. "Kicking Φθόνος: Apollo and His Chorus in Callimachus' Hymn 2." *Classical Philology* 103 (2008): 354–73.

Clauss, James. "Lies and Allusions: The Addressee and Date of Callimachus' Hymn to Zeus." *Classical Antiquity* 5 (1986): 155–70.

Cuypers, Martijn. "The Philosophy of Callimachus' *Hymn to Zeus*." In *Callimachus II*, edited by M. Annette Harder et al., 95–116. Leuven: Peeters, 2004.

D'Alessio, Giovan Battista. "Reconstructing Pindar's First *Hymn*: The Theban 'Theogony' and the Birth of Apollo."

In *Apolline Politics and Poetics*, edited by Lucia Atha-
nassaki, Richard P. Martin, and John F. Miller, 129–48.
Athens: Hellenic Ministry of Culture, 2009.

Faraone, C. "Boubrostis, Meat Eating and Comedy: Ery-
sichthon as Famine Demon in Callimachus' *Hymn to
Demeter*." In *Gods and Religion in Hellenistic Poetry*,
edited by M. Annette Harder, et. al., 61-80. Leuven:
Peters, 2012.

Faulkner, Andrew. "The Collection of Homeric Hymns
from the Seventh to the Third Centuries BC." In *The
Homeric Hymns: Interpretive Essays*, edited by Andrew
Faulkner, 175–205. Oxford: Oxford University Press,
2011.

Furley, William D., and Jan Maarten Bremer. *Greek
Hymns: Selected Cult Songs from the Archaic to the
Hellenistic Period*. 2 vols. Tübingen: Mohr Siebeck,
2001.

Hunter, Richard. "Writing the God: Form and Meaning in
Callimachus, *Hymn to Athena*." *Materiali e discussioni
per l'analisi dei testi classici* 29 (1992): 9–34.

Hunter, Richard, and Theresa Fuhrer. "Imaginary Gods?
Poetic Theology in the *Hymns* of Callimachus." In *Cal-
limaque*, edited by Franco Montanari and Luigi Lehnus,
143–75. Genève: Fondation Hardt, 2002.

Lapp, Friedrich. *De Callimachi Cyrenaei tropis et figuris*.
PhD diss., Bonn, 1965.

Legrand, Philippe-Ernest. "Problèmes alexandrins, I:
Pourquoi furent composés les hymnes de Callimaque?"
Revue des études anciennes 3 (1901): 281–312.

Petrovic, Ivana. "Callimachus and Contemporary Reli-
gion: The *Hymn to Apollo*." In *Brill's Companion to*

Callimachus, edited by Benjamin Acosta-Hughes et al.,
264–85. Leiden: Brill, 2011.

Vamvouri Ruffy, Maria. *La fabrique du divin: Les hymnes
de Callimaque à la lumière des hymnes homériques et
des hymnes épigraphiques.* Liege: Centre international
d'étude de la religion grecque antique, 2004.

HYMNUS I
IN IOVEM

Ζηνὸς ἔοι τί κεν ἄλλο παρὰ σπονδῇσιν ἀείδειν
λώϊον ἢ θεὸν αὐτόν, ἀεὶ μέγαν, αἰὲν ἄνακτα,
Πηλαγόνων[1] ἐλατῆρα, δικασπόλον Οὐρανίδῃσι;
πῶς καί νιν, Δικταῖον ἀείσομεν ἠὲ Λυκαῖον;
5 ἐν δοιῇ μάλα θυμός, ἐπεὶ γένος ἀμφήριστον.
Ζεῦ, σὲ μὲν Ἰδαίοισιν ἐν οὔρεσί φασι γενέσθαι,
Ζεῦ, σὲ δ᾽ ἐν Ἀρκαδίῃ· πότεροι, πάτερ, ἐψεύσαντο;
"Κρῆτες ἀεὶ ψεῦσται"· καὶ γὰρ τάφον, ὦ ἄνα, σεῖο
Κρῆτες ἐτεκτήναντο· σὺ δ᾽ οὐ θάνες, ἐσσὶ γὰρ αἰεί.
10 ἐν δέ σε Παρρασίῃ[2] Ῥείη τέκεν, ἧχι μάλιστα

---

[1] Πηλαγόνων *Et. Gen.* B: πηλογόνων Ψ
[2] Παρρασίῃ corr. La.: παρνασίη Ψ: παρρησιας *Dieg.* 11.15

---

[1] The Giants (*Suda* π 1504), the Titans (Strabo 7.40), the
Macedonians (Steph. Byz. π 135 Billerbeck s.v. *pelagonia*), or the
"Mud-born" (Schol.).   [2] The children of Uranus, also known
as the Titans (Aesch. *PV* 207), whom Zeus drove from heaven
(Hes. *Theog.* 820).   [3] An inscription from the site of the
temple of Zeus Dictaeus at Palaecastro in Crete (*IC* 3.2.2) is a
hymn to the "son of Cronus," that is, Zeus, who is not named there
directly, but only addressed as *kouros* (youth).   [4] Lycaeus is a
mountain in Arcadia where there was an altar of Zeus Lycaeus
(Polyb. 4.33.2; Paus. 8.38.7) and a sacred precinct (Paus. 8.38.6).

HYMN I
TO ZEUS

What better to sing at libations for Zeus than the god himself, forever great, forever king, router of the Pelagonians,[1] scourge of the Uranidae?[2] And how will we sing him? As Dictean[3] Zeus or Lycean?[4] My heart is much in doubt since his birth story is disputed.[5] Zeus, some say you were born on the mountains of Ida;[6] others, Zeus, in Arcadia. Which, Father, have lied? "Cretans are always liars."[7] They even built a tomb[8] for you, Lord, but you did not die, you are forever.

[10] In Arcadian Parrhasia[9] Rhea bore you, where

[5] A near quotation of Antagoras of Rhodes (fr. 1.1 Powell), expressing doubt about the parentage of Eros.

[6] Here, a mountain in Crete (Diod. Sic. 5.70.4), though in Homer Ida is a mountain near Troy, which was also associated with Zeus (*Il.* 14.157).

[7] A direct quote from Epimenides of Crete, a poet of theogonies, who says that he slept for many years in the cave of Dictean Zeus, where he met in a dream the goddesses Truth and Justice (B1 DK). His verse in turn recalls Hesiod, from a passage on poetic lying and truth telling (*Theog.* 26–28).

[8] The tomb of Zeus was said to be located in the Idaean cave (Porph. *Pyth.* 17), near Cnossus (Lact. *Div. inst.* 1.11.46) or elsewhere in Crete.

[9] City in Arcadia (Schol. D ad Hom. *Il.* 2.608; Steph. Byz. π 58 Billerbeck s.v.).

ἔσκεν ὄρος θάμνοισι περισκεπές· ἔνθεν ὁ χῶρος
ἱερός, οὐδέ τί μιν κεχρημένον Εἰλειθυίης
ἑρπετὸν οὐδὲ γυνὴ ἐπιμίσγεται, ἀλλά ἑ Ῥείης
ὠγύγιον καλέουσι λεχώιον Ἀπιδανῆες.

15 ἔνθα σ' ἐπεὶ μήτηρ μεγάλων ἀπεθήκατο κόλπων,
αὐτίκα δίζητο ῥόον ὕδατος, ᾧ κε τόκοιο
λύματα χυτλώσαιτο, τεὸν δ' ἐνὶ χρῶτα λοέσσαι.

Λάδων ἀλλ' οὔπω μέγας ἔρρεεν οὐδ' Ἐρύμανθος,
λευκότατος ποταμῶν, ἔτι δ' ἄβροχος ἦεν ἅπασα

20 Ἀζηνίς·[3] μέλλεν δὲ μάλ' εὔυδρος καλέεσθαι
αὖτις· ἐπεὶ τημόσδε, Ῥέη ὅτε λύσατο μίτρην,
ἦ πολλὰς ἐφύπερθε σαρωνίδας ὑγρὸς Ἰάων
ἤειρεν, πολλὰς δὲ Μέλας ὤκχησεν ἁμάξας,
πολλὰ δὲ Καρίωνος ἄνω διεροῦ περ ἐόντος

25 ἰλυοὺς ἐβάλοντο κινώπετα, νίσσετο δ' ἀνήρ
πεζὸς ὑπὲρ Κραθίν τε πολύστιόν τε Μετώπην
διψαλέος· τὸ δὲ πολλὸν ὕδωρ ὑπὸ ποσσὶν ἔκειτο.

καί ῥ' ὑπ' ἀμηχανίης σχομένη φάτο πότνια Ῥείη·
"Γαῖα φίλη, τέκε καὶ σύ· τεαὶ δ' ὠδῖνες ἐλαφραί."

30 εἶπε καὶ ἀντανύσασα θεὰ μέγαν ὑψόθι πῆχυν
πλῆξεν ὄρος σκήπτρῳ· τὸ δέ οἱ δίχα πουλὺ διέστη,

---

[3] Ἀζηνίς Schol. Dionys. Per. 415: ἀρκαδίη Ψ

---

[10] Goddess of birth (Hom. *Il.* 16.187–88).

[11] The Peloponnesians, from Apollo's son Apis, a physician who rid the land of monsters (Aesch. *Suppl.* 260–70).

[12] Arcadian river (Hes. *Theog.* 344).   [13] Arcadian river, coupled with the Ladon (Antip. Sid. *Anth. Pal.* 6.111.1).

there was a hill sheltered completely by shrubs. Hence the place is holy; no creeping thing or woman in need of Eileithyia[10] approaches it, but the Apidaneans[11] call it the ancient childbed of Rhea. There, when your mother received you from her great womb, at once she sought a stream of water in which she could wash away the afterbirth and bathe your body.

[18] But mighty Ladon[12] did not yet flow, nor Erymanthus,[13] clearest of rivers, and all of Azenis[14] was still dry. It would be called well watered in the future. Since then, when Rhea loosened her belt, wet Iaon[15] raised up many hollow oaks, and Melas[16] carried many wagons. And though Carnion[17] is wet now, then many serpents made their dens upstream. And a man could go on foot above the river Crathis[18] and pebbly Metope,[19] thirsty, though an abundance of water lay under his feet.

[28] And gripped by helplessness, Queen Rhea said, "Dear Earth, give birth! Yes, you. Your labor pains are light." The goddess spoke, and lifting up her mighty arm, she struck the mountain with her staff and it split in two

---

[14] Section of Arcadia near Elis, whose name is derived from a word meaning "dry" (Eust. ad Dionys. Per. 415).

[15] Arcadian river (Dionys. Per. 416) first mentioned here.

[16] Arcadian river (Dionys. Per. 416) first mentioned here, named "black," meaning "opaque" (opposite of the Erymanthus, above, 18–19) or "deep" (Hesych.).

[17] Arcadian river first mentioned here, possibly Pausanias' Carnion (Paus. 8.34.5).

[18] One of several rivers of this name (Hdt. 1.145).

[19] River in Stymphalia and daughter of the river god Ladon (*Hymn* 1.18 above; cf. Pind. *Ol.* 6.84).

ἐκ δ' ἔχεεν μέγα χεῦμα· τόθι χρόα φαιδρύνασα,
ὦνα, τεὸν σπείρωσε, Νέδη δέ σε δῶκε κομίσσαι[4]
κευθμὸν ἔσω Κρηταῖον, ἵνα κρύφα παιδεύοιο,
35 πρεσβυτάτη Νυμφέων, αἵ μιν τότε μαιώσαντο,
πρωτίστη γενεὴ μετά γε Στύγα τε Φιλύρην τε.
οὐδ' ἁλίην ἀπέτεισε θεὴ χάριν, ἀλλὰ τὸ χεῦμα
κεῖνο Νέδην ὀνόμηνε· τὸ μέν ποθι πουλὺ κατ' αὐτὸ
Καυκώνων πτολίεθρον, ὃ Λέπρειον πεφάτισται,
40 συμφέρεται Νηρῆι, παλαιότατον δέ μιν ὕδωρ
υἱωνοὶ[5] πίνουσι Λυκαονίης ἄρκτοιο.
εὖτε Θενὰς ἀπέλειπεν ἐπὶ Κνωσοῖο φέρουσα,
   Ζεῦ πάτερ, ἡ Νύμφη σε (Θεναὶ δ' ἔσαν ἐγγύθι
      Κνωσοῦ),
τουτάκι τοι πέσε, δαῖμον, ἀπ' ὀμφαλός· ἔνθεν ἐκεῖνο
45 Ὀμφάλιον μετέπειτα πέδον καλέουσι Κύδωνες.

---

[4] κομίσσαι αβγδ: κομίζειν ζ, Mineur
[5] υἱωνοὶ corr. La.: γυιωνοί Ψ

---

[20] The nymph who gave her name to both the river and the town (Paus. 4.33.1, 8.38.3).
[21] Cave in "Crete," but Cretea is also a town on Mt. Lycaeum where the inhabitants claim that baby Zeus was raised (Paus. 8.38.2).
[22] The oldest of the daughters of Ocean (Hes. *Theog.* 361, 777) and a river in Arcadia.
[23] Daughter of Ocean seduced by Cronus while the infant Zeus was in his Dictean cave (Ap. Rhod. 2.1231–35).

for her; and from it a great flood poured. There, after she washed your body, Lord, she swaddled you, and gave you to Neda[20] to carry to a hiding place within Crete,[21] so that you would be brought up in secret, Neda, the oldest of the nymphs who once delivered you, firstborn after Styx[22] and Philyra.[23] Nor did the goddess repay her with minimal thanks, but named that stream Neda. And this, rushing in flood down to the very city of the Cauconians,[24] which is called Lepreon,[25] joins with Nereus,[26] that most ancient water, which the descendants of the Bear,[27] daughter of Lycaon, drink.

[43] Father Zeus, when the nymph carrying you left Thenae for Cnossus (for Thenae was near Cnossus),[28] then your navel, Lord, fell away. Since then the Cydones[29] have called that plain Omphalium (of the Navel).[30] Then, Zeus,

---

[24] Named from king Caucon, son of Lycaon of Arcadia (Apollod. *Bibl*. 3.8.1). It was located in Triphylia between Elis, Arcadia, and Messenia.

[25] A town in Elis not far from the river Neda, founded by the Minyae after ousting the Cauconians (Hdt. 4.148).

[26] The sea (Lyc. *Alex*. 164).

[27] Callisto, daughter of Lycaon and mother of Arcas (Paus. 8.3.6).

[28] There is a Thenae in Arcadia and another in Crete (Steph. Byz. θ 23 Billerbeck s.v.). With this geographical imprecision, Callimachus moves the birth story from Arcadia to Crete (Stephens 2003, 103).

[29] The Cydones, who inhabited the Cretan city of Cydonia, were migrants from Arcadia, but some Cretans rejected the claim (Paus. 8.53.4).

[30] Several places claimed to be the navel of the world, notably Delphi (Pind. *Pyth*. 4.73–74; Paus. 10.16.3).

CALLIMACHUS

Ζεῦ, σὲ δὲ Κυρβάντων ἑτάραι προσεπηχύναντο
Δικταῖαι Μελίαι, σὲ δ᾽ ἐκοίμισεν Ἀδρήστεια
λίκνῳ⁶ ἐνὶ χρυσέῳ, σὺ δ᾽ ἐθήσαο πίονα μαζόν
αἰγὸς Ἀμαλθείης, ἐπὶ δὲ γλυκὺ κηρίον ἔβρως.
50 γέντο γὰρ ἐξαπιναῖα Πανακρίδος ἔργα μελίσσης
Ἰδαίοις ἐν ὄρεσσι, τά τε κλείουσι Πάνακρα.
οὖλα δὲ Κούρητές σε περὶ πρύλιν ὠρχήσαντο
τεύχεα πεπλήγοντες,⁷ ἵνα Κρόνος οὔασιν ἠχήν
ἀσπίδος εἰσαΐοι καὶ μή σεο κουρίζοντος.
55 καλὰ μὲν ἠέξευ, καλὰ δ᾽ ἔτραφες, οὐράνιε Ζεῦ,
ὀξὺ δ᾽ ἀνήβησας, ταχινοὶ δέ τοι ἦλθον ἴουλοι.
ἀλλ᾽ ἔτι παιδνὸς ἐὼν ἐφράσσαο πάντα τέλεια·
τῷ τοι καὶ γνωτοὶ προτερηγενέες περ ἐόντες
οὐρανὸν οὐκ ἐμέγηραν ἔχειν ἐπιδαίσιον οἶκον.
60 δηναιοὶ δ᾽ οὐ πάμπαν ἀληθέες ἦσαν ἀοιδοί·
φάντο πάλον Κρονίδῃσι διάτριχα δώματα νεῖμαι·
τίς δέ κ᾽ ἐπ᾽ Οὐλύμπῳ τε καὶ Ἀΐδι κλῆρον ἐρύσσαι,
ὃς μάλα μὴ νενίηλος; ἐπ᾽ ἰσαίῃ γὰρ ἔοικε

⁶ λίκνῳ Schol. ad Eur.: λείκνῳ Ψ
⁷ πεπλήγοντες corr. La. et η: πεπληγότες Ψ

31 Cyrbantes, an alternate spelling of Corybantes, were Asian attendants of Cybele sometimes assimilated to the Curetes, Cretan followers of Rhea. Euripides (Bacch. 120–25) also locates the Phrygian Corybantes in Crete. 32 Tree nymphs living on Mt. Dikte (Hes. Theog. 187). 33 Daughter of Melisseus, a Cretan king, and sister of the Curetes (Schol.), who attended Zeus in the Idaean cave (Ap. Rhod. 3.133).

the comrades of the Cyrbantes,[31] the Dictean Meliae,[32] took you in their arms, and Adrasteia[33] placed you in a golden cradle, and you suckled the rich breast of the goat Amalthea,[34] and you ate the sweet honeycomb. For suddenly the works of the Panacrian bee appeared on the mountains of Ida, which they call Panacra.[35] And around you the Curetes[36] danced the Prylis[37] in quick tempo, beating their armor, so that Cronus[38] would hear the sound of the shields, not your crying.

[55] You grew well, and you were well brought up, heavenly Zeus; quickly you reached maturity, and swiftly your new beard grew. Though still a child, you planned all things that were fulfilled. That is why your siblings, though older, did not think it too much that you have heaven as your allotted home. The ancient bards were not altogether truthful. They said that homes were distributed to the three sons of Cronus by lot, yet who but a fool would draw lots for Olympus and Hades?[39] It makes sense to shake out

---

[34] Sometimes a nymph, but like Aratus (*Phaen.* 163–64), Callimachus presents her as a goat.

[35] A mountain in Crete mentioned only in Steph. Byz. π 112 Billerbeck s.v., which refers back to this passage.

[36] Young male attendants of Rhea, though the dancing Curetes of Hes. fr. 123 M.-W. are gods.

[37] A dance in armor (Schol.) either Cyprian (Arist. fr. 519) or Cretan (Schol. T ad Hom. *Il.* 12.77).

[38] Father of Zeus, who ate his children as they were born (Hes. *Theog.* 459–67).

[39] The drawing of the lots among Zeus, Poseidon, and Hades is recounted in Homer (*Il.* 15.187–92). In Hesiod the other gods invite Zeus to become their king (*Theog.* 881–85).

πήλασθαι· τὰ δὲ τόσσον ὅσον διὰ πλεῖστον ἔχουσι.
65 ψευδοίμην, ἀίοντος ἅ κεν πεπίθοιεν ἀκουήν.
οὔ σε θεῶν ἐσσῆνα πάλοι θέσαν, ἔργα δὲ χειρῶν,
σή τε βίη τό τε κάρτος, ὃ καὶ πέλας εἶσαο δίφρου.
θήκαο δ' οἰωνῶν[8] μέγ' ὑπείροχον ἀγγελιώτην
σῶν τεράων· ἅ τ' ἐμοῖσι φίλοις ἐνδέξια φαίνοις.
70 εἵλεο δ' αἰζηῶν ὅ τι φέρτατον· οὐ σύ γε νηῶν
ἐμπεράμους, οὐκ ἄνδρα σακέσπαλον, οὐ μὲν ἀοιδόν·
ἀλλὰ τὰ μὲν μακάρεσσιν ὀλίζοσιν αὖθι παρῆκας
ἄλλα μέλειν ἑτέροισι, σὺ δ' ἐξέλεο πτολιάρχους
αὐτούς, ὧν ὑπὸ χεῖρα γεωμόρος, ὧν ἴδρις αἰχμῆς,
75 ὧν ἐρέτης, ὧν πάντα· τί δ' οὐ κρατέοντος ὑπ' ἰσχύν;
αὐτίκα χαλκῆας μὲν ὑδείομεν Ἡφαίστοιο,
τευχηστὰς δ' Ἄρηος, ἐπακτῆρας δὲ Χιτώνης
Ἀρτέμιδος, Φοίβου δὲ λύρης εὖ εἰδότας οἴμους·
"ἐκ δὲ Διὸς βασιλῆες," ἐπεὶ Διὸς οὐδὲν ἀνάκτων
80 θειότερον· τῷ καί σφε[9] τεὴν ἐκρίναο λάξιν.
δῶκας δὲ πτολίεθρα φυλασσέμεν, ἵζεο δ' αὐτός
ἄκρησ' ἐν πολίεσσιν, ἐπόψιος οἵ τε δίκησι
λαὸν ὑπὸ σκολιῆσ' οἵ τ' ἔμπαλιν ἰθύνουσιν·
ἐν δὲ ῥυηφενίην ἔβαλές σφισιν, ἐν δ' ἅλις ὄλβον·

---

[8] οἰωνῶν corr. Stephanus: οἰωνόν Ψ
[9] σφε P.Oxy. 2258 A fr. 1 recto: σφι Ψ sed corr. Bentley

---

[40] Force and Power appear as agents of Zeus in Hesiod (*Theog.* 383–88).
[41] The eagle is associated with Zeus and omens from Zeus in Homer (*Il.* 8.247–50).

lots for equal things, but the discrepancy between these is very great. May the lies I tell persuade the listener's ear! Lots did not make you chief of the gods, but the works of your hands, your force, and the power that you set near your throne.[40] And you made the most eminent of birds the messenger of your portents.[41] May the signs that you reveal be favorable to my friends.

[70] You chose the best of men; not those skilled in the use of ships, not the one who carries a shield, nor the singer. These you immediately gave over to lesser gods to care for, and you gave the rest to others, but you chose those who rule cities, under whose hand is the farmer, the expert in the spear, the oarsman, everything. For what is not under the power of the ruler? For smiths we say belong to Hephaestus; armed men, to Ares; hunters, to Artemis who wears the chiton;[42] and those who know well the paths of the lyre belong to Phoebus.

[79] "Kings are from Zeus,"[43] since nothing that belongs to Zeus is more divine than rulers. For this you chose them for your own portion. You gave them cities to guard, and you yourself sit on the acropolis observing who guides the people with justice and who, on the contrary, rules crookedly.[44] You cast riches among them and blessings

---

[42] In Callimachus' *Hymn to Artemis*, the goddess asks her father, Zeus, for a *chiton* that reaches to the knee with an embroidered border to wear while hunting (*Hymn* 3.11).

[43] A direct quotation of Hesiod (*Theog.* 96) from a passage on the power of poets, whose patrons are the Muses and Apollo.

[44] The language of straight and crooked ruling and Zeus' role observing kings is also found in Hesiod (*Op.* 225–69).

85 πᾶσι μέν, οὐ μάλα δ' ἶσον. ἔοικε δὲ τεκμήρασθαι
ἡμετέρῳ μεδέοντι· περιπρὸ γὰρ εὐρὺ βέβηκεν.
ἑσπέριος κεῖνός γε τελεῖ τά κεν ἦρι[10] νοήσῃ·
ἑσπέριος τὰ μέγιστα, τὰ μείονα δ', εὖτε νοήσῃ.
οἱ δὲ τὰ μὲν πλειῶνι, τὰ δ' οὐχ ἑνί, τῶν δ' ἀπὸ
    πάμπαν
90 αὐτὸς ἄνην ἐκόλουσας, ἐνέκλασσας δὲ μενοινήν.

    χαῖρε μέγα, Κρονίδη πανυπέρτατε, δῶτορ ἑάων,
δῶτορ ἀπημονίης. τεὰ δ' ἔργματα τίς κεν ἀείδοι;
οὐ γένετ', οὐκ ἔσται· τίς κεν Διὸς ἔργματ' ἀείσει;[11]
χαῖρε, πάτερ, χαῖρ' αὖθι· δίδου δ' ἀρετήν τ' ἄφενός
    τε.
95 οὔτ' ἀρετῆς ἄτερ ὄλβος ἐπίσταται ἄνδρας ἀέξειν
οὔτ' ἀρετὴ ἀφένοιο· δίδου δ' ἀρετήν τε καὶ ὄλβον.

10 ἦρι corr. T in marg.: ἠοῖ Ψ
11 ἀείσει a et La.: ἀείσοι Ψ

1a *Dieg.* 11.8–19

    Ζηνὸς ἔοι τί κεν ἄλλο παρὰ σπονδῇσιν ἀείδειν·

Ἐνταῦθα Ἀρκάδες καὶ Κρῆτες ἀντιποιοῦνται [10] τῆς
Διὸς γενέσεως ἑκάτεροι λέγοντες παρ' αὐτοῖς γεγεν-
νῆσθαι τὸν θεόν (Κρῆτες δὲ καὶ τάφον αὐτοῦ ἐπι-
δεικνύντες, το[ῦ]τό γε ψευδόμενοι), ἀφορμὴν τοιαύτην
εἰληφότες· τῆς γὰρ Παρρασίας μοίρας ἔν τινι ὄρει
θαμνώδει ἀποτεκοῦσα Ῥέα τὸν Δία Νέδῃ μιᾷ τῶν
Ὠκεανίδων εἴσω τῆς Κρήτης φέρειν ἐνεχείρισεν,
ὅπως κρύφα τρέφοιτο ἐκεῖσε.

aplenty to all, but not equally. Let us take as proof our ruler,[45] who strides far out in front. In the evening he brings to pass what he thought of in the morning; in the evening, the greatest things, lesser things as soon as he thinks of them. Others achieve something in a year, some things not in one; you yourself have cut off the fulfillment of others altogether, and have frustrated their desire.

[91] Loudly hail, supreme son of Cronus, giver of good fortune, giver of safety. Who could sing of your works? He does not exist nor will he. Who will sing of the works of Zeus? Hail, Father, hail again. Give us excellence and wealth. For without excellence, prosperity cannot benefit men, nor can excellence without wealth. Give excellence and prosperity.

[45] One of the early Ptolemies. Callimachus wrote under Ptolemy II Philadelphus and Ptolemy III Euergetes. See discussion in the Introduction.

1a *Diegeseis*

What would be better to sing at libations for Zeus . . .

At that time the Arcadians and the Cretans disagreed about the birth of Zeus, each one saying that the god was born in their territory (the Cretans, who lied about this, even displayed his tomb) for they presumed an origin story such as this: After Rhea gave birth on the scrubby mountain of Parrhasia, she gave Zeus to Neda one of the Oceanids to carry inside of Crete so that he could be brought up there in secret.

1b Schol. Ψ

1a   Πότερον Ζηνὸς σπονδῇσιν ἢ Ζηνὸς τί λώϊον
ἀείδειν;

1b   ⟨ἔοι⟩· εἴη.

1c   ⟨ἔοι τί κεν ἄλλο⟩· ἤγουν τί ἔοικεν (sic) ἄλλο.

3   ⟨Πηλαγόνων⟩· τῶν γιγάντων· παρὰ τὸ ἐκ
πηλοῦ γενέσθαι, τουτέστι τῆς γῆς.

4a   Δικταῖον ὄρος Κρήτης, Λύκαιον δὲ τῆς Ἀρ-
καδίας.

4b   Δικταῖον δὲ ὄρος Κρήτης καὶ Λυκαῖον τὸν ἐξ
ὄρους Ἀρκαδίας ὄντα.

4c   Δικταῖον· Κρῆτα· Δίκτη γὰρ ὄρος Κρήτης.
Λυκαῖον· Ἀρκάδα· Λύκαιον Ἀρκαδίας ὄρος.

5   ἀμφήριστον· ἀντὶ τοῦ ἀμφίλογον.

6   Ἴδη ὄρος Κρήτης καὶ Τροίας· νῦν δὲ τὸ
Κρήτης φησι.

7   ἐν ἤθει ἀναγνωστέον τὸ πότεροι.

8a   παροιμία ἐστὶ "κρητίζειν" ἐπὶ τοῦ ψεύδεσθαι,
ἀπὸ Ἰδομενέως τοῦ Κρητὸς ῥηθεῖσα, ὃς λαχὼν μερί-
σαι τοῖς Ἕλλησι τὰ λάφυρα τῆς Ἰλίου τὰ κρείσσω
ἑαυτῷ περιεποιήσατο.

8b   ⟨τάφον⟩· ἐν Κρήτῃ ἐπὶ τῷ τάφῳ τοῦ Μίνωος
ἐπεγέγραπτο "Μίνωος τοῦ Διὸς τάφος"· τῷ χρόνῳ
δὲ τὸ "Μίνωος τοῦ" ἀπηλείφθη ὥστε περιλειφθῆναι
"Διὸς τάφος." ἐκ τούτου οὖν λέγουσι Κρῆτες τὸν τά-
φον τοῦ Διός. ἢ ὅτι Κορύβαντες λαβόντες αὐτὸν ἐπὶ
τῷ κρύψαι διὰ τὸν Κρόνον προσεποιήσαντο τάφον
αὐτῷ ποιεῖν.

1b Ψ Scholia

1a   What to sing at libations for Zeus, or what is better to sing [at libations] for Zeus?

1b   *eoi*: would be.

1c   *eoi ti ken allo*: that is to say what other thing would be fitting?

3   *Pēlagonōn*: of the Gigantes; like being from mud, that is, from the earth.

4a   The Dictean mountain [is] in Crete; the Lycean, in Arcadia.

4b   The Dictean mountain of Crete and Lycaon is from the mountain of Arcadia.

4c   *Dictaion*: Cretan. Dicte is a mountain of Crete. *Lykaion*: Arcadian. The Lycean mountain of Arcadia.

5   *amphēriston* (disputed): instead of *amphilogon*.

6   Ida is a mountain in Crete and in Troy. Here he means the one in Crete.

7   *poteroi* should be read as which of the two places.

8a   The maxim is "to Cretanize," to act like a Cretan, i.e., to lie, from the story of Idomeneus the Cretan who, when he obtained the spoils of Troy to share with the Greeks, kept the largest part for himself.

8b   *taphon* (a tomb): there is an inscription on the tomb of Minos in Crete, "the tomb of Minos son of Zeus." In time "of Minos" was wiped off and "tomb of Zeus" was left. From this the Cretans say that it is the tomb of Zeus. Or because the Corybantes, after they had taken him to hide him on account of Cronus, pretended to make a tomb for him.

10a   ὄρος Ἀρκαδίας ὁ Παρνασός.

10b   ὄρος Ἀρκαδίας τὸ Παρράσιον ἀπὸ Παρ⟨ρ⟩άσου τοῦ Λυκάονος.

12   Εἰλειθυίης ἤγουν γεννήσεως.

12–13   οὔτε ἑρπετὸν οὔτε γυνὴ χρῄζουσα τοῦ τεκεῖν ἐπιμίσγεται. ἢ οὕτως †οἷον χρῄζειν† Εἰλειθυίας τουτέστι γεννήσεως. ὅτι πᾶν ζῷον εἰσιὸν ἐκεῖ μεμολυσμένον ἄγονον ἐγίνετο καὶ σκιὰν τὸ σῶμα αὐτοῦ οὐκέτι ἐποίει.

14   ⟨Ἀπιδανῆες⟩ οἱ ἀρχαῖοι Ἀρκάδες.

17–18   λύματα· καθάρματα· τὸ δὲ χυτλώσαιτο ἀντὶ τοῦ ἀπολούσαιτο· Ἐρύμανθος δὲ ποταμὸς Ἀρκαδίας.

21   ὕστερον· μετὰ τὸ τεκεῖν τὴν Ῥέαν.

22–23   ⟨σαρωνίδας⟩ δρῦς· παρὰ τὸ σεσηρότα καὶ συνεστραμμένον τὸν φλοιὸν ἔχειν. τὸ δὲ ἤειρεν καὶ ὤκχησεν ἀντὶ τοῦ ἐβάστασεν.

24–25a   ⟨Καρίωνος⟩ λείπει ἡ ὑπέρ· πολλὰ δ᾽ ὑπὲρ τοῦ Καρίωνος κινώπετα ἤγουν ἑρπετά, παρὰ τὸ ἐν τῷ πέδῳ κινεῖσθαι, ἐβάλοντο ἰλυοὺς ἤτοι φωλεούς.

24–25b   λείπει—Καρίωνος ἑρπετὰ τοὺς φωλεοὺς ἐποίησαν. τὰ θηρία, οἱονεὶ κινόπεδα, παρὰ τὸ ἐν τῷ ἐδάφει κινεῖσθαι· τὸ δὲ νίσσετο ἀντὶ τοῦ ἤρχετο, ἐπορεύετο.

24–25c   κινώπετα· τὰ ἐν τῷ πέδῳ κινούμενα θηρία.

25   ⟨ἰλυούς⟩ καταδύσεις.

26   Κρᾶθις ποταμὸς Ἀρκαδίας καὶ ἡ Μετώπη· τὸ δὲ πολύστειον πολύψηφον καὶ πολυπάτητον.

10a   Parnassus: a mountain of Arcadia.

10b   The Parrhasion mountain of Arcadia, from Lycaon of Parrhasus.

12   Or rather the engendering of Eileithuia.

12–13   No creeping thing nor woman needing to give birth spends time there. Or in this way having need of Eileithuia, that is to say, birth. That every living thing entering there became polluted and sterile and its body no longer made a shadow.

14   *Apidanēes*: the ancient Arcadians.

17–18   *lumata*: purifications. *chytlōsaito* (that she might cleanse herself) instead of *apolousaito*. Erymanthus, a river in Arcadia.

21   *hysteron* (the afterbirth): after giving birth to Rhea.

22–23   *sarōnidas*: oaks; from having bark that is polished and compressed. *ēeiren* (raised up) and *ōcchesen* instead of *ebastasen*.

24–25a   *Cariōnos*: the preposition *hyper* is missing [in the text]. Above the *Cariōn* many creeping things, that is to say, serpents made their lairs or dens instead of slithering in the plain.

24–25b   It is missing [in the text]. Serpents (*kinopeta*) made their lairs above the *Cariōn*. Such wild beasts as serpents are named for slithering (*kineisthai*) on the ground. *nisseto* (he went) instead of *ērcheto*, *eporeueto*.

24–25c   *kinōpeta* (serpents): the wild beasts that slither on the plain.

25   *ilyous* (dens): holes.

26   Crathis, a river of Arcadia and the Metope; stony, with many pebbles and much-trodden.

32–33 τὸν σὸν χρῶτα, ὦ ἄνα, σπείρωσε φαιδρύνασα.

33a ⟨ὦνα⟩· ἴσ(ως) ὦ ἄνα (sic).

33b ⟨σπείρωσε⟩· εἵλιξε· παρὰ τὸ σπειρόω, τὸ εἱλίσσω· ὅθεν σπείρημα, τὸ σπαρτί(ον).

33c ⟨Νέδῃ⟩· ὄνομα νύμφης Ὠκεανίνης θρεψαμένης τὸν Δία.

34 ⟨κευθμόν⟩· σπήλαιον.

35 ⟨μαιώσαντο⟩· ἔθρεψαν.

36 ⟨Φιλύρην⟩· μητέρα Χείρωνος τοῦ Κενταύρου.

37 ⟨τὸ χεῦμα⟩· τὸ ἐν Ἀρκαδίᾳ.

38 ⟨τὸ μέν⟩· τὸ χεῦμα.

39 ὄρος Ἀρκάδων ὁ Καύκων. Λέπριον δὲ ἀπὸ Λεπρέα τοῦ Ποσειδῶνος, ὃς προκαλεσάμενος εἰς ἀδηφαγίαν Ἡρακλέα καὶ ὑπ᾽ ἐκείνου ἡττηθεὶς ἐφονεύθη.

40 ⟨Νηρῆι⟩· τῇ θαλάσσῃ.

41 ⟨Λυκαονίης ἄρκτοιο⟩· τῆς πρῴην λεγομένης Καλλιστοῦς, Λυκάονος θυγατρός· ἐξ ἧς καὶ Διὸς μεταβληθέντος εἰς Ἄρτεμιν γεννᾶται ὁ Ἀρκάς, ἀφ᾽ οὗ οἱ Ἀρκάδες.

42a ⟨εὖτε⟩· ὅτε.

42b Θενάς· πόλις καὶ ἄλσος.

44a ⟨τουτάκι⟩· τὸ τηνικαῦτα.

44b ⟨τουτάκι⟩· ἤγουν τότε.

45 ⟨Κύδωνες⟩· ἔθνος Κρήτης.

46a ⟨ἑτάραι⟩· φίλαι.

46b ⟨προσεπηχύναντο⟩· ἤγουν εἰς τοὺς πήχεις ἔλαβον.

32–33   Your body O Lord, she washed and swaddled.

33a   *ōna*: perhaps *Ō ana* (O Lord).

33b   *speirōse*: she swaddled. From *speirōse* (to wind). And from this, *speirēma*, *spartion*.

33c   *Nedēi*: the name of a nymph, daughter of Ocean, who brought up Zeus.

34   *keuthmon*: a cave.

35   *maiōsanto*: they attended.

36   *Philurēn*: mother of Chiron the Centaur.

37   *to cheuma* (the spring): the one in Arcadia.

38   *to men* (this one): the spring.

39   *Caucōn* is a mountain in Arcadia. *Leprion* from Leprea son of Poseidon who challenged Heracles in gluttony, and being defeated, was killed by that man.

40   *Nērēi*: the sea.

41   *Lykaoniēs arktoio*: Callisto is mentioned just now, daughter of Lycaon. From her and Zeus, who was turned against Artemis, Arcas was born, and from him the Arcadians [have their name].

42a   *eute*: when.

42b   *Thenas*: city and grove.

44a   *toutaki*: at that time.

44b   *toutaki*: that is to say, then.

45   *Kydōnes*: a people of Crete.

46a   *(h)etarai*: friends.

46b   *prosepēchynanto*: that is they took him into their arms.

47a <μελίαι>· νύμφαι.

47b <Ἀδρήστεια>· ἡ Νέμεσις.

47c <Ἀδρήστεια>· ἀδελφὴ Κουρήτων.

48 λίκνον ἢ τὸ κόσκινον· τὸ γὰρ παλαιὸν ἐν κοσκίνῳ κατεκοίμιζον τὰ βρέφη πλοῦτον καὶ καρποὺς οἰωνιζόμενοι· ἢ τὸ κουνίον, ἐν ᾧ τὰ παιδία τιθέασιν.

49a <Ἀμαλθείης>· οὕτως ἐκαλεῖτο ἡ αἴξ ἡ τὸν Δία θρέψασα· λέγεται δὲ ἀπὸ μὲν τοῦ ἑνὸς κέρατος ἀμβροσίαν ῥεῖν, ἀπὸ δὲ τοῦ ἄλλου νέκταρ.

49b <ἔβρως>· ἔφαγες.

50a <ἐξαπιναῖα>· τουτέστιν ἐγένετο ἐξαίφνης ἡ Ἴδη πλέα μέλιτος.

50b Πανακρίδος δὲ μελίσσης ἤγουν τῆς τὰ ἄκρα τῶν βοτανῶν δρεπομένης ἄπαντα, ἢ ἀπὸ Πανάκρου, ὄρους Κρήτης.

52a <οὖλα>· †κατὰ κλῆρον, ὑγιῶς.

52b <πρύλιν>· ἐνόπλιον.

55 <καλά>· ἀντὶ τοῦ καλῶς.

57 <παιδνός>· παῖς νέος.

59 <ἐπιδαίσιον>· οὐ μεμερισμένον.

60 <δηναιοί>· παλαιοί.

62–63a τίς δ᾽ ἂν φρονῶν ἐπὶ τῷ Ὀλύμπῳ καὶ τῷ Ἅιδη κληρωθῆναι ἠνέσχετο;

62–63b νενίηλος· ὁ ματαιόφρων, ὁ ἐστερημένος τοῦ αἰόλλειν καὶ κινεῖν τὸν νοῦν.

63–64 ὁ κλῆρος ἐπ᾽ ἴσων πραγμάτων χωρεῖ· ὁ οὐρανὸς δὲ καὶ ὁ ᾅδης τοσοῦτον διαφέρουσιν ὅσον καὶ διεστήκασιν.

198

47a   *meliai*: nymphs.

47b   *Adrēsteia*: Nemesis.

47c   *Adrēsteia*: sister of the Couretes.

48   *liknon* or *koskinon* (winnowing fan or sieve): in antiquity babies were lulled to sleep in a winnowing fan foretelling wealth and plenty. Or a cone in which they place the children.

49a   *Amaltheiēs*: the name of the goat who nourished Zeus. It is said that ambrosia flows from one of her horns, and from the other, nectar.

49b   *ebrōs*: you ate.

50a   *exapinaia*: that is to say suddenly it happened that Ida was full of honey.

50b   Of the Panacrian bee plucking all the tops of the plants, or from Panacrus, a mountain in Crete.

52a   *oula*: vigorously, soundly.

52b   *prylin*: [dance] in armor.

55   *kala*: instead of *kalōs* (well).

57   *paidnos*: a young child.

59   *epidaision* (allotted): not distributed.

60   *dēnaioi* (long-lived): ancient.

62–63a   Someone thinking to draw lots for Olympus or Hades is considered.

62–63b   *neniēlos*: weak-minded, unable to shift and move one's mind.

63–64   A lot determines equal things. Heaven and Hades differ as much as they are distant from one another.

65a   λείπει "λέγων."

65b   ⟨πεπίθοιεν⟩· πείσειαν.

66a   ἐσσὴν κυρίως ὁ βασιλεὺς τῶν μελισσῶν, νῦν δὲ ὁ τῶν ἀνδρῶν.

66b   ⟨ἐσσῆνα⟩· θεόν.

67   τὸ κράτος πλησίον ἵδρυσας τοῦ δίφρου.

68   ⟨οἰωνόν⟩· τὸν ἀετόν.

70   ⟨αἰζηῶν⟩· νῦν καθόλου λέγει τῶν ἀνθρώπων.

71   ⟨ἐμπεράμους⟩· τοὺς ἐμπείρους.

72   ⟨ὀλίζοσιν⟩· μικροῖς.

74   ⟨γεωμόρος⟩· γεωργός.

76a   ⟨ὑδείομεν⟩· λέγομεν.

76b   ὑμνοῦμεν.

77a   ⟨ἐπακτῆρας⟩· κυνηγέτας.

77b   Νηλεὺς ὁ Κόδρου ἀποικίαν θέμενος ἀπὸ Ἀθηνῶν ἔλαβε χρησμὸν ἐγεῖραι ξόανον τῇ Ἀρτέμιδι ἀπὸ παγκάρπων ξύλων. καὶ δήποτε ἑορτῆς τελουμένης τῇ Ἀρτέμιδι ἐν τῇ Χιτώνῃ (ἔστι δὲ δῆμος τῆς Ἀττικῆς) ἀπελθὼν εὗρε δρῦν πάμπολυν καὶ διάφορον ἔχουσαν ἠρτημένον καρπόν. καὶ ἐκ τούτου ἐποίησεν ἄγαλμα τῇ θεᾷ καὶ οὕτω μετῴκησεν ἐν Μιλήτῳ. ἀπὸ τοῦ δήμου οὖν ἔσχε τὴν ὀνομασίαν ἡ Ἄρτεμις· ἢ ὅτι τικτομένων τῶν βρεφῶν ἀνετίθεσαν τὰ ἱμάτια τῇ Ἀρτέμιδι.

80   ⟨λάξιν⟩· λαχμόν, κλήρωσιν.

81   ἐν ταῖς ἀκροπόλεσι καθέζῃ ὁρῶν τὰ δίκαια.

65a   The word "saying" is missing.

65b   *pepithoien*: may they persuade.

66a   *essēn*: properly the king of the bees, now the king of men.

66b   *essēna*: a god.

67   You set the full power beside your throne.

68   *oiōnon* (bird): the eagle.

70   *aizēōn*: he speaks now in general of men.

71   *emperamous*: experts.

72   *olizosin*: minor.

74   *geōmoros*: farmer.

76a   *(h)ydeiomen*: we say.

76b   We sing.

77a   *epaktēras*: hunters.

77b   Neleus the son of Codrus who established a colony on behalf of the Athenians received an oracle to set up a statue for Artemis of wood covered with fruit. And after a time while creating a festival for Artemis in-the-Chiton (it is a deme of Attica), he went out and found a very large oak which had various fruit fastened on it. From this he made a statue of the goddess and so he settled in Miletus. From this deme Artemis has her title. Or because when babies are born they lay upon the cloaks of Artemis.

80   *laxin*: an allotment, choosing by lot.

81   In the acropolis he sits observing acts of justice.

84 ῥυηφενίην ἤγουν πλοῦτον· σύγκειται δὲ ἡ λέξις παρὰ τὸ ῥύδην καὶ ἄφενος, τουτέστι τὴν τοῦ πλούτου ῥύσιν.

86 περὶ τοῦ Πτολεμαίου ταῦτα λέγει.

87 ⟨κεῖνος⟩· ὁ Πτολεμαῖος.

89a ⟨οἱ δέ⟩· οἱ ἄλλοι βασιλεῖς δηλονότι.

89b ⟨πλειῶνι⟩· τῷ ἐνιαυτῷ.

90a ⟨αὐτός⟩· ὦ Πτολεμαῖε.

90b ⟨αὐτός⟩· ὦ Ζεῦ.

90c ⟨ἄνην⟩· ἤγουν ἄνυσιν, τελείωσιν.

95 καὶ Ὅμηρος· "πλούτῳ δ᾽ ἀρετὴ καὶ κῦδος ὀπηδεῖ," καὶ Ἡσίοδος, καὶ Σαπφώ "ὁ πλοῦτος ἄνευ ἀρετῆς οὐκ ἀγαθὸς σύνοικος, ἡ δ᾽ ἐξ ἀμφοτέρων κρᾶσις."

84   *r(h)uēphenia*, or rather wealth: the word is composed from *r(h)udē* (flowing) and *aphenos* (wealth), that is to say the flow of riches.

86   He says these things about Ptolemy.

87   *keinos* (that one): Ptolemy.

89a   *(h)oi de*: clearly the other kings.

89b   *pleiōni*: in a year.

90a   *autos*: O Ptolemy.

90b   *autos*: O Zeus.

90c   *anēn*: fulfillment or rather accomplishment.

95   And Homer: "Excellence and fame attend upon wealth," and Hesiod (*Op.* 313). And Sappho says "Wealth without excellence is not a good housemate, but the mixture of both" (fr. 148 Voigt).

HYMNUS II

IN APOLLINEM

Οἷον ὁ τὠπόλλωνος ἐσείσατο δάφνινος ὅρπηξ,
οἷα[1] δ᾽ ὅλον τὸ μέλαθρον· ἑκὰς ἑκὰς ὅστις ἀλιτρός.
καὶ δή που τὰ θύρετρα καλῷ ποδὶ Φοῖβος ἀράσσει·
οὐχ ὁράᾳς; ἐπένευσεν ὁ Δήλιος ἡδύ τι φοῖνιξ
5 ἐξαπίνης, ὁ δὲ[2] κύκνος ἐν ἠέρι καλὸν ἀείδει.
αὐτοὶ νῦν κατοχῆες ἀνακλίνασθε[3] πυλάων,[4]
αὐταὶ δὲ κλῃῖδες· ὁ γὰρ θεὸς[5] οὐκέτι μακράν·[6]
οἱ δὲ νέοι μολπήν τε καὶ ἐς χορὸν ἐντύνασθε.[7]
ὡπόλλων οὐ παντὶ φαείνεται, ἀλλ᾽ ὅτις[8] ἐσθλός·
10 ὅς μιν ἴδῃ,[9] μέγας οὗτος, ὃς οὐκ ἴδε, λιτὸς ἐκεῖνος.
ὀψόμεθ᾽, ὦ Ἑκάεργε, καὶ ἐσσόμεθ᾽ οὔποτε λιτοί.
μήτε σιωπηλὴν κίθαριν μήτ᾽ ἄψοφον ἴχνος
τοῦ Φοίβου τοὺς παῖδας ἔχειν ἐπιδημήσαντος,

---

[1] οἷα δ᾽ La.: οἶο δ᾽ Ψ: οἷον prop. Valckenaer
[2] ὁ δὲ Ψ: οτε P.Oxy. 2258A fr. 2 recto   [3] ἀνακλίνασθε
Schol. ad Theoc. Id.: ἀνακλίνεσθε Ψ   [4] πυλάων Ψ:]θυραων
sscr. πυλαων P.Oxy. 2258A fr. 2 recto: θυράων Schol. K ad Theoc.
Id. 11.12   [5] ὁ γὰρ θεὸς ψ: επειθεος[P.Oxy. 2258A fr. 2 recto
[6] μακράν Ψ: μακρην P.Oxy. 2258A fr. 2 recto
[7] ε]ντυνασθε P.Oxy. 2258A fr. 2 recto: ἐντύνεσθε Ψ
[8] ὅτις Ψ: οστις P.Oxy. 2258A fr. 2 recto
[9] ἴδῃ Ψ: ι]δεν P.Oxy. 2258A fr. 2 recto

204

HYMN II
TO APOLLO

How the laurel[1] branch of Apollo shakes! How the whole building! Away, away whoever is sinful. Now for sure Phoebus is kicking the doors with his handsome foot. Do you not see? The Delian palm[2] nods[3] sweetly and at once the swan[4] in the air sings something lovely. Now, gate bolts, push yourselves back! And bars! The god is no longer far away.

[8] Young men, prepare for the song and dance. Apollo does not appear to everyone, but only to the fortunate. Whoever sees him is great. Whoever does not is worthless. We will see you, O Far-worker, and we will never be worthless. Do not let the young men keep their lyres silent or their dance steps quiet when Apollo visits, if they mean

---

[1] Associated with Apollo's cult at Delphi (Ar. *Plut.* 213).

[2] A landmark on Delos that Leto held as she gave birth to Apollo (*Hymn. Hom. Ap.* 3.16–18; Hom. *Od.* 6.162–63; *Hymn* 4.209–11).

[3] The palm tree nods assent as gods are typically said to do (Hom. *Il.* 15.75; *Hymn* 3.28).

[4] The swan is associated with Apollo in Plato (*Phd.* 85a–b) and in Callimachus' *Hymn to Delos* (*Hymn* 4.249–52).

CALLIMACHUS

εἰ τελέειν μέλλουσι γάμον πολιήν τε κερεῖσθαι,
15 ἑστήξειν δὲ τὸ τεῖχος ἐπ᾽ ἀρχαίοισι θεμέθλοις.
ἠγασάμην τοὺς παῖδας, ἐπεὶ χέλυς οὐκέτ᾽ ἀεργός.
    εὐφημεῖτ᾽ ἀίοντες ἐπ᾽ Ἀπόλλωνος ἀοιδῇ.
εὐφημεῖ καὶ πόντος, ὅτε κλείουσιν ἀοιδοί
ἢ κίθαριν ἢ τόξα, Λυκωρέος ἔντεα Φοίβου.
20 οὐδὲ Θέτις Ἀχιλῆα κινύρεται αἴλινα μήτηρ,
ὁππόθ᾽ "ἱὴ παιῆον ἱὴ παιῆον" ἀκούσῃ.
καὶ μὲν ὁ δακρυόεις ἀναβάλλεται ἄλγεα πέτρος,
ὅστις ἐνὶ Φρυγίῃ διερὸς λίθος ἐστήρικται,
μάρμαρον ἀντὶ γυναικὸς ὀϊζυρόν τι χανούσης.
25 "ἱὴ ἱὴ" φθέγγεσθε· κακὸν μακάρεσσιν ἐρίζειν.
ὃς μάχεται μακάρεσσιν, ἐμῷ βασιλῆι μάχοιτο·
ὅστις ἐμῷ βασιλῆι, καὶ Ἀπόλλωνι μάχοιτο.
τὸν χορὸν ὡπόλλων, ὅ τι οἱ κατὰ θυμὸν ἀείδει,
τιμήσει· δύναται γάρ, ἐπεὶ Διὶ δεξιὸς ἧσται.
30 οὐδ᾽ ὁ χορὸς τὸν Φοῖβον ἐφ᾽ ἓν μόνον ἦμαρ ἀείσει,
ἔστι γὰρ εὔυμνος· τίς ἂν οὐ ῥέα Φοῖβον ἀείδοι;
    χρύσεα τὠπόλλωνι τό τ᾽ ἐνδυτὸν ἥ τ᾽ ἐπιπορπίς
ἥ τε λύρη τό τ᾽ ἄεμμα τὸ Λύκτιον ἥ τε φαρέτρη,

---

5 Apollo's title refers to a village at the summit of Mt. Parnassus named Lycoreia after Apollo's son Lycorus or because its inhabitants were led there by wolves (Paus. 10.6.2–3).

6 Thetis was in mourning after Apollo killed her son Achilles (prospectively at Hom. *Il.* 18.35–64).

7 This refrain characterizes the paean, the traditional hymn to Apollo (Hom. *Il.* 1.472–74; cf. *Hymn. Hom. Ap.* 3.514–19 on its origin).

206

to conclude a marriage and live long enough to get their gray hair cut, and if the wall is to stand on its ancient foundations. Well done young men! since your lyre is no longer idle.

[17] Be silent when you hear the song of Apollo; for the sea is silent when the bards celebrate either the cithara or the bow, the weapons of Lycorean[5] Apollo. Neither does his mother Thetis[6] sing her laments for Achilles when she hears, "Hie Paieon, Hie Paieon."[7] And the weeping rock puts off its pain, the damp stone that is set up in Phrygia, a marble like a woman gaping in misery.[8]

[25] Cry "Hie Hie." It is evil to challenge the Blessed Ones. Whoever fights with the Blessed Ones would fight with my king.[9] Whoever fights with my king would fight even with Apollo. Apollo will honor the chorus that sings according to his heart: he can, for he sits on the right hand of Zeus. Nor will the chorus sing of Phoebus for only one day, for he is amply sung. Who could not easily sing of Apollo?

[32] Of gold are Apollo's outfit and cloak, his lyre, his Lyctian[10] bowstring, and his quiver. Golden too are his

---

[8] Niobe, whose six sons and daughters were killed by the arrows of Apollo and Artemis. She turned to stone in her perpetual grief, and the rock's dripping water was said to be her tears (Hom. *Il.* 24.602–17). Both she and Thetis are traditional paradigms of grief whose stories illustrate Apollo's power.

[9] The identification of "my king" has been a point of contention. The scholiast suggests Ptolemy III Euergetes, and this seems likely. See Introduction.

[10] From Lyctus, a city in northern Crete known for its archers (Paus. 4.19.4).

χρύσεα καὶ τὰ πέδιλα· πολύχρυσος γὰρ Ἀπόλλων
35 καὶ πουλυκτέανος·[10] Πυθῶνί κε τεκμήραιο.
καὶ μὲν[11] ἀεὶ καλὸς καὶ ἀεὶ νέος· οὔποτε Φοίβου
θηλείαις οὐδ᾽ ὅσσον ἐπὶ χνόος ἦλθε παρειαῖς,
αἱ δὲ κόμαι θυόεντα πέδῳ λείβουσιν ἔλαια·
οὐ λίπος Ἀπόλλωνος ἀποστάζουσιν ἔθειραι,
40 ἀλλ᾽ αὐτὴν πανάκειαν· ἐν ἄστεϊ δ᾽ ᾧ κεν ἐκεῖναι
πρῶκες ἔραζε πέσωσιν, ἀκήρια πάντ᾽ ἐγένοντο.
τέχνῃ δ᾽ ἀμφιλαφὴς οὔτις τόσον ὅσσον
Ἀπόλλων·
κεῖνος ὀϊστευτὴν ἔλαχ᾽ ἀνέρα, κεῖνος ἀοιδόν
(Φοίβῳ γὰρ καὶ τόξον ἐπιτρέπεται καὶ ἀοιδή),
45 κείνου δὲ θριαὶ καὶ μάντιες· ἐκ δέ νυ Φοίβου
ἰητροὶ δεδάασιν ἀνάβλησιν θανάτοιο.
Φοῖβον καὶ Νόμιον κικλήσκομεν ἐξέτι κείνου,
ἐξότ᾽ ἐπ᾽ Ἀμφρυσσῷ ζευγίτιδας ἔτρεφεν ἵππους
ἠίθεου ὑπ᾽ ἔρωτι κεκαυμένος Ἀδμήτοιο.
50 ῥεῖά κε βουβόσιον τελέθοι πλέον, οὐδέ κεν αἶγες
δεύοιντο βρεφέων ἐπιμηλάδες,[12] ᾗσιν Ἀπόλλων
βοσκομένῃσ᾽ ὀφθαλμὸν ἐπήγαγεν· οὐδ᾽ ἀγάλακτες

---

[10] καιπου[. . . . .]ανος P.Oxy 2258A fr. 2 verso: καί τε πολυ-
κτέανος Ψ
[11] καιμεν[P.Oxy. 2258A fr. 2 verso: καὶ κεν Ψ
[12] ἐπιμηλάδες Ψ: μενεμμηλάδες Schol. EeQ

---

[11] Delphi's riches are attested in Homer (Il. 9.404–5; cf.
Hymn. Hom. Herm. 4.178–81).

sandals. Apollo has much gold and many possessions. Let Pytho be proof.[11] He is forever handsome and forever young. No down has ever appeared on his girlish cheeks. His locks drip scented oil on the ground. The hair of Apollo does not drip oil, but Heal-all[12] herself. And in the city where that dew falls to earth, everything is free of harm.

[42] No one is as greatly skilled as Apollo. To him belongs the archer, to him, the singer, for to Phoebus is entrusted archery and song. The Thriae[13] and seers are his; from Phoebus physicians know how to defer death.

[47] We call him Phoebus and Nomius[14] from the time when he reared yoked horses by the Amphryssus[15] burning with love for young Admetus.[16] Easily would the herd become greater; nor would the goats, guardians of the flock, lack young whenever Apollo casts his eye on them as they graze. Nor would sheep be milkless, nor infertile,

[12] Panaceia, a minor healing deity and daughter of Asclepius, (Ar. *Plut.* 702). Also the name of various plants thought to have healing properties.

[13] Three nymphs associated with Mt. Parnassus who instructed Apollo in the use of pebbles as a form of divination by lots (*Hymn. Hom. Herm.* 4.552–57).

[14] "Pastoral" Apollo (cf., e.g., Theoc. *Id.* 25.21–22). He shared the title with his son Aristaeus (Pind. *Pyth.* 9.64–65; Ap. Rhod. 2.506–7).

[15] River in Thessaly (Lucan 6.368). Homer alludes to the story but sets it in Pereia (*Il.* 2.763–67).

[16] King of Pherae in Thessaly, and husband of Alcestis. Apollo entered his service after killing the Cyclopes (Apollod. *Bibl.* 3.10.4) or their sons (Schol. ad Eur. *Alc.* 1).

οἴες οὐδ᾽ ἄκυθοι, πᾶσαι δέ κεν εἶεν ὕπαρνοι,
ἡ δέ κε μουνοτόκος διδυματόκος¹³ αἶψα γένοιτο.

55 Φοίβῳ δ᾽ ἑσπόμενοι πόλιας διεμετρήσαντο
ἄνθρωποι· Φοῖβος γὰρ ἀεὶ πολίεσσι φιληδεῖ
κτιζομένῃσ᾽, αὐτὸς δὲ θεμείλια Φοῖβος ὑφαίνει.
τετραέτης τὰ πρῶτα θεμείλια Φοῖβος ἔπηξε
καλῇ ἐν Ὀρτυγίῃ περιηγέος ἐγγύθι λίμνης.

60 Ἄρτεμις ἀγρώσσουσα καρήατα συνεχὲς αἰγῶν
Κυνθιάδων φορέεσκεν, ὁ δ᾽ ἔπλεκε βωμὸν Ἀπόλλων,
δείματο μὲν κεράεσσιν ἐδέθλια, πῆξε δὲ βωμόν
ἐκ κεράων, κεραοὺς δὲ πέριξ ὑπεβάλλετο τοίχους.
ὧδ᾽ ἔμαθεν τὰ πρῶτα θεμείλια Φοῖβος ἐγείρειν.

65 Φοῖβος καὶ βαθύγειον ἐμὴν πόλιν ἔφρασε Βάττῳ
καὶ Λιβύην ἐσιόντι κόραξ ἡγήσατο λαῷ,
δεξιὸς οἰκιστῆρι, καὶ ὤμοσε τείχεα δώσειν
ἡμετέροις βασιλεῦσιν· ἀεὶ δ᾽ εὔορκος Ἀπόλλων.
ὤπολλον, πολλοί σε Βοηδρόμιον καλέουσι,

70 πολλοὶ δὲ Κλάριον, πάντη δέ τοι οὔνομα πουλύ·
αὐτὰρ ἐγὼ Καρνεῖον· ἐμοὶ πατρώιον οὕτω.

---

¹³ διδυματόκος coni. Stephanus, Williams: διδυμοτόκος Ψ: διδυμητόκος anonym. ap. L. van Santen

---

¹⁷ The Sacred Lake (Hdt. 2.170; *Hymn* 4.261) was a landmark in Delos, here identified with Ortygia. At *Hymn. Hom. Ap.* 3.16, Ortygia is the birthplace of Artemis, in contrast to Apollo's birthplace in Delos.

¹⁸ Delian, from the hill Cynthus on Delos.

¹⁹ The Altar of Horn was an important landmark on Delos

but all would have lambs beneath them, and she who had
just one lamb would at once have two.

[55] And Phoebus men follow when they map out
cities. Phoebus always enjoys founding cities. Phoebus
himself weaves the foundations. At age four Phoebus built
his first foundations in lovely Ortygia near the round
lake.[17] Artemis, constantly hunting, kept bringing the
heads of Cynthian[18] goats, and Apollo wove an altar. He
built the shrine with horns, framed an altar from the
horns, and surrounded it with walls of horn.[19] In this way
Phoebus learned to raise his first foundations.

[65] Phoebus showed Battus[20] my fertile city,[21] and as
a raven[22] he led the people as they entered Libya, an omen
propitious to the founder, and he swore that he would give
walls to our kings.[23] Apollo's oaths are always fulfilled.
Apollo, many call you Boedromius;[24] many call you Cla-
rius,[25] and everywhere you have many names. But I call
you Carneius,[26] for this is my heritage.

(Ov. *Her.* 21.99–100; Plut *Thes.* 21.2) along with the Circular
Lake and the Palm Tree (*Hymn* 2.2 above, 2.59).
    [20] Founder of Cyrene; sometimes called Aristoteles (Hdt.
4.150–61). Cyrene was the birthplace of Callimachus, who calls
himself a "son of Battus" in a mock epitaph (*Epig.* 35). Battus
received three oracles from Apollo over the course of the founda-
tion (Hdt. 4.155–57).   [21] Cyrene, a Greek city in North Africa
in modern Libya. In antiquity it was famously fertile (Pind. *Pyth.*
4.6, 9.6–7).   [22] Presumably Apollo himself, often associated
with the raven (e.g., Hdt. 4.15).   [23] The Battiads.   [24] Apollo
the "Helper" (Paus. 9.17.2).   [25] Clarius was an oracle of Apollo
near Colophon (Tac. *Ann.* 2.54).
    [26] Dorian title of Apollo common in the Peloponnese (Pind.
Pyth. 5.80).

Σπάρτη τοι, Καρνεῖε, τόδε[14] πρώτιστον ἔδεθλον,
δεύτερον αὖ Θήρη, τρίτατόν γε μὲν ἄστυ Κυρήνης.
ἐκ μέν σε Σπάρτης ἕκτον γένος Οἰδιπόδαο
75 ἤγαγε Θηραίην ἐς ἀπόκτισιν· ἐκ δέ σε Θήρης
οὖλος Ἀριστοτέλης Ἀσβυστίδι πάρθετο γαίηι,
δεῖμε δέ τοι μάλα καλὸν ἀνάκτορον, ἐν δὲ πόληι
θῆκε τελεσφορίην ἐπετήσιον, ἧι ἔνι πολλοί
ὑστάτιον πίπτουσιν ἐπ' ἰσχίον, ὦ ἄνα, ταῦροι.
80 ἰὴ ἰὴ Καρνεῖε πολύλλιτε,[15] σεῖο δὲ βωμοί
ἄνθεα μὲν φορέουσιν ἐν εἴαρι τόσσα περ Ὧραι
ποικίλ' ἀγινεῦσι ζεφύρου πνείοντος ἐέρσην,
χείματι δὲ κρόκον ἡδύν· ἀεὶ δέ τοι ἀέναον πῦρ,
οὐδέ ποτε χθιζὸν περιβόσκεται ἄνθρακα τέφρη.
85 ἦ ῥ' ἐχάρη μέγα Φοῖβος, ὅτε ζωστῆρες Ἐνυοῦς
ἀνέρες ὠρχήσαντο μετὰ ξανθῆισι Λιβύσσης,
τέθμιαι εὖτέ σφιν Καρνειάδες ἤλυθον ὧραι.
οἱ δ' οὔπω πηγῆισι[16] Κύρης ἐδύναντο πελάσσαι
Δωριέες, πυκινὴν δὲ νάπαις[17] Ἄζιλιν ἔναιον.
90 τοὺς μὲν ἄναξ ἴδεν αὐτός, ἑῆι δ' ἐπεδείξατο νύμφηι

[14] τόδε Ψ sed suspectum. τό γε prop. Ernesti: πόρε Williams
[15] πολύλ(λ)ιτε La. η: πολύλλιστε Ψ
[16] πηγῆισι Κύρης corr. Schneider: πηγῆς κυρῆς Ψ: πηγαῖσι κυρήνης Schol. (DEGQ) ad Pind. Pyth. 4.523
[17] νάπαις Ψ: νάπησ' Pfeiffer

---

[27] Modern Thira, an island in the Cyclades also known as Santorini.
[28] Theras, who lead the colonists to Thera, was a descendant

212

[72] Sparta, Carneius, was your first foundation. The second was Thera,[27] but the third, the city of Cyrene. From Sparta the sixth generation descended from Oedipus[28] led you to the Theran colony, and from Thera vigorous Aristoteles established you in the land of the Asbystae,[29] and built you a temple of great beauty. And in the city he founded an annual rite in which many a bull falls on its haunches, o lord, for the last time.

[80] Hie, Hie, Carneius of many prayers. Your altars bear flowers in the spring, as many multicolored blossoms as the Horae[30] bring when the Zephyr[31] breathes dew. In winter they bring sweet crocus. Your eternal flame is forever, nor do its ashes feed around yesterday's coal. Phoebus rejoiced greatly when the men, belted for Enyo,[32] danced with the blond Libyan women at the traditional season of the Carneia.[33] Not yet could the Dorians approach the springs of Cyre,[34] but they lived in the dense woodland of Azilis.[35] And the Lord himself saw them and

of Oedipus through his son Polynices and his descendants Thersander, Tisamenus, and Autesion (Hdt. 4.147).

[29] Original inhabitants of the Cyrenaica (Hdt. 4.170; Lyc. *Alex*. 895–96). [30] Minor goddesses who personify the seasons (Hes. *Op*. 75). [31] God of the west wind and messenger of spring (Hes. *Theog*. 379). [32] A war goddess (Hom. *Il*. 5.333). The men are Theran warriors dancing in armor.

[33] The Carneian festival began in Sparta on the seventh day of the month of Carneius and lasted for nine days (Ath. 4.141f; Plut. *Quaest. conv.* 717d). [34] The Fountain of Apollo near his temple in Cyrene (Hdt. 4.158).

[35] Herodotus, who calls the area Aziris, says the Therans remained there for six years before going to the site of Cyrene (Hdt. 4.157–58).

στὰς ἐπὶ Μυρτούσσης κερατώδεος, ἦχι[18] λέοντα
Ὑψηὶς κατέπεφνε βοῶν σίνιν Εὐρυπύλοιο.
οὐ κείνου χορὸν εἶδε[19] θεώτερον ἄλλον Ἀπόλλων,
οὐδὲ πόλει τόσ᾽ ἔδειμεν[20] ὀφέλσιμα, τόσσα Κυρήνῃ,
95 μνωόμενος προτέρης ἁρπακτύος. οὐδὲ μὲν αὐτοί
Βαττιάδαι Φοίβοιο πλέον θεὸν ἄλλον ἔτισαν.

"ἰὴ ἰὴ παιῆον" ἀκούομεν, οὕνεκα τοῦτο
Δελφός τοι πρώτιστον ἐφύμνιον εὕρετο λαός,
ἦμος ἑκηβολίην χρυσέων ἐπεδείκνυσο τόξων.
100 Πυθώ τοι κατιόντι συνήντετο δαιμόνιος θήρ,
αἰνὸς ὄφις. τὸν μὲν σὺ κατήναρες ἄλλον ἐπ᾽ ἄλλῳ
βάλλων ὠκὺν ὀϊστόν, ἐπηΰτησε δὲ λαός·
"ἰὴ ἰὴ παιῆον, ἵει βέλος, εὐθύ σε μήτηρ
γείνατ᾽ ἀοσσητῆρα"· τὸ δ᾽ ἐξέτι κεῖθεν ἀείδῃ.
105 ὁ Φθόνος Ἀπόλλωνος ἐπ᾽ οὔατα λάθριος εἶπεν·
"οὐκ ἄγαμαι τὸν ἀοιδὸν ὃς οὐδ᾽ ὅσα πόντος ἀείδει."
τὸν Φθόνον ὡπόλλων ποδί τ᾽ ἤλασεν ὧδέ τ᾽ ἔειπεν·
"Ἀσσυρίου ποταμοῖο μέγας ῥόος, ἀλλὰ τὰ πολλά

---

[18] ἦχι Ψ: ἔνθα Schol. ad Pind.
[19] εἶδε a La.: ἴδε Ψ
[20] ἔδειμεν Ψ, Williams: ἔνειμεν coni. La.

---

[36] The hill of myrtle (Ap. Rhod. 2.505). In the imperial period there was a cult of Apollo Myrtoos there (*CIG* 3.5138).

[37] The nymph Cyrene, who is not named in the hymn. Hypseus, her father, was king of the Lapithae in Thessaly (Pind. *Pyth*. 9.13–14).

[38] Legendary king of Libya (Pind. *Pyth*. 4.33) who offered his

showed them to his bride, standing on the horn-shaped hill of Myrtussa,[36] where Hypseus' daughter[37] killed the lion that ravaged the herds of Eurypylus.[38] Apollo has seen no other chorus more divine than that one, nor has he given so many benefits to a city as he has for Cyrene, remembering the earlier rape.[39] Nor have the descendants of Battus themselves honored another god more than Phoebus.

[97] We hear "Hie, Hie, Paieon," because the Delphian people first invented this refrain for you, when you demonstrated the shooting of the golden bow. A demonic beast met you when you were going down to Pytho, a dreadful reptile. And you killed him shooting swift arrows[40] one after another, and the people shouted "Hie, Hie, Paieon, shoot an arrow!" Your mother bore you as a helper,[41] and ever since you are celebrated in this way.

[105] Envy secretly spoke into the ear of Apollo, "I do not admire the singer who does not sing as much as the sea." Apollo struck Envy with his foot and said, "Great is the flood of the Assyrian river,[42] but it hauls much refuse

kingdom to anyone who could kill a lion that was destroying his land. In this version, the nymph Cyrene slew the lion and won the kingdom (Acasander in *BNJ* 469 F 4 = Schol. ad Ap. Rhod. 2.498). In earlier versions Cyrene killed the lion in Thessaly and came to Libya later (Pind. *Pyth*. 9.26–28).

39 Callimachus pointedly refrains from telling the story of Apollo's sexual encounter with the virginal Cyrene (Pind. *Pyth*. 9.26–28).

40 The story is told at *Hymn. Hom. Ap*. 3.355–74. The place was called Pytho after the rotting of the snake's corpse.

41 Apollo describes himself similarly in Homer (*Il*. 15.254).

42 Euphrates (Schol. ad Strabo 16.1).

λύματα γῆς καὶ πολλὸν ἐφ᾽ ὕδατι συρφετὸν ἕλκει.
110 Δηοῖ δ᾽ οὐκ ἀπὸ παντὸς ὕδωρ φορέουσι μέλισσαι,
ἀλλ᾽ ἥτις καθαρή τε καὶ ἀχράαντος ἀνέρπει
πίδακος ἐξ ἱερῆς ὀλίγη λιβὰς ἄκρον ἄωτον."
χαῖρε, ἄναξ· ὁ δὲ Μῶμος, ἵν᾽ ὁ Φθόνος,[21] ἔνθα
νέοιτο.

[21] φθόνος I, Ald., Schol. ad Greg. Naz.: φθόρος Ψ

2a *Dieg.* 11.20–12.1

'Οἷον ὁ τὠπόλλωνος ἐσείσατο δάφνινος
    ὄρπηξ' . . .

Προτερατευσάμενος ὡς ἐντεθεασμένων καὶ τῶν ἀψύ-
χων ἐπὶ παρουσίᾳ τοῦ Ἀπόλλωνος δαφνίνων τε κλά-
δων σειομένων καὶ αὐτοῦ τοῦ τεμένους, ἐπιλέγει δεῖν
χορεύειν τοὺς παῖδας καὶ κιθαρίζειν, γεγαληνῶσθαι
δὲ καὶ τὸ πέλαγος ἐφ᾽ ὕμνῳ τοῦ θεοῦ καὶ τοὺς περι-
παθεῖς ἀνέχειν τοῦ (25) θρηνεῖν. προσιστορεῖ δὲ καὶ
τὸ πολύτεχνον τοῦ θεοῦ ὅτι καὶ τοξότης ἀγαθός ἐστι
καὶ ἰατρὸς καὶ μάντις καὶ ἐπόπτης τῆς τροφῆς τῶν
θρεμμάτων, καὶ ὡς χαίρει πόλεων κτίσεσιν οὐδ᾽ ἀρχι-
τεκτονίας ἀπολείπεται· ἔτι δὲ τετραέτης ὢν ἐν τῇ
Δήλῳ βωμὸν ἐκ κεράτων (30) κατεσκευάσατο. καὶ εἰ-
δὼς† ὅτι Κυρήνης τὴν κτίσιν Βάττῳ τῷ Θηραίῳ δι-
εσήμηνε, κόρακα παρασχόμενος ἡγεμόνα· ὡς πρῶτον
μὲν ἐν Σπάρτῃ ἐτετίμητο, δεύτερον δὲ ἐν (12.1) Θήρᾳ,
τρίτον δὲ ἐν Κυρήνηι μετὰ τὰς ἀποικία[σ .] τον λέ-
οντα...... Βάττῳ...... μενον

216

from the land and garbage in its water. Bees[43] carry water
to Deo[44] not from every source, but pure and immaculate
it flows from a holy spring, a tiny trickle, the topmost
flower." Hail, King! And Blame, may he go there, where
Envy dwells.

[43] Variously understood as priestesses of Demeter (Porph. *de
antr. nymph*. 8), or poets (Bacchyl. 10.10; Ar. *Av*. 748–51).

[44] An alternative name of Demeter (*Hymn. Hom. Dem*. 2.47).

2a *Diegeseis*

How the laurel branch of Apollo shakes!

Talking marvels, how even inanimate things make noise at
the arrival of Apollo, the laurel branches shake themselves
and from his sacred precinct he says that it is necessary for
the boys to dance and play the cithara, and the sea to be
calmed at the hymn for the god and those who are suf-
fering to hold back from grieving. And he tells about the
many skills of the god that he is a good bowman and phy-
sician and seer and manager of animal husbandry, and how
he rejoices in the founding of cities and does not cease
from construction. While he was still four years old he
built an altar of horns in Delos. And knowing about the
foundation of Cyrene he marked it out for Battus of Thera,
furnishing a crow as a guide. In this way he was honored
first in Sparta, second in Thera, and third in Cyrene among
the colonies . . . the lion . . . . . . Battus . . .

2b Schol. in *P.Oxy.* 2258A fr. 2

3   ]τοτη.[

4   [.]εν Δηλ[ ] γὰρ ἱερὰ [....]ους δε.[
    ἐν Δή[λ]ῳι [φοῖ]νιξ· κα[ ] ... [ ]Θεοπομπο.[

5   ⟨κύκνος⟩· ἱερὸς γὰρ Ἀπόλ[λωνος]

10   λιτός· ἀν(τὶ) τ(οῦ)....[παραλλη[

13   ἔχειν ...[ἀν(τὶ) τ(οῦ) ἔχετ(ε)[

14   εἰ τελ(έειν) πιθ[ανῶς γάμου τὸ τ[έλος ο[.].
μηλ[

    [ ]λεγοντ[[.]λει[

16   [ ].[ ]...[χελώ[νη· οι. κιθ[άρα]

18   κλείουσ(ιν)· [

25   ]ργ...ιπ[ ].ης θεομαχ[

31   [τ]ίς ἂν [ο]ὐ ῥᾳδίως τὸν Ἀπόλ[λων]α ὑμνοίη;
τοσαῦτα.χο( ).α( )]τις ἂν λέγοι .[.].[.]....]..

32a   ⟨ἐνδυτόν⟩· ὁ χιτών.

32b   ⟨ἐπιπορπίς⟩· [ἡ] πό[ρπη

33a   ⟨ἄεμμα⟩· τ[ὸ] τόξον· κ(αὶ) Φιλί[τας ἐν] Δήμη-
τρι· "αυτα εγε [ ].[.].. γυμνὸν ἄεμμα| [ ]."

33b   ⟨Λύκτιον⟩· Κ]ρητικόν

36–37]ἀεὶ καλ(ός)· οὔποτε Φοίβ(ου)].τ(οῦ) Ἀπόλ-
λωνος].χν(ο)ῦς ἐπῆλθεν].ω[ ].. θηλείαις
][.τ(αι) γυν(αι) [

38   λείβο(υ)σ(ιν)· σ]τάζ[ο]υσιν

39   λίπ(ος)· [ἔ]λ(αι)ον

41   πρῶκες· στ]αγόνες

HYMN II TO APOLLO

2b Oxyrhynchus papyrus (scholia)

3   ...
4   in Delos ... for the sacred ...
     in Delos the palm tree ... Theopompus.
5   *kyknos*: swan, the holy [bird] of Apollo.
10   *litos* (of no account): instead of ... parallel.
13   *echein*: instead of *echete*.
14   if plausibly to fulfill the goal of marriage ...
16   ... *chelōne* (the tortoise shell): ... cithara.
18   *kleiousin* (they celebrate):
25   ... battle with the gods.
31   Who would not easily sing of Apollo? So great ... who could say ...
32a   *endyton*: the chiton.
32b   *epiporpis*: a clasp
33a   *aemma*: the bow. And in the *Demeter* of Philitas: "... uncovered bow"
33b   *Lyktion*: Cretan.
36–37 always beautiful. Not ever of Phoebus ... of Apollo ... has down come to his tender, i.e., womanly [cheeks].
38   *leibousin*: they drip.
39   *lipos*: olive oil.
41   *prōkes*: drops.

2c Comm. in *P.Ant.* 20.1–24

].[

38   [πέδω]ι· τῇ γῇ. λείβουσ[ιν], στάζουσιν

41   ]ϛ. ἔραζε· χαμ[ᾶζε

45   θ]ριαί· μαντικαὶ ψῆφ[οι

48   Ἀμφρυσσῷ· ποταμὸς Θεσσαλίας. Ζ[ευγίτι-
δας· ὑπὸ ζυγὸν ἀ-

50–51 γ[ομένας. βο]υβόσιον· βουστάσιον. [ἐπιμη-
λάδες·

53–55 †ἔγκυοι†. ἄ]κυθοι ἀνέγκυοι. ὕπ[αρνοι· ἔγκυοι.
διεμετρήσαντο·

56   διέγραφον, διέλαχον. φιληδεῖ· [

57–59 ὑφαίνε[ι· κα]τασκευάζει. περιη[γέος· κυκλοτε-
ροῦς λίμνης,

60   ἥτις ἐστὶν ἐν Δήλῳ. ἀγρώσσουσα[· ἀγρεύ-
ουσα. καρήατα· γρά-

61   φεται δὲ κα[ὶ κε]ράατα. συνε[χές· ἀδιάλει-
πτον. Κυνθιάδων·

62?   Κύνθος γ[ὰ]ρ ὄρος Δήλου. π[ῆξε(?)]

65   βαθύγειον· εὔγειον. ἔφ[ρασε Βάττῳ· τῷ Ἀρι-
στοτέλει·

66   ο[ὕ]τω γὰρ ἐκαλεῖτο διὰ τὸ βα[τταρίζειν αὐ-
τόν. κόραξ· ὄ[ρ]νεον οὕτως ὀνομαζόμ[ενον παρὰ τὸ
κορόν· ὁ γὰρ Ἀριστοτέλει τῆς εἰς Λιβύην ἢ ἐπὶ Κυ-
[ρήν]η[ν] ἀποικίας ἡγήσατο.

69   Βοηδρόμιον· οὕτως ἐκαλεῖ[το] Βοηδρομιῶνος
μ[η]ρὸς ιδι[

2c Antinoöpolis papyrus (commentary)

].[

38   *pedoi*: on the ground; *leibousin*, they drop.

41   *eraze*: on the earth.

45   *thriai*: mantic stones.

48   *Amphryssōi*: river of Thessaly. *zeugitidas*: suffering under the yoke.

50–51   *Boubosion*: ox stall. *epimēlades* (of the flock):

53–55   *akythoi*: without offspring. *(h)yparnoi*, with lambs underneath. *diemetrēsanto* (they measured out):

56   *diegraphon, dielachon*: they delineated, divided up. *philēdei* (he takes pleasure in):

57–59   *(h)yphainei*: he constructs. *periēgeos*: the circular lake,

60   which is in Delos. *agrōssousa*: hunting. *karēata* (heads):

61   He marks out the altar of horns. *suneches*: incessantly. *Kynthiadōn*:

62?   Cynthus is a mountain of Delos. *pēxe* (he fitted)

65   *bathygeion*: fertile. He tells of Battus: Aristoteles.

66   He was called this because he stuttered. *korax* (the crow): the bird was named on account of its insolence. It was the leader of the colony into Libya or Cyrene for Aristoteles.

69   *Boēdromion* is the name of a month.

70   πολεμων τοῖς Ἀθηναίοις [Κλάριον]·

71   ἀπὸ Κλάρου τοῦ (?) Κολοφῶνος· Κ[αρνεῖον
δὲ αὐτὸν προσαγορεύουσι ἀπὸ Κάρνου τοῦ θε[οπρό-
που.

74   ἕκτον γένος Οἰδιπόδαο. ὁ Θήρας· οὗτος γὰρ
Α[ὐτεσίωνος τοῦ Τισαμενοῦ τοῦ Θερσάνδρου τοῦ
Πολυνείκους.[

76?   γὰρ ο[ἱ] νεώτεροι ἐξελέξα.[

2d Schol. Ψ

1   Οἷον· ἀντὶ τοῦ οἴως, ὅπως. ἔστι δὲ θειασμός.
λέγεται δὲ τῶν μαντευομένων θεῶν τὰ θεῖα καὶ ἐπιδη-
μεῖν καὶ ἀποδημεῖν. καὶ ὅταν μὲν ἐπιδημῶσι, τὰς μαν-
τείας ἀληθεῖς εἶναι· ὅταν δὲ ἀποδημῶσι, ψευδεῖς. ὡς
γοῦν ἐπιδημοῦντος τοῦ θεοῦ ταῦτά φησιν ὁ Καλλίμα-
χος.

4   ⟨φοῖνιξ⟩· δεικτικῶς λέγεται, ὅτι παρὰ τῷ δέν-
δρῳ τούτῳ ἐγέννησεν ἡ Λητὼ τὸν Ἀπόλλω.

5   ἱερὸν ὄρνεον Ἀπόλλωνός ἐστιν ὁ κύκνος.

6a   ⟨αὐτοί⟩· ἀντὶ τοῦ αὐτόματοι.

6b   ⟨ἀνακλίνεσθε⟩ Ὅμηρος· "ἠμὲν ἀνακλῖναι πυ-
κινὸν νέφος."

7   ⟨αὐταί⟩· αὐτόματοι.

8   ⟨νέοι⟩· ὡς τῶν νέων καθιερωμένων τῷ Ἀπόλ-
λωνι.

14   εἰ μέλλουσι καὶ γάμου ἐντὸς?) γενέσθαι καὶ
πολιᾶσαι· καὶ γὰρ ἀκειρεκόμης ὁ Ἀπόλλων.

70   of wars with the Athenians [Clarion]:

71   from Clarus of Colophon. They call it the Carneion from Carnus according to Theopompus.

74   The sixth generation from Oepidus. Theras: this man was the son of Autesion, son of Tisamenos, son of Thersander, son of Polynices.

76?   For the younger [poets] refute . . .

2d Ψ Scholia

1   (h)oion: instead of (h)oiōs and (h)opōs. It is inspiration. It is said that the divinity of the mantic gods is both present and absent. Whenever it is present, the prophecies are true and whenever it is absent, they are false. Callimachus says these things so that the god will be present.

4   phoinix (the palm): it is said categorically that Leto gave birth to Apollo beside this tree.

5   The holy bird of Apollo is the swan.

6a   autoi: instead of automatoi.

6b   anaklinesthe (you open yourselves): Homer (Il. 5.751): "whether to throw open the thick cloud or to shut it."

7   autai: of their own accord.

8   neoi: as the youths who are devoted to Apollo.

14   If they are about to be within a marriage and grow gray. For Apollo has unshorn hair.

15   ⟨ἐστήξειν⟩· ἀπὸ τοῦ ἵστημι παρακείμενος
ἔστηκα. ἀπὸ τούτου ποιοῦσιν οἱ Συρακούσιοι ἐνε-
στῶτα ἑστήκω, οὗ ὁ μέλλων ἑστήξω, καὶ τὸ ἀπαρέμ-
φατον ἑστήξειν.

16   ⟨χέλυς⟩· ἡ κιθάρα.

18a   ⟨εὐφημεῖ⟩· ἡσυχάζει, γαληνιᾷ.

18b   ⟨κλείουσιν⟩· ὑμνοῦσιν.

19   ⟨Λυκωρέος⟩· τοῦ Ἀπόλλωνος.

20a   ⟨κινύρεται⟩· κλαίει, θρηνεῖ.

20b   ⟨αἴλινα⟩· ἤτοι θρηνητικά.

21   ⟨ἰὴ παιῆον⟩· πρόσφθεγμα καταφρονοῦντος.

22a   ⟨ἀναβάλλεται⟩· ὑπερτίθεται.

22b   ⟨πέτρος⟩· τῆς Νιόβης.

26   ⟨βασιλῆι⟩· τῷ Πτολεμαίῳ τῷ Εὐεργέτῃ· διὰ
δὲ τὸ φιλόλογον αὐτὸν εἶναι ὡς θεὸν τιμᾷ (v. ad test.
I).

32   ἐνδυτόν· τὸ ἱμάτιον· ἐπιπορπὶς δὲ ἡ περόνη,
ἡ λεγομένη φίβλα.

33   ἄεμμα· ἡ νευρά· παρὰ τὸ ἑκατέρωθεν δεδέ-
σθαι. Λύκτος δέ ἐστι πόλις Κρήτης.

35   ⟨Πυθῶνί⟩· Ὅμηρος· "οὐδ' ὅσα λάϊνος οὐδὸς
ἀφήτορος ἐντὸς ἐέργει | Φοίβου Ἀπόλλωνος Πυθοῖ
ἔνι."

37a   ⟨θηλείαις⟩· ἁπαλαῖς.

37b   ⟨χνόος⟩· ψόφος, ξυσμός.

38   ⟨ἔλαια⟩· ση(μείωσαι), ὅτι τὰ ἔλαια πληθυντι-
κῶς παρ' οὐδενὶ ἄλλῳ εὕρηται.

40   ⟨πανάκειαν⟩· τὴν ἴασιν.

15   *estēxein*: from (*h*)*istēmi* parallel to (*h*)*estēka*.
From this [form] the Syracusans make *enestōta* and
(*h*)*estēko*, the future form of which is (*h*)*estēxo*, and the
infinitive (*h*)*estēxein*.

16   *chelus*: the cithara.

18a   *euphēmei*: it is quiet, peaceful.

18b   *kleiousin*: they sing.

19   *Lykōreos*: of Apollo.

20a   *kinyretai*: she laments, she wails.

20b   *ailina*: inclined to mourn.

21   *iē paiēon*: a salutation.

22a   *anaballetai*: she defers.

22b   *petros*: of Niobe.

26   *basilēi*: by Ptolemy Euergetes. On account of his
love of learning he is honored like a god.

32   *endyton*: a cloak. *Epiporpis*: the pin called
phibla.

33   *aemma*: a string to be tied on each side. *Lyktos*
is a city in Crete.

35   *Pythōni*: Homer (*Il.* 9.404–5): "nor however
much the marble threshold of the archer Phoebus Apollo
holds in rocky Pytho."

37a   *thēleiais*: tender.

37b   *chnoos* (down): noise, itching.

38   *elaia*: note that the plural *elaia* is not found any-
where else.

40   *panakeian*: remedy.

41   πρῶκες· δρόσοι σταγόνες· ἀκήρια δέ, ἀσθενῆ
τὰ νοσήματα ἢ μᾶλλον ἄνοσα καὶ ἄφθαρτα πάντα
γίνεται.

42a   τέχνη δ' ἀμφιλαφής· ἔστι γὰρ τοξότης, ἀοι-
δός, μάντις, ἰατρὸς καὶ ποιμήν.

42b   ⟨ἀμφιλαφής⟩· πλούσιος.

42c   ⟨ἀμφιλαφής⟩· βοηθός.

45   ⟨θριαί⟩· μαντικαὶ ψῆφοί εἰσιν αἱ θριαί. λέγε-
ται δὲ αὐτὰς εὑρῆσθαι ὑπό τινων τριῶν νυμφῶν. διὰ
τοῦτο καὶ θριαὶ ὠνομάσθησαν οἱονεὶ τριαί.

48   ⟨ἐπ' Ἀμφρυσσῷ⟩· Ἀμφρυσσὸν οἱ μὲν ποτα-
μὸν Θεσσαλίας, οἱ δὲ πόλιν· ζευγίτιδας δὲ τὰς ὑπὸ
ζυγὸν ἀγομένας.

49   ⟨ἠϊθέου⟩· ἀγάμου, ἄπαιδος.

50a   βουβόσιον· ὁ τόπος ἔνθα οἱ βόες νέμονται.
τὸ δ' ἐπιμηλάδες ἀντὶ τοῦ αἱ μετὰ τῶν μήλων νεμό-
μεναι· καὶ γὰρ καὶ τὰς αἶγας μῆλα λέγουσιν, ὡς
Ὅμηρος ἐπεξηγούμενος τί εἰσι μῆλά φησι· "μῆλ' ὄϊές
τε καὶ αἶγες." ἂν δὲ ἐμμηλάδες γράφηται, ἀντὶ τοῦ
θήλειαι ἐστίν.

50b   ⟨ἐπιμηλάδες⟩· αἱ γόνιμοι.

53   ἄκυθοι· ἤγουν ἄγονοι· κεῦθος γὰρ λέγεται τὸ
κύημα.

59   ⟨ἐν Ὀρτυγίῃ περιηγέος⟩· κυκλοτεροῦς. οὕτω
γὰρ στρογγύλη λίμνη ἐν Ὀρτυγίᾳ καλεῖται. Ὀρτυγία·
δὲ ἡ Δῆλος ἀπὸ τοῦ τὴν Λητὼ εἰς ὄρτυγα μεταβλη-
θεῖσαν εἰς τὴν Δῆλον ἐλθεῖν φεύγουσαν τὴν Ἥραν.

61   ⟨Κυνθιάδων⟩· Κύνθος ὄρος τῆς Δήλου.

41   *prōkes*: drops of dew. Unharmed, diseases are feeble or rather all things are free of illness and uncorrupted.

42a   *technē d' amphilaphēs*: he is a bowman, singer, seer, physician, and herdsman.

42b   *amphilaphēs*: wealthy.

42c   *amphilaphēs*: helpful.

45   *thriai*: the *thriai* are mantic stones. It is said that they were discovered by three nymphs. On account of this they were called *thriai* since there were three.

48   *ep' Amphrussō*: some say that the Amphryssus is a river in Thessaly, others say it is a city; *zeugitidas* means laboring under the yoke.

49   *ēitheou*: unmarried, childless.

50a   *boubosion*: a place where cows feed. *epimēlades*, instead of the [goats] pasturing with the sheep. They call goats *mēla*, as Homer says (*Od.* 9.184), explaining what *mēla* are: "flocks, sheep and goats." He writes *emmēlades* instead of female.

50b   *epimēlades*: fertile.

53   *akythoi*: that is to say, unfruitful. A fetus is called *keuthos*.

59   *en Ortugiē periēgeos*: circular. This is the name of the circular lake in Ortygia. *Ortygia*: Delos, from Leto's being hindered from going into Ortygia (Delos) when fleeing from Hera.

61   *Kynthiadōn*: Mt. Cynthus in Delos.

65   λέγεται ὅτι ὁ Βάττος οὗτος ἄφωνος ἦν. ἀπῆλ-
θεν οὖν εἰς τὸ τοῦ Ἀπόλλωνος ἱερὸν ἐπὶ τῷ τὸν θεὸν
ἐρωτῆσαι περὶ τῆς φωνῆς. ὁ δὲ ἔχρησεν αὐτῷ οὐκέτι
περὶ φωνῆς, ἀλλὰ περὶ μετοικίας. καὶ ὁ Βάττος πει-
σθεὶς τῷ χρησμῷ ἦλθεν εἰς τὴν Λιβύην. λέγεται δὲ
εἶναι πολλοὺς λέοντας ἐν τῇ χώρᾳ ταύτῃ. ἐπιδημήσας
οὖν ὁ Βάττος, καὶ λέοντα αἰφνηδὸν θεασάμενος τῇ
τοῦ φόβου ἀνάγκῃ βιασθεὶς φθέγξασθαι διέρρηξε
τὴν φλέβα, ἥτις τὴν ἐκείνου φωνὴν ἐπεῖχε, καὶ οὕτω
φωνήεις ἐγένετο καὶ τὴν Κυρήνην ἔκτισεν, ὅθεν ἐστὶν
ὁ Καλλίμαχος.

66   <κόραξ>· ὡς ἀνακείμενος τῷ Ἀπόλλωνι ὁ κό-
ραξ.

68   <ἡμετέροις βασιλεῦσι>· τῷ Πτολεμαίῳ.

69   <Βοηδρόμιον>· πολέμου ἐπελθόντος τοῖς Ἀθη-
ναίοις ἔχρησεν αὐτοῖς ὁ θεός, μετὰ βοῆς ἐπιθέσθαι
τοῖς πολεμίοις· οἱ δὲ τοῦτο ποιήσαντες ἐνίκησαν, ὅθεν
Βοηδρόμιος Ἀπόλλων.

70   <Κλάριον>· μαντικόν(?).

71   <Καρνεῖον>· ἀπὸ Κάρνου τοῦ μάντεως τοῦ
ἀναιρεθέντος ὑπὸ Ἀλήτου, ὃς ἦν τῶν Ἡρακλειδῶν.
ὀργισθεὶς οὖν ὁ Ἀπόλλων λοιμὸν ἐνέβαλεν.

74   <Οἰδιπόδαο>· Οἰδίποδος μὲν Πολυνείκης, οὗ
Θέρσανδρος, οὗ Τισαμενός, οὗ Αὐτεσίων, οὗ Θήρας,
ὃς ἀπῴκησεν εἰς Θήραν τὴν νῆσον τὴν νῦν οὕτω κλη-
θεῖσαν.

76   <Ἀριστοτέλης>· ὁ αὐτὸς καὶ Βάττος λέγεται.
οὖλος δὲ ὁ ὑγιής, ὡς πρὸς τὴν φωνήν. καὶ γὰρ ὁ

65   He says that this Battus was mute. He went into the shrine of Apollo to ask the god about his voice. And he replied to him not about his voice, but about founding a colony. And Battus, who was persuaded by the oracle, went into Libya. He says that there are many lions in that place. And Battus, resided there and seeing a lion suddenly was forced to speak by the necessity of fear and ruptured the vein that held back his voice, and in this way became articulate and founded Cyrene where Callimachus came from.

66   *korax*: the crow offered by Apollo.

68   (*h*)*ēmeterois basileusi* (our kings): Ptolemy.

69   *Boēdromion*: when war was coming to the Athenians the god commanded them to set upon the enemies with a shout (*boēs*). They did this and were victorious, and from this, Apollo is called *Boēdromios*.

70   *Klarion*: prophetic(?).

71   *Karneion*: from Carnus, the seer who was killed by Aletes, who was one of the Heraclidae. Apollo, who was angry, cast down a plague.

74   *Oidpodao*: Polynices the son of Oedipus, from him Thersander, from him Tisamenus, from him Autesion, and from him Theras who established a settlement on the island which is now called Thera.

76   *Aristotelēs*: he says that this is Battus. He was entirely healthy in respect to his voice. And an oracle given

δοθεὶς αὐτῷ χρησμὸς τοῦτο παρεμφαίνει· "Βάττ', ἐπὶ
φωνὴν ἦλθες· ἄναξ δέ σε Φοῖβος ἀνώγει ἐς Λιβύην
ἐλθεῖν μηλοτρόφον οἰκιστῆρα." Ἀσβυστίδα δὲ τὴν
λευκὴν λέγει παρὰ τὴν ἄσβεστον. τοιαύτη γὰρ ἡ Λι-
βύη λευκόγειος.

78   ⟨τελεσφορίην⟩· ἑορτήν, θυσίαν.

83   κρόκος τὸ ἄνθος παρὰ τὸ ἐν κρύει θάλλειν.

85   ⟨ζωστῆρες⟩· περιφραστικῶς οἱ πολεμικοί.

86   ὡς ἐπιτελούντων καὶ ἐν τῇ Λιβύῃ ἑορτὴν
Καρνείῳ Ἀπόλλωνι.

87   ⟨τέθμιαι⟩· νόμιμοι, ὡρισμέναι.

88 sq.   ⟨Κυρῆς⟩· κρήνη ἐν Κυρήνῃ. Δωριέας δὲ τοὺς
Ἡρακλείδας λέγει τοὺς ἀπὸ Σπάρτης μετοικήσαντας
εἰς Θήραν καὶ ἀπὸ Θήρας εἰς Κυρήνην.

89   ⟨Ἄζιλιν⟩· ὄρος καὶ ποταμὸς Λιβύης.

90a   ⟨ἄναξ⟩· ἤγουν ὁ Ἀπόλλων.

90b   ⟨νύμφῃ⟩· τῇ Κυρήνῃ.

91   ἐπὶ Μυρτούσσης· ὄρος Λιβύης· κερατώδεος
δὲ τῆς κέρατα ἐχούσης ἤτοι ἀκρωρείας. φαίνεται δὲ ἡ
Κυρήνη ὡς φονεύσασα ἐν τῇ Λιβύῃ λέοντά τινα βλά-
πτοντα τὰς βοῦς τοῦ Εὐρυπύλου· ἦν δὲ αὕτη κυνηγέ-
τις, θυγάτηρ Ὑψέως.

92   ⟨Ὑψηΐς⟩· ἡ Κυρήνη.

94   ⟨τόσσα⟩· ὅσσα.

95   ⟨ἁρπακτύος⟩· τῇ Κυρήνῃ κυνηγετούσῃ ἐν
τῷ ὄρει τῷ Πηλίῳ τῆς Θεσσαλίας συνεκαθεύδησεν
Ἀπόλλων, ἐξ ἧς τίκτεται ὁ Ἀρισταῖος.

to him revealed this, "Battus, you came here for your voice. Lord Phoebus orders you to go into sheep rearing Libya as a colonist." He calls it white Asbystis and also *asbestus*. Such is white-soiled Libya.

78   *telephoriēn*: festival, sacrifice.

83   *krokos*: a flower, from flourishing in the frost.

85   *zōstēres*: periphrastically, warriors.

86   to prescribe a festival in Libya for Apollo Carneius.

87   *tethmiai*: customs, ordinations.

88 sq.   *Kyrēs*: a spring in Cyrene. He says that the Dorian Heraclidae came as colonists from Sparta into Thera and from Thera into Cyrene.

89   *Azilin*: mountain and river of Libya.

90a   *anax*: or rather Apollo.

90b   *nymphēi*: Cyrene.

91   *epi Myrtoussēs*: a mountain in Libya; *keratōdeos* from having horns on its peaks. Cyrene appears because she killed a lion in Libya who was harming the herds of Euripylus. She was a huntress, the daughter of Hypseus.

92   (H)*ypseïs*: Cyrene.

94   *tossa*: (h)*ossa*.

95   (h)*arpaktyos*: Apollo raped Cyrene who was hunting on mount Pelion in Thessaly and gave birth to Aristaeus.

106   ἐγκαλεῖ διὰ τούτων τοὺς σκώπτοντας αὐτὸν
μὴ δύνασθαι ποιῆσαι μέγα ποίημα, ὅθεν ἠναγκάσθη
ποιῆσαι τὴν Ἑκάλην.
108   ‹Ἀσσυρίου ποταμοῖο›· τὸν τῶν Περσῶν λέ-
γει τὸν καλούμενον Εὐφράτην.

106   On account of these things he blames those who mocked him on account of not being able to write a long poem, and from this he was forced to write the *Hecale*.

108   *Assyriou potamoio*: the river of the Persians he says is called the Euphrates.

HYMNUS III
IN ARTEMIN

Ἄρτεμιν (οὐ γὰρ ἐλαφρὸν ἀειδόντεσσι λαθέσθαι)
ὑμνέομεν, τῇ τόξα λαγωβολίαι τε μέλονται
καὶ χορὸς ἀμφιλαφὴς καὶ ἐν οὔρεσιν ἑψιάασθαι,
ἀρχμενοι[1] ὡς ὅτε[2] πατρὸς ἐφεζομένη γονάτεσσι

5 παῖς ἔτι κουρίζουσα τάδε προσέειπε γονῆα·
"δός μοι παρθενίην αἰώνιον, ἄππα, φυλάσσειν,
καὶ πολυωνυμίην, ἵνα μή μοι Φοῖβος ἐρίζῃ,
δὸς δ' ἰοὺς καὶ τόξα—ἔα πάτερ, οὔ σε φαρέτρην
οὐδ' αἰτέω μέγα τόξον· ἐμοὶ Κύκλωπες ὀιστοὺς

10 αὐτίκα τεχνήσονται, ἐμοὶ δ' εὐκαμπὲς ἄεμμα·
ἀλλὰ φαεσφορίην τε καὶ ἐς γόνυ μέχρι χιτῶνα
ζώννυσθαι λεγνωτόν, ἵν' ἄγρια θηρία καίνω.
δὸς δέ μοι ἑξήκοντα χορίτιδας Ὠκεανίνας,
πάσας εἰνέτεας, πάσας ἔτι παῖδας ἀμίτρους·

15 δὸς δέ μοι ἀμφιπόλους Ἀμνισίδας εἴκοσι νύμφας,
αἵ τε μοι ἐνδρομίδας[3] τε καὶ ὁππότε μηκέτι λύγκας
μήτ' ἐλάφους βάλλοιμι, θοοὺς κύνας εὖ κομέοιεν.

---

1 αρχμενοι P.Oxy. 3328 col. II, corr. Blomfield: ἀρχόμενοι Ψ
2 ὡς ὅτε Ψ: καὶ ὅτε δ: ὡς ποτε prop. Hermann
3 ἐνδρομίδας Et. Gen.: ἐνδρομάδας Ψ

234

HYMN III
TO ARTEMIS

Artemis we hymn, for it is no small matter for singers to forget her. Bows and shooting hare are her concern, frequent dancing, and playing in the mountains, beginning from the time she sat on her father's knees, still a little girl speaking childishly, and said these things to her begetter: "Give me virginity to keep forever, papa, and to have many titles, so that Apollo will not rival me. Give me arrows and bows, but wait, father, I am not asking for a quiver or a great bow: for me the Cyclops will make arrows straight away, and for me a well-bent bow. [11] But let me be the Bringer-of-Light,[1] and let me belt on a chiton to the knee, with a colored border so that I can kill wild beasts. And give me sixty daughters of Ocean for my chorus, all nine years old and all unmarried. And give me twenty nymphs, daughters of Amnisus,[2] as attendants, who will take good care of my boots and swift dogs when I am no longer shooting at lynx or deer.

[1] Artemis Phosphorus (*Hymn* 3.204 below; cf. Eur. *IT* 21).

[2] A river in Crete. Callimachus also associates Artemis with the Cretan plain of Amnisus (*Ia*. 202.1). Eileithyia, goddess of childbirth, was also worshipped there as early as the Bronze Age (Linear B tablet KN Gg 705; *Od*. 19.188).

CALLIMACHUS

δὸς δέ μοι οὔρεα πάντα· πόλιν δέ μοι ἥντινα
  νεῖμον
ἥντινα λῇς· σπαρνὸν γὰρ ὅτ᾽ Ἄρτεμις ἄστυ
  κάτεισιν·
20 οὔρεσιν οἰκήσω, πόλεσιν δ᾽ ἐπιμείξομαι ἀνδρῶν
μοῦνον ὅτ᾽ ὀξείῃσιν[4] ὑπ᾽ ὠδίνεσσι γυναῖκες
τειρόμεναι καλέωσι[5] βοηθόον, ᾗσί με Μοῖραι
γεινομένην τὸ πρῶτον ἐπεκλήρωσαν ἀρήγειν,
ὅττι με καὶ τίκτουσα καὶ οὐκ ἤλγησε φέρουσα
25 μήτηρ, ἀλλ᾽ ἀμογητὶ φίλων ἀπεθήκατο γυίων."
  ὣς ἡ παῖς εἰποῦσα γενειάδος ἤθελε πατρός
ἅψασθαι, πολλὰς δὲ μάτην ἐτανύσσατο χεῖρας[6]
μέχρις ἵνα ψαύσειε. πατὴρ δ᾽ ἐπένευσε γελάσσας,
φῆ δὲ καταρρέζων· "ὅτε[7] μοι τοιαῦτα θέαιναι
30 τίκτοιεν, τυτθόν κεν ἐγὼ ζηλήμονος Ἥρης
χωομένης ἀλέγοιμι.[8] φέρευ, τέκος, ὅσσ᾽ ἐθελημός
αἰτίζεις, καὶ δ᾽ ἄλλα πατὴρ ἔτι μείζονα δώσει.
τρὶς δέκα τοι πτολίεθρα καὶ οὐχ ἕνα πύργον
  ὀπάσσω,
τρὶς δέκα τοι πτολίεθρα, τὰ μὴ θεὸν ἄλλον ἀέξειν
35 εἴσεται, ἀλλὰ μόνην σὲ καὶ Ἀρτέμιδος καλέεσθαι·
πολλὰς δὲ ξυνῇ πόλιας διαμετρήσασθαι
μεσσόγεως νήσους τε· καὶ ἐν πάσῃσιν[9] ἔσονται
Ἀρτέμιδος βωμοί τε καὶ ἄλσεα. καὶ μὲν ἀγυιαῖς
ἔσσῃ καὶ λιμένεσσιν ἐπίσκοπος." ὣς ὁ μὲν εἰπών
40 μῦθον ἐπεκρήηνε καρήατι. βαῖνε δὲ κούρη

---

[4] ὀξείῃσιν corr. Pf.: ὀξεσσιν Ψ: ὀξείαισιν BCK La.

236

[18] And give me all the mountains, and give as my share whatever city you want, for seldom will Artemis go down to a city. I will live on the mountains and visit the cities of men only when women suffering from sharp birth pains call for help. For these the fates assigned me from my very birth to bring aid, since my mother when she gave birth to me and carried me did not suffer, but took me from her own womb without pain."

[26] The child speaking in this way wished to touch the beard of her father, but in vain she kept stretching out her hands so that she could grasp it. Her father smiled, nodded assent, and as he stroked her spoke: "When goddesses bear such children to me I care little about the jealousy of angry Hera. Take, child, whatever you ask, heartily, and your father will give you even more. Three times ten cities and not just one tower will I give to you, three times ten cities that will not know how to glorify any other god but you alone, and they will be called 'of Artemis.' And many cities to be shared in common with other gods, inland cities and islands. In all there will be altars and groves of Artemis, and you will be the guardian of streets and harbors." So he spoke, and confirmed his word with a nod of his head.

[40] And the girl went to the white mountain of Crete,

---

5 κ[α]λέωσι *P.Mil.Vogl.* 42 col. II: καλέουσι Ψ

6 ἐτανύσσατο χεῖρας Ψ: aliter *P.Oxy.* 2258A fr. 3 verso

7 οτε *P.Mil.Vogl.* 42 col. II: ὅτε La.: ὅτι Ψ

8 ἀλέγοιμι Ψ: aliter *P.Mil.Vogl.* 42 col. II

9 ἐ]ν[πα]σηι[σιν *P.Mil.Vogl.* 42 col. II, *P.Gen.* inv. 209: ἀπά-σησιν Ψ corr. T in marg.

Λευκὸν ἔπι Κρηταῖον ὄρος κεκομημένον ὕλῃ,
ἔνθεν ἐπ᾽ Ὠκεανόν· πολέας δ᾽ ἐπελέξατο[10] νύμφας,
πάσας εἰνέτεας, πάσας ἔτι παῖδας ἀμίτρους·
χαῖρε δὲ Καίρατος ποταμὸς μέγα, χαῖρε δὲ Τηθύς,
45 οὕνεκα θυγατέρας Λητωίδι πέμπον[11] ἀμορβούς.

    αὖθι δὲ Κύκλωπας μετεκίαθε· τοὺς μὲν ἔτετμε
νήσῳ ἐνὶ Λιπάρῃ (Λιπάρῃ νέον, ἀλλὰ τότ᾽ ἔσκεν
οὕνομά οἱ Μελιγουνίς) ἐπ᾽ ἄκμοσιν[12] Ἡφαίστοιο
ἑσταότας περὶ μύδρον· ἐπείγετο γὰρ μέγα ἔργον·
50 ἱππείην τετύκοντο Ποσειδάωνι ποτίστρην.
αἱ νύμφαι δ᾽ ἔδδεισαν, ὅπως ἴδον αἰνὰ πέλωρα
πρηόσιν Ὀσσαίοισιν[13] ἐοικότα (πᾶσι δ᾽ ὑπ᾽ ὀφρύν
φάεα μουνόγληνα σάκει ἴσα τετραβοείῳ
δεινὸν ὑπογλαύσσοντα) καὶ ὁππότε δοῦπον ἄκουσαν
55 ἄκμονος ἠχήσαντος ἐπὶ[14] μέγα πουλύ τ᾽ ἄημα
φυσάων αὐτῶν τε βαρὺν στόνον· αὖε γὰρ Αἴτνη,
αὖε δὲ Τρινακρίη[15] Σικανῶν ἕδος, αὖε δὲ γείτων
Ἰταλίη, μεγάλην δὲ βοὴν ἐπὶ Κύρνος ἀύτει,

---

10 ἐπελέξατο Ψ: ἀπ[ε]λεξαο P.Gen. inv. 209
11 πέμπον Schol. ad Nic. Th. 349: πέμπεν Ψ, P.Gen. inv. 209
12 ἄκμοσιν Ψ, P.Gen. inv. 209:]οσ P.Mil.Vogl. 42 col. II,
ἄκμον]ος prop. Pfeiffer   13 Ὀσσαίοισιν corr. Meineke:
Ὀσσαίοις P.Ant. 20 recto: Ὀσσείοισιν Ψ
14 ἐπὶ T in marg.: ἐπεὶ Ψ   15]ινακριη P.Ant. 20 recto,
Τρινακρίη E in marg., η: Τρινακίη Ψ

---

3 A river in Crete and an ancient name of Cnossus (Strabo
10.4.8).

coiffed with woods, and from there to Ocean. And she chose many nymphs all nine years old, all unmarried girls. And the river Caeratus[3] was happy in a big way, and Tethys[4] rejoiced because they were sending their daughters as attendants to the daughter of Leto.[5]

[46] Then she visited the Cyclopes. And she found them on the island of Lipare[6] (modern-day Lipare, but then its name was Meligunis) at the anvils of Hephaestus, standing around a mass of molten metal. They were rushing to finish a big project. They were making a horse trough for Poseidon. The nymphs were afraid when they saw the monsters, dreadful like the crags of Ossa[7] (for under their brows all had a single eye as big as a shield of four bull hides, glancing terribly from under), and when they heard the crash of the anvil echoing mightily, the great blast of the bellows, and their deep groaning. For Etna[8] cried out and Trinacria, the seat of the Sicani,[9] shouted, their neighbor Italy screamed, and Cyrnus[10] gave

[4] Sister and wife of Ocean (*Hymn* 4.17; Ap. Rhod. 3.244); daughter of Gaea and Uranus (Hes. *Theog.* 132–36).

[5] Daughter of Phoebe and Coeus (Hes. *Theog.* 404–8; *Hymn. Hom. Ap.* 3.62). Mother of Artemis and Apollo (*Hymn* 4.326).

[6] Island near Sicily and Hiera, where Hephaestus was thought to have his forge (Thuc. 3.88.2–3; *Aet.* 113e).

[7] Mountain in Thessaly. Otis and Ephialtes tried to reach the heavens by piling Ossa on Olympus and Pelion on Ossa (Apollod. *Bibl.* 1.7.4).

[8] An active volcano in Sicily (*Hymn* 4.141) and another site of Hephaestus' forge (Aesch. *PV* 365–74; Pind. *Pyth.* 1.20–28).

[9] First settlers of Sicily after the Cyclopes and the Laestrygonians (Thuc. 6.2.1–2). They named the island Sicania, but its ancient name was Trinacria.   [10] Ancient Corsica (Hdt. 1.165).

εὖθ᾽ οἵγε ῥαιστῆρας ἀειράμενοι ὑπὲρ ὤμων
60 ἢ χαλκὸν ζείοντα καμινόθεν ἠὲ σίδηρον
ἀμβολαδὶς τετύποντες ἐπὶ[16] μέγα μυχθίσσειαν.[17]
    τῷ σφέας οὐκ ἐτάλασσαν ἀκηδέες Ὠκεανῖναι
οὔτ᾽ ἄντην ἰδέειν οὔτε κτύπον οὔασι δέχθαι.
οὐ νέμεσις· κείνους γε καὶ αἱ μάλα μηκέτι τυτθαί
65 οὐδέποτ᾽ ἀφρικτὶ μακάρων ὁρόωσι θύγατρες.
ἀλλ᾽ ὅτε κουράων τις ἀπειθέα μητέρι τεύχοι,
μήτηρ μὲν Κύκλωπας ἑῇ ἐπὶ παιδὶ καλιστρεῖ,
Ἄργην ἢ Στερόπην· ὁ δὲ δώματος ἐκ μυχάτοιο
ἔρχεται Ἑρμείης σποδιῇ κεχριμένος[18] αἰθῇ·
70 αὐτίκα τὴν κούρην μορμύσσεται, ἡ δὲ τεκούσης
δύνει ἔσω κόλπους θεμένη ἐπὶ φάεσι χεῖρας.
    κούρα, σὺ δὲ προτέρω περ, ἔτι τριέτηρος ἐοῦσα,
εὖτ᾽ ἔμολεν Λητώ σε μετ᾽ ἀγκαλίδεσσι φέρουσα,
Ἡφαίστου καλέοντος ὅπως ὀπτήρια δοίη,
75 Βρόντεώ σε στιβαροῖσιν ἐφεσσαμένου γονάτεσσι,
στήθεος ἐκ μεγάλου λασίης ἐδράξαο χαίτης,
ὤλοψας δὲ βίηφι· τὸ δ᾽ ἄτριχον εἰσέτι καὶ νῦν
μεσσάτιον στέρνοιο μένει μέρος, ὡς ὅτε κόρσῃ[19]
φωτὸς ἐνιδρυθεῖσα κόμην ἐπενείματ᾽ ἀλώπηξ.
80 τῷ μάλα θαρσαλέη σφε τάδε προσελέξαο[20]
    τῆμος·
"Κύκλωπες, κἠμοί[21] τι Κυδώνιον εἰ δ᾽ ἄγε τόξον

---

[16] ἐπὶ corr. Stephanus: ἐπεὶ Ψ
[17] μυχθίσσειαν corr. Meineke: μυχθίσσαιεν P.Ant.: μοχθίσσειαν Ψ: μοχθήσειαν a La.
[18] κεχριμένος E, T in marg.: κεχρημένος Ψ

240

out a great noise, when lifting their hammers above their shoulders, and laboring greatly, they struck with a rhythmic swing the bronze sizzling from the furnace or the iron.

[62] And so the daughters of Ocean did not dare look them in the face without concern, nor bear the din in their ears. No blame for that: the daughters of the blessed ones never look at them without fear even when they are no longer small. When one of the girls would disobey her mother, the mother would call in the Cyclopes, Arges or Steropes,[11] to her daughter, and from the innermost chamber of the house Hermes would come, smeared with burned ashes. At once he frightens the girl and she sinks into the lap of her mother, putting her hands over her eyes.

[72] And you, girl, were even younger, only three years old, when Leto came carrying you in her arms at the bidding of Hephaestus so that he could give you presents, and Brontes set you on his sturdy knees, you grasped the shaggy hair from his great chest and plucked it out by force. And the midpart of his chest remains hairless even now, just as when the mange settling onto the temples of a man eats away at his hair.

[80] Therefore very boldly did you address them this way: "Cyclopes, for me too make something Cydonian,[12]

---

[11] Two of the three Cyclopes whose names are listed by Hesiod (*Theog.* 139–40). The third, Brontes, appears below (*Hymn* 3.75).

[12] Cretan (Schol.). For Cydonian bows, cf. *Fr. Inc. Sed.* 560.

---

19 κόρσῃ T in marg., Bentley: κόρσην Ψ, Mair

20 προσελέξαο E: προσελέξατο Ψ

21 κῆμοί corr. Meineke: καιμο[ι P.Gen. inv. 209: κἀμοι L in marg.: ἢ ἤ μοί Ψ

ἠδ᾽ ἰοὺς κοίλην τε κατακληῖδα βελέμνων
τεύξατε· καὶ γὰρ ἐγὼ Λητωιὰς ὥσπερ Ἀπόλλων.
αἱ δέ κ᾽ ἐγὼ τόξοις μονιὸν δάκος ἤ τι πέλωρον
85 θηρίον ἀγρεύσω, τὸ δέ κεν Κύκλωπες ἔδοιεν."
ἔννεπες· οἱ δ᾽ ἐτέλεσσαν· ἄφαρ δ᾽ ὡπλίσσαο,
     δαῖμον.
    αἶψα δ᾽ ἐπὶ σκύλακας πάλιν ἤιες· ἵκεο δ᾽ αὖλιν
Ἀρκαδικὴν ἔπι Πανός. ὁ δὲ κρέα λυγκὸς ἔταμνε
Μαιναλίης, ἵνα οἱ τοκάδες κύνες εἶδαρ ἔδοιεν.
90 τὶν δ᾽ ὁ γενειήτης δύο μὲν κύνας ἥμισυ πηγούς,
τρεῖς δὲ παρουαίους,[22] ἕνα δ᾽ αἰόλον, οἵ ῥα λέοντας
αὐτοὺς αὖ ἐρύοντες, ὅτε δράξαιντο δεράων,
εἷλκον[23] ἔτι ζώοντας ἐπ᾽ αὔλιον, ἑπτὰ δ᾽ ἔδωκε
θάσσονας αὐράων Κυνοσουρίδας, αἵ ῥα διῶξαι
95 ὤκισται νεβρούς τε καὶ οὐ μύοντα λαγωόν
καὶ κοίτην ἐλάφοιο καὶ ὑστριχος ἔνθα καλιαί
σημῆναι καὶ ζορκὸς ἐπ᾽ ἴχνιον ἡγήσασθαι.
    ἔνθεν ἀπερχομένη (μετὰ καὶ κύνες ἐσσεύοντο)
εὗρες ἐπὶ προμολῆσ᾽ ὄρεος τοῦ Παρρασίοιο
100 σκαιρούσας ἐλάφους, μέγα τι χρέος· αἱ μὲν ἐπ᾽
        ὄχθης[24]
αἰὲν ἐβουκολέοντο μελαμψήφιδος Ἀναύρου,
μάσσονες ἢ ταῦροι, κεράων δ᾽ ἀπελάμπετο χρυσός·
ἐξαπίνης δ᾽ ἔταφές τε καὶ ὃν ποτὶ θυμὸν ἔειπες·

---

[22] παρουαίους em. Schneider: παρουατίους Ψ
[23] εἷλκον T in marg.: εἷλον Ψ
[24] ὄχθης αβγ: ὄχθης δζη

whether it is a bow or arrows or a hollow container for
them! For I am a child of Leto like Apollo, and if I ever
hunt with bows a wild animal or some monstrous beast,
the Cyclopes will eat it." You spoke, and they brought it to
pass.

[87] And at once, Goddess, you armed yourself, and at
once you returned to your dogs. And you went to the Ar-
cadian hut of Pan. He was cutting the meat of a Maena-
lian[13] lynx so that the breeding bitches could eat it for
food. And the bearded[14] one gave you two half-white dogs,
three chestnut, one speckled, which take down even lions,
when they grasp them by the throat, and drag them still
living to the fold. He gave seven Cynosurian[15] dogs, faster
than the winds, which are the swiftest to pursue fawns and
the hare who never sleeps; and to mark out the lair of the
stag, and the burrows of the porcupine, and to lead on the
track of the gazelle.

[98] And departing from there, with the hounds follow-
ing, you found, on the approaches to Mt. Parrasius,[16] frisk-
ing deer, a great herd, which always pastured on the banks
of the black-pebbled Anaurus,[17] larger than bulls, and
from their horns shone gold. And at once you were aston-
ished and spoke to your own heart, "This would be a first

---

[13] Maenalus is a Mt. in Arcadia. (Pind. *Ol.* 9.59; Ap. Rhod.
1.168).

[14] Pan's beard (*Hymn. Hom. Pan* 19.39).

[15] Spartan (Schol.).

[16] In Arcadia (Schol. ad Call. *Hymn* 1.10; Hesych. s.v. Παρ-
ράσιον).

[17] In Thessaly. Jason carried the disguised Hera across it (Ap.
Rhod. 3.67–73).

CALLIMACHUS

"τοῦτό κεν Ἀρτέμιδος πρωτάγριον ἄξιον εἴη."

105 πέντ' ἔσαν αἱ πᾶσαι· πίσυρας δ' ἕλες ὦκα θέουσα
νόσφι κυνοδρομίης, ἵνα τοι θοὸν ἅρμα φέρωσι.
τὴν δὲ μίαν Κελάδοντος ὑπὲρ ποταμοῖο φυγοῦσαν
Ἥρης ἐννεσίῃσιν, ἀέθλιον Ἡρακλῆι
ὕστερον²⁵ ὄφρα γένοιτο, πάγος Κερύνειος²⁶ ἔδεκτο.

110 Ἄρτεμι Παρθενίη Τιτυοκτόνε, χρύσεα μέν τοι
ἔντεα καὶ ζώνη, χρύσεον δ' ἐζεύξαο δίφρον,
ἐν δ' ἐβάλευ χρύσεια, θεή, κεμάδεσσι χαλινά.
ποῦ δέ σε τὸ πρῶτον κερόεις ὄχος ἦρξατ' ἀείρειν;
Αἵμῳ ἐπὶ Θρήικι, τόθεν βορέαο κάταιξ
115 ἔρχεται ἀχλαίνοισι δυσαέα κρυμὸν ἄγουσα.
ποῦ δ' ἔταμες πεύκην, ἀπὸ δὲ φλογὸς ἥψαο ποίης;
Μυσῷ ἐν Οὐλύμπῳ, φάεος δ' ἐνέηκας αὐτμήν
ἀσβέστου, τό ῥα πατρὸς ἀποστάζουσι κεραυνοί.
ποσσάκι δ' ἀργυρέοιο, θεή, πειρήσαο τόξου;
120 πρῶτον ἐπὶ πτελέην, τὸ δὲ δεύτερον ἧκας ἐπὶ δρῦν,
τὸ τρίτον αὖτ' ἐπὶ θῆρα. τὸ τέτρατον οὐκέτ' †ἐπὶ
δρῦν†,²⁷
ἀλλά †μιν²⁸ εἰς ἀδίκων ἔβαλες πόλιν, οἵ τε περὶ
σφέας

²⁵ ὕστερον Schol. ad Ap. Rhod. 1.996: ὕστατον Ψ
²⁶ Κερύνειος P.Amh. 20, Ψ: Κεραύνιος Schol. ad Ap. Rhod.
1.996, La.
²⁷ Repetitum e fine v. 120 in Ψ: ἔπαισας vel ἔπαιξας prop.
Barber. Post v. 121 versum excidisse suspicati sunt Schneider,
Wilamowitz, et al.
²⁸ Corruptum nisi versus deest.

catch worthy of Artemis." There were five in all. Running swiftly you took four, without the dogs giving chase, to pull your swift chariot. One fled across the Celadonian[18] river, at the suggestion of Hera, so that it could be a future labor for Heracles. And the Ceryneian[19] hill received her.

[110] Artemis, Maiden, Slayer of Tityus,[20] golden was your gear and belt, and you yoked a chariot of gold. On to the deer you fit golden bridles, Goddess. And where first did your horned team begin to carry you? To Thracian Haemus[21] from where the gusts of Boreas come bringing an ill-blowing frost to the cloakless. Where did you cut the pine, and from what flame did you kindle it? On Mysian[22] Olympus, and you put in it the breath of unquenchable fire, which the thunderbolts of your father distill.

[119] How often, goddess, did you put your silver bow to the test? First at an elm, and second you shot at an oak, third at a wild beast, and the fourth time not at an oak, but you shot at a city of unjust men, who committed many

---

[18] In western Arcadia (Hom. *Il.* 7.133), tributary of the Alpheus, which Heracles crossed when he chased Artemis' Ceryneian hind (Paus. 8.38.9).

[19] One of the labors of Heracles required that he bring the Ceryneian hind to Mycenae alive. It had golden horns and was sacred to Artemis (Pind. *Ol.* 3.26–30).

[20] A giant who assaulted Leto (Hom. *Od.* 11.576–81) while on the way to Pytho. He was killed by Artemis (Pind. *Pyth.* 4.90–91) or Apollo (Ap. Rhod. 1.759–62).

[21] The "bloody" mountain in Thrace near which Typhon fought Zeus (Apollod. *Bibl.* 1.6.3).

[22] The Mt. Olympus in northwestern Anatolia (Hdt. 1.36).

οἵ τε περὶ ξείνους ἀλιτήμονα πολλὰ τέλεσκον.
σχέτλιοι, οἷς τύνη χαλεπὴν ἐμμάξεαι ὀργήν·
125 κτήνεά φιν λοιμὸς²⁹ καταβόσκεται, ἔργα δὲ πάχνη,
κείρονται δὲ γέροντες ἐφ' υἱάσιν, αἱ δὲ γυναῖκες
ἢ βληταὶ θνήσκουσι λεχωίδες ἠὲ φυγοῦσαι
τίκτουσιν τῶν οὐδὲν ἐπὶ σφυρὸν ὀρθὸν ἀνέστη.

οἷς δέ κεν εὐμειδής τε καὶ ἵλαος αὐγάσσηαι,
130 κείνοις εὖ μὲν ἄρουρα φέρει στάχυν, εὖ δὲ γενέθλη
τετραπόδων, εὖ δ' οἶκος³⁰ ἀέξεται· οὐδ' ἐπὶ σῆμα
ἔρχονται πλὴν εὖτε πολυχρόνιόν τι φέρωσιν·
οὐδὲ διχοστασίη τρώει γένος, ἥ τε καὶ εὖ περ
οἴκους ἑστηῶτας ἐσίνατο· ταὶ δὲ θυωρόν
135 εἰνάτερες γαλόῳ τε μίαν πέρι δίφρα τίθενται.
πότνια, τῶν εἴη μὲν ἐμοὶ φίλος ὅστις ἀληθής,
εἴην δ' αὐτός, ἄνασσα, μέλοι δέ μοι αἰὲν ἀοιδή·
    τῇ ἔνι μὲν Λητοῦς γάμος ἔσσεται, ἐν δὲ σὺ
        πολλή,
ἐν δὲ καὶ Ἀπόλλων, ἐν δ' οἵ σεο πάντες ἄεθλοι,
140 ἐν δὲ κύνες καὶ τόξα καὶ ἄντυγες, αἵ τε σε ῥεῖα
θηητὴν φορέουσιν ὅτ' ἐς Διὸς οἶκον ἐλαύνεις.
ἔνθα τοι ἀντιόωντες ἐνὶ προμολῇσι δέχονται
ὅπλα μὲν Ἑρμείης Ἀκακήσιος, αὐτὰρ Ἀπόλλων
θηρίον ὅττι φέρῃσθα–πάροιθέ γε, πρίν περ ἱκέσθαι
145 καρτερὸν Ἀλκείδην· νῦν δ' οὐκέτι Φοῖβος³¹ ἄεθλον

---

²⁹ λοιμὸς η, E: λιμὸς Ψ   ³⁰ οἶκος Meineke (cf. Hes.
Op. 244): ὄλβος Ψ   ³¹ φ[οιβοσαεθλο]ντουτον P.Amh. 20:
τοῦτον ἄεθλον φοῖβος Ψ

246

sinful acts against one another and against foreigners, wicked men on whom you would inflict your terrible anger. Plague feeds on their cattle, frost, on their fieldwork, old men cut their hair for their sons, and the women are either struck down in childbirth and perish, or avoiding that, bear none but those who do not stand straight on their ankles.

[129] But those on whom you look smiling and gracious, their field bears corn in abundance, abundant is their stock of four-footed beasts, and their wealth increases abundantly. Nor do they go to the cemetery except when they bring the very old. Nor does discord, which has harmed even well-established houses, ruin the family, but brothers' wives and sisters-in-law[23] set their chairs around one sacrificial table. Among these, Queen, may he be whoever is my true friend, and of these may I be myself, Queen, and may song always be my care.

[138] And in my song will be the marriage of Leto, and you will be in it often, and Apollo will be in it, and all of your accomplishments, and the dogs and the bow will be in it, and your chariots, which easily carry you spectacularly when you drive to the house of Zeus. And there, meeting you in the entrance, Hermes Acacesios[24] takes your armor, and Apollo, whatever beast you bring—in the past, that is, before the strong son of Alcides[25] arrived. But

---

[23] The kinship terms are Homeric (*Il.* 6.378).

[24] Epithet of Hermes, perhaps equivalent to Hermes ἀκά-κητα, the "gracious one" (Hom. *Il.* 16.185, *Od.* 24.10; Hes. fr. 137.1 M.-W.).

[25] Heracles. He was named Alcides or Alcaeus for his grandfather Alcaeus (Apollod. *Bibl.* 2.4.12).

τοῦτον ἔχει, τοῖος γὰρ ἀεὶ Τιρύνθιος ἄκμων
ἔστηκε πρὸ πυλέων ποτιδέγμενος, εἴ τι φέρουσα
    νεῖαι πῖον ἔδεσμα· θεοὶ δ' ἐπὶ πάντες ἐκείνῳ
ἄλληκτον γελόωσι, μάλιστα δὲ πενθερὴ αὐτή,
150 ταῦρον ὅτ' ἐκ δίφροιο μάλα μέγαν ἢ ὅγε[32] χλούνην
κάπρον ὀπισθιδίοιο φέροι ποδὸς ἀσπαίροντα·
κερδαλέῳ μύθῳ σε, θεή, μάλα τῷδε πινύσκει·
"βάλλε κακοὺς ἐπὶ θῆρας, ἵνα θνητοί σε βοηθὸν
ὡς ἐμὲ κικλήσκωσιν. ἔα πρόκας ἠδὲ λαγωοὺς
155 οὔρεα βόσκεσθαι· τί δέ[33] κεν πρόκες ἠδὲ λαγωοὶ
ῥέξειαν; σύες ἔργα, σύες φυτὰ λυμαίνονται.
καὶ βόες ἀνθρώποισι κακὸν μέγα· βάλλ' ἐπὶ καὶ
    τούς."
ὣς ἔνεπεν, ταχινὸς δὲ μέγαν περὶ θῆρα πονεῖτο.
οὐ γὰρ ὅγε Φρυγίη περ ὑπὸ δρυὶ γυῖα θεωθεὶς
160 παύσατ' ἀδηφαγίης· ἔτι οἱ πάρα νηδὺς ἐκείνη,
τῇ ποτ' ἀροτριόωντι συνήντετο Θειοδάμαντι.
    σοὶ δ' Ἀμνισιάδες μὲν ὑπὸ ζεύγληφι λυθείσας
ψήχουσιν κεμάδας, παρὰ δέ σφισι πουλὺ νέμεσθαι
Ἥρης ἐκ λειμῶνος ἀμησάμεναι φορέουσιν
165 ὠκύθοον[34] τριπέτηλον, ὃ καὶ Διὸς ἵπποι ἔδουσιν·
ἐν καὶ χρυσείας ὑποληνίδας ἐπλήσαντο
ὕδατος, ὄφρ' ἐλάφοισι ποτὸν θυμάρμενον εἴη.
    αὐτὴ δ' ἐς πατρὸς δόμον ἔρχεαι· οἱ δέ σ' ἐφ'
    ἕδρην

---

[32] ὅγε corr. La.: ὅτε Ψ   [33] τί δέ κεν La.: τί κεν Ψ
[34] ὠκύθοον Hesych.: ὠκύθεον Ψ, P.Ant. 179

now no longer does Phoebus have this task, for in that role an anvil of Tiryns[26] stands before the gates, waiting to see if you come bringing some fat tidbit.

[148] And all the gods laugh at him endlessly, especially his own mother-in-law,[27] when he carries a very large bull from the car, or a wild boar by the hind foot, gasping. And with this clever speech he admonishes you, Goddess, "Shoot at evil beasts, so that mortals may call you a helper, as they call me. Let the deer and the rabbits feed on the mountains. What harm could deer or rabbits do? Boars ravage cultivated land, boars destroy crops, and oxen are a great bane of humanity. Shoot at them!" So he spoke, and quickly he set to work on the great beast. Though his limbs were deified under a Phrygian oak[28] he has not ceased from gluttony. He still has the belly with which he once met the plowman Thiodamas.[29]

[162] For you the daughters of Amnisus rub down the hinds loosed from the yoke, and for them they distribute much quick-growing clover, gathering and carrying it from the meadow of Hera, clover that the horses of Zeus also eat. And they fill the golden troughs with water so that the deer would have a heart-pleasing drink.

[168] And you yourself go into the house of your father.

---

[26] City in the Argolid where Heracles' tormenter Eurystheus was king (Hom. *Il.* 19.122–33).

[27] Hera, the mother of Heracles' wife, Hebe (Hom. *Od.* 11.601–4).

[28] Where Heracles was immolated in Trachis (Schol.).

[29] King of the Dryopes, whose oxen Heracles slaughtered to feed his hungry son Hyllus (*Aet.* 24–25d; Ap. Rhod. 1.1211–14).

CALLIMACHUS

πάντες ὁμῶς καλέουσι· σὺ δ᾽ Ἀπόλλωνι παρίζεις.
170 ἡνίκα δ᾽ αἱ νύμφαι σε χορῷ ἔνι κυκλώσονται
ἀγχόθι πηγάων Αἰγυπτίου Ἰνωποῖο
ἢ Πιτάνη (καὶ γὰρ Πιτάνη σέθεν) ἢ ἐνὶ Λίμναις,
ἢ ἵνα, δαῖμον, Ἁλὰς Ἀραφηνίδας οἰκήσουσα
ἦλθες ἀπὸ Σκυθίης, ἀπὸ δ᾽ εἴπαο τέθμια Ταύρων,
175 μὴ νειὸν τημοῦτος ἐμαὶ βόες εἵνεκα μισθοῦ
τετράγυον τέμνοιεν ὑπ᾽ ἀλλοτρίῳ ἀροτῆρι·
ἦ γάρ κεν γυιαί τε καὶ αὐχένα κεκμηυῖαι
κόπρον ἔπι προγένοιντο, καὶ εἰ Στυμφαίιδες εἶεν
εἰναετιζόμεναι κεραελκέες, αἳ μέγ᾽ ἄρισται
180 τέμνειν ὦλκα βαθεῖαν· ἐπεὶ θεὸς οὔποτ᾽ ἐκεῖνον
ἦλθε παρ᾽ Ἥλιος καλὸν χορόν, ἀλλὰ θεῆται
δίφρον ἐπιστήσας, τὰ δὲ φάεα μηκύνονται.
  τίς δέ νύ τοι νήσων, ποῖον δ᾽ ὄρος εὔαδε
    πλεῖστον,
  τίς δὲ λιμήν, ποίη δὲ πόλις; τίνα δ᾽ ἔξοχα[35] νυμφέων
185 φίλαο καὶ ποίας ἡρωίδας ἔσχες ἑταίρας;
εἰπέ, θεή, σὺ μὲν ἄμμιν, ἐγὼ δ᾽ ἑτέροισιν ἀείσω.

[35] ἔξοχα I, S: ἔξοχον Ψ

---

[30] A river of Delos said to be fed by the Nile (*Hymn* 4.206).
[31] City on the Eurotas near Sparta featuring a shrine of Artemis (Paus. 3.16.9).
[32] Athenian Limnae (Schol.) or Limnae in Sparta, where rites of Artemis were held (Paus. 3.16.9).
[33] Attic deme with a temple of Artemis Tauropolus (Strabo 9.1.22).

250

And all the gods offer you a seat, but you sit beside Apollo. But when the nymphs circle you in the dance, near the fountains of Egyptian Inopus,[30] or Pitane[31] (for Pitane is yours), or in Limnae,[32] or when, Goddess, you came from Scythia to dwell in Alae Araphenides,[33] renouncing the rites of the Taurians.[34] Then may my bulls not plow four *guai* of fallow land[35] for a wage from a foreign plowman, or else surely lame and weary in the neck they would come to the dunghill, even if they were Stymphaeans[36] nine years old, drawing by the horns, which are much the best to plow a deep furrow. For the god Helios[37] never passes by the lovely dance, but stops his chariot to watch, and the light of day grows longer.

[183] Now what islands are yours? What mountain pleases you the most? What lake? What city? Which of the nymphs do you love the most? And what heroines do you have as companions? Tell me, Goddess, and what you tell me I will sing to others. Of islands, Doliche,[38] of cities

---

[34] Human sacrifices for Artemis (Hdt. 4.103).

[35] A *guas* is a measure of land, and this verse is a reference to a Homeric passage (*Od.* 18.366–75) in which Odysseus challenges Eurymachus to a plowing contest on a field of the same size.

[36] Proverbially cows from Epirus so large one had to stand to milk them (Ar. *Hist. an.* 522b14–25).

[37] The sun god (*Hymn. Hom. Hel.* 31.1–19). The speed of his journey across the sky determines the length of the day.

[38] An island among the Sporades once named Icarus or Icaria by Heracles after Icarus, son of Daedalus, who landed there after he flew too near the sun during an escape from Crete (Apollod. *Bibl.* 2.6.3). There was a shrine there of Artemis Tauropolis (Strabo 14.1.19).

CALLIMACHUS

νήσων μὲν Δολίχη, πολίων δέ τοι εὔαδε Πέργη,
Τηΰγετον δ' ὀρέων, λιμένες γε μὲν Εὐρίποιο.
ἔξοχα δ' ἀλλάων Γορτυνίδα φίλαο νύμφην,
190 ἐλλοφόνον Βριτόμαρτιν εὔσκοπον· ἧς ποτε Μίνως
πτοιηθεὶς ὑπ' ἔρωτι κατέδραμεν οὔρεα Κρήτης.
ἡ δ' ὁτὲ³⁶ μὲν λασίῃσιν ὑπὸ δρυσὶ κρύπτετο νύμφη,
ἄλλοτε δ' εἰαμενῇσιν· ὁ δ' ἐννέα μῆνας ἐφοίτα
παίπαλά τε κρημνούς τε καὶ οὐκ ἀνέπαυσε διωκτύν,
195 μέσφ' ὅτε μαρπτομένη καὶ δὴ σχεδὸν ἥλατο πόντον
πρηόνος ἐξ ὑπάτοιο καὶ ἔνθορεν εἰς ἁλιήων
δίκτυα, τά σφ' ἐσάωσαν· ὅθεν μετέπειτα Κύδωνες
νύμφην μὲν Δίκτυναν, ὄρος δ' ὅθεν ἥλατο νύμφη
Δικταῖον καλέουσιν, ἀνεστήσαντο δὲ βωμοὺς
200 ἱερά τε ῥέζουσι· τὸ δὲ στέφος ἤματι κείνῳ
ἢ πίτυς ἢ σχῖνος, μύρτοιο δὲ χεῖρες ἄθικτοι·
δὴ τότε γὰρ πέπλοισιν ἐνέσχετο μύρσινος ὄζος
τῆς κούρης, ὅτ' ἔφευγεν· ὅθεν μέγα χώσατο μύρτῳ.
Οὖπι ἄνασσ' εὐῶπι φαεσφόρε, καὶ δέ σε κείνης
205 Κρηταέες καλέουσιν ἐπωνυμίην ἀπὸ νύμφης.

---

³⁶ ὁτὲ E, I: ὅτε Ψ

---

39 A city in Pamphylia possessing a well-known temple of Artemis (Strabo 14.4.2).

40 Where Artemis hunted boars (Hom. *Od.* 6.102–4).

41 The port of the city of Muniche on the strait near Aulis with a temple of Artemis containing two marble statues and relics of the visit of Agamemnon and his fleet before their departure for Troy (Paus. 9.19.6).

Perge[39] is pleasing to you, of mountains, Taygeton,[40] of harbors, Euripus.[41]

[189] Above the others, you love the nymph of Gortyn,[42] fawn-slaying Britomartis,[43] the keen sighted, for love of whom Minos, distraught, roamed the mountains of Crete. But the nymph would hide under the bushy oaks and sometimes in the wetlands, and for nine months he ranged about the crags and the cliffs and did not stop the pursuit until almost caught, she leaped into the sea from the top of the headland, and sprang into the nets of the fishermen, which saved her. From this thereafter they call the nymph Dictyna, and the mountain from which the nymph leaped, Dictaeon, and they established altars and perform holy rites. And the garland on that day is pine or mastic, but the hands are untouched by myrtle. For a branch of myrtle had been caught in the girl's dress as she fled, hence she was greatly angered at the myrtle. And Queen Upis[44] of the radiant face, the Cretans name you too after the nymph.

[42] A city in Crete founded by Gortys of Tegea that had rejected Leto when she was looking for a place to give birth to Apollo. Gortys left Tegea following a visit from Apollo and Artemis (Paus. 8.53.1–4).

[43] A Minoan-Mycenean goddess identified with Artemis the Huntress (Eur. *Hipp.* 1130, *IT* 126–27; Aristoph. *Ran.* 1358–59). The story of Minos' pursuit is in Strabo 10.4.12.

[44] *Hymn* 4.292. A cult name shared by Artemis and a Hyperborean maiden closely connected with her, who was remembered with rites and hymns in Delos (Hdt. 4.35).

CALLIMACHUS

καὶ μὴν Κυρήνην ἑταρίσσαο, τῇ ποτ' ἔδωκας
αὐτὴ θηρητῆρε δύω κύνε, τοῖς ἔνι κούρη
Ὑψηὶς παρὰ τύμβον Ἰώλκιον ἔμμορ' ἀέθλου.
καὶ Κεφάλου ξανθὴν ἄλοχον Δηιονίδαο,
210 πότνια, σὴν ὁμόθηρον ἐθήκαο· καὶ δέ σέ φασι
καλὴν Ἀντίκλειαν ἴσον φαέεσσι φιλῆσαι.
αἱ πρῶται θοὰ τόξα καὶ ἀμφ' ὤμοισι φαρέτρας
ἰοδόκους ἐφόρησαν· †ἀσύλλωτοι[37] δέ φιν ὦμοι
δεξιτεροὶ καὶ γυμνὸς ἀεὶ παρεφαίνετο μαζός.
215 ἤνησας δ' ἔτι πάγχυ ποδορρώρην Ἀταλάντην
κούρην Ἰασίοιο συοκτόνον Ἀρκασίδαο,
καί ἑ κυνηλασίην τε καὶ εὐστοχίην ἐδίδαξας.
οὔ μιν ἐπίκλητοι Καλυδωνίου ἀγρευτῆρες
μέμφονται κάπροιο· τὰ γὰρ σημήια νίκης
220 Ἀρκαδίην εἰσῆλθεν, ἔχει δ' ἔτι θηρὸς ὀδόντας·
οὐδὲ μὲν Ὑλαῖόν τε καὶ ἄφρονα Ῥοῖκον ἔολπα
οὐδέ περ ἐχθαίροντας ἐν Ἄϊδι μωμήσασθαι
τοξότιν· οὐ γάρ σφιν λαγόνες συνεπιψεύσονται,
τάων Μαιναλίη νᾶεν φόνῳ ἀκρώρεια.

37 ἀσύλλωτοι Ψ: ἀσύλωτοι La. η: ἀσίλλωτοι prop. Mair

45 Nymph who became the wife of Apollo after killing a lion
either in Thessaly or at the site of the city of Cyrene in Libya,
birthplace of Callimachus (Hes. fr. 215 M.-W.; *Hymn* 2.90–92).
46 Father of Cyrene and king of the Lapithae (Pind. *Pyth.*
9.12–17).   47 The tomb of Pelias (Schol.), king of Iolcus in
Thessaly. Perhaps it was a prize in a footrace.
48 Procris, daughter of Erechtheus (Paus. 9.19.1), a huntress
to whom Artemis gave a dog that never lost his prey and a javelin

[206] And you chose Cyrene[45] as a comrade, to whom you yourself once gave two hunting dogs, with which the daughter of Hypseus[46] won a prize beside the Iolcian[47] tomb. And the blond wife of Cephalus,[48] son of Deioneus, Queen, you made your fellow hunter. And they say that you loved lovely Anticleia[49] as much as your own eyes. These first carried the swift bows and the arrow-holding quivers on their shoulders, the quiver strap slung over the right shoulder, and one breast always exposed.

[215] And you amply praised swift-footed Atalanta,[50] the boar-slayer, daughter of Arcadian Iasius,[51] and taught her hunting with dogs and good archery. Nor did those invited to hunt the Calydonian boar fault her, for the victory prizes came into Arcadia, which still has the tusks of the beast.[52] Nor would Hylaeus and witless Rhoecus[53] although hating her in Hades, find fault, I daresay, with her archery. For their flanks that watered the Maenalian[54] peaks with their gore will not join them in falsehood.

that never missed its mark to woo back her husband, Cephalus, who was having an affair with Eos, the Dawn (Hyg. *Fab*. 189; Ov. *Met*. 7.694–757). Deioneus was the son of Aeolus and ruler of Phocis (Apollod. *Bibl*. 1.9.4).   [49] Mother of Odysseus (Hom. *Od*. 11.85), but perhaps this reference is to another Anticleia.

[50] Participant in the famous hunt of the Calydonian boar who was the first to hit it and won the prize of honor, the head and the hide (Paus. 8.45.2).

[51] Son of Lycurgus, king of Arcadia (Apollod. *Bibl*. 3.9.2).

[52] The tusks were displayed in a temple of Athena Alea in Tegea but were later carried off by the emperor Augustus (Paus. 8.46.1).   [53] Centaurs who insulted Atalanta and were killed by her (Apollod. *Bibl*. 3.9.2).

[54] An area in Arcadia (Paus. 3.11.7) associated with Atalanta (Eur. *Phoen*. 1162; Ap. Rhod. 1.769–70).

CALLIMACHUS

225   πότνια πουλυμέλαθρε, πολύπτολι, χαῖρε, Χιτώνη
Μιλήτῳ ἐπίδημε· σὲ γὰρ ποιήσατο Νηλεύς
ἡγεμόνην, ὅτε νηυσὶν ἀνήγετο Κεκροπίηθεν.
Χησιὰς Ἰμβρασίη πρωτόθρονε, σοὶ δ' Ἀγαμέμνων
πηδάλιον νηὸς σφετέρης ἐγκάτθετο νηῷ

230   μείλιον ἀπλοΐης, ὅτε οἱ κατέδησας ἀήτας,
Τευκρῶν ἡνίκα νῆες Ἀχαιίδες ἄστεα κήδειν
ἔπλεον ἀμφ' Ἑλένῃ Ῥαμνουσίδι θυμωθεῖσαι.

    ἦ μέν τοι Προῖτός γε δύω ἐκαθίσσατο νηούς,
ἄλλον μὲν Κορίης, ὅτι οἱ συνελέξαο κούρας

235   οὔρεα πλαζομένας Ἀζήνια,[38] τὸν δ' ἐνὶ Λούσοις
Ἡμέρῃ, οὕνεκα θυμὸν ἀπ' ἄγριον εἵλεο παίδων.

    σοὶ καὶ Ἀμαζονίδες πολέμου ἐπιθυμήτειραι
ἔν κοτε παρραλίῃ Ἐφέσῳ βρέτας ἱδρύσαντο
φηγῷ ὑπὸ πρέμνῳ, τέλεσεν δέ τοι ἱερὸν Ἱππώ·

240   αὐταὶ δ', Οὖπι ἄνασσα, περὶ πρύλιν ὠρχήσαντο

---

[38] Ἀζήνια corr. Holstenius, et al.: Ἀζείνια Ψ

55 Title of Artemis also in Callimachus' *Hymn to Zeus* (*Hymn* 1.77–78). It may be derived from the name of the Attic deme Chitone, (Schol.), but is usually understood as a reference to her signature short chiton (above, *Hymn* 3.11–12).

56 Site of a temple of Artemis Chitone with a festival called the Neleis (Plut. *De mul. vir.* 16. 254a).

57 Son of Codrus, king of Athens and founder of Miletus (Hdt. 9.97).

58 Athens, understood here by a reference to its mythical first king and culture hero (Hdt. 8.44). The Athenians are called Cecropidae in Callimachus' *Hymn to Delos* (*Hymn* 4.315).

256

[225] Queen with many temples, many cities, hail, Chitone,[55] sojourner in Miletus.[56] Neleus[57] followed you when he led out his ships from the land of Cecrops.[58] Lady of Chesion, of Imbrasus,[59] throned preeminently,[60] to you Agamemnon dedicated the rudder of his ship in your temple for a mild sailing, when you bound the winds for him, when the Achaean ships sailed out to harass the cities of the Trojans, angry about Ramnusian[61] Helen.

[233] For you Proetus[62] set up two temples: one "Of the Maiden" because you gathered his daughters, who were wandering on the Azenian[63] mountains, and the other, in Lousi[64] to the "Benign One" because you removed the spirit of wildness from his children's hearts.

[237] To you the Amazons too, who are eager for war, once in Ephesus beside the sea set up a wooden image under an oak trunk, and Hippo[65] performed something holy for you, and they themselves, Queen Upis, danced the Prylis[66] around the image, first armed with shields, and

---

[59] Cult titles of Artemis from geographical features of Samos: Chesias, an acroterium of Samos and the river Imbrasia (Schol.).

[60] Cult title of Artemis at Ephesus (Paus. 10.38.6).

[61] Rhamnus was a deme of Athens with a temple of Nemesis, who, like Leda, laid an egg from which Helen hatched (Apollod. *Bibl.* 3.10.7).

[62] King of Argos (*Aet.* 54a.10). His mad daughters were cured by Artemis (Bacchyl. 11.83–112).

[63] In Arcadia (*Hymn* 1.20).

[64] Area named for a river in Arcadia with which Proetus purified himself before praying to Artemis (Bacchyl. 11.96–97).

[65] Perhaps the Amazon Hippolyte, daughter of Ares and mother of Hippolytus (Eur. *Hipp.* 10–11; Apollod. *Bibl.* 2.5.9).

[66] A ritual dance in armor (cf. *Hymn* 1.52, with note).

πρῶτα μὲν ἐν σακέεσσιν ἐνόπλιον, αὖθι δὲ κύκλῳ
στησάμεναι χορὸν εὐρύν· ὑπήεισαν δὲ λίγειαι
λεπταλέον σύριγγες, ἵνα ῥήσσωσιν[39] ὁμαρτῇ
(οὐ γάρ πω νέβρεια δι᾽ ὀστέα τετρήναντο,
245 ἔργον Ἀθηναίης ἐλάφῳ κακόν)· ἔδραμε δ᾽ ἠχώ
Σάρδιας ἔς τε νομὸν Βερεκύνθιον. αἱ δὲ πόδεσσιν
οὖλα κατεκροτάλιζον, ἐπεψόφεον δὲ φαρέτραι.
κεῖνο δέ τοι μετέπειτα περὶ βρέτας εὐρὺ θέμειλον
δωμήθη, τοῦ δ᾽ οὔτι θεώτερον ὄψεται ἠώς
250 οὐδ᾽ ἀφνειότερον· ῥέα κεν Πυθῶνα παρέλθοι.

τῷ ῥα καὶ ἠλαίνων ἀλαπαξέμεν ἠπείλησε
Λύγδαμις ὑβριστής· ἐπὶ δὲ στρατὸν ἱππημολγῶν
ἤγαγε[40] Κιμμερίων ψαμάθῳ ἴσον, οἵ ῥα παρ᾽ αὐτόν
κεκλιμένοι ναίουσι βοὸς πόρον Ἰναχιώνης.
255 ἆ δειλὸς βασιλέων, ὅσον ἤλιτεν· οὐ γὰρ ἔμελλεν
οὔτ᾽ αὐτὸς Σκυθίηνδε παλιμπετὲς οὔτε τις ἄλλος
ὅσσων ἐν λειμῶνι Καϋστρίῳ ἔσταν ἄμαξαι
νοστήσειν· Ἐφέσου γὰρ ἀεὶ τεὰ τόξα πρόκειται.

πότνια Μουνιχίη λιμενοσκόπε, χαῖρε, Φεραίη.

---

[39] ῥήσσωσιν corr. F. de Jan: πλήσσωσιν Ψ
[40] ἤγαγε Ψ: ἤλασε Et. Gud.

---

[67] A mountain in Phrygia associated with Cybele (Strabo 10.3.17) and known for its flutes ([Plut. De fluv. 10.4.2).

[68] Apollo's shrine at Delphi named for the rotting flesh of the snake Typhon (Hymn. Hom. Ap. 3.355–74).

[69] Cimmerian king who burned the temple of Artemis at Ephesus (Strabo 1.3.21).

again in a circle, forming up a broad chorus, and the clear-sounding pipes played along elegantly, so that they could dance in step. For not yet did they perforate the bones of fawns, the work of Athena, an evil for the deer. And the echo reached to Sardis and the range of Berecynthus.[67] And with their feet they beat the earth loudly, and their quivers rattled. And afterward around that image a shrine of broad foundation was built, and dawn will see nothing more divine than this nor richer. Easily it would surpass Pytho.[68]

[251] For that reason Lygdamis,[69] hybristic, wandering in his mind, threatened to sack it. Against it he lead an army of Cimmerian[70] mare milkers, in number like sand, who live hard by the banks of the Strait of the Cow,[71] daughter of Inachus.[72] Ah, wretched among kings, how greatly he sinned! For neither was he himself destined to return to Scythia nor anyone else whose wagons stood in the Caystrian[73] meadow. For your arrows are evermore set as a bulwark before Ephesus.

[259] Munychian Queen,[74] watcher of the harbors,

[70] Scythian nomads who harassed the Lydians and Greeks in the 7th c. BC (Strabo 14.1.40).

[71] The Bosporus named for Io, whom Zeus turned into a cow. She crossed it as she fled the jealous Hera from Greece to Egypt (Aesch. *PV* 729–34).

[72] Legendary king of Argos (Paus. 2.15.4).

[73] A river near Sardis in Lydia (Strabo 13.4.5). In Homer, the Greek armies are compared with birds flocking in the meadow by the Cayster (*Il.* 2.459–68; Bornmann 125–26).

[74] Artemis had a temple at Munychia in Attica (Paus. 1.1.4), and another temple for Artemis Munychia was founded by Agamemnon at Pygela near Ephesus (Strabo 14.1.20).

260   μή τις ἀτιμήσῃ τὴν Ἄρτεμιν (οὐδὲ γὰρ Οἰνεῖ
βωμὸν ἀτιμάσσαντι καλοὶ πόλιν ἦλθον ἀγῶνες),
μηδ᾽ ἐλαφηβολίην μηδ᾽ εὐστοχίην ἐριδαίνειν
(οὐδὲ γὰρ Ἀτρεΐδης ὀλίγῳ ἐπὶ κόμπασε μισθῷ),
μηδέ τινα μνᾶσθαι τὴν παρθένον (οὐδὲ γὰρ Ὦτος,
265   οὐδὲ μὲν Ὠαρίων ἀγαθὸν γάμον ἐμνήστευσαν),
μηδὲ χορὸν φεύγειν ἐνιαύσιον (οὐδὲ γὰρ Ἱππώ
ἀκλαυτὶ περὶ βωμὸν ἀπείπατο κυκλώσασθαι)·
χαῖρε μέγα, κρείουσα, καὶ εὐάντησον ἀοιδῇ.

3a Comm. in *P.Ant.* 20 recto, 1–28

                     ].ι̣.̣οι̣στ[
                     ].ι̣ ἐπέτρε̣ψ[
37   ] μεσσόγεως· μ[εσοιγαίους]
41   Λευ]κόν· ὄρος Κρήτ[ης]
44   ]ιοις. Καίρατος· ποτ[αμὸς Κρήτης.
47–48   Λιπάρῃ ἔνι· Λιπάρη γὰρ] νῆσος Σικελίας,
ἥτις πρ[ότερον Με-

hail, Pherian![75] Let none disparage Artemis. Unpleasant struggles came to the city of Oeneus,[76] who dishonored her altar. And do not compete with her in shooting stags nor in bowmanship. The son of Atreus[77] bragged about it with no small requital. Nor should anyone woo the maiden. For neither Otus[78] nor Orion[79] won a good marriage. And do not avoid the annual chorus, for not without tears did Hippo refuse to dance around her altar. Hail great ruler and receive this song graciously.

[75] Artemis Pheraea was worshipped by the Athenians, Sicyonians, and Argives, who claimed that her cult image was brought from Pherae in Thessaly (Paus. 2.23.5).

[76] Son of Ares who organized the hunt for the Calydonian boar, which had been sent by Artemis to punish him for neglecting to honor her (Apollod. *Bibl.* 1.8.2).

[77] Agamemnon. His shooting of Artemis' sacred deer and his boasting about it led to her detaining the Greek fleet at Aulis and the sacrifice of his daughter Iphigeneia (Soph. *El.* 566–72).

[78] One of the giants who planned to carry off Artemis by piling Mt. Ossa on Olympus and Pelion on Ossa to reach the heavens. They were killed by Artemis on Naxos (Apollod. *Bibl.* 1.7.4).

[79] A giant and hunting companion of Artemis whom she killed (Apollod. *Bibl.* 1.4.3). Various reasons are alleged (cf., e.g., Hom. *Od.* 5.121).

3a Antinoöpolis papyrus (commentary)

	] he gave [her]
37	] *messogeōs*: interior land.
41	*Leu]kon*: a mountain in Crete.
44	] *Kairatos*: a river in Crete.
47–48	*Liparē eni*: Lipare is an island of Sicily which was founded

51   [λιγουνίς]ις πεποιημένην. [πέλ]ωρα·

52   ὑπερφυεῖς καὶ φοβερού]ς. Ὀσσαίοσιν· τῆς
Ὄσσης· Ὄσσα δὲ

53   [Θεσσαλίας. μουνόγληνα· μον]όκορα. τετρα-
βοείῳ· τεραπτύχῳ

55   [ὑπογλαύσσοντα· ὑποβλέπον]τα. ἄημα· πνεῦ-
μ[α. Τρ]ινακρίη·

56   γ΄ ἔχουσα ἄκρας Λιλύβαιο]ν, Πάχυνον, Πε-
λωρί[δα]. <Αἴτνη]

                    ]μενοι Ἱέρων [Αἴτ]ρην Σικελι-
59–61   ῥαιστῆ]ρας· σφύρας. ἀ[μ]βολαδίς

61   ]ντες· μυχθίσσαιεν· στενάξεια(ν)

65–68 ἀφρικτ]ί· χωρὶς φόβου. μυχάτοιο

70   ]...λωεδει. μορμύσσεται· φόβεθρον

74   ]...μα ὑπὲρ τοῦ ἰδεῖν δῶρα

76–77   λα]σίου· δασέος. ὤλοψας·

78–79 ἀπέτιλας. μεσσάτιον·]μέσον. ἐπενείματο· ἐπε-
νεμήθη.

79 ἀλώπηξ·] ἐπὶ τῆς κεφαλῆς [...]..[[.]]οπερ
          ὁ γὰρ τόπος, ἔνθα ἄ]ν ἀλώπη[ξ ο]ὐρήσῃ ἢ
πορεύση-

81–84 ται, ἄγονος γίγνεται.] Κυδώνιον· Κρητικόν.
μονιὸν δάκος·

86 ὗς ἄγριος ὃς ἂν μὴ συν]αγελάζηται ἑτέροις.
ὡπλίσσαο

89 καθωπλίσω. Μαιναλίης· Μαί]ναλον γὰρ ὄρος Πε-
λοποννήσ(ου)

90   ].επε.η. πηγούς· λευκούς

262

51   before Meligounis. *pelōra*:
52   huge and fearful. *Ossaioisin*: of Ossa. Ossa
53   of Thessaly. *mounoglēna*: one-eyed. *tetraboeiō*:
of four bull hides.
55   (*h*)*ypoglaussonta*: glowering menacingly. *aēma*:
breath. Trinacria:
56   having the headlands of Lilybaeum, Pachynus,
and Pelorias. Etna, [of the sacred Sicil- . . .
59–61   *raistēras*: hammers. *amboladis* (with uplifted
arms)
61   *muxthissaien*: they snorted
65–68   *aphrikti*: without fear. *mychatoio* (from the in-
nermost part of the house)
70   *mormyssetai*: fearful.
74   gifts on the occasion of seeing you.
76–77   *lasiou*: shaggy. *ōlopsas*: you plucked out.
78–79   *messation*: middle. *epeneimato*: it grazed,
79   *alōpēx*: mange on the head
the place where mange creeps or goes along.
81–84   It becomes unfruitful. *Kydōnion*: Cretan. *mo-
nion dakos* (a solitary or savage beast):
86   a wild boar which does not herd together with
others. (*h*)*ōplissao*:
89   you were equipped. *Mainaliēs*: Mt. Mainalon in
the Peloponnese.
90   *pēgous*: white . . . on black

]‚ει δὲ ἐπὶ τοῦ μέλανος τη.εξ

92   αὐερύ]οντες· εἰς τοὐπίσω ἕλκοντες.

92–94 δεράων· αὐχέ]νων. θάσσονας· ταχινούς

3b Schol. in *P.Cair.* 47993b

48   Μελιγουν(ὶς) τὸ πρότερο(ν) ἐκαλεῖτο ἡ νῦν
     Λιπάρα

50   τετύκο(ντο)· κατεσκεύαζον

52   ⟨πρηόσιν Ὀσσαίοισιν⟩· Ὄσσα Θεσσαλ[ί]ας
ὄρο(ς) ὑψηλότατ(ον)· πρηόνες οἱ ὑψηλότατοι κ(αὶ) πε-
τρώδεις τ(ῶν) ὀρῶ(ν) λόφοι

3c Schol. in *P.Oxy.* 2258A fr. 2

84   ⟨μονιὸν δάκος⟩· κάπ]ροι ἰδικ[ῶς   ]αι
γὰρ ἀλλη[

85   ]‚ε[‚]‚Κύκλωπες[
     ]‚ε‚

87   ]‚και σκύλακας[
     ]‚ἐπορεύου
       ]….[

110*   ]‚ταιηα‚[

113   ] κερόε(ις) ὄχος· [‚‚]‚[
     ]νο‚ λοφ(ων)‚κερα[
     ]   [

116   ] φλογ(ός)· ‚‚[
      ]‚ε‚[

92   *aueruontes*: drawing back
92–94   *deraōn*: by the neck. *thassonas*: swift.

3b Cairo papyrus (scholia)

48   What is now Lipara was earlier called Meligou-
nis.
50   *tetukonto*: they were making
52   *prēosin Ossaioisin*: Ossa is the highest mountain
in Thessaly; the loftiest headlands and rocky crests of the
mountain.

3c Oxyrhynchus papyrus

84   *monion dakos* (solitary or savage beast): properly
boars . . . for other[
85   the Cyclopes
87   and puppies
        you furnished
               ].…[
110*   ] *taiēa* [
113   *keroe(is) ochos* (horned chariot):
        loph(ōn) kera (of the horned hills)
116   *phlog(os)* (a flame):

3d Comm. in *P.Amh*. 20 recto, 1–20

109   πάγος Κερύνειος· ἀκρωτήρ[ιον Ἀρκα]δίας
οὕτω καλούμενον.

107   τὴν δὲ μίαν Κελ‚άδοντο‚ς· δυνά[μ]εθα εἰπεῖν
τὸ κελάδοντ[ος ἀντὶ] ἐπιθέτου καὶ

114   λέγειν ποτ[α]μὸν Ἀρκ[αδίας ‚‚] κύριον. Αἵμῳ

117   ἐπὶ Θρήϊκι· ὄρει Θρ[ᾴ]κ[ης. Μυσῷ ϛʹ διά]
φοροι Ὄλυμποι

145–46   ὄρη. νῦν δ᾽ οὐκέτι Φ‚οῖβος ἄεθλο‚ν τοῦτον
ἔχει·

146   φρόντισμα ἐνδ‚‚‚[‚‚‚‚‚‚‚‚‚‚]μενη. Τιρύν-
          θιος ἄκμων· ἀκάματος [ὁ Ἡρακλῆς]· Τίρυνς
γὰρ

138   πόλις Ἄργους. γάμος ἔ‚σσεται· ‚‚]ησεται.
Ἀκα-

143   κήσιος λέγεται ἢ ἐπ[ίκλην διὰ] τὸ ἐν ὄρει
Ἀκακησίῳ ‚‚‚‚]‚ονα[‚‚‚‚‚ἢ ὅτ]‚ι ἀναίτιός ἐστι

161   κακοῦ τινος. συνήντετο] ‚Θειοδ‚άμαντι· Θειο-
          δάμας Δρυόπων βασιλεύς· οἱ]δὲ Δρύοπ[ε]ς
                        Τυφρ]ηστὸν ὄρος
                        Ἡρα]κλῆς τίνων
                            ]. ζυγὸν καὶ
                            ]σεν γὰρ ἀρο-
                            ]‚‚μὴ δοῦνα[ι
                            ]‚‚λαδ‚οντο[
                  ]‚αν‚‚‚‚[

3d Amherst papyrus (commentary)

109   *pagos Keryneios*: a ridge of Ceryneia, called the highest of Arcadia.

107   *tēn de mian Keladontos*: the one of Celadon. We are able to say "of Celadon" instead the adjective [Celadonian].

114   the river of Arcadia . . . properly. Haemus

117   in Thrace: a mountain in Thrace. *Mysō*: Mysian Olympus. There are six different Olympus

145–46   mountains. Now Phoebus no longer has this task.

146   a speech . . . The Tirynthian
           anvil: Heracles. Tiryns,

138   city of Argos. There will be a marriage.

143   [Hermes] is called *Akakēsios* either on account of being on Mt. Acacesius or because he is guiltless of

161   some evil. He met *Thiodamas*: Thiodamas was king of the Dryopes. The Dryopes
                             Mt. Typhrestus
                             Heracles of some
                             yoke and
                             not to give
                             . . .

172   ὅθεν λιμν.ι[......]τος. Πιτ.ά.νη· πόλις Λακε-
δαί-

173   [μο]νος. Ἀλ.ὰς Ἀραφην.ίδ.ας· δῆμ]ος Ἀττι-
κῆς.

176–78   τετράγυον· [τεσσαρῶν γυῶν]. Στ.υμ.φαΐδες·
Ἠπειρωτικαί· Στ[ύμφαι πόλις Θεσ]πρωτίας, Στυμ-

174   φαῖον δὲ ὄρ[ος. Ταύρων· Ταύρο]ι ἔθνος Σκυ-
θίας·

       ἡ δὲ ἱστορ[ία ἔχει οὕτως· μέ]λλουσαν θύε-
σθαι

       τὴν Ἰφιγένει[αν ἡ Ἄρτ]εμις [ἁ]ρπάξασα
ἀπήγαγεν

       εἰς Ταύρους .[.....]....ι.[.].[.]ισομενη τῆς
Ἀρτέμι-

       δος τοὺς π.ρ.[.........]......αυτη· ἡ δὲ Ἰ-
φιγένεια ε.[   ].ε[
ἐκ τῆς ἐλεφα[ντίνης ὠμοπλάτης
[ση]μεῖον ε[
ἡ Ἄρτεμις .[
ἀγαγεῖν τὰ α[
Κλειτόδημος π[
πρόσταξιν α.[
δ]αίμονος. .
..]τειδητ.[

172   from this [. . .] *Pitanē*: city of Lacedaemonia.

173   *Alas Araphēnidas*: a deme of Attica.

176–78 *tetragyon*: of four acres. *Stymphaiüdes*: Epeiroti-
cae (of Epirus). *Stymphai*: a city of Thesprotia; Mt. Stym-
phaion.

174   *Taurōn*: The Taurians are a Scythian people.
        The history is this: they were about to sacrifice
        Iphigeneia
        and Artemis snatched her up and brought her to
        the Taurians . . .
        of Artemis . . . Iphigeneia . . .
        from an ivory shoulder
        a sign
        Artemis
        to carry off
        Cleitodemus
        a command
        of the god
        . .]*teidēt*.[

CALLIMACHUS

3e Schol. Ψ

1   Τὸ ἑξῆς· Ἄρτεμιν ὑμνοῦμεν ἀρχόμενοι.
3   ἐψιάασθαι· διατρίβειν, παίζειν.
4   Ὅμηρος· "οὐδέ τί μιν παῖδες ποτὶ γούνασιν."
8   ⟨ἔα⟩ τὸ ἔᾱ δασυνόμενον μὲν καὶ ὀξυνόμενον
τὰ ἴδια ἢ τὰ ἀγαθὰ δηλοῖ, ψιλούμενον δὲ καὶ παρο-
ξυνόμενον τὸ συγχώρει καὶ δίδου· καὶ τὸ
ὑπῆρχον δέ, "εἰ τότε κοῦρος ἔα."
10   ⟨ἄεμμα⟩· ἡ νευρά.
11   φαεσφορίην· ἢ ὅτι λαμπαδοῦχος (ἡ αὐτὴ γὰρ
τῇ Ἑκάτῃ) ἢ ὅτι τοὺς μαιευομένους προάγει εἰς φῶς.
12   λεγνωτόν· τὸ ἔχον ᾤαν, τουτέστι τὸ ἀπολή-
γον τοῦ ἱματίου. λέγναι γὰρ αἱ ᾤαι, τὰ λώματα, οἱ
κροσσοί, ἅπερ Ὅμηρος θυσάνους καλεῖ· "τῆς ἑκατὸν
θύσανοι."
14   ⟨ἀμίτρους⟩· ἀζώστους, μὴ διαπεπαρθενευμέ-
νας. μίτρας γὰρ ἐζώννυντο, ἃς ἔλυον ὅταν ἔμελλον
διαπαρθενεύεσθαι, ἢ ὅτι οἱ ἄγαμοι γυμνοὶ ἐβάδιζον.
15   ⟨Ἀμνισίδας⟩· Κρητικάς. Ἀμνισὸς γὰρ ποτα-
μὸς Κρήτης.
16a   ⟨ἐνδρομίδας⟩· τὰ ὑποδήματα.
16b   τὸ δὲ ἑξῆς· αἴτε μοι, ὁπότε δὴ μὴ λύγκας
⟨βάλλοιμι⟩, ἐνδρομίδας
τε καὶ θοοὺς κύνας εὖ κομέοιεν.
18   ⟨ἥντινα⟩· περιττὸν τὸ ἥν.

3e Ψ Scholia

1   Take the words in this order: We sing of Artemis at the beginning.

3   *epsiaasthai*: to waste time, to play.

4   Homer (*Il.* 5.408): "nor do his children ever prattle about his knees."

8   *ea*, *ea* being aspirated and accented with an acute makes clear what is unusual or good; [in comparison with the synonyms] *sugchōrei* and *didou* [which] are unaspirated with an acute accent on the penultimate. And the traditional meaning, "if ever I was a young man" (Hom. *Il.* 4.321).

10   *aemma*: bow.

11   *phaesphoriēn*: either because she is a bearer of light (the same as Hecate) or because she brings newborns into the light.

12   *legnōton*: having a fringe, that is to say, the border of the cloak. The fringes, the borders, the tassels that Homer (*Il.* 2.448) calls *thysanoi*: "the hundred tassels of the [*aegis*]."

14   *amitrous*: without belts, virgins. For their belts are cinched, which they loosen when they are about to have sex or because the unmarried girls go about unclad.

15   *Amnisidas*: Cretan. The Amnisus is a river of Crete.

16a   *endromidas*: sandals

16b   Take the words in this order: who, whenever I do not shoot at Lynx, would take good care of my boots and swift dogs.

18   *(h)ēntina*: whichever, an expanded form of which.

19a   λῇς ἀντὶ τοῦ θέλῃς κατὰ ἀποβολὴν τῆς θε
συλλαβῆς. κέχρηται πολλαχοῦ τῇ λέξει καὶ ὁ Θε-
όκριτος· "λῇς ποτὶ τᾶν νυμφᾶν, λῇς, αἰπόλε;"

19b   ⟨σπαρνόν⟩· σπάνιον.

21   ⟨ὠδίνεσσι⟩· ἡ αὐτὴ γάρ ἐστι τῇ Εἰλειθυίᾳ.

28   ⟨μέχρις ἵνα⟩· περιττὸν τὸ μέχρις.

30   ⟨τυτθόν⟩· ἀντὶ τοῦ οὐδὲ τυτθόν.

35   ⟨καὶ Ἀρτέμιδος καλέεσθαι⟩· ἀπὸ κοινοῦ τὸ
εἴσεται.

36   ⟨πολλὰς δὲ ξυνῇ⟩· ἀπὸ κοινοῦ τὸ ὀπάσω σοι,
μετὰ τὰς λ´· κοινῇ δέ σοι καὶ τῷ Ἀπόλλωνι πολλάς.

40   ⟨ἐπεκρήηνε καρήατι⟩· Ὅμηρος· "ὅ τι κεν κε-
φαλῇ κατανύσω."

41   ⟨Λευκόν⟩ ὄρος Κρήτης. ἑνικῶς οὕτως εἴρηκε,
Λευκὰ δὲ ὄρη λέγονται πληθυντικῶς.

44   ⟨Καίρατος⟩· ποταμὸς Κρήτης καὶ πόλις ἡ
κερατοφόρος οὕτω λεγομένη.

45a   ἀμορβούς· ἤγουν ἀκολούθους· παρὰ τὸ ἅμα
πορεύεσθαι.

45b   ὀπαδούς· ἐκ τοῦ ἅμα ὀρούεσθαι.

46 sqq.   τὸ ἑξῆς· τοὺς μὲν ἔτεμεν ἐπ᾽ ἄκμοσιν Ἡφαί-
στοιο.

47   νῆσός ἐστιν ἡ Λιπάρη πλησίον Σικελίας,
ἔνθα ἦν τὰ χαλκεῖα Ἡφαίστου. ἔστι δὲ μία τῶν Αἰο-
λίδων. λέγεται δέ, ὅτι σίδηρα διάφορα θέντες ἐν αὐτῇ
ναῦται ἕωθεν εὑρήκασιν αὐτὰ ἐκ τῆς ἀναδόσεως τοῦ

19a   *lēs*, instead of *thelēs* (you wish), following the removal of the syllable *the*. It is used often in writing, for example Theocritus (*Id.* 1.12): "Do you wish, by the nymphs, do you wish, goatherd?"

19b   *sparnon*: rare.

21   *ōdinessi*: birth pains. She herself is [an aid to] Eileithuia.

28   *mechris (h)ina*: an expanded form of *mechris* (as far as).

30   *tutthon* (little): instead of not a bit of.

35   *kai Artemidos kaleesthai* (and to be called "of Artemis"): and some will be in common [with other gods].

36   *pollas de xynē* (many in common): I will give to you, in common, after the thirty; many in common to you and Apollo.

40   *epekrēēne karēati* (he brought to pass with his head): Homer: "He nodded in assent with his head" (*Il.* 1.527).

41   *Leukon*: a mountain in Crete. The singular is written in this way, the Leuca mountains are spelled in the plural.

44   *Kairatos*: a river in Crete and a city called "horned" in this way.

45a   *amorbous*: that is to say, a follower, from *(h)ama poreuesthai* (to go along with).

45b   *opadous* (attendants): from following together.

46 sqq.   Follow this order: he found them at the anvils of Hephaestus.

47   Lipare is an island close to Sicily, where the metalworks of Hephaestus were. It is one of the Aeolians. It is said that after putting on it different things made of iron sailors found them at dawn from the exhalations of

πυρὸς ἀναλιπανθέντα. καὶ διὰ τοῦτο ἐκλήθη ἡ νῆσος Λιπάρα· < … > διὰ τὸ αὐτὰ διάφορα ὄντα ἓν γενέσθαι (?).

49   μύδρον· τὸν πεπυρακτωμένον σίδηρον, παρὰ τὸ μύρεσθαι καὶ διαρρεῖν.

52   <πρηόσιν Ὀσσαίοισιν>· Ὄσσα ὄρος Θεσσαλίας.

53   <φάεα μουνόγληνα> καὶ Ἡσίοδος· "κυκλοτερὴς ὀφθαλμὸς ἔεις."

54   ὑπογλαύσσοντα· ἤγουν ὑποβλέποντα, ὅθεν καὶ γλαύκ<ι>ος.

56a   <βαρὺν στόνον>· ἀπὸ κοινοῦ τὸ αἱ νύμφαι ἔδεισαν.

56b   <Αἴτνη>· ὄρος Σικελίας.

58   <Κύρνος>· νῆσος πρὸ τῆς Σικελίας ἡ Κύρνος ἐστίν.

59   <εὖθ' οἵ γε ῥαιστῆρας>· τὸ ἑξῆς· ἐπεὶ μέγα πολύ τ' ἄημα, εὖθ' οἵ γε ῥαιστῆρας. λέγει δὲ τὰς σφύρας ῥαιστῆρας παρὰ τὸ ῥαίειν καὶ φθείρειν τὰ ὑποπίπτοντα.

61   <ἀμβολαδίς>· ἐκ διαδοχῆς.

62a   <ἐτάλασσαν>· ἔτλησαν.

62b   <ἀκηδέες>· ἄφοβοι.

67   <καλιστρεῖ>· καλεῖ.

69   <αἰθῇ>· τῇ κεκαυμένῃ, τῇ μελαίνῃ.

70   <μορμύσσεται>· ἐκφοβεῖ.

74   ὀπτήρια· τὰ ὑπὲρ τοῦ ἰδεῖν δῶρα.

77   ὤλοψας· ἤτοι ἀπέτιλας, ἐλέπισας.

the radiant fire. And on account of this the island was called Lipara . . . on account of these different things being one.

49   *mydron*: molten iron, from *muresthai* and *diarrein*.

52   *prēosin Ossaioisin*: Mt. Ossa in Thessaly.

53   *phaea mounoglēna* (one glowing eye): and Hesiod (*Theog.* 145): "a circular eye," etc.

54   (*h)ypoglaussonta*: glancing furtively, and from this, *glaukios*.

56a   *baryn stonon* (deep groan): colloquial. What the nymphs feared.

56b   Etna: mountain in Sicily.

58   *Kyrnos*: Cyrnus (Corsica) is an island in front of Sicily.

59   *euth' (h)oi ge rhaistēras* (straightway they [lifted] the hammers): Use this word order: since the blast was great, when they lifted the hammers. He calls hammers *rhaistēras* from *rhaiein* and *phtheirein* the things collapsing underneath [them].

61   *amboladis* (in turn): from *diadoches*.

62a   *etalassan*: they suffered.

62b   *akēdees*: without fear.

67   *kalistrei*: *kalei* (she calls).

69   *aithē*: burned, blackened.

70   *mormussetai*: he frightens.

74   *optēria*: gifts on the occasion of seeing.

77   *ōlopsas*: that is to say, plucked, skinned.

79   ἀλώπηξ· πάθος περὶ τὴν κεφαλὴν γινόμενον,
ἀπὸ μεταφορᾶς τοῦ ζῴου· †τὸ γὰρ ζῷον τοῦτο λέγε-
ται† ἔνθα ἂν οὐρήσῃ, ἄγονος ὁ τόπος τῷ ἔτει ἐκείνῳ
γίνεται.

81   Κυδώνιον· ἔθνος Κρήτης, ἀφ' οὗ Κρητικόν.

82   ⟨κατακληῖδα⟩· τὴν φαρέτραν.

84   ⟨μονιὸν δάκος⟩· μονιὸν τὸ κατὰ μόνας νεμό-
μενον· δάκος δὲ τὸ θηρίον.

88   ⟨λυγκός⟩· εἶδος θηρίου ὁ λύγξ, οὗ τὸ οὖρον
πήγνυται, ὃ καλοῦσι λυγκούριον.

89   ⟨Μαιναλίης⟩· ὄρος Ἀρκαδίας.

90   ⟨πηγούς⟩· λευκούς. καὶ Ὅμηρος "πηγεσι-
μάλλῳ."

94   ⟨Κυνοσουρίδας⟩· τὰς ἀπὸ κυνῶν καὶ ἀλωπέ-
κων τικτομένας κύνας, ἢ τὰς Λακωνικάς. Κυνοσουρὶς
γὰρ τόπος Λακωνικός.

95   ⟨λαγωόν⟩· ὁ γὰρ λαγωὸς καὶ ἐν τῷ κοιμᾶ-
σθαι οὐ μύει.

96   ⟨ὕστριχος⟩· ὕστριξ θηρίον τι τραχύτατον.

98   ⟨ἀπερχομένη⟩· σοὶ τῇ Ἀρτέμιδι.

99a   ⟨προμολῆς'⟩· ταῖς διεξόδοις.

99b   ⟨Παρρασίοιο⟩· ὄρος Ἀρκαδίας.

101   ⟨Ἀναύρου⟩· ποταμὸς Θεσσαλίας ὁ Ἄναυρος.

102   ⟨κεράων⟩· σημείωσαι ὅτι τὰς θηλείας ἐλά-
φους κερατοφόρους εἶπεν.

107   ⟨Κελάδοντος⟩· ποταμὸς Ἀρκαδίας.

109   ⟨Κερύνειος⟩· λόφος Ἀρκαδίας.

HYMN III TO ARTEMIS

79   *alōpēx* (mange): a condition that occurs around the head, an animal metaphor . . . where it arises the place becomes sterile in that year.

81   *Kydōnion*: a people of Crete, from which comes *Krētikon*.

82   *kataklēida*: the quiver.

84   *monion dakos* (the solitary or savage beast): living alone by itself. The beast is wild.

88   *lynkos*: the lynx is a kind of wild beast, whose tail is stiff. They call it *lygkourion*.

89   *Mainaliēs*: a mountain of Arcadia.

90   *pēgous*: white. And Homer (*Il.* 3.197): "with thick fleece."

94   *kynosouridas*: the dogs born from dogs and foxes, or the Laconian dogs. Cynosouris is a place in Laconia.

95   *lagōon*: the hare that does not close its eyes in sleep.

96   *(h)ystrichos*: the wild porcupine, the roughest thing.

98   *aperchomenē*: to you, Artemis.

99a   *promolēs*: the approaches.

99b   *Parrasioio*: a mountain in Arcadia.

101   *Anaurou*: The Anaurus is a river in Thessaly.

102   *keraōn*: notice that he said the female deer have horns.

107   *Keladon*: a river of Arcadia.

109   *Keryneios*: a ridge in Arcadia.

110   ⟨Τιτυοκτόνε⟩· Τιτυὸς βιασάμενος Λητὼ ἀνῃρέθη ὑπὸ Ἀπόλλωνος καὶ Ἀρτέμιδος.

112   ⟨κεμάδεσσι⟩· ἐλάφοις.

114a   ⟨Αἵμῳ⟩· ὄρος Θρᾴκης.

114b   καταῖξ δὲ ἡ λεγομένη καταιγίς.

114c   ⟨καταῖξ⟩· λαῖλαψ.

117   ⟨Μυσῷ⟩· ἔστι γὰρ καὶ ἄλλος Μακεδονίας.

124   ⟨ἐμμάξεαι⟩· ἐμβάλῃς.

125   φιν· χωρὶς τοῦ σ διὰ τὸ μέτρον.

127   ἢ βληταί· ἤγ(ουν) βεβλημέναι ὑπὸ τῆς Ἀρτέμιδος.

133   ⟨τρώει⟩· τρύχει, φθείρει.

134   ⟨θυωρόν⟩· θυωρὸς ἡ φιλικὴ τράπεζα, κυρίως δὲ ἡ θεοῖς ἀνατιθεμένη. τὸ δὲ ἑξῆς· περὶ μίαν θυωρὸν τὰ δίφρα τίθενται αἱ εἰνάτερες καὶ αἱ γαλόῳ.

136 sq.   εἴη μοι φίλος ὅστις ὑπὸ σοῦ προνοεῖται, εἴην δὲ καὶ αὐτός.

140   ⟨ἄντυγες⟩· ἀπὸ τῆς ἄντυγος τὸ ὅλον ἅρμα σημαίνει.

143   Ἀκακήσιος· ἀπὸ ὄρους Ἀρκαδίας, ἢ ὁ μηδενὸς κακοῦ παραίτιος ὤν.

146   ⟨Τιρύνθιος ἄκμων⟩· ὁ μὴ καμὼν ἐπὶ τοῖς ἄθλοις Ἡρακλῆς.

149   ⟨πενθερή⟩· ἡ Ἥρα.

152   πινύσκει· σωφρονίζει, κολακεύει ὁ Ἡρακλῆς.

154a   ⟨ἔα πρόκας⟩· διὰ τὴν ἀδηφαγίαν τὰ μείζω τῶν ζῴων αὐτὴν κελεύει ἀγρεύειν.

154b   ⟨πρόκας⟩· νεβρούς.

110   *Tityoktone*: Tityus who assaulted Leto was killed by Apollo and Artemis.

112   *kemadessi*: deer.

114a   *(H)aimōi*: a mountain in Thrace.

114b   *kataix*: the squall that was mentioned.

114c   *kataix*: a hurricane.

117   *Mysōi*: There is another in Macedonia.

124   *emmaxeai*: you inflicted.

125   *fin*: separated from the sigma on account of the meter.

127   *ē blētai*: that is to say, stricken by Artemis.

133   *trōei*: it wastes, it destroys.

134   *thyōron*: the friendly offering table, which properly holds offerings for the gods. Use this word order: Around the one table they take their seats, the wives of the brothers and the husband's sisters.

136 sq.   May he be a friend to me whoever takes thought for you, and may I be myself.

140   *attyges* (rim): by the rim he signifies the whole chariot.

143   *Akakēsios* (Hermes): from a mountain in Arcadia, or being an accessory to no evil.

146   *Tirynthios akmōn* (the Anvil of Tiryns): Heracles not worn out by his labors.

149   *pentherē*: Hera.

152   *pinuskei*: he learns wisdom, Heracles flatters [her].

154a   *ea prokas* (hold back on the deer): on account of his gluttony he orders her to hunt the larger animals.

154b   *prokas*: deer.

158   ⟨περὶ θῆρα πονεῖτο⟩· ἐσθίων.

159   ⟨Φρυγίη⟩· Φρυγία ὄρος Τραχῖνος, ἔνθα ἑκάη
ὁ Ἡρακλῆς.

161   ⟨Θειοδάμαντι⟩· βασιλεὺς Δρυόπων ὁ Θειοδά-
μας.

165   ⟨ὠκύθοον τριπέτηλον⟩· ταχέως ἀνατέλλον
τρίφυλλον.

166   ⟨ὑποληνίδας⟩· πυέλους, ποτίστρας.

170 sqq. τὸ ἑξῆς· ἡνίκα αἱ νύμφαι—, μὴ νειὸν τημοῦ-
τος (175).

171   ⟨Ἰνωποῖο⟩· Ἰνωπὸς ποταμὸς Δήλου. Αἰγύ-
πτιος δὲ διὰ τὸν Νεῖλον, ὅτι καὶ αὐτὸς †ἐκεῖ† πλημυ-
ρεῖ. ἢ ὅτι λέγεται ἐκ τοῦ ὕδατος τοῦ Νείλου μετέχειν
λαθραίως.

172a   ⟨Πιτάνη⟩· πόλις Λακεδαιμονίας.

172b   ⟨Λίμναις⟩· Λίμναι δῆμος Ἀττικῆς, ἔνθα τι-
μᾶται ἡ Ἄρτεμις.

173   ⟨Ἁλὰς Ἀραφηνίδας⟩· δύο Ἁλαὶ δῆμοι τῆς
Ἀττικῆς, Ἁλαὶ Ἀραφηνίδες καὶ Ἁλαὶ Αἰξωνίδες.

174   τέθμια Ταύρων· τὰ νόμιμα τῶν Σκυθῶν ἤγουν
τὸ θύειν τοὺς ξένους.

175   ⟨τημοῦτος⟩· τηνικαῦτα.

176 sqq. τὸ ἑξῆς· ἡνίκα αἱ νύμφαι τὴν Ἄρτεμιν τῷ
χορῷ κυκλώσονται, μὴ γένοιτο τὰς ἐμὰς βοῦς ἐπ᾽ ἀλ-
λοτρίῳ μισθῷ ἐργάζεσθαι· καὶ γὰρ ὁ ἥλιος ἐπέχει τὸν
ἑαυτοῦ δρόμον καὶ αὐτὸς ἐφορῶν τὸν χορὸν τῶν νυμ-
φῶν, ὥστε εἶναι πολὺ τὸ τῆς ἡμέρας διάστημα.

177   ⟨γυιαί⟩· χωλαί.

158   *peri thēra poneito* (he labored around the beasts): eating.

159   *Phrygiē*: Phrygia is a mountain of Trachis, where Heracles was immolated.

161   *Theiodamanti*: Thiodamas was king of the Dryopians.

165   *ōkythoon tripetelon* (swift-growing clover): quickly the clover grows.

166   *(h)ypolēnidas*: a tub, a drinking trough.

170 sqq.   Without the asides the sentence goes: When the nymphs—, not lately, then (175).

171   *Inōpoio*: Inopus is a river in Delos. It is Egyptian because it floods like the Nile, or because it is said that it shares the Nile's water out of sight.

172a   *Pitanē*: a Lacedaemonian city.

172b   *Limnais*: Limnae is a deme of Attica where Artemis is honored.

173   *Alas Araphēnidas*: There are two demes named Alae in Attica, *Alai Araphēnides* and *Alai Aixōnides*.

174   *tethmia Taurōn*: the custom of Scythians to sacrifice strangers.

175   *tēmoutos*: then.

176 sqq.   Use this word order: when the nymphs circle Artemis in the dance may it not be that my oxen work for a stranger's wage. And the sun stops in his track watching the dance of the nymphs so that there is a long extension of the day.

177   *guiai*: limbs.

178a   ⟨κόπρον⟩· τὴν ἔπαυλιν.

178b   ⟨Στυμφαΐδες⟩· Ἠπειρωτικαί· Στύμφαι γὰρ χωρίον τῆς Ἠπείρου· λέγεται δὲ καλὰς βοῦς ἔχειν τὴν Ἤπειρον.

179   κεραελκέες· διὰ τὸ τοῖς κέρασιν ἕλκειν τὸ ἄροτρον.

187   ⟨Πέργη⟩· μητρόπολις Παμφυλίας.

188a   ⟨Τηΰγετον⟩· ὄρος Λακεδαίμονος.

188b   ⟨Εὐρίποιο⟩· ὁ μεταξὺ Εὐβοίας καὶ Βοιωτίας ῥοῦς. καλεῖται δὲ οὕτως ἡ Εὔβοια· λέγεται δὲ καὶ Μάκρις διὰ τὸ ἐπὶ μῆκος αὐτὴν κεῖσθαι.

189   ⟨Γορτυνίδα⟩· Κρητικήν, ἀπὸ τόπου.

190a   ⟨ἐλλοφόνον⟩· νεβροκτόνον.

190b   ⟨Βριτόμαρτιν⟩· Βριτόμαρτις ὄνομα κύριον τῆς νύμφης, ἀφ' ἧς καὶ ἡ Ἄρτεμις ἐν Κρήτῃ Βριτόμαρτις τιμᾶται, ὡς Διογενιανός.

194   ⟨παίπαλα⟩· τόπους τραχεῖς.

204   ⟨Οὖπι⟩· Οὖπις ἐπίθετον Ἀρτέμιδος· ἢ παρὰ τὸ ὀπίζεσθαι τὰς τικτούσας αὐτήν, ἢ παρὰ τὴν θρέψασαν αὐτὴν Οὖπιν ἢ διὰ τὰς Ὑπερβορέους κόρας, Οὖπιν, Ἑκαέργην, Λοξώ, ἃς ἐτίμησεν Ἀπόλλων καὶ Ἄρτεμις· καὶ ἀπὸ μὲν τῆς μιᾶς Οὖπις ἡ Ἄρτεμις, Λοξίας δὲ καὶ Ἑκάεργος ἐκ τῶν λοιπῶν ὁ Ἀπόλλων.

208a   ⟨Ὑψηίς⟩· ἡ Κυρήνη.

208b   τύμβον Ἰώλκιον· τὸν τοῦ Πελίου· ἐν Ἰωλκῷ γὰρ ὁ Πελίας.

209   ⟨Κεφάλου ξανθὴν ἄλοχον⟩· τὴν Πρόκριν.

178a   *kopron*: dung

178b   *Stymphaiides*: Epirioticae. Stymphae is a place in Epirus. He says that Epirus has lovely cattle.

179   *keraelkees*: on account of dragging the plow by the horns.

187   *Pergē*: the mother city of Pamphylia.

188a   *Tēugeton*: A Lacedaemonian mountain.

188b   *Euripoio*: the strait between Euboea and Boeotia. From this it is called Euboea. He mentions Makris because it lies lengthwise.

189   *Gortynida*: Crete, from the place.

190a   *ellophonon*: fawn-slayer.

190b   *Britomartin*: Britomartis is the proper name of a nymph from whom Artemis Britomartis is honored in Crete, according to Diogenes (fr. 20).

194   *paipala*: rough places.

204   *Oupi*: Upis is an epithet of Artemis. Either by caring for those giving birth or from Upis, the one who brought her up, or on account of the Hyperborean girls: Upis, Hecaerge and Loxo whom Apollo and Artemis honored. From Upis alone, Artemis, from the rest, Loxo and Hecaergus, Apollo.

208a   *(H)ypsēis*: Cyrene.

208b   *tymbon Iōlkion* (the Iolcian tomb): the one of Pelius, the Pelias in Iolcus.

209   *Kephalou xanthēn alochon* (the blonde wife of Cephalus): Procris.

211 ⟨Ἀντίκλειαν⟩· ἢ τὴν μητέρα Ὀδυσσέως ἢ
ἄλλην τινά.

215 ⟨ποδορρώρην⟩· τὴν τοῖς ποσὶν ὀρούουσαν
καὶ ὁρμῶσαν.

221 ⟨Ὑλαῖον⟩· Ὑλαῖος καὶ Ῥοῖκος Κένταυροι
περὶ Ἀρκαδίαν, οὓς ἀνεῖλεν Ἀταλάντη βιασαμένους
αὐτήν.

224a ⟨τάων⟩· τῶν λαγόνων τῶν Κενταύρων.

224b ⟨Μαιναλίη⟩· ὄρος Ἀρκαδίας.

224c ναεν· ἔσταξεν, ἔβρεξεν, ὅθεν καὶ νᾶμα καὶ
νασμός.

228 Χησιάς· ⟨Χήσιον⟩ ἀκρωτήριον τῆς Σάμου
καὶ Ἴμβρασος ποταμὸς Σάμου.

232 ⟨Ῥαμνουσίδι⟩· Ῥαμνοῦς δῆμος Ἀττικῆς,
ἔνθα τῇ Νεμέσει ὁ Ζεὺς συνεκαθεύδησεν, ἥτις ἔτεκεν
ᾠόν, ὅπερ εὑροῦσα ἡ Λήδα ἐθέρμανε καὶ ἐξέβαλε
τοὺς Διοσκούρους καὶ τὴν Ἑλένην.

235a ⟨Ἀζήνια⟩· ὄρος Ἀρκαδίας.

235b ⟨ἐνὶ Λούσοις⟩· ἡ εὐθεῖα τὰ Λοῦσα οὐδετέρως,
ὡς Ἡρωδιανός.

236 ⟨θυμὸν ἀπ' ἄγριον εἵλεο παίδων⟩· τοῦ Προί-
του μανεῖσαι αἱ τρεῖς θυγατέρες πάλιν διὰ τῆς Ἀρτέ-
μιδος ἡμερώθησαν. ὁ δὲ κτίζει ἱερὰ δύο, ἓν μὲν Κο-
ρίης, ἓν δὲ Ἡμέρης, διότι τὰς κόρας ἡμέρωσεν.

238 ⟨παρραλίη Ἐφέσῳ⟩· τῇ παραθαλασσίῃ.

239 Ἱππώ· μία τῶν Ἀμαζόνων.

245 ⟨ἔργον Ἀθηναίης⟩· Ἀθηνᾶ γὰρ ἔφορος πά-
σης τέχνης.

284

211   *Antikleia*: the mother of Odysseus or some other woman.

215   *podorrōrēn*: with feet rushing headlong and darting forward.

221   *(H)ylaion*: Hylaeus and Roecus, Centaurs in Arcadia, whom Atalanta killed after they assaulted her.

224a   *taōn*: of the flanks of the Centaurs.

224b   *Mainaliē*: a mountain in Arcadia.

224c   *naen*: it dripped, it rained, and from this *nāma* and *nasmos*.

228   *Chēsias*: (Chesion) the peak of Samos and the Imbrasus river of Samos.

232   *Rhamnousidi*: Rhamnus is a deme in Attica, where Zeus had sex with Nemesis, who gave birth to an egg, which Leda discovered, kept warm, and produced the Dioscuri and Helen.

235a   *Azēnia*: a mountain in Arcadia.

235b   *en Lousois*: the nominative is *ta Lousa*, like a neuter, according to Herodian.

236   *thymon ap' agrion (h)eileo paidōn* (you took away the wild heart of the girls): the three mad daughters of Proetus were tamed in turn by Artemis. He founded two shrines, one for Coria and one for Hemera, because she pacified the girls.

238   *parraliē Ephesō*: by the shore.

239   *Hippō*: one of the Amazons.

245   *ergon Athēnaiēs*: Athena is the guardian of every art.

246a   ⟨Σάρδιας⟩· πόλις Λυδίας.

246b   Βερεκύνθιον· μεταξὺ Λυδίας καὶ Φρυγίας.

250   Ὅμηρος· "οὐδ' ὅσα λάϊνος οὐδὸς ἀφήτορος."

251   ⟨ἠλαίνων⟩· μωραίνων.

253   ⟨Κιμμερίων⟩· Σκυθῶν.

254   ⟨βοὸς πόρον Ἰναχιώνης⟩· τῆς Ἰοῦς τῆς εἰς βοῦν μεταμορφθείσης. Βόσποροι δὲ εἰσὶ δύο, ὅ τε Βυζάντιος καὶ ὁ Κιμμέριος.

259   Μουνιχίῃ· ἤτοι Ἀττική· Μουνιχία γάρ ἐστι μέρος τοῦ Πειραιῶς τοῦ λιμένος τῶν Ἀθηνῶν.

246a   *Sardias*: a city of Lydia.

246b   *Berekynthion*: between Lydia and Phrygia.

250   Homer (*Il.* 9.404): "Not as much as the marble threshold of the Archer."

251   *ēlainon*: being mad.

253   *Kimmeriōn*: Scythians.

254   *Boos poron Inachiōnes*: of Io [daughter of Inachus] who was changed into a heifer. There are two Bosporuses: one Byzantine and the other Cimmerian.

259   *Mounichiō*: truly, Attica. Mounichia is part of the Peiraeus harbor of Athens.

HYMNUS IV
IN DELON

Τὴν ἱερήν, ὦ θυμέ, τίνα χρόνον †ηποτ†[1] ἀείσεις
Δῆλον Ἀπόλλωνος κουροτρόφον; ἦ μὲν ἅπασαι
Κυκλάδες, αἳ νήσων ἱερώταται εἰν ἁλὶ κεῖνται,
εὔυμνοι· Δῆλος δ᾽ ἐθέλει τὰ πρῶτα φέρεσθαι
5 ἐκ Μουσέων, ὅτι Φοῖβον ἀοιδάων[2] μεδέοντα
λοῦσέ τε καὶ σπείρωσε καὶ ὡς θεὸν ᾔνεσε πρώτη.
ὡς Μοῦσαι τὸν ἀοιδὸν ὃ μὴ Πίμπλειαν ἀείσῃ
ἔχθουσιν, τὼς Φοῖβος ὅτις Δήλοιο λάθηται.
Δήλῳ νῦν οἴμης ἀποδάσσομαι, ὡς ἂν Ἀπόλλων
10 Κύνθιος[3] αἰνήσῃ με φίλης ἀλέγοντα τιθήνης.
    κείνη δ᾽ ἠνεμόεσσα καὶ ἄτροπος †οἷά θ᾽†[4]
        ἁλιπλήξ
αἰθυίης καὶ μᾶλλον ἐπίδρομος ἠέπερ ἵπποις
πόντῳ ἐνεστήρικται· ὃ δ᾽ ἀμφί ἑ πουλὺς ἑλίσσων
Ἰκαρίου πολλὴν ἀπομάσσεται ὕδατος ἄχνην·
15 τῷ σφε καὶ ἰχθυβολῆες ἁλίπλοοι ἐννάσσαντο.
ἀλλά οἱ οὐ νεμεσητὸν ἐνὶ πρώτῃσι λέγεσθαι,
ὁππότ᾽ ἐς Ὠκεανόν τε καὶ ἐς Τιτηνίδα Τηθὺν

---

[1] ἢ πότ᾽ a La. δ: ἤ ποτ᾽ ΕΠζ: εἴ ποτε Reiske: ἠπύτ᾽ Mineur
[2] ἀοιδάων La. η: ἀοιδέων Ψ   [3] Κύνθιος corr. La.: καύριος Ψ   [4] οἷά θ᾽ Ψ: αἶά θ᾽ coni. Mineur

288

HYMN IV
TO DELOS

At what time or when will you sing, o my heart, of holy Delos, nurse of Apollo? Certainly all of the Cyclades, most holy of islands that lie in the sea, are often hymned. But Delos stands to take first prize from the Muses, because she bathed Phoebus, lord of minstrels, swaddled him, and first hailed him as a god. As the Muses hate the singer who does not sing of Pimpleia,[1] Phoebus hates those who forget Delos. Now I will award to Delos her share of song, so that Apollo Cynthius[2] may praise me for respecting his dear nurse.

[11] She is set in the sea, windy and barren, sea swept, a fitter course for gulls than for horses. And the sea, whirling greatly around her, casts off its copious foam of Icarian[3] water. On that account seafaring fishermen have settled there. But she should not be grudgingly named among the foremost, for whenever the islands gather to Ocean and to Tethys,[4] the Titan's child, she always travels

---

[1] Fountain in Pieria sacred to the Muses (Strabo 10.3.17).

[2] Mt. Cynthus in Delos, where Artemis hunted goats to build the horned altar (*Hymn* 2.61).

[3] Part of the Aegean named for Icarus, son of Daedalus, who lost his life there when his handmade wings malfunctioned (Strabo 14.1.19; Diod. Sic. 4.77.6).

[4] The child of Gaius and Uranus (Hes. *Theog.* 132–36).

CALLIMACHUS

νῆσοι ἀολλίζονται, ἀεὶ δ' ἔξαρχος ὁδεύει.
ἡ δ' ὄπιθεν⁵ Φοίνισσα μετ' ἴχνια Κύρνος ὁπηδεῖ

20 οὐκ ὀνοτὴ καὶ Μάκρις Ἀβαντιὰς Ἑλλοπιήων
Σαρδώ θ' ἱμερόεσσα καὶ ἣν ἐπενήξατο Κύπρις
ἐξ ὕδατος τὰ πρῶτα, σαοῖ δέ μιν ἀντ' ἐπιβάθρων.
κεῖναι μὲν πύργοισι περισκεπέεσσιν ἐρυμναί,
Δῆλος δ' Ἀπόλλωνι· τί δὲ στιβαρώτερον ἕρκος;

25 τείχεα μὲν καὶ λᾶες ὑπὸ ῥιπῆς⁶ κε πέσοιεν
Στρυμονίου βορέαο· θεὸς δ' ἀεὶ ἀστυφέλικτος·
Δῆλε φίλη, τοῖός σε βοηθόος ἀμφιβέβηκεν.

εἰ δὲ λίην πολέες σε περιτροχόωσιν ἀοιδαί,
ποίῃ ἐνιπλέξω σε; τί τοι θυμῆρες ἀκοῦσαι;

30 ἦ ὡς⁷ τὰ πρώτιστα μέγας θεὸς οὔρεα θείνων
ἄορι τριγλώχινι τό οἱ Τελχῖνες ἔτευξαν
νήσους εἰναλίας εἰργάζετο, νέρθε δὲ πάσας
ἐκ νεάτων ὤχλισσε καὶ εἰσεκύλισε θαλάσσῃ;
καὶ τὰς μὲν κατὰ βυσσόν,⁸ ἵν' ἠπείροιο λάθωνται,

35 πρυμνόθεν ἐρρίζωσε· σὲ δ' οὐκ ἔθλιψεν ἀνάγκη,

---

⁵ ὄπιθεν corr. β La. I: ὄπισθεν Ψ
⁶ ὑπὸ ῥιπῆς corr. Meineke: ὑπαὶ ῥιπῆς Ψ: υπ]οριπαις[
P.Oxy. 2225 col. I
⁷ ἦ ὡς T in marg.: χ' ὡς Ψ
⁸ βυσσόν corr. Dindorf: βυθόν Ψ

---

⁵ Corsica, settled first by Phoenicians (Hdt. 1.165).
⁶ Euboea. Macris, daughter of Aristaeus, nursed Dionysus in a cave there before they were sent away by Hera (Ap. Rhod. 4.1128–38). The island was also called Abantis (Hes. fr. 296 M.-W.; Hom. *Il.* 2.536).

290

in the lead. Phoenician Cyrnus,[5] not to be scorned, follows after her footsteps, Abantian Macris[6] of the Ellopians,[7] lovely Sardo,[8] and the island to which Cypris[9] swam when she first emerged from the sea. She keeps it safe as a landing fee. Those are defended by circling towers, but Delos, by Apollo. What fortification is stronger? Walls and rocks may fall by the blast of Strymonian[10] Boreas, but the god is unshaken forever. Dear Delos, such is the helper that protects you!

[28] If so many songs circle round you, what kind shall I weave about you? What would you love to hear? Is it how at the very first the Great God,[11] striking the mountains with the three-pronged sword that the Telchines[12] forged for him, created the islands in the deep, and from their deepest foundations pried them all up and rolled them into the sea? And he rooted them in the depths from their foundations so that they would forget the mainland. But

[7] The people of Euboea named for Ellops, son of Ion (Strabo 10.1.3).

[8] Sardinia (Paus. 10.17.2).

[9] Aphrodite, who in one tradition emerged from the sea near Cyprus (Hes. *Theog.* 191–99).

[10] Strymon, a river in northeastern Thrace (Hes. *Theog.* 337–39). Boreas is the north wind.

[11] Apparently, a primeval Poseidon whose weapon is the trident and who is associated with earthquakes and island building (Hom. *Od.* 13.159–64).

[12] Mythical metalworkers and wizards usually located at Rhodes. Elsewhere Callimachus calls them insolent sorcerers (*Aet.* 75.64–69) and ignoramuses, who are no friends of the Muses (*Aet.* 1.1–8).

CALLIMACHUS

ἀλλ᾽ ἄφετος πελάγεσσιν ἐπέπλεες· οὔνομα δ᾽ ἦν τοι
Ἀστερίη τὸ παλαιόν, ἐπεὶ βαθὺν ἥλαο τάφρον
οὐρανόθεν φεύγουσα Διὸς γάμον ἀστέρι ἴση.
τόφρα μὲν οὔπω τοι χρυσέη ἐπεμίσγετο Λητώ,
40 τόφρα δ᾽ ἔτ᾽ Ἀστερίη σὺ καὶ οὐδέπω ἔκλεο Δῆλος.

πολλάκι σ᾽ ἐκ⁹ Τροιζῆνος †ἀποξανθοιο¹⁰ πολίχνης
ἐρχόμενοι Ἐφύρηνδε Σαρωνικοῦ ἔνδοθι κόλπου
ναῦται ἐπεσκέψαντο, καὶ ἐξ Ἐφύρης ἀνιόντες
οἱ μὲν ἔτ᾽ οὐκ ἴδον αὖθι, σὺ δὲ στεινοῖο παρ᾽ ὀξύν
45 ἔδραμες Εὐρίποιο πόρον καναχηδὰ ῥέοντος,
Χαλκιδικῆς δ᾽ αὐτῆμαρ ἀνηναμένη ἁλὸς ὕδωρ
μέσφ᾽ ἐς Ἀθηναίων προσενήξαο Σούνιον ἄκρον
ἢ Χίον ἢ νήσοιο διάβροχον ὕδατι μαστόν
Παρθενίης (οὔπω γὰρ ἔην Σάμος), ἧχί σε νύμφαι
50 γείτονες Ἀγκαίου Μυκαλησσίδες ἐξείνισσαν.
ἡνίκα δ᾽ Ἀπόλλωνι γενέθλιον οὖδας ὑπέσχες,
τοῦτό τοι ἀντημοιβὸν ἁλίπλοοι οὔνομ᾽ ἔθεντο,

⁹ πολλάκι σ᾽ ἐκ in marg. T: πολλάκις ἐκ Ψ: πολλάκι σε
Reiske   ¹⁰ ἀπὸ ξάνθοιο Ψ: ἀπὸ Ξάνθοιο schol.: ἀπὸ
ζαθέοιο prop. Meineke

13 Daughter of Coeus and Phoebe. She is a sister of Leto (Hes. *Theog.* 404–410), though here Callimachus ignores their relationship. In Pindar (*Pae.* 7b fr. 52h, 43–48), Asteria is thrown into the sea after rejecting Zeus' advances and is transformed into a "conspicuous rock."

14 In the northeastern Peloponnese across the Saronic Gulf from Athens (Strabo 8.6.14). It was the birthplace of Theseus, the Athenian hero whose story is below (*Hymn* 4.307–16).

292

no constraint pressured you, but you floated freely on the high seas. Your ancient name was Asteria,[13] since you leaped into that deep trench like a star from heaven when you fled from marriage with Zeus. Until then golden Leto did not socialize with you. Until then you were still Asteria and were not yet called Delos.

[41] Often sailors saw you in the Saronic Gulf as they came from the town of fair-haired Troezen[14] to Ephyra,[15] and when they returned from Ephyra they no longer saw you there, for you had run along the quickly moving, noisily rushing strait of narrow Euripus.[16] And on the same day, after abandoning the waters of the Sea of Chalcis, you swam to the Athenians' Cape Sounion[17] or to Chios or to the water-soaked breast of the island of Parthenia (for it was not yet Samos),[18] where the nymphs of Mycalessus,[19] neighbors of Ancaeus,[20] received you. But when you offered your land to Apollo for his birth, the sailors gave you this name in exchange, since you no longer floated "un-

[15] An ancient name of Corinth (Paus. 2.1.1; Strabo 8.3.5).

[16] Separates the two parts of the gulf of Euboea, called here the Sea of Chalcis, after the city of that name located just south of the strait. Apparently the floating island cannot fit through the narrow strait and so sails south toward Cape Sounion near Athens.

[17] Promontory at the southernmost point of the Attic peninsula.

[18] Parthenia was an ancient name of Samos (Schol. ad Ap. Rhod. 1.187), an Aegean island off the coast of Ionia. Samos was an important Ptolemaic naval base, and the eastern leg of Delos' journey is a gesture to either Ptolemy II or Ptolemy III.

[19] A mythical king of Mycale, a promontory on the mainland opposite Samos.

[20] King of Samos (Ap. Rhod. 2.865–66).

οὕνεκεν οὐκέτ' ἄδηλος ἐπέπλεες, ἀλλ' ἐνὶ πόντου
κύμασιν Αἰγαίοιο ποδῶν ἐνεθήκαο ῥίζας.

55   οὐδ' Ἥρην κοτέουσαν ὑπέτρεσας· ἡ μὲν ἀπάσαις
δεινὸν ἐπεβρωμᾶτο λεχωίσιν αἳ Διὶ παῖδας
ἐξέφερον, Λητοῖ δὲ διακριδόν,[11] οὕνεκα μούνη
Ζηνὶ τεκεῖν ἤμελλε φιλαίτερον Ἄρεος υἷα.
τῷ ῥα καὶ αὐτὴ μὲν σκοπιὴν ἔχεν αἰθέρος εἴσω

60   σπερχομένη μέγα δή τι καὶ οὐ φατόν, εἶργε δὲ
          Λητώ
τειρομένην ὠδῖσι· δύω δέ οἱ εἴατο φρουροί
γαῖαν ἐποπτεύοντες, ὁ μὲν πέδον ἠπείροιο
ἥμενος ὑψηλῆς κορυφῆς ἔπι Θρήικος Αἵμου
θοῦρος Ἄρης ἐφύλασσε σὺν[12] ἔντεσι, τὼ δέ οἱ ἵππω

65   ἑπτάμυχον βορέαο παρὰ σπέος ηὐλίζοντο·
ἡ δ' ἐπὶ νησάων ἑτέρη σκοπὸς αἰπειάων[13]
ἧστο κόρη Θαύμαντος ἐπαΐξασα Μίμαντι.
ἔνθ' οἱ μὲν πολίεσσιν ὅσαις ἐπεβάλλετο Λητώ
μίμνον ἀπειλητῆρες, ἀπετρώπων δὲ δέχεσθαι.

70   φεῦγε μὲν Ἀρκαδίη, φεῦγεν δ' ὄρος ἱερὸν Αὔγης
Παρθένιον, φεῦγεν δ' ὁ γέρων μετόπισθε Φενειός,[14]
φεῦγε δ' ὅλη Πελοπηὶς ὅση παρακέκλιται Ἰσθμῷ,

---

[11] διακριδόν Ψ: διακριτον P.Bodl. f. 109p verso
[12] ἐφύλασσε σὺν S La. η: ἐφύλασσε δὲ σὺν Ψ
[13] αι]πειαων P.Bodl. f. 109p verso: ευρειάων Ψ
[14] Φενειός corr. Arnaldus: φεναιός Ψ: φανιο[P.Oxy. 2225
col. II

seen"[21] but planted the roots of your feet in the waves of the Aegean Sea.

[55] Nor did you shrink back from furious Hera, who roared terribly at all the women who bore the children of Zeus, and especially at Leto, because she alone was to bear to Zeus a son dearer than Ares. And so Hera herself kept watch in the sky, greatly, even unspeakably angry, and she barred Leto, who was distressed with birth pains. And she had two lookouts to keep watch on the earth. Bold Ares, sitting on the high peak of Thracian Haemus,[22] kept an armed watch on the plain of the continent, and his horses were stabled beside the seven-chambered cave of Boreas. The other, the daughter of Thaumas,[23] was the lookout over the far-flung islands. She sat on Mimas,[24] where she had rushed. And there they waited, threatening whatever cities Leto approached and preventing them from receiving her.

[70] Arcadia fled, and Parthenium, the holy mountain of Auge,[25] fled, and the old man Pheneius[26] fled behind her, and the whole Peloponnesus that lies along the isth-

---

[21] "Unseen" translates ἄδηλος, which contrasts with the island's new name, Δῆλος (conspicuous). Before Leto's arrival Delos was hard to see because she was in constant motion.

[22] A mountain range in northern Thrace (*Hymn* 3.114).

[23] Iris (Hes. *Theog.* 780).

[24] Hill in Asia Minor opposite Chios.

[25] Daughter of Aleus, king of Tegea, who bore Telephus to Heracles on Mt. Parthenium against her father's wishes (Paus. 8.48.7).

[26] The city Pheneus or a river named for it (Paus. 8.13.6).

ἔμπλην Αἰγιαλοῦ γε καὶ Ἄργεος· οὐ γὰρ ἐκείνας
ἀτραπιτοὺς ἐπάτησεν, ἐπεὶ λάχεν Ἴναχον Ἥρη.
75 φεῦγε καὶ Ἀονίη τὸν ἕνα δρόμον, αἱ δ' ἐφέποντο
Δίρκη τε Στροφίη τε μελαμψήφιδος ἔχουσαι
Ἰσμηνοῦ χέρα πατρός, ὁ δ' εἵπετο πολλὸν ὄπισθεν
Ἀσωπὸς βαρύγουνος, ἐπεὶ πεπάλακτο κεραυνῷ.
ἡ δ' ὑποδινηθεῖσα χοροῦ ἀπεπαύσατο νύμφη
80 αὐτόχθων Μελίη καὶ ὑπόχλοον ἔσχε παρειὴν
ἥλικος ἀσθμαίνουσα περὶ δρυός, ὡς ἴδε χαίτην
σειομένην Ἑλικῶνος. ἐμαὶ θεαὶ εἴπατε Μοῦσαι,
ἦ ῥ' ἐτεὸν ἐγένοντο τότε δρύες ἡνίκα Νύμφαι;
'Νύμφαι μὲν χαίρουσιν, ὅτε δρύας ὄμβρος ἀέξει,
85 Νύμφαι δ' αὖ κλαίουσιν, ὅτε δρυσὶ μηκέτι¹⁵ φύλλα.'
    ταῖς μὲν ἔτ' Ἀπόλλων ὑποκόλπιος αἰνὰ χολώθη,
φθέγξατο δ' οὐκ ἀτέλεστον ἀπειλήσας ἐπὶ Θήβῃ·
"Θήβη τίπτε τάλαινα τὸν αὐτίκα πότμον ἐλέγχεις;
μήπω μή μ' ἀέκοντα βιάζεο μαντεύεσθαι.
90 οὔπω μοι Πυθῶνι μέλει τριποδήιος ἕδρη,
οὐδέ τί πω τέθνηκεν ὄφις μέγας, ἀλλ' ἔτι κεῖνο

---

¹⁵ μ[ηκετι P.Oxy. 2225 col. III: οὐκέτι Ψ

²⁷ An ancient name of Achaea (Paus. 7.1.1).
²⁸ River and early king of Argos who allotted Argos to Hera in a dispute with Poseidon (Paus. 2.15.4).
²⁹ Boeotia (Fr. Inc. Sed. 572).
³⁰ A river or spring near Thebes (Eur. Bacch. 519–33).
³¹ Unknown. Perhaps a generic "winding" river (Stephens, 193).

mus fled, except Aegialus[27] and Argos. For she did not
tread on those paths, since Hera had been allotted Ina-
chus.[28] And Aonia[29] too fled along the same course, and
there followed Dirce[30] and Strophia,[31] holding the hand
of their father, black-pebbled Ismenus,[32] and further back
Aesopus[33] followed with heavy knees, since he was crip-
pled by a thunderbolt. And the earthborn nymph Melia,[34]
who was whirling about, ceased from the dance, her
cheeks turned pale, and she gasped in fear for her coeval
oak when she saw the locks of Helicon tremble. My god-
desses, Muses, say whether it is true that the oaks were
created at the same time as the nymphs? The nymphs are
happy when the rain increases the oaks; and again the
nymphs weep when the oaks no longer have leaves.

[86] And Apollo, still in the womb, was very angry at
them. He threatened Thebe[35] and uttered no idle threat:
"Thebe, you wretch, why do you inquire after your fate
that soon will come? Do not yet force me to make a proph-
ecy unwillingly. Not yet is the tripod seat at Pytho my
concern, nor has the great serpent[36] yet perished, but still

---

[32] River in Thebes, son of Aesopus (Apollod. *Bibl.* 3.12.6), or
Apollo and Melia (Pind. *Pyth.* 11.4–6).

[33] Boeotian river. Zeus abducted his daughter Aegina and
struck him with a thunderbolt when he gave chase (Schol.).

[34] Daughter of Ocean, but here a tree nymph (Hes. *Theog.*
187).

[35] Daughter of Aesopus (Pind. *Isth.* 8.16–21) and eponym of
Thebes.

[36] Typhoeus. The snake that Apollo will kill before founding
his oracle at Delphi, which was called Pytho after its rotting
corpse (*Hymn. Hom. Ap.* 3.355–74).

θηρίον αἰνογένειον ἀπὸ Πλειστοῖο καθέρπον
Παρνησὸν νιφόεντα περιστέφει ἐννέα κύκλοις·
    ἀλλ᾽ ἔμπης ἐρέω τι τομώτερον ἢ ἀπὸ δάφνης.
95 φεῦγε πρόσω· ταχινός σε κιχήσομαι αἵματι λούσων
τόξον ἐμόν· σὺ δὲ τέκνα κακογλώσσοιο γυναικός
ἔλλαχες. οὐ σύ γ᾽ ἐμεῖο φίλη τροφὸς οὐδὲ Κιθαιρών
ἔσσεται· εὐαγέων δὲ καὶ εὐαγέεσσι μελοίμην."
    ὣς ἄρ᾽ ἔφη. Λητὼ δὲ μετάτροπος αὖτις ἐχώρει.
100   ἀλλ᾽ ὅτ᾽ Ἀχαιιάδες μιν ἀπηρνήσαντο πόληες
ἐρχομένην, Ἑλίκη τε Ποσειδάωνος ἑταίρη
Βοῦρά τε Δεξαμενοῖο βοόστασις Οἰκιάδαο,
ἂψ δ᾽ ἐπὶ Θεσσαλίην πόδας ἔτρεπε· φεῦγε δ᾽
        Ἄναυρος
καὶ μεγάλη Λάρισα καὶ αἱ Χειρωνίδες ἄκραι,
105 φεῦγε δὲ καὶ Πηνειὸς ἑλισσόμενος διὰ Τεμπέων·
Ἥρη, σοὶ δ᾽ ἔτι τῆμος ἀνηλεὲς ἦτορ ἔκειτο
οὐδὲ κατεκλάσθης τε καὶ ᾤκτισας, ἡνίκα πήχεις
ἀμφοτέρους ὀρέγουσα μάτην ἐφθέγξατο τοῖα·
"Νύμφαι Θεσσαλίδες, ποταμοῦ γένος, εἴπατε πατρί

---

37 River flowing from Mt. Parnassus near Delphi (Aesch.
Eum. 27).   38 Mount above Delphi, proverbially snowy
(*Hymn. Hom. Ap.* 3.282; Soph. *OT* 474–76).

39 Niobe, who boasted that her children were better than
Leto's (*Hymn* 2.22–24; cf. Hom. *Il.* 24.602–17). They were killed
by the arrows of Apollo and Artemis. This may also be a reference
to the banishment of Arsinoe I (Mineur, 128).

40 Niobe's sons were killed by Apollo on this mountain in
Boeotia (Apollod. *Bibl.* 3.5.6).   41 City on the Achaean coast
with a cult of Poseidon (Hom. *Il.* 20.403–5).

that beast with its terrible jaws, creeping down from Pleis-
tus,[37] surrounds snowy Parnassus[38] with his nine coils.

[94] But I will say something much clearer than proph-
ecies from the laurel branch. Flee onward! And I will over-
take you quickly, washing my bow in blood. For in your
charge are the children of a woman with an evil tongue.[39]
You will not be my dear nurse, nor will Cithaeron.[40] Being
pure, I should be in the care of the pure." So he spoke.
And Leto turned and went back.

[100] But when the Achaean cities refused her as
she arrived—Helice,[41] the companion of Poseidon, and
Bura,[42] the cowshed of Dexamenus, the son of Oeceus[43]—
she turned her feet back again toward Thessaly. And
Anaurus[44] fled and great Larissa[45] and the cliffs of Chi-
ron[46] fled, and the Peneius[47] too, snaking through Tempe.[48]
Hera, even then your heart still stayed pitiless; neither did
you break down nor take pity, when stretching out both of
her arms Leto spoke in vain: "Thessalian nymphs, descen-
dants of a river, tell your father to put to bed his great

---

[42] City of Achaea, destroyed with Helice in an earthquake of
373 BC.   [43] Father and son were kings of Olenus in Achaea
(Paus. 7.18.1). Dexamenus was called "the Receiver" for hosting
Heracles, but here the name is ironic.

[44] River in Thessaly (Ap. Rhod. 3.67–73) over which Jason
carried the disguised Hera.

[45] City in Thessaly on the river Peneius named for the nymph
Larissa (Paus. 2.24.1).

[46] Mt. Pelion, where the Centaur Chiron was born.

[47] River in Thessaly and grandfather of Cyrene, wife of Apollo
(Hymn 2.90–95).

[48] Valley through which the Peneius flows between Mt. Olym-
pus and Mt. Ossa (Hdt. 7.173).

110 κοιμῆσαι μέγα χεῦμα, περιπλέξασθε γενείῳ
λισσόμεναι τὰ Ζηνὸς ἐν ὕδατι τέκνα τεκέσθαι.
Πηνειὲ Φθιῶτα, τί νῦν ἀνέμοισιν ἐρίζεις;
ὦ πάτερ, οὐ μὴν ἵππον ἀέθλιον ἀμφιβέβηκας.
ἦ ῥά τοι ὧδ' αἰεὶ ταχινοὶ πόδες, ἢ ἐπ' ἐμεῖο
115 μοῦνον ἐλαφρίζουσι, πεποίησαι δὲ πέτεσθαι
σήμερον ἐξαπίνης;" ὁ δ' ἀνήκοος. "ὦ ἐμὸν ἄχθος,
ποῖ σε φέρω; μέλεοι γὰρ ἀπειρήκασι τένοντες.
Πήλιον ὦ Φιλύρης νυμφήιον, ἀλλὰ σὺ μεῖνον,
μεῖνον, ἐπεὶ καὶ θῆρες ἐν οὔρεσι πολλάκι σεῖο
120 ὠμοτόκους ὠδῖνας ἀπηρείσαντο λέαιναι."
    τὴν δ' ἄρα καὶ Πηνειὸς ἀμείβετο δάκρυα λείβων·
"Λητοῖ, Ἀναγκαίη μεγάλη θεός. οὐ γὰρ ἔγωγε
πότνια σὰς ὠδῖνας ἀναίνομαι (οἶδα καὶ ἄλλας
λουσαμένας ἀπ' ἐμεῖο λεχωίδας)· ἀλλά μοι Ἥρη
125 δαψιλὲς ἠπείλησεν. ἀπαύγασαι, οἷος ἔφεδρος
οὔρεος ἐξ ὑπάτου σκοπιὴν ἔχει, ὅς κέ με ῥεῖα
βυσσόθεν ἐξερύσειε. τί μήσομαι; ἦ ἀπολέσθαι
ἡδύ τί τοι Πηνειόν; ἴτω πεπρωμένον ἦμαρ·
τλήσομαι εἵνεκα σεῖο, καὶ εἰ μέλλοιμι ῥοάων
130 διψαλέην ἄμπωτιν ἔχων αἰώνιον ἔρρειν
καὶ μόνος ἐν ποταμοῖσιν ἀτιμότατος καλέεσθαι.
ἠνίδ' ἐγώ· τί περισσά; κάλει μόνον Εἰλήθυιαν."
εἶπε καὶ ἠρώησε μέγαν ῥόον.
                                        ἀλλά οἱ Ἄρης
Παγγαίου προθέλυμνα καρήατα μέλλεν ἀείρας
135 ἐμβαλέειν δίνῃσιν, ἀποκρύψαι δὲ ῥέεθρα·
ὑψόθε δ' ἐσμαράγησε καὶ ἀσπίδα τύψεν ἀκωκῇ

stream, entwine your hands in his beard and beg that the children of Zeus be born in his waters. Phthiotian Peneius, why now do you fight with the winds? O father, you do not ride a race horse. Are your feet always so swift? Or only from me are they light, and you suddenly take flight today?" He did not hear. "O my burden, where should I take you? My pitiful sinews refuse to go on. O Pelion, bridal chamber of Philyra,[49] please stay. Stay, since in your mountains even wild lionesses often deposit their labor of premature births."

[121] And Peneius answered her, pouring out tears, "Leto, Necessity is a great goddess. It is not I who refuse your birth pangs, queen, for I know others who have washed their afterbirth in me. But Hera has threatened me in a big way. You see what sort of watcher is positioned on the highest mountain, who easily could pull me from the depths. What should I plan to do? Is it agreeable to you that Peneius should perish? Let the fated day go forward! I will endure for your sake, even if I must limp along thirsty and with eternal ebbing of my streams, and alone be called the least honored of rivers. Here I am. What's left? Just call Eileithyia."[50] He spoke and stayed his great stream.

[133] But Ares was about to raise up the peaks of Pangaeum[51] from their foundations and cast them into Peneius' eddies and hide his streams. And from on high he made a thunderous din and struck his shield with the point

---

[49] Mother of Chiron by Cronus who fled from Rhea to give birth on Mt. Pelion (Ap. Rhod. 2.1231–41). [50] Goddess of childbirth (Hom. *Il*. 16.187–88). [51] A mountain in Thrace associated with the sons of Boreas (Pind. *Pyth*. 4.180–83).

δούρατος· ἡ δ᾽ ἐλέλιξεν ἐνόπλιον· ἔτρεμε δ᾽ Ὄσσης
οὔρεα καὶ πεδίον Κραννώνιον αἵ τε δυσαεῖς
ἐσχατιαὶ Πίνδοιο, φόβῳ δ᾽ ὠρχήσατο πᾶσα
140 Θεσσαλίη· τοῖος γὰρ ἀπ᾽ ἀσπίδος ἔβραμεν[16] ἦχος.
ὡς δ᾽, ὁπότ᾽ Αἰτναίου ὄρεος πυρὶ τυφομένοιο
σείονται μυχὰ πάντα, κατουδαίοιο γίγαντος
εἰς ἑτέρην Βριαρῆος ἐπωμίδα κινυμένοιο,
θερμάστραι τε βρέμουσιν ὑφ᾽ Ἡφαίστοιο πυράγρης
145 ἔργα θ᾽ ὁμοῦ, δεινὸν δὲ πυρίκμητοί τε λέβητες[17]
καὶ τρίποδες πίπτοντες ἐπ᾽ ἀλλήλοις ἰαχεῦσιν,
τῆμος ἔγεντ᾽ ἄραβος σάκεος τόσος εὐκύκλοιο.

Πηνειὸς δ᾽ οὐκ αὖτις ἐχάζετο, μίμνε δ᾽ ὁμοίως
καρτερὸς ὡς τὰ πρῶτα, θοὰς δ᾽ ἐστήσατο δίνας,
150 εἰσόκε οἱ Κοιηὶς ἐκέκλετο· "σῴζεο χαίρων,
σῴζεο· μὴ σύ γ᾽ ἐμεῖο πάθῃς κακὸν εἵνεκα τῆσδε
ἀντ᾽ ἐλεημοσύνης· χάριτος δέ τοι ἔσσετ᾽ ἀμοιβή."
ἦ καὶ πολλὰ πάροιθεν ἐπεὶ κάμεν ἔστιχε νήσους
εἰναλίας·[18] αἱ δ᾽ οὔ μιν ἐπερχομένην ἐδέχοντο,
155 οὐ λιπαρὸν νήεσσιν Ἐχινάδες ὅρμον ἔχουσαι,
οὐδ᾽ ἥτις Κέρκυρα φιλοξεινωτάτη ἄλλων,

---

[16] ἔβραμεν ΒΠδζ: ἔβραχεν α La.   [17] Λέβητες Ψ: λεβη]
τος P.Oxy. 2225 col. IV   [18] εἰναλίας corr. La.: εἰναλίδας Ψ

---

[52] A mountain in Thessaly. Otus and Ephialtes tried to reach
heaven by piling Ossa on Olympus and Pelion on Ossa (Apollod.
Bibl. 1.7.4). Ossa, Crannon, and Pindus form a line between Ares'
seat on Mt. Pangaeum and the river Peneius (Stephens, 202 with
map 6).

of his spear. And it rang out war. The hills of Ossa[52] trembled and the plain of Crannon, and the stormy foothills of Pindus, and all of Thessaly danced in fear. Such a din shook from his shield, as when all the recesses of Mt. Etna,[53] smoking with fire, are shaken, when the giant under the earth, Briareus,[54] moves onto his other shoulder, and the ovens roar with the tongs of Hephaestus, and the metalworks all together, cauldrons made in fire and tripods, falling on one another, ring out terribly. Such was the ringing of the well-rounded shield.

[148] But Peneius did not fall back, but remained as strong as at first, and he stopped his swift eddies, until the daughter of Coeus[55] called to him, "Save yourself, farewell! Save yourself. Do not suffer evil for my sake on account of this pity of yours. For your kindness there will be a reward." She spoke, and she was very weary when she came to the sea islands, but they did not receive her on arrival, not the Echinades,[56] which have a smooth anchorage for ships, not Cercyra,[57] the most hospitable of all

---

[53] A mountain with an active volcano in Sicily, traditional location of Hephaestus' forge (Aesch. *PV* 365–74; Pind. *Pyth.* 1.20–28; *Aet.* 113e).

[54] One of the Hundred-handers (Hom. *Il.* 1.401–4; Hes. *Theog.* 149–50). Typhoeus or Typhon was usually located under Etna (Pind. *Ol.* 4.6–7).

[55] Leto (Hes. *Theog.* 404–8; *Hymn. Hom. Ap.* 3.62).

[56] Small islands near the mouth of the Achelous that once had good harbors (Hom. *Il* 2.625–29; Hes. fr. 193.16–18 M.-W.). They had silted up by Callimachus' time.

[57] Sometimes identified with Scheria, the island of the Phaeacians, who were so hospitable to Odysseus in Book 6 of the *Odyssey*.

Ἶρις ἐπεὶ πάσῃσιν ἐφ᾽ ὑψηλοῖο Μίμαντος
σπερχομένη μάλα δεινὸν[19] ἀπέτρεπεν·[20] αἱ δ᾽ ὑπ᾽
    ὁμοκλῆς
πασσυδίῃ[21] φοβέοντο κατὰ ρόον ἥντινα τέτμοι.
160   ὠγυγίην δή᾽πειτα Κόων Μεροπηίδα νῆσον
ἵετο,[22] Χαλκιόπης ἱερὸν μυχὸν ἡρωίνης.
ἀλλά ἑ παιδὸς ἔρυκεν ἔπος τόδε· "μὴ σύ γε, μῆτερ,
τῇ με τέκοις. οὔτ᾽ οὖν ἐπιμέμφομαι οὐδὲ μεγαίρω
νῆσον, ἐπεὶ λιπαρή τε καὶ εὔβοτος, εἴ νύ τις ἄλλη·
165   ἀλλά οἱ ἐκ Μοιρέων τις ὀφειλόμενος θεὸς ἄλλος
ἐστί, Σαωτήρων ὕπατον γένος· ᾧ ὑπὸ μίτρην
ἵξεται οὐκ ἀέκουσα Μακηδόνι κοιρανέεσθαι
ἀμφοτέρη μεσόγεια καὶ αἱ πελάγεσσι κάθηνται,
μέχρις ὅπου περάτη τε καὶ ὁππόθεν ὠκέες ἵπποι
170   Ἥλιον φορέουσιν· ὁ δ᾽ εἴσεται ἤθεα πατρός.
    καί νύ ποτε ξυνός τις ἐλεύσεται ἄμμιν ἄεθλος
ὕστερον, ὁππόταν οἱ μὲν ἐφ᾽ Ἑλλήνεσσι μάχαιραν
βαρβαρικὴν καὶ Κελτὸν ἀναστήσαντες Ἄρηα
ὀψίγονοι Τιτῆνες ἀφ᾽ ἑσπέρου ἐσχατόωντος
175   ρώσωνται νιφάδεσσιν ἐοικότες ἢ ἰσάριθμοι
τείρεσιν, ἡνίκα πλεῖστα κατ᾽ ἠέρα βουκολέονται,[23]

---

[19] δεινο[P.Oxy. 2225 col. V: πολλὸν Ψ
[20]]τρεπεν P.Oxy. 2225 col. V: ἀπέτραπεν Ψ
[21] πασσυδίῃ con. La.: πασσυδι[P.Oxy. 2225 col. V:]ασσυδ[
P.Oxy. 2258A fr. 5 verso: πανσυδίη Ψ
[22] ἵ]ετο P.Oxy. 2225 col. V suppl. Lobel: ἵκετο Ψ et P.Oxy.
2258A fr. 5 verso   [23] Post 176 duo vv. lacunosi in P.Oxy.
2225 col. V, suppl. Pfeiffer: φρούρια Ψ

other islands, since Iris on high Mimas, terribly angry at
all of them, turned them away. And whichever she reached,
at the threat they quickly fled down the stream.

[160] And then to Ogygian Cos, the island of Merops,[58]
she came, the holy sanctum of the heroine Chalciope,[59]
but this word from her child drew her back, "Mother, do
not give birth to me here. I do not blame the island nor do
I bear any grudge, since it is as rich and well-pastured as
any other. But to her is owed by the Fates some other
god,[60] the highest lineage of the Saviors.[61] Under their
crown will come, not unwilling to be ruled by a Macedo-
nian, both the continents and lands that sit in the sea, as
far as the extremities of the universe and whence the swift
horses carry Helios.[62] And he will realize his father's ways.

[171] Yes, and some day afterward a general conflict
will come upon us, when the later-born Titans,[63] raising
up against the Greeks a barbarian sword and Celtic war,
from the farthest west rushing like snow or equal in num-
ber to the heavenly bodies when they flock most thickly in
the sky.

---

[58] In the sea opposite Halicarnassus. Named after the daugh-
ter of Merops (*Hymn. Hom. Ap.* 3.42–56; Thuc. 8.41.2).

[59] Daughter of Eurypylus, king of Cos (Apollod. *Bibl.* 2.7.8).

[60] Ptolemy II Philadelphus, born on Cos in 308/9 BC (Parian
Marble 120, *BNJ* 239 B 19).

[61] *Soteres* (Saviors) was a cult title of Ptolemy I and his wife,
Berenice I.

[62] The sun god (*Hymn. Hom. Hel.* 31.1–19).

[63] The Gauls or Celts, who were defeated in an attack against
Delphi in 279/8 (Paus. 10.22.12–23.14).

177a παῖδ[ες   ].. σα[ ]. [ ]
177b Δωρι . [.] . [   ] . οσα[ ]ς
 καὶ πεδία Κρισσαῖα καὶ Ἡφαί[στο]ιο φάρ[αγγ]ες[24]
 ἀμφιπεριστείνωνται,[25] ἴδωσι δὲ πίονα καπνόν[26]
180 γείτονος αἰθομένοιο, καὶ οὐκέτι μοῦνον ἀκουῇ,
 ἀλλ᾽ ἤδη παρὰ νηὸν ἀπαυγάζοιντο[27] φάλαγγας
 δυσμενέων, ἤδη δὲ παρὰ τριπόδεσσιν ἐμεῖο
 φάσγανα καὶ ζωστῆρας ἀναιδέας ἐχθομένας τε
 ἀσπίδας, αἱ Γαλάτῃσι κακὴν ὁδὸν ἄφρονι φύλῳ
185 στήσονται· τέων αἱ μὲν ἐμοὶ γέρας, αἱ δ᾽ ἐπὶ Νείλῳ
 ἐν πυρὶ τοὺς φορέοντας ἀποπνεύσαντας ἰδοῦσαι
 κείσονται βασιλῆος ἀέθλια πολλὰ καμόντος.
 ἐσσόμενε Πτολεμαῖε, τά τοι μαντήια Φοίβου.[28]
 αἰνήσεις μέγα δή τι τὸν εἰσέτι γαστέρι μάντιν
190 ὕστερον ἤματα πάντα.

       σὺ δὲ ξυμβάλλεο, μῆτερ·
 ἔστι διειδομένη τις ἐν ὕδατι νῆσος ἀραιή,
 πλαζομένη πελάγεσσι· πόδες δέ οἱ οὐκ ἐνὶ χώρῃ,
 ἀλλὰ παλιρροίῃ ἐπινήχεται ἀνθέρικος ὥς,
 ἔνθα νότος, ἔνθ᾽ εὖρος, ὅπη φορέῃσι θάλασσα.
195 τῇ με φέροις· κείνην γὰρ ἐλεύσεαι εἰς ἐθέλουσαν."

 αἱ μὲν τόσσα λέγοντος ἀπέτρεχον εἰν ἁλὶ νῆσοι·
 Ἀστερίη φιλόμολπε, σὺ δ᾽ Εὐβοίηθε κατήιεις,
 Κυκλάδας ὀψομένη περιηγέας, οὔτι παλαιόν,

---

[24] Ἡφαί[στο]ιο φάρ[αγγ]ες *P.Oxy.* 2225 col. V suppl. Lobel,
Pfeiffer: ἤπειροι tum spatium Ψ: ἠπείροιο φάραγγες LMNOT
[25] ἀμφιπεριστείνωνται corr. anon. Bernensis: -στείνονται Ψ

boys ...

Dorian ...

and the Crissian plains[64] and the ravines of Hephaestus. Pressed on all sides, they will see the rich smoke [180] of their burning neighbor, and no longer only hear of it. But already beside the temple they might glimpse the phalanxes of the enemies, and already beside my tripods, the swords, cruel belts and hostile shields, which will make for an evil journey for the Galatians,[65] a foolish tribe. And some of these will be a prize of honor for me. Others, having seen those wearing them perish in fire, will be laid at the Nile, prizes for a king who labored much. Ptolemy yet to be, these are Phoebus' prophecies for you. Greatly will you praise the seer in the belly, in all the days to come.

[190] But take note, mother: there is a slender island to be seen wandering in the sea. Her feet are not in one place, but she swims in the backflow like an asphodel, wherever the south wind, the east wind, or the sea take her. Take me there, for you will be going to one who wishes it."

[196] After he had spoken this much, the other islands in the sea ran away. But you, Asteria, lover of song, came down from Euboea, to visit the circular Cyclades. Not long

---

[64] In the foothills of Mt. Parnassus near Delphi (Hdt. 8.32; Soph. *El.* 730).   [65] The Gallic invaders. Some who later settled in Asia Minor became known as Galatians.

---

[26] καπνον *P.Oxy.* 2225 col. V: καρπόν Ψ

[27] ἀπαυγάζοιντο Ψ: απαυγαζαντο *P.Oxy.* 2225 col. V

[28] Φοιβ]ου *P.Oxy.* 2225 col. VI suppl. Lobel et coni. La.: φαίνω Ψ

ἀλλ' ἔτι τοι μετόπισθε Γεραίστιον εἵπετο φῦκος·

200 ὡς δ' ἴδες, [ὥσ] ἔστης [   ]ιδου[.]α[29]

θαρσαλέη τάδ' ἔλεξας[30] [   ].... ρ'[[31]]

δαίμον·[32] ὑπ' ὠδίνεσσι βαρυνομένην ὁρόωσα·

"Ἥρη, τοῦτό με ῥέξον ὅ τοι φίλον· οὐ γὰρ ἀπειλάς

ὑμετέρας ἐφύλαξα· πέρα, πέρα εἰς ἐμέ, Λητοῖ."

205   ἔννεπες· ἡ δ' ἀρητὸν ἄλης ἀπεπαύσατο

       †λυγρῆς,[33]

ἕζετο δ' Ἰνωποῖο παρὰ ῥόον ὅν τε βάθιστον

γαῖα τότ' ἐξανίησιν, ὅτε πλήθοντι ῥεέθρῳ

Νεῖλος ἀπὸ κρημνοῖο κατέρχεται Αἰθιοπῆος·

λύσατο δὲ ζώνην, ἀπὸ δ' ἐκλίθη ἔμπαλιν ὤμοις

210 φοίνικος ποτὶ πρέμνον ἀμηχανίης ὑπὸ λυγρῆς

τειρομένη· νότιος δὲ διὰ χροὸς ἔρρεεν ἱδρώς.

εἶπε δ' ἀλυσθενέουσα·[34] "τί μητέρα, κοῦρε, βαρύνεις;

αὕτη τοι, φίλε, νῆσος ἐπιπλώουσα θαλάσσῃ.

γείνεο, γείνεο, κοῦρε, καὶ ἤπιος ἔξιθι κόλπου."

215   νύμφα Διὸς βαρύθυμε, σὺ δ' οὐκ ἄρ' ἔμελλες

       ἄπυστος

δὴν ἔμεναι· τοίη σε προσέδραμεν ἀγγελιῶτις,

εἶπε δ' ἔτ' ἀσθμαίνουσα, φόβῳ δ' ἀνεμίσγετο μῦθος·

"Ἥρη τιμήεσσα, πολὺ προὔχουσα θεάων,

---

29 Versum om. Ψ: ὡς δ' ἴδες, [ὥσ] ἔστης P.Oxy. 2225 col. V
suppl. Pfeiffer   ἔστης δ' ἐν μέσσῃσι LMNOT]ιδου[σ]α
P.Oxy. 2225 col. VI: κατοικτ(ε)ιρουσα LMNOT
30 Θαρσαλεηταδελεξασ P.Oxy. 2225 col. VI: om. Ψ

ago, the Geraestian[66] seaweed still followed behind you.
As you saw, you stopped . . .
Taking heart, you spoke thus . . .
seeing the goddess oppressed with birth pains, "Hera, do
to me what you wish. I will not regard your threats. Cross
over, cross over to me, Leto."

[205] You spoke, and she gratefully stopped her griev-
ous wandering, then sat beside the stream of Inopus[67]
which the earth sends forth in deepest flood when the Nile
comes down in full torrent from the Aethiopian height.
She loosened her belt and leaned back her shoulders
against the trunk of a palm tree, distressed by grievous
helplessness. And damp sweat poured over her body like
rain. Though weak, she spoke. "Why, child, do you weigh
down your mother? There, dear, is your island floating in
the sea. Be born, be born, my child, and go forth gently
from the womb."

[215] Furious wife of Zeus, you were not to remain
uninformed for long, so swift a messenger had run to you.
And she spoke still panting, her speech tinged with fear,
"Honored Hera, much the best of the goddesses, I am

---

[66] Hill and harbor in southern Euboea with a temple of Po-
seidon (Hom. *Od.* 3.177–79). [67] River in Delos associated
with Apollo's birth (*Hymn. Hom. Ap.* 3.18). In myth it was con-
nected underground to the Nile (*Hymn* 3.171).

---

[31] fin. φλέξας (τάδε λέξας T in marg.) ἐπεὶ περικαίεο
πυρί Ψ   [32] δαιμον P.Oxy. 2225 col. VI: τλήμον' Ψ
[33] λυγρῆς Ψ: δηρῆς Mineur   [34] αλ[υσθ]ενεο[υσα P.Oxy.
2225 suppl. Lobel: ἀλυσθμαίνουσα Ψ

309

σὴ μὲν ἐγώ, σὰ δὲ πάντα, σὺ δὲ κρείουσα κάθησαι
220 γνησίη Οὐλύμποιο, καὶ οὐ χέρα δείδιμεν ἄλλην
θηλυτέρην, σὺ δ᾿, ἄνασσα, τὸν αἴτιον εἴσεαι ὀργῆς.
Λητώ τοι μίτρην ἀναλύεται ἔνδοθι νήσου.
ἄλλαι μὲν πᾶσαί μιν ἀπέστυγον οὐδ᾿ ἐδέχοντο·
Ἀστερίη δ᾿ ὀνομαστὶ παρερχομένην ἐκάλεσσεν,
225 Ἀστερίη, πόντοιο κακὸν σάρον· οἶσθα καὶ αὐτή.
ἀλλά, φίλη, δύνασαι γάρ, ἀμύνειν35 πότνια δούλους
ὑμετέροις, οἳ σεῖο πέδον πατέουσιν ἐφετμῇ."

ἦ καὶ ὑπὸ χρύσειον ἐδέθλιον ἷζε κύων ὥς,
Ἀρτέμιδος ἥτις τε, θοῆς ὅτε παύσεται ἄγρης,
230 ἵζει θηρήτειρα παρ᾿ ἴχνεσιν, οὔατα δ᾿ αὐτῆς
ὀρθὰ μάλ᾿, αἰὲν ἑτοῖμα θεῆς ὑποδέχθαι ὁμοκλήν·
τῇ ἰκέλη Θαύμαντος ὑπὸ θρόνον ἷζετο κούρη.
κείνη δ᾿ οὐδέ ποτε σφετέρης ἐπιλήθεται ἕδρης,
οὐδ᾿ ὅτε οἱ ληθαῖον ἐπὶ πτερὸν ὕπνος ἐρείσῃ,
235 ἀλλ᾿ αὐτοῦ μεγάλοιο ποτὶ γλωχῖνα θρόνοιο
τυτθὸν ἀποκλίνασα καρήατα λέχριος εὕδει.
οὐδέ ποτε ζώνην ἀναλύεται οὐδὲ ταχείας
ἐνδρομίδας, μή οἵ τι καὶ αἰφνίδιον ἔπος εἴπῃ
δεσπότις.
                  ἡ δ᾿ ἀλεγεινὸν ἀλαστήσασα προσηύδα·
240 "οὕτω νῦν, ὦ Ζηνὸς ὀνείδεα, καὶ γαμέοισθε
λάθρια καὶ τίκτοιτε κεκρυμμένα, μηδ᾿ ὅθι δειλαί
δυστοκέες μογέουσιν ἀλετρίδες, ἀλλ᾿ ὅθι φῶκαι
εἰνάλιαι τίκτουσιν, ἐνὶ σπιλάδεσσιν ἐρήμοις.
Ἀστερίῃ δ᾿ οὐδέν τι βαρύνομαι εἵνεκα τῆσδε
245 ἀμπλακίης, οὐδ᾿ ἔστιν ὅπως ἀποθύμια ῥέξω,

yours, all things are yours, and you sit as legitimate ruler
of Olympus. We fear no other female hand. You, Queen,
will know the cause of your anger. Leto is loosening her
belt within an island. All the others abhorred her and did
not receive her. Asteria called her by name as she was
passing by, Asteria, that evil scum of the sea. You know it
yourself. But, dear Queen, defend your servants (for you
are able), who walk the earth at your command."

[228] So she spoke, and sat beside the golden throne
like Artemis' dog which, when it ceases from the swift
hunt, sits beside her feet, a hunter, with her ears straight,
ever ready to receive the goddess' order. Like her the
daughter of Thaumas sat beside the throne. She never
forgets her station, not even when sleep presses upon her
its forgetful wing, but there by the edge of the great throne
itself, inclining her head a little at a slant, she sleeps.
Never does she loosen her belt or her swift boots, in case
the queen might give her some sudden order.

[239] And Hera, grievously distraught, spoke. "Now, O
shameful creatures of Zeus, may you all marry secretly and
give birth in hiding, not even where poor corn mill-women
labor with difficult births, but where the seals in the sea
give birth, on desolate rocks. But I am not at all angry at
Asteria on account of this lapse, nor will I do anything as

---

35 ἀμύνειν, πότνια, δούλοις/ ὑμετέροις Ψ: ἀμύνεο, πότνια,
δούλους/ ὑμετέρους coni. Maas

τόσσα δέοι³⁶ (μάλα γάρ τε κακῶς ἐχαρίσσατο
    Λητοῖ)·
ἀλλά μιν ἔκπαγλόν τι σεβίζομαι, οὕνεκ' ἐμεῖο
δέμνιον οὐκ ἐπάτησε, Διὸς δ' ἀνθείλετο πόντον."
    ἡ μὲν ἔφη· κύκνοι δὲ †θεοῦ μέλποντες ἀοιδοί†³⁷
250 Μηόνιον Πακτωλὸν ἐκυκλώσαντο λιπόντες
ἑβδομάκις περὶ Δῆλον, ἐπήεισαν δὲ λοχείῃ
Μουσάων ὄρνιθες, ἀοιδότατοι πετεηνῶν
(ἔνθεν ὁ παῖς τοσσάσδε λύρῃ ἐνεδήσατο χορδάς
ὕστερον, ὁσσάκι κύκνοι ἐπ' ὠδίνεσσιν ἄεισαν)·
255 ὄγδοον οὐκέτ' ἄεισαν, ὁ δ' ἔκθορεν, αἱ δ' ἐπὶ μακρόν
νύμφαι Δηλιάδες, ποταμοῦ γένος ἀρχαίοιο,
εἶπαν Ἐλειθυίης ἱερὸν μέλος, αὐτίκα δ' αἰθήρ
χάλκεος ἀντήχησε διαπρυσίην ὀλολυγήν.
οὐδ' Ἥρη νεμέσησεν, ἐπεὶ χόλον ἐξέλετο Ζεύς.
260   χρύσεά τοι τότε πάντα θεμείλια γείνετο Δῆλε,
χρυσῷ δὲ τροχόεσσα πανήμερος ἔρρεε λίμνη,
χρύσειον δ' ἐκόμησε γενέθλιον ἔρνος ἐλαίης,
χρυσῷ δὲ πλήμυρε βαθὺς Ἰνωπὸς ἑλιχθείς.
αὐτὴ δὲ χρυσέοιο ἀπ' οὔδεος εἵλεο παῖδα,
265 ἐν δ' ἐβάλευ κόλποισιν, ἔπος δ' ἐφθέγξαο τοῖον·
"ὦ μεγάλη, πολύβωμε, πολύπτολι, πολλὰ φέρουσα,
πίονες ἤπειροί τε καὶ αἳ περιναίετε νῆσοι,
αὕτη ἐγὼ τοιήδε· δυσήροτος, ἀλλ' ἀπ' ἐμεῖο
Δήλιος Ἀπόλλων κεκλήσεται, οὐδέ τις ἄλλη
270 γαιάων τοσσόνδε θεῷ πεφιλήσεται ἄλλῳ,
οὐ Κερχνὶς κρείοντι Ποσειδάωνι Λεχαίῳ,

unpleasant as I should, since it was very wrong of her to
favor Leto. No, I honor her very highly for not trampling
on my bed but preferring the sea to Zeus."

[249] She spoke. And swans, the minstrels of the god,
leaving Maeonian Pactolus,[68] circled seven times around
Delos. They sang at the birth, the birds of the Muses, most
musical of winged creatures. Hence the divine child later
on strung just so many strings on the lyre, as many as the
swans sang at his birth. They had not yet sung the eighth
when he leaped out, and the Delian nymphs, born of the
ancient river, intoned the holy song of Eileithyia, and at
once the bronze sky echoed their piercing cry. Nor was
Hera angry, since Zeus had taken away her anger.

[260] Then, Delos, all of your foundations became
golden, the round lake flowed all day long with gold, and
your birthday shoot of olive bloomed gold, and with gold
the eddying depths of Inopus flowed, and you yourself
took the child from the golden earth and put him in your
lap, and made this speech, "O great Earth, with many al-
tars, many cities, bounteous produce! And you rich conti-
nents and the islands that surround them! I myself am like
this: hard for plowing. Yet from me Apollo will be called
Delius, and no other land will be so beloved by another
god: not Cerchnis, by the ruler Poseidon of Lechaeum;[69]

---

[68] A river near Sardis in Lydia known for its swans (Ap. Rhod.
4.1300–1302).

[69] The two harbors of Corinth, Cenchreae and Lechaeum
were named for sons of Poseidon (Paus. 2.2.3).

---

37 θεοῦ μέλποντες ἀοιδοί Ψ: θεοῦ μέλποντες μέλλοντος
ἀοιδοί Dyck: θεὸν μέλποντες ἀοιδαῖς Ruhken: θεοῦ μέλλοντες
ἀοιδοί Wilamowitz

313

CALLIMACHUS

οὐ πάγος Ἑρμείῃ Κυλλήνιος, οὐ Διὶ Κρήτη,
ὡς ἐγὼ Ἀπόλλωνι· καὶ ἔσσομαι οὐκέτι πλαγκτή."
ὧδε σὺ μὲν κατέλεξας· ὁ δὲ γλυκὺν ἔσπασε μαζόν.

275 τῷ καὶ νησάων ἁγιωτάτη ἐξέτι κείνου
κλῄζῃ, Ἀπόλλωνος κουροτρόφος· οὐδέ σ' Ἐννώ
οὐδ' Ἀΐδης οὐδ' ἵπποι ἐπιστείβουσιν Ἄρηος·
ἀλλά τοι ἀμφιετεῖς δεκατηφόροι αἰὲν ἀπαρχαί
πέμπονται, πᾶσαι δὲ χοροὺς ἀνάγουσι πόληες,

280 αἵ τε πρὸς ἠοίην αἵ θ' ἕσπερον αἵ τ' ἀνὰ μέσσην
κλήρους ἐστήσαντο, καὶ οἳ καθύπερθε βορείης
οἰκία θινὸς ἔχουσι, πολυχρονιώτατον αἷμα.
οἱ μέν τοι καλάμην τε καὶ ἱερὰ δράγματα πρῶτοι
ἀσταχύων φορέουσιν· ἃ Δωδώνηθε Πελασγοί

285 τηλόθεν ἐκβαίνοντα πολὺ πρώτιστα δέχονται,
γηλεχέες θεράποντες ἀσιγήτοιο λέβητος·
δεύτερον Ἴριον ἄστυ καὶ οὔρεα Μηλίδος αἴης
ἔρχονται· κεῖθεν δὲ διαπλώουσιν Ἀβάντων
εἰς ἀγαθὸν πεδίον Ληλάντιον· οὐδ' ἔτι μακρός

290 ὁ πλόος Εὐβοίηθεν, ἐπεὶ σέο γείτονες ὅρμοι.
πρῶταί τοι τάδ' ἔνεικαν ἀπὸ ξανθῶν Ἀριμασπῶν
Οὖπίς τε Λοξώ τε καὶ εὐαίων Ἑκαέργη,

---

70 Hermes' birthplace in Arcadia (*Hymn. Hom. Herm.* 4.1–2).
71 God of war (Hom. *Il.* 5.592–93; *Hymn* 2.85–86).
72 The earliest Greeks (Hdt. 1.56–58).
73 Oracle of Zeus in Epirus (Hdt. 2.55).
74 The Pelasgian interpreters of Zeus' oracle at Dodona who slept on the ground (Hom. *Il.* 16.232–35). The gong produced by

314

not the hill of Cyllene,[70] by Hermes; not Crete, by Zeus, as I by Apollo. And I will no longer be wandering." So you spoke, and he drew on your sweet breast.

[275] And so from that day you are called the holiest of islands, the nurse of Apollo. Neither does Enyo,[71] nor Ares, nor the horses of Ares tread on you. But to you every year tithes of first fruits are sent, and all the cities send choruses, those that have established estates toward the east, and those toward the west, and those in the south, and those who have homes above the shore of Boreas, the most long-lived race. These first bring the stalk to you and holy sheaths of corn, which coming from so far away the Pelasgians[72] from Dodona[73] receive first of all. They sleep on the earth, servants of the unsilent caldron.[74]

[287] Second they come to the holy city and the mountains of the Malian land.[75] And from there they sail into the good Lelantian[76] plain of the Abantes.[77] Then it is no long sail from Euboea, since your harbors are neighbors. The first who brought these offerings to you from the blond Arimaspi[78] were Upis, Loxo, and blessed Hec-

---

striking the sacred caldron with a whip or alternatively by a row of tripods, which had some unknown role in the ritual, became proverbial for someone who never stopped talking (Strabo 7.3; Steph. Byz. δ 146 Billerbeck s.v. Δωδώνη).

[75] Located at the mouth of the river Spercheios with a coast along the western Aegean.

[76] Between Chalcis and Eretria (*Hymn. Hom. Ap.* 3.220).

[77] Ionian tribe living in Euboea (Hdt. 1.146).

[78] Mythical people with one eye who lived south of the Hyperboreans (Hdt. 4.27).

θυγατέρες Βορέαο, καὶ ἄρσενες οἱ τότ᾽ ἄριστοι
ἠιθέων· οὐδ᾽ οἵγε παλιμπετὲς οἴκαδ᾽ ἵκοντο,
295 εὔμοιροι δ᾽ ἐγένοντο, καὶ ἀκλεὲς οὔποτ᾽ ἐκεῖνοι.[38]
ἦ τοι Δηλιάδες μέν, ὅτ᾽ εὐηχὴς ὑμέναιος
ἤθεα κουράων μορμύσσεται, ἥλικα χαίτην
παρθενικαῖς, παῖδες δὲ θέρος τὸ πρῶτον ἰούλων
ἄρσενες ἠιθέοισιν ἀπαρχόμενοι φορέουσιν.
300 Ἀστερίη θυόεσσα, σὲ μὲν περί τ᾽ ἀμφί τε νῆσοι
κύκλον ἐποιήσαντο καὶ ὡς χορὸν ἀμφεβάλοντο·
οὔτε σιωπηλὴν οὔτ᾽ ἄψοφον οὖλος ἐθείραις
Ἕσπερος, ἀλλ᾽ αἰεί σε καταβλέπει ἀμφιβόητον.
οἱ μὲν ὑπαείδουσι νόμον Λυκίοιο γέροντος,
305 ὅν τοι ἀπὸ Ξάνθοιο θεοπρόπος ἤγαγεν Ὠλήν·
αἱ δὲ ποδὶ πλήσσουσι χορίτιδες ἀσφαλὲς οὖδας.
δὴ τότε καὶ στεφάνοισι βαρύνεται ἱρὸν ἄγαλμα
Κύπριδος ἀρχαίης ἀριήκοον, ἥν ποτε Θησεύς
εἵσατο, σὺν παίδεσσιν ὅτε Κρήτηθεν ἀνέπλει.
310 οἱ χαλεπὸν μύκημα καὶ ἄγριον υἷα φυγόντες
Πασιφάης καὶ γναμπτὸν ἕδος σκολιοῦ λαβυρίνθου,
πότνια, σὸν περὶ βωμὸν ἐγειρομένου κιθαρισμοῦ
κύκλιον ὠρχήσαντο, χοροῦ δ᾽ ἡγήσατο Θησεύς.

---

[38] ἐκεῖνοι Ψ: ἔσονται Mineur: κεῖνται Maas

---

[79] Upis is also a cult title of Artemis (*Hymn* 3.204, 240). Loxo and Hecaerge are feminine versions of epithets of Apollo, Loxias and Hecaergos.

[80] The evening star, i.e., the planet Venus.

aerge,[79] the daughters of Boreas, and the males who were then the best of the youth. They did not come home again, but they had propitious fates, and never will they be without fame. Indeed the daughters of Delos, when the lovely-sounding marriage hymn frightens the sensitive girls, bring offerings of their hair to the maidens, and the young males offer to the youths the first harvest of the down from their cheeks.

[300] Fragrant Asteria, around you the islands made a circle as if they had arranged a chorus. Nor does Hesperus[80] with curly hair see you silent or noiseless, but always surrounded by sound. They sing the song of the old man of Lycia, the very one that the seer Olen[81] brought from Xanthus. The chorus girls strike with their feet the solid ground. Then too is laden with crowns the holy statue of ancient Cypris,[82] widely known, which Theseus[83] brought when he sailed from Crete with the youths. Escaping the terrible bellowing and the wild son of Pasiphaë,[84] and the coiled lair of the crooked labyrinth, Queen, around your altar with raised lyre they danced in a circle, and Theseus

[81] An early Greek poet from Xanthus in Lydia, author of hymns to Apollo (Hdt. 4.35).

[82] Aphrodite, who emerged from the sea near Cyprus (Hes. *Theog.* 191–99).

[83] Athenian hero who slew the Minotaur and rescued the Athenian youths who were sent to the monster as tribute (Pl. *Phdr.* 58b).

[84] The Minotaur, half-man, half-bull, was the offspring of Pasiphaë, wife of King Minos of Crete, and a bull given to Minos by Poseidon for sacrifice (Apollod. *Bibl.* 3.1.4).

ἔνθεν ἀειζώοντα θεωρίδος ἱερὰ Φοίβῳ
315 Κεκροπίδαι πέμπουσι τοπήια νηὸς ἐκείνης.
    Ἀστερίη πολύβωμε πολύλλιτε, τίς δέ σε ναύτης
ἔμπορος Αἰγαίοιο παρήλυθε νηὶ θεούσῃ;
οὐχ οὕτω μεγάλοι μιν ἐπιπνείουσιν ἀῆται,
χρειὼ δ᾽ ὅττι τάχιστον ἄγει πλόον, ἀλλὰ τὰ λαίφη
320 ὠκέες ἐστείλαντο καὶ οὐ πάλιν αὖτις ἔβησαν,
πρὶν μέγαν ἢ σέο βωμὸν ὑπὸ πληγῇσιν ἑλίξαι
ῥησσόμενον καὶ πρέμνον ὀδακτάσαι ἁγνὸν ἐλαίης
χεῖρας ἀποστρέψαντας· ἃ Δηλιὰς εὕρετο νύμφη
παίγνια κουρίζοντι καὶ Ἀπόλλωνι γελαστύν.
325   ἱστίη ὦ νήσων εὐέστιε, χαῖρε μὲν αὐτή,
χαίροι δ᾽ Ἀπόλλων τε καὶ ἣν ἐλοχεύσατο[39] Λητώ.

[39] ἐλοχεύσατο Ψ: ἐλοχεύσαο Wilamowitz, Pfeiffer

4a Schol. Ψ

1   ⟨Τίνα⟩· κατὰ τίνα.
7   ⟨Πίμπλειαν⟩· ὄρος Θρᾴκης ἱερὸν Μουσῶν.
11a   ἄτροπος: ἤγουν ἀκίνητος καὶ ἄσειστος· ἡ
γὰρ Δῆλος οὐδέποτε σειομένη τινάσσεται. φησὶ δὲ
καὶ Θουκυδίδης ὅτι σεισμὸς γενόμενος τοσοῦτον ἦν
μέγας ὡς καὶ τὴν Δῆλον νῆσον σεισθῆναι.
11b   ἄλλως. ἄτροπος· ἤγουν ἀγεώργητος· μὴ τρε-
πομένη καὶ μεταβαλλομένη ἐν τῷ ἀροῦσθαι· τραχεῖα
γάρ.
11c   ἁλιπλὴξ· δὲ ὑπὸ τῆς ἁλὸς πληττομένη.

lead the chorus. Hence the Cecropidae[85] send ever-living offerings of the tribute-bearing ship to Phoebus: the rigging of that vessel.

[316] Asteria of many altars and many prayers, what maritime trader of the Aegean ever passes by you in a speeding ship? Even if strong winds blow on him, and need urges the quickest possible sailing, they speedily furl the sails and do not board again until they have circled the great altar buffeted by blows and bitten the sacred trunk of the olive with hands tied behind. These things the Delian nymph invented as games and amusement for the young Apollo.

[325] O prosperous hearth of the islands, hail to you, to Apollo, and to her whom Leto bore.

[85] The Athenians. Cecrops was an early king of Athens (Hdt. 8.44).

4a Ψ Scholia

1   *tina*: at what [time].
7   *Pimpleian*: a mountain in Thrace holy to the Muses.
11a   *atropos*: unmoving and unshaking. Delos, unmoved, is never shaken. But Thucydides says (2.8.3) that there was an earthquake so great that the Delian temple was shaken.
11b   *allōs. atropos*: another meaning is untilled: that is to say, uncultivated. Not altered and changed in plowing: rough.
11c   *(h)aliplēx*: struck by the sea.

12   ⟨αἰθυίης⟩· λάροις.

14a   ⟨ἀπομάσσεται⟩· ἀπορρίπτει.

14b   ⟨ἄχνην⟩· ἀφρόν.

18   οὐχ ὅτι αἱ νῆσοι ἀθροίζονται, ἀλλ' οἱ ἔξαρ-
χοι θεοί.

19   ⟨Κύρνος⟩ ἡ νῦν †Τύρος† καλουμένη.

20a   ⟨Μάκρις Ἀβαντιάς⟩· ἡ Εὔβοια.

20b   ⟨Ἑλλοπιήων⟩· τῶν Εὐβοέων.

21   ⟨ἣν ἐπενήξατο Κύπρις⟩· ἡ Κύπρος.

22   ⟨σαοῖ⟩· σώζει.

23   ⟨ἐρυμναί⟩· ἠσφαλισμέναι.

26   ⟨Στρυμονίου⟩· Στρυμὼν ποταμός ἐστι καὶ
πόλις Θρᾴκης.

28   ⟨πολέες⟩· αἱ Πινδάρου καὶ Βακχυλίδου. ἔδει
δὲ εἰπεῖν πολλαί.

30   λέγεται γὰρ ὅτι ὁ Ποσειδῶν τῇ τριαίνῃ ἀπο-
σπῶν τὰς νήσους ἐποίει.

31   ⟨ἄορι τριγλώχινι⟩· τῇ τριαίνῃ.

41   ⟨ἀπὸ Ξάνθοιο πολίχνης⟩· ἀπό τινος Ξάνθου
βασιλεύσαντος Τροιζῆνος.

46   ⟨Χαλκιδικῆς⟩· Χαλκὶς πόλις Εὐβοίας.

47   Σούνιον· ἀκρωτήριον τῆς Ἀττικῆς.

48a   ⟨νήσοιο . . . Παρθενίης⟩· τῆς Σάμου.

48b   ⟨διάβροχον⟩· τὸν γόνιμον.

50   ⟨Ἀγκαίου⟩· Ἀγκαῖος βασιλεὺς Σάμου.

57   ⟨διακριδόν⟩· κατ' ἐξοχήν, μεγάλως.

60   ⟨σπερχομένη⟩· ὀργιζομένη.

61   ⟨εἵατο⟩· ἐκαθέζοντο.

12   *aithyiēs*: gulls
14a   *apomassetai*: it wipes off.
14b   *achnēn*: foam.
18   Not that the islands would gather together, but that the gods are the leaders.
19   *Kyrnos*: the one now called †Tyros.†
20a   *Makris Abantias*: Euboea.
20b   *Ellopieōn*: of the Euboeans.
21   *en epenēxato Kypris* (which Cypris first swam to): Cyprus.
22   *saoi*: she keeps safe.
23   *erumnai*: secure.
26   *Stymoniou*: Strymon is a river and city of Thrace.
28   *polees*: [the spelling] of Pindar and Bacchylides. One ought to write *pollai*.
30   He says that Poseidon made the islands separating them with his trident.
31   *aori triglōchini*: the trident.
41   *apo Xanthoio polichnēs*: from a certain Xanthus, who was king of Troezen.
46   *Chalkidikēs*: Chalcis, a city of Euboea.
47   *Sounion*: the cape of Attica.
48a   *nēsoio . . . Pantheniēs*: of Samos.
48b   *diabrochon*: fruitful.
50   *Ankaious*: King Ancaeus of Samos.
57   *diakridon*: distinctly, to an extreme.
60   *sperchomenē*: being angry.
61   *eiato*: they sat.

CALLIMACHUS

63   ⟨Αἵμου⟩· ὄρος Θράκης ὁ Αἷμος.

65   ⟨ἑπτάμυχον⟩· πολύμυχον.

66   ⟨νησάων⟩· παραλόγως ἔχει τὴν διαίρεσιν νη-
σάων. οὐ γὰρ ἀπὸ τῶν εἰς αῑ ἐστίν.

67a   ⟨κόρη⟩· ἡ Ἶρις.

67b   ⟨Μίμαντι⟩· ὄρος ⟨ἀντικρὺ⟩ Χίου.

71a   ⟨Παρθένιον⟩· ὄρος Ἀρκαδίας τὸ Παρθένιον,
ἔνθα τὴν Αὔγην τοῦ Ἀλεοῦ τὴν θυγατέρα, ἱέρειαν τῆς
Ἀθηνᾶς, ἔφθειρεν Ἡρακλῆς.

71b   ⟨Φενειός⟩· πόλις Ἀρκαδίας ἀρχαία.

73a   ⟨ἔμπλην⟩· χωρίς.

73b   ⟨Αἰγιαλοῦ⟩· Ὅμηρος· "Αἰγιαλόν τ᾽ ἀνὰ
πάντα."

75   ⟨Ἀονίη⟩· Ἀονίαν τὰς Θήβας λέγει.

76   ⟨Δίρκη τε Στροφίη τε⟩· κρῆναι ἐν Θήβαις
ταῖς Βοιωτίαις.

77   ⟨Ἰσμηνοῦ⟩· Ἰσμηνὸς ποταμὸς Θηβῶν καὶ
Ἀσωπός.

78   ⟨ἐπεὶ πεπάλακτο κεραυνῷ⟩· ἐπεὶ τὴν θυγα-
τέρα αὐτοῦ Αἴγιναν ἁρπαγεῖσαν ὑπὸ Διὸς ἀπήγγειλε
Σίσυφος, ὁ δὲ ἤρξατο καταδιώκειν αὐτόν, Ζεὺς δὲ ὀρ-
γισθεὶς ἐκεραύνωσεν αὐτόν.

79   ⟨ὑποδινηθεῖσα⟩· ὑπότρομος γενομένη.

80   ⟨μελίη⟩· τὸ ἑξῆς ⟨. . .⟩ οὐκ ἔστι κύριον, ἀλλὰ
ἁπλῶς εἴρηται περὶ πάσης μελίας.

82   ⟨Ἑλικῶνος⟩· ὄρος Βοιωτίας.

86   ⟨ταῖς μέν⟩· ταῖς μὴ δεξαμέναις δηλαδὴ τὴν
Λητώ.

63   (*H*)*aimou*: Haemus, a mountain in Thrace.

65   (*h*)*eptamychon*: with seven recesses.

66   *nēsaōn*: irregularly *nēsaōn* has a diaeresis. It is not from *tōn* into *ai*.

67a   *korē*: Iris.

67b   *Mimanti*: a mountain opposite Chios.

71a   *Parthenion*: the Parthenion is a Mountain in Arcadia, where Heracles killed Auga the daughter of Aleus, priestess of Athena.

71b   *Pheneios*: ancient city of Arcadia.

73a   *emplēn*: except

73b   *Aigialou*: Homer (*Il.* 2.575): "across all Aegialus."

75   *Aoniē*: he calls Thebes Aonia.

76   *Dirkē te Strophiē te*: springs in Theban Boeotia.

77   *Ismēnou*: the Ismenus is a river of Thebes and Asopus.

78   *epei pepalakto keraunō*: when Sisyphus announced that his daughter Aegina had been abducted by Zeus he began to pursue him and Zeus, being angry, struck him with his thunderbolt.

79   *hypodinētheisa*: having become tremulous.

80   *meliē*: use this order . . . it is not correct, but he writes plainly about all the ash trees.

82   (*H*)*elikōnos*: a Boeotian mountain.

86   *tais men*: clearly the ones who had not received Leto.

88   τὸ ἑξῆς· ὦ Θήβη, τί αὐτίκα ἐλέγχεις τὸν ἐσό-
μενόν σοι πότμον;

91   <ὄφις μέγας>· ὁ Δελφύνης.

92   <ἀπὸ Πλειστοῖο>· Πλειστὸς ποταμὸς Φωκί-
δος παρὰ τὸν Παρνασὸν ῥέων, ὅς ἐστιν ὄρος Φωκί-
δος.

94   <τομώτερον>· σαφέστερον, ὀξύτερον.

96   <κακογλώσσοιο>· τῆς Νιόβης· ἐν Θήβαις
γὰρ κατῴκει.

97   <Κιθαιρών>· ὄρος Θηβῶν.

101   <Ἑλίκη>· πόλις Ἀχαΐας.

102   <Βούρά τε Δεξαμενοῖο>· Βούρα πόλις Ἀχα-
ΐας· ᾤκησε δὲ αὐτὴν Δεξαμενὸς ὁ Κένταυρος. ἐκεῖ δὲ
αὐτοῦ τὰ βουστάσια ἐφυλάττετο· διὸ καὶ Βούρα ὠνο-
μάσθη.

104a <Λάρισα>· πόλις Θεσσαλίας.

104b Χειρωνίδες ἄκραι: τὸ Πήλιον ὄρος Θεσσα-
λίας, διὰ τὸ τὸν Χείρωνα ἐκεῖσε οἰκῆσαι.

105a <Πηνειός>· ποταμὸς Θεσσαλίας.

105b <Τεμπέων>· ὄρη Θεσσαλίας.

105c <Τεμπέων>· ὄρη Κιλικίας πλησίον Θεσσα-
λίας.

105d <Τεμπέων>· Τέμπη αἱ στενώταται διεκβολαὶ
τῶν Θεσσαλίας ὀρῶν.

109   <Θεσσαλίδες>· αἱ παρὰ τὸν Πηνειόν.

112   <ἀνέμοισιν ἐρίζεις>· ἐν τῷ τρέχειν.

115   <πεποίησαι>· προσπεποίησαι τὸ ὀξέως τρέ-
χειν.

88   Use this order: O Thebes, why do you ask now about the fate coming to you?

91   *ophis megas*: Delphynes.

92   *apo Pleistoio*: Pleistus, a river of Phocis, flowing beside Parnasus, which is a mountain of Phocis.

94   *tomōteron*: more clearly, more sharply.

96   *kakoglōssoio*: of Niobe. She lived in Thebes.

97   *Kitharōn*: a mountain in Thebes.

101   *Helikē*: an Achaean city.

102   *Boura te Dexamenoio*: Boura is an Achaean city. Dexamenus, the Centaur, lived there. There he guarded his ox stall. On account of this it was named Boura.

104a   *Larisa*: a city of Thessaly.

104b   *Cheirōnides akrai*: Mt. Pelion in Thessaly because Chiron lived there.

105a   *Pēneios*: a river of Thessaly.

105b   *Tempeōn*: a mountain of Thessaly.

105c   *Tempeōn*: a mountain of Cilicia near Thessaly.

105d   *Tempeōn*: the narrowest passes of the mountains of Thessaly.

109   *Thessalides*: the [nymphs] who lived beside the Peneius.

112   *anemoisin erizeis*: he challenges the winds in running.

115   *pepoiēsai*: to gain the power to run swiftly.

118 ⟨Φιλύρης νυμφήϊον⟩· ἐν τῷ Πηλίῳ γὰρ ὁ
Κρόνος τῇ Φιλύρᾳ μιγεὶς ποιεῖ τὸν Χείρωνα.

122 ⟨Ἀναγκαίη⟩· τὸ τοῦ ποιητοῦ· "ἀναγκαίη γὰρ
ἐπείγει." ἡ γὰρ Ἀνάγκη μεγάλη θεός ἐστι.

125 ⟨ἀπαύγασαι⟩· θέασαι.

126 τὸν Ἄρην λέγει.

130 ⟨διψαλέην ἄμπωτιν⟩· ξηρασίαν.

132 ⟨τί περισσά⟩· φθέγγομαι δηλονότι.

134 ⟨Παγγαίου⟩· Πάγγαιον ὄρος Θρᾴκης.

137 ⟨Ὄσσης⟩· ὄρος Θεσσαλίας.

139 ⟨Πίνδοιο⟩· ὄρος Περραιβικόν.

143 ⟨Βριάρηος⟩· οἱ μέν φασι Βριάρεως, οἱ δὲ
Τυφωέως, οἱ δὲ Ἐγκελάδου.

144 ⟨θερμάστραι⟩· αἱ κάμινοι.

150 ⟨Κοιηΐς⟩· Κοίου γὰρ καὶ Φοίβης ἡ Λητώ.

156 ⟨Κέρκυρα⟩· ἡ Φαιακία.

160–61 ⟨Κόων Μεροπηΐδα νῆσον . . . Χαλκιόπης
ἱερὸν μυχόν⟩· ἢ ὅτι ὑπὸ Μέροπος ἐβασιλεύθη, ἢ ὅτι
Μέροπες αὐτὴν ᾤκησαν· θυγάτηρ δ᾽ Εὐρυπύλου βα-
σιλέως ⟨τῆς⟩ Κῶ (sc. ἡ Χαλκιόπη).

165 ⟨ἐκ Μοιρέων⟩· διὰ τὸ ἐκεῖσε ἀνατραφῆναι τὸν
Φιλάδελφον Πτολεμαῖον ἐν τῇ Κῷ.

166 ⟨ὑπὸ μίτρην⟩· ὑπὸ τὴν βασιλείαν, ὑπὸ τὴν
ἀρχήν.

167 ⟨Μακηδόνι⟩· τῷ Φιλαδέλφῳ Πτολεμαίῳ.

170 ⟨πατρός⟩· τοῦ Σωτῆρος.

174a Τιτῆνες· διὰ τὸ ἐπιχείρημα.

118   *Philyrēs nymphēion*: on Pelion Cronus had sex with Philyra and produced Chiron.

122   *Anagkaiē*: the saying of the poet (Hom. *Il.* 6.85 = *Od.* 19.73): "Necessity presses hard." For Necessity is a great goddess.

125   *apaugasai*: to see.

126   He speaks of Ares.

130   *dipsaleēn ampōtin*: desiccation.

132   *ti perissa*: I speak clearly.

134   *Pangaiou*: the Pangaeum mountain in Thrace.

137   *Ossēs*: a mountain in Thessaly.

139   *Pindoio*: Mt. Perraebicon.

143   *Briarēos*: Some say Briareus, others Typhoeus, and others Enceladus.

144   *thermastrai*: furnaces.

150   *Koiēis*: Leto daughter of Coeus and Phoebe.

156   *Kerkyra*: Phaeacia.

160–61   *Koōn Meropēida nēson, . . . Chalkiopēs (h)ieron muchon*: either because Merops was king or because the Meropes settled it. The daughter of king Eurypylus of Cos, i.e., Chalciope.

165   *ek Moireōn*: on account of Ptolemy Philadelphus being brought up there in Cos.

166   *(h)upo mitrēn*: under the royal diadem, under the rule.

167   *Makēdoni*: Ptolemy Philadelphus.

170   *patros*: [Ptolemy] Soter.

174a   *Titēnes*: on account of the battle.

CALLIMACHUS

174b   ⟨ἑσπέρου⟩· τῆς δύσεως.

175–87   Βρέννος ὁ τῶν Γάλλων βασιλεὺς συλλαβὼν
τοὺς Κελτοὺς ἦλθεν ἐπὶ Πυθῶνα βουλόμενος τὰ χρή-
ματα αὐτῆς ἁρπάσαι. πλησίον δὲ γενομένου αὐτοῦ ὁ
Ἀπόλλων χαλάζῃ χρησάμενος ἀπώλεσε τοὺς πλείους
αὐτῶν. ὀλίγων οὖν παραλειφθέντων Ἀντίγονός τις φί-
λος τοῦ Φιλαδέλφου Πτολεμαίου προξενεῖ αὐτοὺς
αὐτῷ ὥστε ἐπὶ μισθῷ στρατεύεσθαι. καὶ γὰρ ἔχρῃζεν
ὁ Πτολεμαῖος τούτου τοῦ στρατεύματος. οἱ δὲ ὁμοίως
ἠβουλήθησαν καὶ τοῦ Πτολεμαίου ἁρπάσαι τὰ χρή-
ματα. γνοὺς οὖν λαμβάνει αὐτοὺς καὶ ἀπάγει πρὸς τὸ
στόμιον τοῦ Νείλου τὸ λεγόμενον Σεβεννυτικὸν καὶ
κατέκαυσεν αὐτοὺς ἐκεῖσε. ταῦτα οὖν, φησί, ξυνὸν
ἀγῶνα ἔσεσθαι.

184   ⟨Γαλάτῃσιν⟩· τοῖς Γάλλοις.

185   ⟨τέων⟩· ὧντινων ἀσπίδων αἱ μὲν ἐμοὶ εἰς γέ-
ρας, αἱ δὲ τῷ Πτολεμαίῳ δοθήσονται.

191a   ⟨διειδομένη⟩· φαινομένη.

191b   ⟨ἀραιή⟩· λεπτή.

193   ἀνθέρικός ἐστιν ὁ τοῦ ἀσφοδέλου καρπός.

199   ⟨Γεραίστιον⟩· Γέραιστος ἀκρωτήριον Εὐ-
βοίας.

204   ⟨ἐφύλαξα⟩· ἀντὶ τοῦ φυλάξω.

210   ⟨φοίνικος ποτὶ πρέμνον⟩· καὶ Ὅμηρος·
"Δήλῳ δὴ τοῖον Ἀπόλλωνος παρὰ βωμῷ φοίνικος
νέον ἔρνον ἀνερχόμενον."

212   ἀλυσθμαίνουσα· ἤτοι πνευστιῶσα, ἀσθμαί-
νουσα.

328

174b   (h)*esperou*: sunset

175–87   Brennus, the king of the Gauls, assembled the
Celts and went into Pytho, intending to carry off its wealth.
When he was nearby Apollo used hail and slew most of
them. With only a few remaining Antigonus, a friend of
Ptolemy Philadelphus, took charge of them so that they
could be mercenaries for him. And Ptolemy needed this
army. They likewise wanted to carry off the wealth of Ptol-
emy. When he perceived this he took them and led them
to the mouth of the Nile which is called Sebennyticon and
there he immolated them. These things he says will be a
common agony.

184   *Galatēsin*: The Gauls.

185   *teōn*: of whichever shields, some will be prizes
for me and some will be given to Ptolemy.

191a   *dieidomenē*: appearing.

191b   *araiē*, slender.

193   *antherikos*: the fruit of the asphodel.

199   *Geraistion*: Geraestus was a promontory of Eu-
boea.

204   *ephylaxa*: instead of *phylaxō*.

210   *phoinikos poti premnon*: and Homer (*Od.* 6.162–
63): "In Delos once [I saw] such a thing, the young shoot
of a palm springing up beside the altar."

212   *alysthmainousa*: panting, gasping for breath.

215 <νύμφα Διός>· πρὸς τὴν Ἥραν ὁ λόγος.

225 σάρον· τὸ κάλλυντρον.

234 ληθαῖον· τὸ λήθην τῶν κακῶν ἐμποιοῦν.

235 <ποτὶ γλωχῖνα>· πρὸς τὴν γωνίαν τοῦ θρόνου.

236 <λέχριος>· πλαγίως.

238 ἐνδρομίδας· κυρίως τῶν κυνηγῶν τὰ ὑποδήματα.

242 ἀλετρίδες· αἱ θεράπαιναι αἱ ἀλήθουσαι.

246 καίτοι περ κακῶς τῇ Λητοῖ ἐχαρίσατο.

250 <Μηόνιον Πακτωλόν>· ποταμὸς Λυδίας χρυσοῦ ψήγματα φέρων.

251 <ἑβδομάκις> ἑπταμηνιαῖος γὰρ ἐτέχθη ὁ Ἀπόλλων.

256 <ποταμοῦ γένος ἀρχαίοιο>· τοῦ Ἰνωποῦ.

258 <ὀλολυγήν>· τὴν μετὰ εὐφημίας λέγει εὐχήν.

261 <τροχόεσσα . . . λίμνη>· ἡ θάλασσα διὰ τὸ περιτρέχειν κύκλῳ τὴν νῆσον, ἢ λίμνη τις ἐν Δήλῳ περιφερής.

266 <ὦ μεγάλη πολύβωμε>· πρὸς τὴν γῆν λέγει πᾶσαν.

271 Κερχνὶς καὶ Λέχαιον· ἀκρωτήριά εἰσιν, ἔνθα ὁ Ποσειδῶν τιμᾶται.

275 <νησάων>· παραλόγως τὸ νησάων.

280 <ἀνὰ μέσσην>· ἐν μεσημβρίᾳ.

281a <οἳ καθύπερθε Βορείης οἰκία θινὸς ἔχουσι>· οἱ Ὑπερβόρεοι.

281b θῖνα νῦν τὴν ζώνην λέγει ὠκεανοῦ.

215   *nympha Dios*: the expression relates to Hera.
225   *saron*: brush.
234   *lēthaion*: bringing about the forgetting of evils.
235   *pote glōchina*: by the edge of the throne.
236   *lechrios*: aslant.
238   *endromidas*: properly the sandals of hunters.
242   *aletrides*: the enslaved women who grind grain.
246   She would do a favor for Leto basely.
250   *Mēonion Paktōlon*: a river in Lydia carrying chips of gold.
251   *(h)ebdomakis*: Apollo was born in the seventh month.
256   *potamou genos archaioio*: the Inopus.
258   *ololugēn*: [a cry] which he calls euphemistically a prayer.
261   *trochoessa . . . limnē*: the sea because it goes around the island in a circle or a certain round lake on Delos.
266   *Ō megalē polybōme*: he speaks of the whole earth.
271   *Kerchnis kai Lechaion*: they are capes, where Poseidon is honored.
275   *nēsaōn*: a unique form.
280   *ana messēn*: in midday.
281a   *(h)oi kathyperthe boreiēs oikia thinos exousi* (those who dwell beyond the northlands): the Hyperboreans.
281b   He calls what is now the shore the belt of Ocean.

CALLIMACHUS

283–85 λέγεται ὅτι οἱ Ὑπερβόρεοι δῶρα πέμπουσι τῷ Ἀπόλλωνι, ἅτινα δέχονται πρῶτοι οἱ Δωδωναῖοι.

286a γηλεχέες· οὓς Ὅμηρός φησι χαμαιεύνας.

286b ⟨ἀσιγήτοιο λέβητος⟩· ὅθεν Δωδωναῖον χαλκεῖον.

287 ⟨Μηλίδος⟩· Μηλὶς πόλις Τραχῖνος.

289 ἐν Εὐβοίᾳ πεδίον Ληλάντιον ἀπὸ Ληλάντου βασιλέως.

291 ⟨Ἀριμασπῶν⟩· ἔθνος τῶν Ὑπερβορέων.

292a ⟨Οὖπίς τε⟩· αἱ τρεῖς κόραι τῶν Ὑπερβορέων Σκυθῶν·

292b εὐαίων δὲ ἡ μακαρία.

295 †⟨εὔμοιροι⟩· εὔφημοι†.

296 ⟨ὑμέναιος⟩· καιρὸς τοῦ γάμου.

298 ⟨παρθενικαί⟩· ἀπὸ κοινοῦ τὸ φορέουσιν.

299 ⟨ἄρσενες⟩· οἱ καθαροί.

302 ⟨οὖλος ἐθείραις⟩· ὁ ὁλόκληρος ταῖς θριξί, τουτέστιν ὁ λαμπρὸς ταῖς ἀκτῖσιν.

305 Ὠλὴν γάρ τις Λύκιος εὗρε τὸν ὕμνον τοῦτον.

308 ⟨ἄγαλμα Κύπριδος ἀρχαίης⟩ ἀριήκοον· Ἀφροδίτης ἱερὸν ἐν Δήλῳ ὅπερ Θησεὺς ἔκτισε διὰ τὸ εὐχερῶς τὴν Ἀριάδνην ὀλισθῆσαι εἰς πόθον τὸν Θησέως καὶ χειρώσασθαι τὸν Μινώταυρον.

314a τοῦτο καὶ Πλάτων ἔφη ἐν τῷ Φαίδωνι.

314b τὸ ἑξῆς· θεωρίδος νηός, νῦν τῆς τὰ ἱερὰ φερούσης· κυρίως δὲ θεωρὸς ὁ τὰ τοῦ θεοῦ ὡρῶν ὅ ἐστι φυλάσσων, ἐκ δὲ τούτου ὁ ἱερεύς.

283–85 He says that the Hyperboreans send gifts to Apollo, which the Dodoni receive first.

286a *gēlechees*: which in Homer (*Il.* 16.235) means "sleeping on the ground."

286b *asigētoio lebētos*: from which comes the expression Dodonian cauldron.

287 *Mēlidos*: Trachinos, a city of Melis.

289 In Euboia the Lelantian plain from King Lelantus.

291 *Arimaspōn*: a people of the Hyperboreans.

292a *Oupis te*: the three girls of the Scythian Hyperboreans.

292b *euaiōn*: blissfulness.

295 †*eumoiroi*: auspicious.†

296 (*H*)*ymenaios*: the season of marriage.

298 *parthenikai*: commonly, what they convey.

299 *arsenes*: ritually pure.

302 *oulos etheirais*: with wooly hair, that is to say radiant with rays.

305 A certain Olen, a Lycian, devised this hymn.

308 *agalma Kypridos archaiēs ariēkoon*: the shrine of Aphrodite in Delos that Theseus built on account of Ariadne recklessly falling in love with Theseus and subduing the Minotaur.

314a Plato says this in the *Phaedo* (58a–b).

314b Take it in this order: of the sacred ship, now of the one carrying sacred items. Properly the *theōros* is the one who sees the possessions of the god, who is watching over [them] and from this, the name of the priest.

314c   ἱερὰ τριήρης.

315   τοπήια· ὅπλα νεώς, Λάκωνες· σχοινία, κάλοι.

316   ⟨τίς δέ σε⟩· ἀντὶ τοῦ οὐδείς.

321–23   ἐν Δήλῳ περὶ τὸν βωμὸν τοῦ Ἀπόλλωνος
ἔθος ἦν τρέχειν καὶ τύπτειν τὸν βωμὸν μάστιγι καὶ
ἀποδάκνειν ἐξηγκωνισμένους ἐκ τῆς ἐλαίας.

322a   ⟨ῥησσόμενον⟩· πλησσόμενον.

322b   ⟨ὀδακτάσαι⟩· δράξασθαι, δακεῖν.

325a   ⟨ἱστίη ὢ νήσων⟩· ἑστία ἐστὶ μέντοι κυρίως
ὁ βωμὸς ὁ ἐν μέσῳ τῷ δόμῳ ἑστώς· ἐπειδὴ οὖν ἡ
Δῆλος ἐν μέσῳ τῶν Κυκλάδων ἕστηκε, δοκεῖ ὥσπερ
ἑστία τις καὶ βωμὸς εἶναι.

325b   ⟨εὐέστιε⟩· εὔοικε.

314c   (h)*iera triēres*: the holy trireme.

315   *topēia*: the gear of the ship, a Laconian [word]: rope, cables.

316   *tis de se*: instead of *oudeis* (no one).

321–23   In Delos it was the custom to run around the altar of Apollo and to strike the altar with a whip and to take a bite from the olive tree with arms bent back.

322a   *rhēssomenon*: striking.

322b   *odaktasai*: grab by the throat, bite.

325a   (h)*istiē Ō nēsōn*: the hearth (*hestia*) is properly an altar standing in the middle of the house. Since Delos stood in the middle of the Cyclades it seems that it is a hearth and an altar.

325b   *euestie*: well-inhabited.

HYMNUS V
IN LAVACRUM PALLADIS

Ὅσσαι λωτροχόοι τᾶς Παλλάδος ἔξιτε πᾶσαι,
    ἔξιτε· τᾶν ἵππων ἄρτι φρυασσομενᾶν
τᾶν ἱερᾶν ἐσάκουσα, καὶ ἁ θεὸς εὔτυκος ἕρπεν·[1]
    σοῦσθέ νυν, ὦ ξανθαὶ σοῦσθε Πελασγιάδες.
5 οὔποκ' Ἀθαναία μεγάλως ἀπενίψατο πάχεις,
    πρὶν κόνιν ἱππειᾶν ἐξελάσαι λαγόνων·
οὐδ' ὅκα δὴ λύθρῳ πεπαλαγμένα πάντα φέροισα
    τεύχεα τῶν ἀδίκων ἦνθ' ἀπὸ γαγενέων,
ἀλλὰ πολὺ πράτιστον ὑφ' ἅρματος αὐχένας ἵππων
10   λυσαμένα παγαῖς ἔκλυσεν Ὠκεανῶ
ἱδρῶ καὶ ῥαθάμιγγας, ἐφοίβασεν δὲ παγέντα
    πάντα χαλινοφάγων ἀφρὸν ἀπὸ στομάτων.
ὦ ἴτ' Ἀχαιιάδες, καὶ μὴ μύρα μηδ' ἀλαβάστρως
    (συρίγγων ἀίω φθόγγον ὑπαξόνιον),[2]
15 μὴ μύρα λωτροχόοι τᾷ Παλλάδι μηδ' ἀλαβάστρως
    (οὐ γὰρ Ἀθαναία χρίματα μεικτὰ φιλεῖ)

---

[1] ἕρπεν corr. Schneider: ἕρπει Ψ
[2] ὑπαξόνιον EQS Pol.: ὑπαξονίων αεΠ La. ζ

---

[1] The Pelasgians were thought to be the ancestors of the Ar-
gives (Aesch. *Suppl.* 250–53; Hdt. 1.56–58), and the two terms

HYMN V
ON THE BATH OF PALLAS

You bath attendants of Pallas, come out, all of you come out! Just now I heard the whinnying of the sacred mares, and the Goddess is ready to move. Hurry now, hurry, you fair-haired Pelasgian[1] women. Never did Athena wash her own huge arms before brushing the dust from the flanks of her horses. Not even when she returned from the lawless earthborn giants,[2] bringing her armor all smeared with gore, but first of all she freed the necks of the horses from the chariot and with springs of Ocean she washed away the flecks of sweat and she washed all the clotted foam from their mouths that champ the bit.

[13] Come out, daughters of Achaea,[3] and do not bring myrrh nor alabaster (I hear the sound of the naves beneath the wagon), bath pourers, bring not myrrh nor alabaster for Pallas, for Athena does not like mixed unguents, and

became poetic equivalents. The identity of the women locates the ceremony in Argos and accounts for the hymn's Doric dialect.

[2] The Giants, offspring of Gaia, the earth (Hes. *Theog*. 183–85), engaged in a primordial battle with the Olympians, in which Athena killed Pallas and used his flayed skin as a shield (Apollod. *Bibl*. 1.6.1–2).

[3] A region in the northern Peloponnese. Perhaps the poet intended to distinguish these women from the inhabitants of Thessalian Argos (Bulloch, 122).

CALLIMACHUS

οἴσετε μηδὲ κάτοπτρον· ἀεὶ καλὸν ὄμμα τὸ τήνας.
    οὐδ᾽ ὅκα τὰν Ἴδᾳ³ Φρὺξ ἐδίκαζεν ἔριν,
οὔτ᾽ ἐς ὀρείχαλκον μεγάλα θεὸς οὔτε⁴ Σιμοῦντος
20   ἔβλεψεν δίναν ἐς διαφαινομέναν·
οὐδ᾽ Ἥρα· Κύπρις δὲ διαυγέα χαλκὸν ἑλοῖσα
    πολλάκι τὰν αὐτὰν δὶς μετέθηκε κόμαν.
ἁ δὲ δὶς ἑξήκοντα διαθρέξασα διαύλως,
    οἷα παρ᾽ Εὐρώτᾳ τοὶ Λακεδαιμόνιοι
25 ἀστέρες, ἐμπεράμως ἐνετρίψατο⁵ λιτὰ λαβοῖσα⁶
    χρίματα, τᾶς ἰδίας ἔκγονα φυταλιᾶς,
ὦ κῶραι, τὸ δ᾽ ἔρευθος ἀνέδραμε, πρώϊον οἵαν
    ἢ ῥόδον ἢ σίβδας κόκκος ἔχει χροιάν.
τῷ καὶ νῦν ἄρσεν⁷ τι κομίσσατε μῶνον ἔλαιον,
30   ᾧ Κάστωρ, ᾧ καὶ χρίεται Ἡρακλέης·
οἴσετε καὶ κτένα οἱ παγχρύσεον, ὡς ἀπὸ χαίταν
    πέξηται, λιπαρὸν σμασαμένα πλόκαμον.
ἔξιθ᾽, Ἀθαναία· πάρα τοι καταθύμιος ἴλα,
    παρθενικαὶ μεγάλων παῖδες Ἀρεστοριδᾶν·⁸

---

3 Ἴδᾳ corr. Stanley, Bentley: ἴδαν Ψ
4 οὔτ᾽ . . . . οὔτε Meineke1: οὐδ᾽ . . . οὐδὲ Ψ
5 ἐνετρίψατο corr. Meineke: ἐτρίψατο Ψ
6 λαβοῖσα Pol. S: βαλοῖσα Fβ La. δ
7 τι corr. Bergk: τε Ψ
8 Ἀρεστοριδᾶν corr. Valckenaer: Ἀκεστοριδᾶν Ψ

---

4 Paris, the "Phrygian" by virtue of Troy's location, judged a beauty contest on Mt. Ida between Athena, Hera, and Aphrodite, whom he chose as the winner (Hom. *Il.* 24.25–30).

338

do not bring a mirror. That face is always lovely. Not even when the Phrygian judged the contest on Ida[4] did the great goddess look into orichale[5] or into the pellucid eddies of the Simois.[6] Nor did Hera. But Cypris[7] took up the shining bronze, and often rearranged the same locks more than once. But Athena, after running twice sixty double laps, skillfully anointed herself, like the Lacedaemonian stars[8] beside the Eurotas,[9] putting on light oils, the products of her own tree.[10] Girls, a blush rose up, like the color of a morning rose or a seed of pomegranate. For that reason bring something masculine, only olive oil that Castor and Heracles used to anoint themselves. Bring her also a comb, the all-golden one, so she can comb out her hair after cleaning her glossy locks.

[33] Come forth, Athena! A heart-pleasing company is nearby, young girls, the maiden daughters of Arestor's

5 An alloy of unknown metals, later thought to be copper and zinc ([Hes.] *Sc.* 122; *Hymn. Hom. Aphr.* 6.9; Pl. *Crit.* 114e).

6 River near Mt. Ida in Troy (Hom. *Il.* 4.475).

7 Aphrodite, who in one tradition emerged from the sea near Cyprus (Hes. *Theog.* 191–99) and had an important cult center there.

8 The Dioscuri, Castor and Pollux, were the twin brothers of Helen of Troy and like her were Spartan (i.e., Lacedaemonian) in origin. They were often represented as stars (Eur. *Hel.* 137–40) and were associated with the constellation Gemini (Arat. *Phaen.* 147).

9 River in Lacedaemonia with the name of an early Spartan king (Paus. 3.1). Ancient Sparta was located on its west bank.

10 The olive was Athena's gift to Athens and associated with her cult on the Acropolis (Hdt. 8.55; Apollod. *Bibl.* 3.14.1).

35 ὠθάνα, φέρεται δὲ καὶ ἁ Διομήδεος ἀσπίς,
    ὡς ἔθος Ἀργείως⁹ τοῦτο παλαιοτέρως
Εὐμήδης ἐδίδαξε, τεῒν κεχαρισμένος ἱρεύς·
    ὅς ποκα βωλευτὸν γνοὺς ἐπί οἱ θάνατον
δᾶμον ἑτοιμάζοντα φυγᾷ τεὸν ἱρὸν ἄγαλμα
40 ᾤχετ᾽ ἔχων, Κρεῖον δ᾽ εἰς ὄρος ᾠκίσατο,
    Κρεῖον ὄρος· σὲ δέ, δαῖμον, ἀπορρώγεσσιν ἔθηκεν
ἐν πέτραις, αἷς νῦν οὔνομα Παλλατίδες.
    ἔξιθ᾽, Ἀθαναία περσέπτολι, χρυσεοπήληξ,
ἵππων καὶ σακέων ἁδομένα πατάγῳ.

45 σάμερον, ὑδροφόροι, μὴ βάπτετε—σάμερον, Ἄργος,
    πίνετ᾽ ἀπὸ κρανᾶν μηδ᾽ ἀπὸ τῶ ποταμῶ·¹⁰
σάμερον αἱ δῶλαι τὰς κάλπιδας ἢ ᾽ς Φυσάδειαν
    ἢ ἐς Ἀμυμώναν οἴσετε τὰν Δαναῶ.
καὶ γὰρ δὴ χρυσῷ τε καὶ ἄνθεσιν ὕδατα μείξας
50 ἡξεῖ φορβαίων Ἴναχος ἐξ ὀρέων
    τἀθάνᾳ τὸ λοετρὸν ἄγων καλόν. ἀλλά, Πελασγέ,
φράζεο μὴ οὐκ ἐθέλων τὰν βασίλειαν ἴδῃς.
    ὅς κεν ἴδῃ γυμνὰν τὰν Παλλάδα τὰν πολιοῦχον,
τὦργος ἐσοψεῖται τοῦτο πανυστάτιον.

---

⁹ Ἀργείως . . . παλαιοτέρως corr. anon. Bern.: Ἀργείων . . .
παλαιοτέρον Ψ
¹⁰ τῶ ποταμῶ corr. anon. Bern.: τῶν ποταμῶν Ψ

---

¹¹ A distinguished Argive ancestor and son of Argus (Ap.
Rhod. 1.112, 1.325). "Arestor's great sons" are the Argives gener-
ally.
¹² A relic of Diomedes, the Argive hero and legendary king

great sons.[11] Athena, the Shield of Diomedes[12] is on its way, in the fashion that Eumedes,[13] the priest who pleased you, taught the ancient Argives the custom. When one day he learned that the people were preparing a plan for his death, he took flight with your holy image and lived on the hill of Creion,[14] Mt. Creion. And you, Goddess, he established on the steep rocks, which now have the name Pallatides.

[43] Come forth, Athena, golden-helmeted sacker-of-cities, who loves the clash of horses and shields. Today, water carriers, do not dip—today, Argos, drink from the springs, not from the river. Today, servants, carry your pitchers either to Physadeia or to Amymone,[15] daughter of Danaus.[16] For after he has mixed his water with gold and flowers, Inachus[17] will come from his pastoral hills, bringing a lovely bath for Athena. But take care, Pelasgian men, that you not look at the queen, even unwittingly. For whoever sees Pallas, Guardian of the City, naked, will look at this Argos for the last time. Queen Athena, do come out,

who brought back the Palladium, a cult statue of Athena, from Troy (Apollod. *Bibl.* 5.13; Conon, *Dieg.* 34).

[13] Eumedes was suspected by the Argives of wishing to betray the Palladium to the Heraclidae (Schol.).

[14] Otherwise unknown.

[15] Springs of Argos named for two of the daughters of Danaus (*Aet.* 65–66).

[16] King of Argos who left Egypt to escape his brother Aegyptus. When Poseidon dried up the rivers in Argos, Danaus sent his fifty daughters to search for water. The springs were revealed, principally to Amymone (Apollod. *Bibl.* 2.1.4).

[17] Legendary king of Argos and his eponymous river (Paus. 2.15.4).

55 πότνι' Ἀθαναία, σὺ μὲν ἔξιθι· μέστα[11] δ' ἐγώ τι
    ταῖσδ' ἐρέω· μῦθος δ' οὐκ ἐμός, ἀλλ' ἑτέρων.
    παῖδες, Ἀθαναία νύμφαν μίαν ἔν ποκα Θήβαις
    πουλύ τι καὶ πέρι δὴ φίλατο τᾶν ἑταρᾶν,
    ματέρα Τειρεσίαο, καὶ οὔποκα χωρὶς ἔγεντο·
60 ἀλλὰ καὶ ἀρχαίων εὖτ' ἐπὶ Θεσπιέων[12]
    <   > ἢ εἰς Ἁλίαρτον ἐλαύνοι
    ἵππως, Βοιωτῶν ἔργα διερχομένα,
    ἢ 'πὶ Κορωνείας, ἵνα οἱ τεθυωμένον ἄλσος
    καὶ βωμοὶ ποταμῷ κεῖντ' ἐπὶ Κουραλίῳ,
65 πολλάκις ἁ δαίμων νιν ἑῶ ἐπεβάσατο δίφρω,
    οὐδ' ὄαροι νυμφᾶν οὐδὲ χοροστασίαι
    ἁδεῖαι τελέθεσκον, ὅκ' οὐχ ἁγεῖτο Χαρικλώ·
    ἀλλ' ἔτι καὶ τήναν δάκρυα πόλλ' ἔμενε,
    καίπερ Ἀθαναίᾳ καταθύμιον ἔσσαν ἑταίραν.
70 δή ποκα γὰρ πέπλων λυσαμένα περόνας
    ἵππω ἐπὶ κράνᾳ Ἑλικωνίδι καλὰ ῥεοίσᾳ
    λῶντο· μεσαμβρινὰ δ' εἶχ' ὄρος ἀσυχία.
    ἀμφότεραι λῶοντο, μεσαμβριναὶ δ' ἔσαν ὧραι,
    πολλὰ δ' ἀσυχία τῆνο κατεῖχεν ὄρος.
75 Τειρεσίας δ' ἔτι μοῦνος[13] ἁμᾶ κυσὶν ἄρτι γένεια
    περκάζων ἱερὸν χῶρον ἀνεστρέφετο·
    διψάσας δ' ἄφατόν τι ποτὶ ῥόον ἤλυθε κράνας,
    σχέτλιος· οὐκ ἐθέλων δ' εἶδε τὰ μὴ θεμιτά.

---

[11] μέστα prop. Pf.: μέσφα Ψ   [12] lacuna in 61 ind.
Wilamowitz: omit. ζ: ἢ 'πὶ Κορωνείας Ψ (= 63 init.): 'πὶ Ἀλαλ-
κομένειον Livrea   [13] μοῦνος Ψ, Mair: μῶνος coni. Ernesti

342

and meantime I will speak to these young women. The
story is not mine, but others'.

[57] Children, once in Thebes Athena loved one nymph
very much, much more than her other companions: the
mother of Teiresias,[18] and they were never apart. But
whenever she drove her horse to ancient Thespiae[19] or
Haliartus, passing through the fields of the Boeotians, or
to Coroneia, where her fragrant grove and altars lie beside
the river Curalius, often the goddess took her aboard
her chariot, and there were no conversations among the
nymphs or pleasant organization of dances when Chariclo
did not take the lead.

[68] Yet even for her many tears awaited, although she
was a comrade who pleased Athena's heart. One day they
loosened the pins of their dresses and bathed in the lovely-
flowing Spring of the Horse[20] on Helicon. A midday calm
took over of the mountain. Both of them were bathing, the
hour was noon, and great peacefulness held that moun-
tain. Only Teiresias, whose beard was just now turning
dark, still roamed the holy place with his dogs. Unspeak-
ably thirsty, he went to the flowing fountain. Poor man!
Unwittingly he saw what was not permitted. Athena was

[18] Chariclo. Teiresias' father was Everes (Apollod. *Bibl.* 3.6.7;
Hyg. *Fab.* 75).

[19] Thespiae, Haliartus, and Coroneia are towns in Boeotia
connected with Athena: Thespiae (Paus. 9.26.6); Coroneia (Al-
caeus 325 Voigt). Haliartus may be a textual error for Alalcome-
nae (Livrea, 31–36), also connected with Athena (Paus. 9.33.5).

[20] Hippocrene, spring on Mt. Helicon in Boeotia frequented
by the Muses (Hes. *Theog.* 1–8).

CALLIMACHUS

τὸν δὲ χολωσαμένα περ ὅμως προσέφασεν Ἀθάνα·
80 "τίς σε, τὸν ὀφθαλμὼς οὐκέτ' ἀποισόμενον,
ὦ Εὐηρείδα, χαλεπὰν ὁδὸν ἄγαγε δαίμων;"
ἁ μὲν ἔφα, παιδὸς δ' ὄμματα νὺξ ἔλαβεν.[14]
ἐστάκη[15] δ' ἄφθογγος, ἐκόλλασαν γὰρ ἀνίαι
γώνατα καὶ φωνὰν ἔσχεν ἀμαχανία.
85 ἁ νύμφα δ' ἐβόασε· "τί μοι τὸν κῶρον ἔρεξας
πότνια; τοιαῦται, δαίμονες, ἐστὲ φίλαι;
ὄμματά μοι τῶ παιδὸς ἀφείλεο.[16] τέκνον ἄλαστε,
εἶδες Ἀθαναίας στήθεα καὶ λαγόνας,
ἀλλ' οὐκ ἀέλιον πάλιν ὄψεαι. ὦ ἐμὲ δειλάν,
90 ὦ ὄρος, ὦ Ἑλικὼν οὐκέτι μοι παριτέ,
ἦ μεγάλ' ἀντ' ὀλίγων ἐπράξαο· δόρκας ὀλέσσας
καὶ πρόκας οὐ πολλὰς φάεα παιδὸς ἔχεις."
ἁ μὲν ⟨ἅμ'⟩[17] ἀμφοτέραισι φίλον περὶ παῖδα
λαβοῖσα
μάτηρ μὲν γοερᾶν οἶτον ἀηδονίδων
95 ἆγε βαρὺ κλαίοισα, θεὰ δ' ἐλέησεν ἑταίραν.
καί νιν Ἀθαναία πρὸς τόδ' ἔλεξεν ἔπος·
"δῖα γύναι, μετὰ πάντα βαλεῦ πάλιν ὅσσα δι'
ὀργάν
εἶπας· ἐγὼ δ' οὔ τοι τέκνον ἔθηκ' ἀλαόν.
οὐ γὰρ Ἀθαναίᾳ γλυκερὸν πέλει ὄμματα παίδων
100 ἁρπάζειν· Κρόνιοι δ' ὧδε λέγοντι νόμοι·
'ὅς κε τιν' ἀθανάτων, ὅκα μὴ θεὸς αὐτὸς ἕληται,
ἀθρήσῃ, μισθῶ τοῦτον ἰδεῖν μεγάλω.'
δῖα γύναι, τὸ μὲν οὐ παλινάγρετον αὖθι γένοιτο
ἔργον, ἐπεὶ Μοιρᾶν ὧδ' ἐπένησε[18] λίνα,

344

furious with him, but spoke nonetheless, "What god led you down this hard road, son of Everes, you who will never recover your eyesight?"

[82] She spoke, and night seized the eyes of the boy. He stood speechless, and pain welded his knees; helplessness held back has voice. The nymph cried out, "What have you done to my boy, Queen? Is this how you goddesses are friends? You took the eyes of my son. Accursed child, you saw the breast and body of Athena, but you will not see the sun again. O poor me. O Mountain, O Helicon, where I can no longer wander, you extorted great things for small. After losing some gazelles and deer—not many—you took the eyes of a child."

[93] Then that mother took her dear boy in both arms and kept up a lament like mournful nightingales, wailing deeply. The goddess was moved to pity for her companion. And Athena spoke these words to her: "Noble lady, take back all these things that you said in anger. It was not I that made your child blind. For it is no joy for Athena in plucking out a child's eyes. The laws of Cronus[21] thus decree: 'Whoever sees any one of the immortals, when the god is not willing, will look at great cost.' Noble lady, this deed cannot be undone, since the thread of the Fates was

---

[21] The youngest of the Titans who ruled over the Golden Age when justice prevailed throughout the universe (Hes. *Op.* 109–26; Pl. *Resp.* 271c–72d, *Leg.* 713e).

---

14 ἔλαβεν corr. anon. in marg. Ald.: ἔβαλεν Ψ

15 ἐστάκη Buttmann: ἐστάθη Ψ   16 ἀφείλεο E in marg.: ἀφείλετο Ψ   17 ἅμ' suppl. Schneider: ἁ μὲν ἀμφοτέραισι Ψ

18 ἐπένησε corr. Bentley: ἐπένευσε Ψ

105 ἁνίκα τὸ πρᾶτόν νιν ἐγείναο· νῦν δὲ κομίζευ,
   ὦ Εὐηρείδα, τέλθος ὀφειλόμενον.
   πόσσα μὲν ἁ Καδμηὶς ἐς ὕστερον ἔμπυρα καυσεῖ,
   πόσσα δ' Ἀρισταῖος, τὸν μόνον εὐχόμενοι
   παῖδα, τὸν ἡβατὰν[19] Ἀκταίονα, τυφλὸν ἰδέσθαι.
110 καὶ τῆνος μεγάλας σύνδρομος Ἀρτέμιδος
   ἔσσεται· ἀλλ' οὐκ αὐτὸν ὅ τε δρόμος αἵ τ' ἐν ὄρεσσι
   ῥυσεῦνται ξυναὶ τᾶμος ἐκαβολίαι,
   ὁππόκα κ' οὐκ[20] ἐθέλων περ ἴδῃ χαρίεντα λοετρά
   δαίμονος· ἀλλ' αὐταὶ τὸν πρὶν ἄνακτα κύνες
115 τουτάκι δειπνησεῦντι· τὰ δ' υἱέος ὀστέα μάτηρ
   λεξεῖται δρυμὼς πάντας ἐπερχομένα·
   ὀλβίσταν δ' ἐρέει σε καὶ εὐαίωνα γενέσθαι
   ἐξ ὀρέων ἀλαὸν παῖδ' ὑποδεξαμέναν.
   ὦ ἑτάρα, τῷ μή τι μινύρεο· τῷδε γὰρ ἄλλα
120 τεῦ χάριν ἐξ ἐμέθεν πολλὰ μενεῦντι γέρα,
   μάντιν ἐπεὶ θησῶ νιν ἀοίδιμον ἐσσομένοισιν,
   ἦ μέγα τῶν ἄλλων δή τι περισσότερον.
   γνωσεῖται δ' ὄρνιχας, ὃς αἴσιος οἵ τε πέτονται
   ἄλιθα[21] καὶ ποίων οὐκ ἀγαθαὶ πτέρυγες.
125 πολλὰ δὲ Βοιωτοῖσι θεοπρόπα, πολλὰ δὲ Κάδμῳ
   χρησεῖ, καὶ μεγάλοις ὕστερα Λαβδακίδαις.

[19] ἡβατὰν corr. Bulloch: ἀβατὰν Ψ
[20] ὁππόκα κ' οὐκ corr. Bulloch: ὁππόταν οὐκ Ψ
[21] ἄλιθα Bulloch: ἤλιθα Ψ

[22] Autonoe, mother of Actaeon. Cadmus was the founder of
Thebes (Hes. Theog. 975-78).

346

spun this way when first you bore him. Now take the payment that is owed, son of Everes.

[107] How many offerings will the daughter of Cadmus[22] burn in the future? How many will Aristaeus?[23] praying to see their only son, youthful Actaeon, blind. And yet he will be the hunting companion of great Artemis. But neither the hunt nor their shared archery in the mountains will save him when he sees, not wishing it, the lovely bath of the goddess.[24] No, his dogs themselves will then dine on the one who before was their master. And the mother will collect the bones of her son, wandering over all the woods. She will say that you are most blessed and happy in life since you got your son, blind, back from the mountains.

[119] My friend, do not lament at all. For him[25] there will be many other honors from me, for your sake. Since I will make him a seer to be sung of by men hereafter, much greater than the others. He will know the birds, which ones are auspicious, which fly in a neutral way, and which flights are ill-omened. And many prophecies for the Boeotians, many for Cadmus will he pronounce, and afterward for the great Labdacidae.[26] And I will give him a large staff

---

[23] Father of Actaeon, son of Apollo and Cyrene (Hes. [*Cat.*] fr. 216 M.-W.). Like his mother and his son, he was associated with hunting.

[24] Actaeon was on Mt. Cithaeron in Boeotia when he saw Artemis in her bath (Apollod. *Bibl.* 3.4.4).

[25] Teiresias.

[26] Labdacus was a grandson of Cadmus and grandfather of Oedipus (Pind. *Isth.* 3.16; Soph. *OT* 487). Labdacidae are Thebans generally.

δωσῶ καὶ μέγα βάκτρον, ὅ οἱ πόδας ἐς δέον ἀξεῖ,
    δωσῶ καὶ βιότω τέρμα πολυχρόνιον,
καὶ μόνος, εὖτε θάνῃ, πεπνυμένος ἐν νεκύεσσι
130   φοιτασεῖ, μεγάλῳ τίμιος Ἀγεσίλᾳ."
ὣς φαμένα κατένευσε· τὸ δ' ἐντελές, ᾧ κ' ἐπινεύσῃ
    Παλλάς, ἐπεὶ μώνᾳ Ζεὺς τόγε θυγατέρων
δῶκεν Ἀθαναίᾳ πατρώια πάντα φέρεσθαι,
    λωτροχόοι, μάτηρ δ' οὔτις ἔτικτε θεάν,
135   ἀλλὰ Διὸς κορυφά. κορυφὰ Διὸς οὐκ ἐπινεύει
    ψεύδεα ⟨   ⟩αι²² θυγάτηρ.
ἔρχετ' Ἀθαναία νῦν ἀτρεκές· ἀλλὰ δέχεσθε
    τὰν θεόν, ὦ κῶραι, τὦργον²³ ὅσαις μέλεται,
σύν τ' εὐαγορίᾳ σύν τ' εὔγμασι σύν τ' ὀλολυγαῖς.
140   χαῖρε, θεά, κάδευ δ' Ἄργεος Ἰναχίω.
χαῖρε καὶ ἐξελάοισα, καὶ ἐς πάλιν αὖτις ἐλάσσαις
    ἵππως, καὶ Δαναῶν κλᾶρον ἅπαντα σάω.

²² ἁ θυγάτηρ F Bulloch: αἱ θυγάτηρ Atη: vers. om. δζ
²³ τὦργον corr. Boissonade: τῶργος Ψ

5a Schol. Ψ

1   ῎Εν τινι ἡμέρᾳ ὡρισμένῃ ἔθος εἶχον αἱ Ἀρ-
γεῖαι γυναῖκες λαμβάνειν τὸ ἄγαλμα τῆς Ἀθηνᾶς καὶ
Διομήδους καὶ ἄγειν ἐπὶ τὸν Ἴναχον ποταμὸν κἀκεῖσε
ἀπολούειν· ὃ δὴ καὶ λουτρὰ ὠνομάζετο τῆς Παλλά-
δος.
2   φρυασσομενᾶν ἤτοι ποιὸν ἦχον ἀποτελου-
σῶν.

that will guide his feet as necessary, and I will give him a very long lifespan. And he alone, when he dies, will go about with intelligence intact among the dead,[27] honored by the great Hagesilas."[28]

[131] She nodded to what she had said. When Pallas nods to something, it is accomplished, since Zeus gave to Athena alone of his daughters all the patriarchal prerogatives. Bath attendants, no mother bore this goddess, but the head of Zeus,[29] and the head of Zeus does not nod to falsehoods. Neither does his daughter.

[137] Athena is coming now for sure. Receive the god, girls, whoever has this task, with fair speech, with prayers, and with cries of thanksgiving. Hail, goddess, and take care of Inachian[30] Argos. Hail when you drive your horses out, and when you drive them back again. Preserve the whole land of the Danaans.[31]

---

[27] In the Homeric underworld (*Od.* 10.490–95).

[28] Rare name for Hades (Ath. 3.99b).

[29] Cf. Hes. *Theog.* 924–28; Pind. *Ol.* 7.36–38.

[30] The Inachus, a river and also an early king of Argos (Paus. 2.15.4).   [31] The descendants of Danaus (i.e., the Argives).

5a Ψ Scholia

1   On a designated day Argive women had a custom of taking the statue of Athena and Diomedes to the river Inachus and bathing it there. This is called the Bath of Pallas.

2   *phruassomenān*: that is to say, rendering such a sound.

CALLIMACHUS

4   σοῦσθε· ὁρμᾶτε, ἀπὸ τοῦ σεύω.

5   ⟨πάχεις⟩· ἀπὸ μέρους τὸ ὅλον.

8   ⟨γηγενέων⟩· τῶν γιγάντων.

11   ⟨ἐφοίβασεν⟩· ἐκάθηρεν.

13–17 ἀπὸ κοινοῦ τὸ οἴσετε.

14   ⟨συρίγγων⟩· τῶν χοινικίδων.

15   ⟨ἀλαβάστρως⟩· τὰς μυροθήκας.

24a   ⟨παρ' Εὐρώτᾳ⟩· ποταμὸς Λακεδαιμονίας.

24b   ⟨τοὶ Λακεδαιμόνιοι ἀστέρες⟩· οἱ Διόσκουροι.

25a   ⟨ἐμπεράμως⟩· ἐμπείρους.

25b   λιτά· ἀσκεύαστα, ἄμεικτα.

28   ⟨σίβδας⟩· ῥοιᾶς.

29   ἄρσεν· ἤτοι καθαρόν, ἄμεικτον.

32   ⟨σμασαμένα⟩· σμηξαμένη.

33   ἴλα· ἡ τῶν νυμφῶν φρατρία καὶ ἄθροισις.

34   ⟨Ἀρεστοριδᾶν⟩· Ἀρεστορίδαι φυλὴ ἐπίσημος ἐν Ἄργει.

37   ⟨Εὐμήδης⟩· ποτὲ τῶν Ἡρακλειδῶν ἐλθόντων κατὰ τῶν Ὀρεστειδῶν Εὐμήδης, ἱερεὺς τῆς Ἀθηνᾶς, ὑπενοήθη ὑπὸ τῶν Ἀργείων ὡς βουλόμενος προδοῦναι τὸ Παλλάδιον τοῖς Ἡρακλείδαις· φοβηθεὶς οὖν ὁ Εὐμήδης ἔλαβε τὸ Παλλάδιον καὶ παρεγένετο εἰς τὸ ὄρος τὸ καλούμενον Ἴφειον.

40   ⟨Κρεῖον⟩· ὄρος Ἄργους.

41   ⟨ἀπορρώγεσσιν⟩· ἐν πέτραις ἐρρηγμέναις.

42   ⟨Παλλατίδες⟩· οὕτω γὰρ καλοῦνται ἀπὸ τῆς Παλλάδος.

45   ⟨Ἄργος⟩· τουτέστιν ὦ Ἀργεῖοι.

4   *sousthe*: hasten, from *seuō*.

5   *pacheis*: the whole from a part.

8   *gēgeneōn*: of the Giants.

11   *ephoibasin*: she cleansed.

13–17   *oisete* is a zeugma.

14   *suriggōn*: of the naves.

15   *alabastrōs*: jars for unguents.

24a   *par' Eurōta*: a river of Lacedaemonia.

24b   *toi Lakedaimonioi asteres*: the Dioscuri.

25a   *emperamōs*: experienced.

25b   *lita*: natural, unmixed.

28   *sibdas*: pomegranate.

29   *arsen*: that is, pure, unmixed.

32   *smasamena*: having cleansed.

33   *ila*: a band and gathering.

34   *Arestoridān*: the Arestoridae are a notable tribe in Argos.

37   *Eumēdēs*: once, after the Heracleidae had gone against the Oresteides, Eumedes, a priest of Athena, was suspected of wanting to betray the Palladion to the Heracleidae. Eumedes, who had become afraid, took the Palladion and went with it into the mountain called Ipheion.

40   *Kreion*: a mountain in Argos.

41   *aporrōgessin*: on the sheer rocks.

42   *Pallatides*: they are called by this name from Pallas.

45   *Argos*: that is to say, O Argives!

47 sq.   ⟨ἢ 'ς Φυσάδειαν ἢ ἐς Ἀμυμώναν⟩· Φυσάδεια καὶ Ἀμυμώνη θυγατέρες Δαναοῦ, ὅθεν τὴν ὀνομασίαν ἔσχον αἱ κρῆναι.

57   ⟨νύμφαν μίαν⟩· τὴν Χαρικλώ, μητέρα Τειρεσίου τοῦ μάντεως.

60–63   Θέσπεια, Κορώνεια, Ἁλίαρτος πόλεις Βοιωτίας.

64   ⟨Κουραλίῳ⟩· ποταμὸς Βοιωτίας.

71   ⟨ἵππω ἐπὶ κράνᾳ⟩· οὕτω καλεῖται Ἵππου κρήνη ἐν Ἑλικῶνι, ἣν ὁ Πήγασος τῇ ὁπλῇ πλήξας ἐποίησεν.

72   ⟨λῶντο⟩· ἐλούοντο.

76a   περκάζων ἤτοι μελαινόμενος ὑπὸ τῆς ἐκφύσεως τῶν τριχῶν.

76b   μελανίζων.

81   ⟨ὦ Εὐηρείδα⟩· Εὐήρους υἱὸς ὁ Τειρεσίας.

87   ⟨ἄλαστε⟩· ἤτοι ἀνεπίληστα ὑπομείνας.

90   ⟨παριτέ⟩· παραβατέ, παροδεύσιμε.

97   ⟨μετὰ πάντα βαλεῦ⟩· τὸ ἑξῆς· μεταβαλεῦ.

106   ⟨τέλθος⟩· χρέος.

108–15   Ἀκταίων υἱὸς Ἀρισταίου καὶ Αὐτονόης. οὗτος ὑπὸ τῶν ἰδίων κυνῶν ἐσπαράχθη διὰ τὸ τὴν Ἄρτεμιν ἰδεῖν γυμνήν.

109   ⟨ἀβατάν⟩· ἡβητήν.

115   ⟨τουτάκι⟩· τηνικαῦτα.

120a   ⟨τεῦ⟩· σοῦ.

120b   ⟨μενεῦντι⟩· μενοῦσι.

124   ⟨ἤλιθα⟩· μάτην.

47 sq.   *ē 's Physadeian ē es Amymōnan*: Physadeia and Amymone, the daughters of Danaus, from whom the fountains were named.

57   *nymphan mian*: Chariclo, the mother of Tiresias the seer.

60–63   *Thespeia, Coroneia, Haliartus*: cities of Boeotia.

64   *Kouraliō*: a river of Boeotia.

71   *(H)ippō epi krana*: the Fountain of the Horse on Helicon has this name because Pegasus made it by striking it with his hoof.

72   *lōnto*: they were bathing.

76a   Ripening, that is to say, growing dark by the growth of hair.

76b   Turning dark.

81   *Ō Euēreida*: Euerous, the son of Tiresias.

87   *alaste*: that is, you endured unforgettable things.

90   *parite*: walk, travel.

97   *meta panta baleu*: use this word order: *metabaleu* (you change).

106   *telthos*: a debt.

108–15   Actaeon was the son of Aristaeus and Autonoe. This man was torn apart by his own dogs on account of seeing Artemis naked.

109   *abatan*: adult.

115   *toutaki*: then.

120a   *teu*: *sou* (of you).

120b   *meneunti*: they will remain.

124   *ēlitha*: in vain.

126   ⟨Λαβδακίδαις⟩· τοῖς περὶ Οἰδίποδα καὶ Ἰο-
κάστην.
130   ⟨Ἀγεσίλᾳ⟩· τῷ Ἅιδῃ, τῷ Πλούτωνι.
139   ⟨ὀλολυγαῖς⟩· εὐχαῖς.
140   ⟨κάδευ⟩· κήδου.

126   *Labdakidais*: the family of Oedipus and Jocasta.
130   *Agesila*: Hades, Pluto.
139   *ololugais*: prayers.
140   *kadeu*: care for.

HYMNUS VI
IN CEREREM

Τῶ καλάθω κατιόντος ἐπιφθέγξασθε, γυναῖκες·
"Δάματερ, μέγα χαῖρε, πολυτρόφε πουλυμέδιμνε."
τὸν κάλαθον κατιόντα χαμαὶ θασεῖσθε, βέβαλοι,
μηδ᾿ ἀπὸ τῶ τέγεος μηδ᾿ ὑψόθεν αὐγάσσησθε
5   μὴ παῖς μηδὲ γυνὰ μηδ᾿ ἃ κατεχεύατο χαίταν,
μηδ᾿ ὅκ᾿ ἀφ᾿ αὐαλέων στομάτων πτύωμες ἄπαστοι.
Ἕσπερος ἐκ νεφέων ἐσκέψατο (πανίκα νεῖται;),
Ἕσπερος, ὅς τε πιεῖν Δαμάτερα μῶνος ἔπεισεν,
ἁρπαγίμας ὅκ᾿ ἄπυστα μετέστιχεν ἴχνια κώρας.
10   πότνια, πῶς σε δύναντο πόδες φέρεν¹ ἔστ᾿ ἐπὶ
      δυθμάς,
ἔστ᾿ ἐπὶ τὼς μέλανας καὶ ὅπα τὰ χρύσεα μᾶλα;
οὐ πίες οὔτ᾿ ἄρ᾿ ἔδες τῆνον χρόνον οὐδὲ λοέσσα.²
τρὶς μὲν δὴ διέβας Ἀχελώιον ἀργυροδίναν,
τοσσάκι δ᾿ ἀενάων ποταμῶν ἐπέρασας ἕκαστον,

¹ πόδες φέρεν Fβ: φέρεν πόδες ut vid. *P.Ant.* 179 fr. 2a
² λοέσσα corr.Wilamowitz (cf. 16): λοέσσω Ψ

---

1 The *kalathos* is a basket with a narrow base sometimes used in cult practices. It might contain sacred objects for the ritual or offerings. As the hymn concludes, it will arrive in a cart pulled by four white horses (*Hymn* 6.120–21).

2 The disheveled appearance of the participants and their fast-

HYMN VI
TO DEMETER

As the basket[1] comes round cry out, women, "Greatly hail, Demeter, nourisher of many, rich in corn." You who are uninitiated will watch the returning basket from the ground. You will not view it from the roof nor from above, not child, nor woman, nor one who has let down her hair, not even when fasting we spit from parched mouths.[2] Hesperus[3] has peered out from the clouds. (When will it come?), Hesperus, who alone persuaded Demeter to drink when she followed the hidden tracks of her ravished daughter.[4]

[10] Queen, how were your feet able to carry you to the west, even to the black men[5] and where the golden apples are.[6] You did not drink nor did you eat, nor during that time did you bathe. Three times you crossed silver-eddying Achelous,[7] and as often you traversed each of the ever-flowing rivers. Three times you sat on the ground by the

---

ing imitate Demeter's condition as she searched for her daughter Persephone (*Hymn. Hom. Dem.* 2.47–50) and is likely a ritual prescription (Hopkinson, 83).   [3] The Evening Star, which marks the end of the ritual and the fast.   [4] Persephone, abducted by Hades.   [5] The Aethiopians (Schol. Ψ).

[6] The Garden of the Hesperides (Hes. *Theog.* 215), said to be located in various places usually in the west.

[7] River in Aetolia often identified with the streams of Ocean or water in general on account of its great size (D'Alessio 2007, vol. 1, 242–43n40 on *Epig.* 5; cf. Hes. *Theog.* 340).

15 τρὶς δ' ἐπὶ Καλλιχόρῳ χαμάδις ἐκαθίσσαο φρητί
   αὐσταλέα ἄποτός τε καὶ οὐ φάγες οὐδὲ λοέσσα.
   μὴ μὴ ταῦτα λέγωμες ἃ δάκρυον ἄγαγε Δηοῖ·
   κάλλιον, ὡς πολίεσσιν ἑαδότα τέθμια δῶκε·
   κάλλιον, ὡς καλάμαν τε καὶ ἱερὰ δράγματα πράτα
20 ἀσταχύων ἀπέκοψε καὶ ἐν βόας ἧκε πατῆσαι,
   ἁνίκα Τριπτόλεμος ἀγαθὰν ἐδιδάσκετο τέχναν·
   κάλλιον, ὡς (ἵνα καί τις ὑπερβασίας ἀλέηται)
   π[   ]ἰδέσθαι³
      οὔπω τὰν Κνιδίαν, ἔτι Δώτιον ἱρὸν ἔναιον,
25 †τὶν δ' αὐτᾷ†⁴ καλὸν ἄλσος ἐποιήσαντο Πελασγοί
   δένδρεσιν ἀμφιλαφές· διά κεν μόλις ἦνθεν ὀιστός·
   ἐν πίτυς, ἐν μεγάλαι πτελέαι ἔσαν, ἐν δὲ καὶ ὄχναι,
   ἐν δὲ καλὰ γλυκύμαλα· τὸ δ' ὥστ' ἀλέκτρινον ὕδωρ

³ π[. . .]ἰδέσθαι Ψ
⁴ τὶν δ'αὐτᾷ Ψ: τῇ δ'αὐτᾷ Wilamowitz: τὶν δ' ἀγνᾷ
Schadewaldt: τᾷ δ' αὐτεῖ Hopkinson

---

8 Where Demeter instructed the Eleusinians to build her
temple (*Hymn. Hom. Dem.* 2.270–72). It became a landmark at
Eleusis (Paus. 1.38.6).

9 Demeter.

10 Demeter as the giver of agriculture (*Hymn. Hom. Dem.*
2.453–56). Here she introduces techniques for harvesting and
threshing.

11 Mythic king of Eleusis connected with Demeter's mysteries
there and the first to teach men agriculture (*Hymn. Hom. Dem.*
2.473–79).

fountain Callichorus,[8] parched and thirsty, but you did not eat or bathe. No, let us not mention what brought a tear to Deo.[9] It is better to tell of how she gave pleasing laws to the cities, how first she cut stalks and holy sheaves of corn, and brought in oxen to tread them,[10] when Triptolemus[11] was taught the good art. Better, how (so that someone might avoid overstepping) . . . to see.[12]

[24] The Pelasgians[13] still lived in holy Dotium,[14] not yet in Cnidia,[15] where they planted a lovely grove wide-abounding in trees. An arrow could scarcely pass through it. In it were pines; great elms were there, pear trees and lovely sweet apples. And water like amber gushed from the trenches. The goddess was crazy about the place, as

[12] On the lacuna see Hopkinson (p. 99). The missing verse introduced the story of Erysichthon, which follows it as an example of the dangers of defying Demeter. Wilamowitz (1924, vol. 2, 30n1) suggests that the space could be filled in this way: π[αῖδα κακὸν Τριόπα σκιοειδέα θῆκεν] ἰδέσθαι (she made the evil son of Triopas look like a shadow).

[13] The earliest Argives and original inhabitants of Thessaly (Aesch. *Suppl.* 250–53; Hdt. 1.57–58, 146).

[14] Plain in east Thessaly and early cult center of Demeter as well as the birthplace of Asclepius (*Hymn. Hom. Asclep.* 16.1–5).

[15] Dorian city on the coast of Ionia, where a temple of Apollo was built by Triopas (Hdt. 1.144; Thuc. 8.35.3), the father of Erysichthon as early as [Hes.] fr. 43a.2–3, 43b, except in Hellanicus (*BNJ* 4 F 7), where his father is Myrmidon. In some versions of this tale, Triopas takes the place of Erysichthon in offending Demeter and is driven destitute from Thessaly to Triopium near Cnidus (Diod. Sic. 5.61.1–2; Hyg. *Poet. astr.* 2.13). The father and the son are conflated by Lycophron (*Alex.* 1391–96).

ἐξ ἀμαρᾶν ἀνέθυε. θεὰ δ' ἐπεμαίνετο χώρῳ
30   ὅσσον Ἐλευσῖνι, Τριόπᾳ θ' ὅσον ὀκκόσον Ἔννᾳ.
     ἀλλ' ὅκα Τριοπίδαισιν ὁ δεξιὸς ἄχθετο δαίμων,
     τουτάκις ἁ χείρων Ἐρυσίχθονος ἅψατο βωλά·
     σεύατ' ἔχων θεράποντας ἐείκοσι, πάντας ἐν ἀκμᾷ,
     πάντας δ' ἀνδρογίγαντας ὅλαν πόλιν ἀρκίος ἆραι,
35   ἀμφότερον πελέκεσσι καὶ ἀξίναισιν ὁπλίσσας,
     ἐς δὲ τὸ τᾶς Δάματρος ἀναιδέες ἔδραμον ἄλσος.
     ἦς[5] δέ τις αἴγειρος, μέγα δένδρεον αἰθέρι κῦρον,
     τῷ ἔπι[6] ταὶ νύμφαι ποτὶ τώνδιον ἑψιόωντο·
     ἁ πράτα πλαγεῖσα κακὸν μέλος ἴαχεν ἄλλαις.
40   ἄσθετο Δαμάτηρ, ὅτι οἱ ξύλον ἱερὸν ἄλγει,
     εἶπε δὲ χωσαμένα· "τίς μοι καλὰ δένδρεα κόπτει;"
        αὐτίκα Νικίππᾳ, τάν οἱ πόλις ἀράτειραν
     δαμοσίαν ἔστασαν, ἐείσατο, γέντο δὲ χειρί
     στέμματα καὶ μάκωνα, κατωμαδίαν δ' ἔχε κλᾷδα.
45   φᾶ δὲ παραψύχοισα κακὸν καὶ ἀναιδέα φῶτα·
     "τέκνον, ὅτις τὰ θεοῖσιν ἀνειμένα δένδρεα κόπτεις,
     τέκνον ἐλίννυσον, τέκνον πολύθεστε τοκεῦσι,
     παύεο καὶ θεράποντας ἀπότρεπε, μή τι χαλεφθῇ
     πότνια Δαμάτηρ, τᾶς ἱερὸν ἐκκεραΐζεις."
50   τὰν δ' ἄρ' ὑποβλέψας χαλεπώτερον ἠὲ κυναγόν

----

[5] ἦς La.: ἦν Ψ
[6] τῷ ἔπι corr. Schneider: τῷ δ' ἔπι P.Ant. 179 fr. 2b et Ψ

much as she loved Eleusis,[16] as much as Triopia,[17] as Enna.[18]

[31] But when their good fortune became angry at the Triopidae, then a terrible plan fastened itself on Erysichthon, and he rushed with twenty servants, all in their prime, all giant men, strong enough to lift up a whole city, armed with double axes and hatchets, and they ran without shame into the grove of Demeter. There was a certain poplar, a huge tree reaching to the sky. At noon the nymphs used to play near it. Struck first, it wailed a sad lament to the others. Demeter sensed that her sacred wood was in pain, and she spoke in anger, "Who is cutting down my lovely trees?"

[42] At once she assumed the form of Nicippe,[19] whom the city had appointed her public priestess. She had in her hand the garlands and poppy, and the key to the shrine hung on her shoulder. She spoke soothingly to the wicked and shameless man: "Child, you who cut the trees dedicated to the gods, child, stop, child much-prayed for by your parents, cease and turn back your servants, so Queen Demeter will not be angry—you are pillaging something sacred to her." But he looked at her more fiercely than a

---

[16] The site of Demeter's important sanctuary near Athens, home of the Eleusinian mysteries. [17] The temple of Apollo founded by Triopas (Theoc. *Id*. 17.68). [18] The site of a temple of Demeter in Sicily visited by Philotera, sister of Ptolemy II and Arsinoe II, in Callimachus' *Apotheosis of Arsinoe* (*Mel*. 228.43–45). [19] "Victory through horses," a name invented by Callimachus possibly in reference to Berenice II (Victory-bringing), the wife of Ptolemy III, whose victory in the four-horse chariot race at Nemea the poet also celebrates (*Aet*. 54).

ὤρεσιν ἐν Τμαρίοισιν ὑποβλέπει ἄνδρα λέαινα
ὠμοτόκος, τᾶς φαντὶ πέλειν βλοσυρώτατον ὄμμα,
"χάζευ," ἔφα, "μή τοι πέλεκυν μέγαν ἐν χροῒ πάξω.
ταῦτα δ᾽ ἐμὸν θησεῖ στεγανὸν δόμον, ᾧ ἔνι δαῖτας
55 αἰὲν ἐμοῖς ἑτάροισιν ἄδην[7] θυμαρέας ἀξῶ."

    εἶπεν ὁ παῖς, Νέμεσις δὲ κακὰν ἐγράψατο φωνάν.
Δαμάτηρ δ᾽ ἄφατόν τι κοτέσσατο, γείνατο δ᾽ ἁ
        θεύς·[8]
ἵματα μὲν χέρσω, κεφαλὰ δέ οἱ ἅψατ᾽ Ὀλύμπω.
οἱ μὲν ἄρ᾽ ἡμιθνῆτες, ἐπεὶ τὰν πότνιαν εἶδον,
60 ἐξαπίνας ἀπόρουσαν ἐνὶ δρυσὶ χαλκὸν ἀφέντες.
ἁ δ᾽ ἄλλως μὲν ἔασεν, ἀναγκαίᾳ γὰρ ἕποντο
δεσποτικὰν ὑπὸ χεῖρα, βαρὺν δ᾽ ἀπαμείψατ᾽ ἄνακτα·
"ναὶ ναί, τεύχεο δῶμα, κύον κύον, ᾧ ἔνι δαῖτας
ποιησεῖς· θαμιναὶ γὰρ ἐς ὕστερον εἰλαπίναι τοι."
65 ἁ μὲν τόσσ᾽ εἰποῖσ᾽ Ἐρυσίχθονι τεῦχε πονηρά.

    αὐτίκα οἱ χαλεπόν τε καὶ ἄγριον ἔμβαλε λιμόν
αἴθωνα κρατερόν, μεγάλα δ᾽ ἐστρεύγετο νούσῳ.
σχέτλιος, ὅσσα πάσαιτο τόσων ἔχεν ἵμερος αὖτις.
εἴκατι δαῖτα πένοντο, δυώδεκα δ᾽ οἶνον ἄφυσσον.

---

[7] ἄδην Ψ: ἄδαν Hopkinson
[8]]δαθεύς P.Oxy. 2226 col. II, Ψ: αὖ θεύς Bergk, Hopkinson

---

[20] A mountain in Epirus near the oracle of Zeus at Dodona,
an archetypically remote place (*Aet.* 23.3).
[21] Nemesis was the recorder of impious speech (Pl. *Leg.*
4.717d).

lioness looks at a hunter in the Tmarian[20] mountains, a lioness who has just given birth, whose eyes they say are grimmest. "Back off," he said, "or I will fix this great ax in your flesh. These will put a roof on my house, where I plan to lay out for my comrades their fill of hearty banquets."

[56] So the boy spoke and Nemesis[21] recorded his evil speech. Demeter was unspeakably angry and became visible as a goddess. Her steps touched the ground but her head reached Olympus.[22] When they saw the goddess, they ran off at once half-dead from fear, leaving the bronze ax-heads in the oaks. She left the others alone, for they followed by necessity under the hand of their master. But she answered their overbearing lord, "Yes, yes, build yourself a house, you dog—dog!—where you will hold your banquets. Constant feasts will be yours in time to come." That much she said, and devised trouble for Erysichthon.

[66] At once she afflicted him with a harsh and savage hunger, burning[23] fiercely, and he was consumed by a terrible disease.[24] Poor man, as much as he ate, he wanted so much again. Twenty servants prepared his banquet, twelve

[22] A typical feature of divine epiphany (e.g., *Hymn. Hom. Dem.* 2.188; Hom. *Il.* 4.443).

[23] Erysichthon was also called Aethon in reference to his blazing hunger (Hes. [*Cat.*] fr. 43a.5–8, 43b–c; Hellanicus *FGH* 4 F 7; Lyc. *Alex.* 1396). Sometimes Aethon is an alternative name for Erysichthon (Hes. [*Cat.*] fr. 43a.37; Ant. Lib. *Met.*17.5; *Suda* αι 142 Αἴθων), but in other traditions the two figures are separate. The *Suda* calls Aethon the son of Helios, which explains his name, but his story is that of Erysichthon's.

[24] Verses 66 to 115 are organized in five sections focused alternatively on Erysichthon and his family (D'Alessio 2007, vol. 1, 204n14).

71 καὶ γὰρ τᾷ Δάματρι συνωργίσθη Διόνυσος·
70 τόσσα Διώνυσον γὰρ ἃ καὶ Δάματρα χαλέπτει.⁹
    οὔτε νιν εἰς ἐράνως οὔτε ξυνδείπνια πέμπον
    αἰδόμενοι γονέες, προχάνα δ' εὑρίσκετο πᾶσα.
    ἦνθον Ἰτωνιάδος νιν Ἀθαναίας ἐπ' ἄεθλα
75 Ὀρμενίδαι καλέοντες· ἀπ' ὧν ἀρνήσατο μάτηρ·
    "οὐκ ἔνδοι, χθιζὸς γὰρ ἐπὶ Κραννῶνα βέβακε
    τέλθος ἀπαιτησῶν ἑκατὸν βόας." ἦνθε Πολυξώ,
    μάτηρ Ἀκτορίωνος, ἐπεὶ γάμον ἄρτυε παιδί,
    ἀμφότερον Τριόπαν τε καὶ υἱέα κικλήσκοισα.
80 τὰν δὲ γυνὰ βαρύθυμος ἀμείβετο δακρύοισα·¹⁰
    "νεῖταί¹¹τοι Τριόπας, Ἐρυσίχθονα δ' ἤλασε κάπρος
    Πίνδον ἀν' εὐάγκειαν, ὁ δ' ἐννέα φάεα κεῖται."
        δειλαία φιλότεκνε, τί δ' οὐκ ἐψεύσαο, μᾶτερ;
    δαίννεν εἰλαπίναν τις· "ἐν ἀλλοτρίᾳ Ἐρυσίχθων."
85 ἄγετό τις νύμφαν· "Ἐρυσίχθονα δίσκος ἔτυψεν,"
    ἢ "ἔπεσ' ἐξ ἵππων," ἢ "ἐν Ὄθρυϊ ποίμνι' ἀμιθρεῖ."
    ἐνδόμυχος δῆπειτα πανάμερος εἰλαπιναστάς

---

⁹ ordinem mutavit Reiske et al.
¹⁰ Δακ]ρυοισα P.Oxy. 2226 col. III: δακρυχέουσα Ψ
¹¹ νεῖται Ψ: νητα[ι P.Oxy. 2226 col. III

---

²⁵ Following Reiske, lines 70 and 71 have been transposed so
that the more general statement precedes the particular example
(Hopkinson, 137–39).
²⁶ The father of Amyntor (Hom. Il. 9.448, 10.266) and the
eponymous founder of Ormenium (Il. 2.734) in eastern Thessaly.
He was related to the family of Triopas through his uncle Aeolus.
²⁷ Athena had a sanctuary at Itone in Thessaly, but this refer-

drew his wine. For Dionysus shares Demeter's anger; whatever enrages Demeter, provokes Dionysus just as much.[25] His embarrassed parents did not send him to dinners or common banquets, and every sort of pretext was found. The sons of Ormenus[26] came to invite him to the games of Itonian Athena,[27] but his mother refused them. "He is not at home, but yesterday he went to Crannon[28] to demand payment on a debt of a hundred oxen." Polyxo,[29] mother of Actorion,[30] came to invite both Triopas and his son, when she was preparing her child's wedding. But the woman replied tearfully with heavy heart: "Triopas will come, but a boar attacked Erysichthon on Pindus[31] of the lovely valleys, and he has been laid up for nine days."

[83] Poor woman, devoted mother, what lie did you not tell? Someone was giving a feast: "Erysichthon is away." Someone was bringing home a bride: "A discus struck Erysichthon," or "He fell from his cart," or "He is counting his flocks on Othrys."[32] And yet within the house the all-

ence is probably to the better-known festival of Athena Itonias at Iton in Boeotia (Ap. Rhod. 1.551; Strabo 9.2.29, 9.5.14), founded by migrants from Thessaly (*RE* 9.2 2374–76).

[28] A town in Thessaly on a plain between the Enipeus and Peneus Rivers (Strabo 9.5.20; *Hymn* 4.138).

[29] Polyxo appears only here.

[30] This Actorion may be Homer's Actor, father of the twins who prevented Nestor from winning a chariot race at the funeral games for Amarynceus in Epeius (Hom. *Il.* 23.638–42).

[31] A mountain chain between Thessaly and Epirus, well known as a hunting ground (Pind. *Pyth.* 9.15–25; Xen. *Cyn.* 11.1).

[32] A mountain in southern Thessaly near Achaea Phthiotis (Hdt. 7.129; Strabo 9.5.14; *RE* 18.2 1873–76).

ἤσθιε μυρία πάντα· κακὰ δ' ἐξάλλετο γαστήρ
αἰεὶ μᾶλλον ἔδοντι, τὰ δ' ἐς βυθὸν οἷα θαλάσσας
90 ἀλεμάτως ἀχάριστα κατέρρεεν εἴδατα πάντα.[12]
ὡς δὲ Μίμαντι χιών, ὡς ἀελίῳ ἔνι πλαγγών,
καὶ τούτων ἔτι μέζον ἐτάκετο, μέστ' ἐπὶ[13] νεύρας[14]
δειλαίῳ ῥινός τε[15] καὶ ὀστέα μῶνον ἐλείφθη.[16]
    κλαῖε μὲν ἁ μάτηρ, βαρὺ δ' ἔστενον αἱ δύ'
        ἀδελφαί
95 χὠ μαστὸς τὸν ἔπωνε καὶ αἱ δέκα πολλάκι δῶλαι.
καὶ δ' αὐτὸς Τρίοπας πολιαῖς ἐπὶ χεῖρας ἔβαλλε,
τοῖα τὸν οὐκ ἀίοντα Ποτειδάωνα καλιστρέων·
"ψευδοπάτωρ, ἴδε τόνδε τεοῦ τρίτον, εἴπερ ἐγὼ μέν
σεῦ τε καὶ Αἰολίδος Κανάκας γένος, αὐτὰρ ἐμεῖο
100 τοῦτο τὸ δείλαιον γένετο βρέφος· αἴθε γὰρ αὐτόν
βλητὸν ὑπ' Ἀπόλλωνος ἐμαὶ χέρες ἐκτερέιξαν·
νῦν δὲ κακὰ βούβρωστις ἐν ὀφθαλμοῖσι κάθηται.
ἢ οἱ ἀπόστασον χαλεπὰν νόσον ἠέ νιν αὐτός
βόσκε λαβών· ἀμαὶ γὰρ ἀπειρήκαντι τράπεζαι.
105 χῆραι μὲν μάνδραι, κενεαὶ δέ μοι αὔλιες ἤδη

[12] εἴδατα πάντα Ψ: ειδαταπολλα P.Oxy. 2226 col. III
[13] μεστεπι P.Oxy. 2226 col. III: μέσφ' ἐπί Ψ
[14] νευράς Ψ: νεύρ..ς P.Oxy. 2226 col. III: νεύροις prop.
Lobel
[15] ρινοστε P.Oxy. 2226 col. III: ἰνές τε Ψ
[16] ἔλ(ε)ιφθεν Ψ: ελειφθη P.Oxy. 2226 col. III

---

[33] εἰλαπιναστάς (banqueter) is a Homeric hapax legomenon
(*Il.* 17.577). The word choice implies a contrast between the wel-

day banqueter[33] ate boundlessly. His vile belly leaped up as he ate more and more. And thanklessly all the food rushed down in vain into a depth like the sea's. Like the snow on Mimas,[34] like a wax doll in the sun,[35] but even more quickly than these he wasted to the very sinews. Only skin and bones were left to the poor man.

[94] His mother wept, and his two sisters groaned deeply, and the nurse whose breast he had suckled, and the ten maidservants over and over. And Triopas himself put his hands on his gray hair and with words like these kept calling on Poseidon, who did not listen: "False father, look at this grandson of yours—if I was born of you and Aeolian Canace,[36] and this wretched baby is mine! I wish that he had been blasted by Apollo and my own hands had buried him. Now he sits before my eyes as an accursed avatar of famishment![37] Either remove this terrible disease from him, or take him yourself and feed him. My tables have given out. The sheepfolds are desolate and my

come companion at the feast described by Homer and Erysichthon, who gorges alone.   34 A cape extending from the shore of Asia Minor opposite Chios. It is proverbially snowy (Ar. *Nub.* 273).   35 This verse twice violates Callimachus' metrical norms (Hopkinson, 152).

36 Canace was the daughter of Aeolus and the mother by Poseidon of Triopas (Diod. Sic. 5.61; Apollod. *Bibl.* 1.7.3–4).

37 Boubrostis, a demon personifying famine, here, literally, "ox hunger," which suits Erysichthon's appetite for farm animals (Faraone 2012). It is also a Homeric hapax legomenon (*Il.* 24.532), illustrating the kind of ill fortune that can come from the two urns of Zeus. The reference contrasts Triopas' desire to be rid of his still-living son with Priam's need to ransom his dead one (Acosta-Hughes and Stephens 2012, 19–20).

τετραπόδων· οὐδὲν[17] γὰρ ἀπαρνήσαντο μάγειροι.
ἀλλὰ καὶ οὐρήας μεγαλᾶν ὑπέλυσαν ἀμαξᾶν,
καὶ τὰν βῶν ἔφαγεν, τὰν Ἑστίᾳ ἔτρεφε μάτηρ,
καὶ τὸν ἀεθλοφόρον καὶ τὸν πολεμήιον ἵππον,
110 καὶ τὰν μάλουριν,[18] τὰν ἔτρεμε θηρία μικκά."
μέστα μὲν ἐν[19] Τριόπαο δόμοις ἔτι[20] χρήματα κεῖτο,
μῶνον[21] ἄρ' οἰκεῖοι θάλαμοι κακὸν ἠπίσταντο.
ἀλλ' ὅκα[22] τὸν βαθὺν οἶκον ἀνεξήραναν[23] ὀδόντες,
καὶ τόχ' ὁ τῶ βασιλῆος ἐνὶ τριόδοισι καθῆστο
115 αἰτίζων ἀκόλως τε καὶ ἔκβολα λύματα δαιτός.
Δάματερ, μὴ τῆνος ἐμὶν φίλος, ὅς τοι ἀπεχθής,
εἴη μηδ' ὁμότοιχος· ἐμοὶ κακογείτονες ἐχθροί.
⟨ ⟩[24] παρθενικαί, καὶ ἐπιφθέγξασθε, τεκοῖσαι·
"Δάματερ, μέγα χαῖρε, πολυτρόφε πουλυμέδιμνε."
120 χὼς αἱ τὸν κάλαθον λευκότριχες ἵπποι ἄγοντι
τέσσαρες, ὣς ἁμὶν μεγάλα θεὸς εὐρυάνασσα
λευκὸν ἔαρ, λευκὸν δὲ θέρος καὶ χεῖμα φέροισα
ἥξεῖ καὶ φθινόπωρον, ἔτος δ' εἰς ἄλλο φυλαξεῖ.
ὡς δ' ἀπεδίλωτοι καὶ ἀνάμπυκες ἄστυ πατεῦμες,

---

[17] οὐδ[εν P.Oxy. 2226 col. IV: ἤδη Ψ
[18] μαλουριν P.Oxy. 2226 col. IV: αἴλουραν Ψ
[19] μεσταμενεν P.Oxy. 2226 col. IV: μεσφ' ὅτε μέν Ψ
[20] ἔτι Lobel: ἔνι Ψ   [21] μωνον P.Oxy 2226 col. IV: μῶ-νοι Ψ   [22] ἀλλ' ὅκα Schneider: αλλοκα P.Oxy. 2226 col. IV: ἀλλ' ὅτε Ψ   [23] ἀνεξήραναν Ernesti: ἀνεξήραιναν Ψ
[24] Init. lacuna Ψ. vv. 118–37: omit. P.Oxy. 2226

---

[38] Goddess of the hearth (*Hymn. Hom. Aphr.* 5.21–33), the very center of the household.

barns are already empty of four-footed creatures, for the
cooks have denied him nothing. They let loose the mules
from the large wagon, and he ate the heifer that his mother
was fattening for Hestia,[38] the race horse and the war
horse, and White Tail,[39] which the little vermin so feared."
While possessions still lay in the house of Triopas, only his
private chambers understood the evil. But when his teeth
had dried up the rich house, then the king's son sat at the
crossroads asking for scraps and garbage cast off from a
feast. Demeter, may that man you hate never be my friend
nor share a wall with me. Bad neighbors are hateful to
me.[40]

[118] . . . .[41] young girls, and respond, mothers. "Deme-
ter, hail greatly, nourisher of many, rich in corn." As the
four white-haired horses bring the basket, so to us may
the great goddess, wide-ruling, come bringing a white[42]
spring, a white harvest, winter and fall, and may she watch
over us for another year. As we walk through the city with-
out sandals and without headbands, so our feet and heads

---

39 *P.Oxy.* 2226 col. IV reads μάλουριν (white tail) but does not
specify the type of aggressive animal. It was apparently glossed as
αἴλουρον (cat), which later migrated into the text of the arche-
type.   40 Here the papyrus (*P.Oxy.* 2226) breaks off, omitting
verses 118 to 137. It begins again with 138, the last line preserved
in the archetype. After this, it adds an additional verse with only
a few letters visible that was not included in the medieval manu-
scripts. There is also an unplaced fragment that cannot be fit into
the extant text. Putting these together Pfeiffer and others con-
cluded that there may once have been an alternative conclusion
to the hymn (Stephens, 297).

41 To fill this lacuna Wilamowitz suggests ἄρχετε (Begin!).

42 "Fortunate," more often used to describe a lucky day
(Aesch. *Pers.* 301; cf. *Aet.* 178.2; *Ia.* 191.37).

125 ὡς πόδας, ὡς κεφαλὰς παναπηρέας ἕξομες αἰεί.
ὡς δ' αἱ λικνοφόροι χρυσῷ πλέα λίκνα φέροντι,
ὡς ἁμὲς τὸν χρυσὸν ἀφειδέα πασεύμεσθα.
μέστα τὰ τᾶς πόλιος πρυτανήια τὰς ἀτελέστως,
τὰς δὲ τελεσφορέας²⁵ ποτὶ τὰν θεὸν ἄχρις ὁμαρτεῖν,
130 αἵτινες ἑξήκοντα κατώτεραι· αἱ δὲ βαρεῖαι,
χἄτις Ἐλειθυίᾳ τείνει χέρα χἄτις ἐν ἄλγει,
ὡς ἅλις, ὡς αὐταῖς ἱθαρὸν²⁶ γόνυ· ταῖσι δὲ Δηὼ
δωσεῖ πάντ' ἐπίμεστα καὶ †ὡς ποτὶ²⁷ ναὸν ἵκωνται.
      χαῖρε, θεά, καὶ τάνδε σάω πόλιν ἔν θ' ὁμονοίᾳ
135 ἔν τ' εὐηπελίᾳ, φέρε δ' ἀγρόθι νόστιμα πάντα·
φέρβε βόας, φέρε μᾶλα, φέρε στάχυν, οἶσε
            θερισμόν,
φέρβε καὶ εἰράναν, ἵν' ὃς ἄροσε τῆνος ἀμάσῃ.
ἵλαθί μοι, τρίλλιστε, μέγα κρείοισα θεάων.

²⁵ τελεφορέας corr. anon. Bern.: τελεφορίας Ψ
²⁶ αυτα]ισιθαρον P.Oxy. 2258A fr. 9 recto c: αὐταν ἱκα-
νόν Ψ   ²⁷ καὶ ὡς ποτὶ Ψ: καὶ ὡς ποκα prop. Meineke:
καὶ αἷς π. fort. Schol.

6a ad vv. 13–16, P.Oxy. 2258 fr. 10 recto; ad vv. 126–30,
fr. 9 recto

                    ]ρ.ε[
                  ]φ[.] .ι.ο.[
15   [Καλ]λίχορον φ[ρέαρ]
                  ]α ζητοῦσα[
                  ]   [
            .   .   .   .

will always be safe. As the basket-carriers carry winnowing baskets full of gold, so may we get gold unstinted. The uninitiated should walk to the town hall, the initiated to the goddess' shrine, if they are below the age of sixty. Those who are heavy, she who stretches her hand to Eileithyia[43] or who is in pain, for them it is enough to go as far as their knees are comfortable. To them Deo will give everything in full measure, just as she gives to those who go to her shrine.[44]

[134] Hail, Goddess, and preserve this city in harmony and in prosperity. And bring everything wholesome from the field. Feed the cows, bring fruit, bring corn, bring the harvest. Especially nurture peace, so that whoever sows may also reap. Be gracious to me, O thrice-prayed for, great Queen of goddesses!

[43] Goddess of childbirth (Hes. *Theog.* 922; Diod Sic. 5.72.5).
[44] Or "just as if they reached her temple" (Hopkinson, 181–82).

6a Oxyrhynchus papyrus

. . .
15   The well Callichoron
16   seeking
. . .

]ַτας [λικ]νοφόρους φέρε[ιν
126   αἰֶ, λικνοφֶ.όֶροֶι χρυσῶ πλέֶα
127   [   ]ω.[   ]καὶ βέλτιον ἔξομεν ἀφ[
128   [   ] πρυτανήϊα ὡς μεγαλασֶ.αֶ[
130   [   ]ֶνειν τὰς [ὑ]πֶὲρ ἑξήκοντα [
          ]   [   ]   [   ] [
                  ]ֶ[

6b Schol. Ψ

1   Ὁ Φιλάδελφος Πτολεμαῖος κατὰ μίμησιν
τῶν Ἀθηνῶν ἔθη τινὰ ἵδρυσεν ἐν Ἀλεξανδρείᾳ, ἐν οἷς
καὶ τὴν τοῦ καλάθου πρόοδον. ἔθος γὰρ ἦν ἐν Ἀθή-
ναις ἐν ὡρισμένῃ ἡμέρᾳ ἐπὶ ὀχήματος φέρεσθαι
κάλαθον εἰς τιμὴν τῆς Δήμητρος.
5   ⟨μηδ' ἃ κατεχεύατο χαίταν⟩· μηδ' ἥτις ἄγα-
μός ἐστιν.
6   μηδὲ ὅταν ἐκ τῶν αὐαλέων χειλέων τοῦ στό-
ματος πτύωμεν ἄπαστοι, τουτέστι μετὰ τὸ δεῖπνον·
τότε γὰρ οὐ μεταλαμβάνομεν σιτίων.
7–9   Ἕσπερος μόνος ἐθεάσατο τὸν κάλαθον ὅστις
ἔπεισε τὴν Δήμητραν μεταλαβεῖν σιτίων μετὰ τὸ
παύσασθαι ζητοῦσαν τὴν κόρην.
11a   ⟨τὼς μέλανας⟩· τοὺς Αἰθίοπας.
11b   ⟨ὄπα τὰ χρύσεα μᾶλα⟩· ἐπὶ τὴν Λιβύην.
12   ⟨λοέσσα⟩· ἀντὶ τοῦ ἐλούσω.
13   ⟨Ἀχελώϊον⟩· ποταμὸς Αἰτωλίας.
15   ⟨Καλλιχόρῳ⟩· Καλλίχορον φρέαρ ἐκαλεῖτο
ἐν Ἐλευσῖνι (ἔστι δὲ καὶ δῆμος Ἀττικῆς).

HYMN VI TO DEMETER

the basket-carriers to carry the . . .
126   the basket-carriers . . . full of gold
127   we will have better
128   Prytaneia, as great
130   the women over sixty

6b Ψ Scholia

1   Ptolemy Philadelphus, in imitation of Athens,
established some customs in Alexandria, and among these
was the Procession of the Basket. In Athens the custom
was that on a designated day a basket was carried on a cart
in honor of Demeter.
5   *mēd' a katecheuato chaitan*: no one who is un-
married.
6   Nor when fasting do we spit from the mouth
through parched lips, that is to say, after dinner. Then we
do not partake of food.
7–9   Hesperus alone has seen the basket, who per-
suaded Demeter to take up food after halting the search
for Kore.
11a   *tōs melanas*: the Ethiopians.
11b   *(h)opa ta chrusea mala*: in Libya.
12   *loessa*: instead of *elousō*.
13   *Achelōion*: a river of Aetolia.
15   *Kallichorōi*: a well was called Callichoron in
Eleusis (it is a deme of Attica).

373

CALLIMACHUS

21   ⟨Τριπτόλεμος⟩· Τριπτόλεμον λέγουσιν υἱὸν
Κελεοῦ ὃν Δημήτηρ ἐδίδαξεν σιτουργίαν.
22   τὸ ἑξῆς· κάλλιον τὰ δράγματα †ἔδειν† ἵνα
καί τις ὑπερβασίας ἀλέηται.
24   ⟨Δώτιον⟩· χώρα Θεσσαλίας.
28   ἀλέκτρινον ὕδωρ· τὸ διαυγές· παρὰ τὸ ἤλεκ-
τρον.
29   ἐξ ἀμαρᾶν Ὅμηρος· "ἀμάρης ἐξ ἔχματα
βάλλων." εἰσὶ δὲ ἀμάραι αἱ ὑδρορρόαι.
30   Ἐλευσὶς †καὶ Ἔννα† δῆμοι τῆς Ἀττικῆς.
38   ⟨ποτὶ τώνδιον ἐψιόωντο⟩· περὶ τὸ ἔνδιον
ἤγουν περὶ τὸ μεσημβρινὸν ἐψιόωντο καὶ ἔπαιζον.
43   ⟨ἐείσατο⟩· ὡμοιώθη.
44   ⟨ἔχε κλᾷδα⟩· εἶχε κλεῖδα ὡς ἱέρεια.
46   ⟨ἀνειμένα⟩· ἀνακείμενα.
47   ⟨πολύθεστε⟩· πολυπόθητε.
73   ⟨προχάνα⟩· πρόφασις.
74 sq.   ⟨Ἰτωνιάδος νιν Ἀθαναίας ἐπ᾽ ἄεθλα Ὀρμενί-
δαι καλέοντες⟩· Ἰτὼν πόλις Θεσσαλίας, ἔνθα τιμᾶται
Ἀθηνᾶ. γένος δὲ ἐπίσημον οἱ Ὀρμενίδαι.
76   ⟨Κραννῶνα⟩· πόλις Θεσσαλίας.
77   ⟨Πολυξώ⟩· ἐπίσημος αὕτη.
79   ⟨υἱέα⟩· τὸν Ἐρυσίχθονα.
81   ⟨νεῖται⟩· ἔρχεται.
84   εἰ ἑστιῶν φίλους τις ἦν, ἐζητεῖτο δὲ Ἐρυσί-
χθων, ἔλεγεν ἡ μήτηρ· "ἐν ἀλλοτρίοις οἰκήμασίν
ἐστιν."
86   ⟨ἀμ.....⟩· ἀριθμεῖ.

21   *Triptolemos*: he mentions Triptolemus the son Celeus whom Demeter taught to raise corn.

22   Use this word order: [it is] better to . . . handfuls so that one may avoid overstepping.

24   *Dōtion*: a place in Thessaly.

28   *alekrinon (h)ydōr*: translucent; like electrum.

29   *ex amaran*: Homer (*Il.* 21.259): "casting off the blockages from the channel." The *amarai* are water channels.

30   *Eleusis*: †and Enna,† demes of Attica.

38   *poti tōndion epsioōnto*: they amused themselves and played at noon, that is, at midday.

43   *eeisato*: she was like.

44   *eche klāida*: she had a key as a priestess.

46   *aneimena*: dedicated to.

47   *polytheste*: much desired.

73   *prochana*: an excuse.

74 sq.   *Itōnidos nin Athanaias ep' aethla Ormenidai kaleontes*: Iton is a city of Thessaly where Athena is honored. The Ormenidae are a well-known family.

76   *Krannōna*: a city of Thessaly.

77   *Poluxō*: she is well known.

79   *(h)uia*: Erysichthon.

81   *neitai*: he goes.

84   If someone were entertaining friends, and he would seek out Erysichthon, his mother would say "he is in another town."

86   [. . .]: he is counting.

88   ἐξάλλετο· ηὐξάνετο ἐπὶ τῷ ἐσθίειν.

90   ⟨ἀλεμάτως⟩· ματαίως.

91   πλαγγών· ἡ κήρινος νύμφη.

95   ⟨χὠ μαστὸς τὸν τὸν ἔπωνε⟩· καὶ ὁ μαστὸς
ὃν ἔπινεν, ἤγουν ἡ τροφός.

97   ⟨καλιστρέων⟩· καλῶν.

99   ⟨Αἰολίδος Κανάκης γένος⟩· ἡ Κανάκη μήτηρ
Τριόπα, θυγάτηρ Αἰόλου.

108   ⟨τὰν Ἑστίᾳ ἔτρεφε μάτηρ⟩· ἥντινα ἔτρεφεν
ἡ αὐτοῦ μήτηρ τῇ Ἑστίᾳ.

110a   ⟨τὰν αἴλουρον⟩· τὸν ἰδιωτικῶς λεγόμενον
κάττον.

110b   ⟨θηρία μικκά⟩· οἱ μύες.

113   ⟨ἀνεξήραινον⟩· ἔρημον ἐποίουν.

115   ⟨ἀκόλως⟩· ἄρτους.

122   ⟨λευκόν⟩· λαμπρόν.

125   ⟨παναπηρέας⟩· ἀβλαβεῖς.

126   ⟨χρυσῷ πλέα λίκνα⟩· ἢ χρυσοῦ πεπληρω-
μένα ἢ ὅτι περιεχρύσουν αὐτὰ δι᾽ εὐπρέπειαν.

127   ⟨πασεύμεθα⟩· κτησόμεθα.

128–32   τὰς μὲν ἀμήτους κελεύω μέχρι τοῦ πρυτα-
νείου παραγενέσθαι· αἵτινες δέ εἰσιν ἑξήκοντα ἐνιαυ-
τῶν ἢ καὶ πλειόνων, ταύτας κελεύω κατὰ τὸ δυνατὸν
ἀκολουθῆσαι τῷ καλάθῳ.

132 sq.   ταῖς ἐλθούσαις καὶ ταῖς μὴ ἐλθούσαις ἴσον
μισθὸν δώσει ἡ Δημήτηρ.

88   *exalleto*: it increased in size by eating.

90   *alematōs*: in vain.

91   *plaggōn*: a wax doll.

95   *chō mastos ton epōne*: the breast that he drank from, that is, the nurse.

97   *kalistreōn*: calling.

99   *Aiolidos Kanakēs genos*: Canace the mother of Triopas, daughter of Aeolus.

108   *tan (H)estiāi etrephe matēr*: which his own mother had brought up [to sacrifice for] Hestia.

110a   *tan ailouron*: idomatically, a cat.

110b   *thēria mikka*: the mice.

113   *anexērainon*: they made him destitute.

115   *akolōs*: bread.

122   *leukon*: shining.

125   *panapēreas*: unharmed.

126   *chrusō plea likna*: either filled with gold or plausibly, that they gilded them.

127   *paseumetha*: let us possess.

128–32   I order the uninitiated to go as far as the Prytaneion. Whoever are sixty years old or pregnant, I order them to follow the basket as far as they are able.

132 sq.   To the ones going [to the temple] and the ones not going Demeter will give an equal reward.

EPIGRAMS

INTRODUCTION

DEVELOPMENT OF THE GENRE

The earliest Greek epigrams are inscriptions on stone that record names of the deceased on grave markers or indicate who made and who received dedications. By the late fourth century BC, collections appeared, especially of short verse inscriptions sometimes attributed to prominent poets like Simonides, who was later credited with inventing the genre. It was not long before poets began composing their own fictitious dedications and epitaphs in verse, usually elegiac couplets, and a new poetic genre took form. By the third century it had expanded to include short display pieces, sympotica, erotica, and other miscellaneous contents. Inspired by the compendia of inscribed epigrams, literary epigrams were also published in collections.[1] An example is the Milan papyrus (*P.Mil.Vogl.* 8.309) of the late third century BC, which contains 112 carefully organized epigrams of Callimachus' older contemporary Posidippus of Pella. There is ample evidence that Callimachus' own epigrams were originally published in a collection like that one,[2] and internal evidence, discussed

---

[1] Reitzenstein 1893, 104–5. See also Meyer 2005, 96–101 for bibliography on early epigram collections.

[2] Callimachus' *Epigrams* are cited in Diog. Laert. 1.79; Ach. Tat. *Vit. Arat.* 4 (*Fr. Doct.* 460); *Suda* μ 194. Commentaries on

below, suggests that it was included in his monumental collected works.

HISTORY AND CONSTITUTION
OF THE TEXT

Hellenistic literary epigrams have survived into our own age thanks to their inclusion in the *Garland* of Meleager, an anthology comprising works of forty-seven authors assembled around 100–90 BC.[3] Meleager not only selected its roughly eight hundred poems from earlier collections, but wove them together in an artful way that obscured their arrangement in his sources. Then the *Garland* itself was merged with anthologies of later epigrams (viz., the *Garland* of Philip, ca. 40 AD; the *Cycle* of Agathias, mid 6th c.), which in turn were combined by Constantinus Cephalas at the beginning of the tenth century AD into a massive collection that we call the *Greek Anthology*. Its principal manuscripts are the tenth-century Codex Palatinus (*Anth. Pal.*) divided between Paris (Bibl. Nat. cod. Gr. suppl. 384) and Heidelberg (cod. Gr. 23), and the shorter codex of Maximus Planudes (*Anth. Plan.*) produced in 1301, now in Venice (cod. Ven. Marc. 481). The latter was published by Lascaris in 1494, and the former

---

them were written by the Hellenistic Archibius (*Suda* α 4105) and Hedylus (*Et. Mag.* s.v. ἀλθτάρχης), while Martial (4.23) and Pliny (*Epist.* 4.4.4–4) refer to them in ways that suggest that they were widely known (Gutzwiller 1998, 19).

[3] On the dates of Meleager's *Garland* and the other anthologies, see Cameron 1993, 49–77, with earlier bibliography, and Argentieri 2007. Meleager identifies forty-seven of his authors by name in his prooemium, to which must be added anonymous others and himself.

by Brunck in 1772–1776, though partial copies (*apographa*) were circulated earlier.

It was from these early editions and a few other ancient sources that scholars collected Callimachus' epigrams beginning in the sixteenth century. The story is told by Pfeiffer (vol. 2, xciii–iv): the second Stephanus edition of Callimachus (1577) contains *Epigrams* 1–25, which were gathered by Nicodemus Frischlin from the *Planudean Anthology*; Anna Fabri (1675) added *Epigrams* 26–51 from an *apographon* of the yet unpublished *Palatine Anthology* provided to her by Pierre Huet; Bentley contributed *Epigrams* 52–58 to Graevius' edition of Callimachus (1697) from the Oxford *apographon* (cod. Graec. Bibl. Bodl. Misc. 98); *Epigrams* 59–62 were added by Ernesti in 1761 from the *apographon* and notes of Salmasius sent to him by Ruhnken; and Blomfield (1815) topped off the collection with *Epigram* 63, which he found in Brunck's *editio princeps* (1772). Meineke (1861) removed some spurious poems and first printed the now canonical *Epigrams* 1–63 plus *dubia*, but Schneider (1873) undid the sequence by reintroducing some of the spurious poems. Mair (1921) followed Schneider, while Wilamowitz (1897) and Cahen (1922) used Meineke's numbering, as did Pfeiffer (1949–1953).

ORGANIZATION OF CALLIMACHUS' BOOK OF *EPIGRAMS*

This edition preserves Pfeiffer's numbering, which follows the order in which the epigrams were first published and in no way reflects their original arrangement in Callimachus' book of *Epigrams*. Meleager's artful integration of them with epigrams by his contemporaries, and the subsuming of the *Garland* itself into later anthologies, all but erased the traces of Callimachus' original composition. Meleager was also selective in his choice of poems, so the majority of Callimachus' epigrams, which probably numbered two hundred or more, have been permanently lost. Nonetheless, it is possible to glean some clues about how the book might have been organized.

Posidippus' epigram book, copied onto the Milan papyrus close to Callimachus' lifetime, and the *Palatine Anthology* as a whole offer useful comparanda. Posidippus' text is divided into at least ten sections labeled by subject, and the *Palatine Anthology* is similarly divided into seven.[4] Posidippus' sections either reflect the topical organization of the *Palatine Anthology* directly (e.g., both include "dedications") or they form a subsection within one of the *Palatine Anthology*'s topics. An example of the latter is Posidippus' "shipwrecks," which is a special type of the *Palatine Anthology*'s "epitaphs." All of Callimachus' extant epigrams fit within four of the *Palatine Anthology*'s categories: epideictic, dedicatory, sympotic, and sepulchral. It is likely, then, that his original book of epigrams was organized in this way with some more precise subsections in the manner of Posidippus.

This type of organization is also evident in two uninterrupted runs of epigrams in the *Palatine Anthology* that have been identified as undigested extracts from Callimachus' original poetry book added to Cephalus' collection from a source other than Meleager's *Garland*.[5] These in-

---

[4] Gow-Page 1965, xlvii.
[5] Gutzwiller 1998, 190–93, 200–213.

clude a run of five dedicatory poems to deities on behalf of family members (*Anth. Pal.* 6.146–50 = *Epig.* 53–57) and another of nine epitaphs (*Anth. Pal.* 7.517–25 = *Epig.* 20, 22, 14, 10, 12, 15, 60, 13, 21). The final poem in this series, *Epigram* 21, an epitaph for the poet's own father, partially quotes the programmatic Prologue of the *Aetia* (1.37–38), while *Epigrams* 1 and 7 also use language from *Aetia* 1 to promote the same aesthetic agenda. The epigrams, then, not only display Callimachus' habit of self-reference, but their connections with the prologues and programs of two of his most important poetry books show that the poet himself thought of them as an organized whole and an integral part of his collected oeuvre.

The connections between the *Epigrams* and Callimachus' *Aetia* and *Iambi* are an invitation to identify characteristics of these works that could inform a hypothetical book of Callimachus' *Epigrams*. These would include programmatic introductions (*Aet.* 1.1; *Ia.* 191); homages to Arsinoe II and Berenice II, in that order (*Aet.* 2a.1, 54–60j); references to Callimachus' other poems (*Ia.* 202.15–17; *Hymn* 1.8–9);[6] traditional meter giving way to metrical experiments (*Ia.* 195–202); smaller units arranged to create variety (*poikilia*), while those with similar subjects or meter are brought together (*Aet.* 100–100a, 101–101b); and ring composition linking beginnings and endings (*Ia.* 191, 203).

Principles of organization that might have informed Callimachus' epigram book can also be gleaned from Po-

---

[6] More examples of Callimachus' self-citation are in Acosta-Hughes 2003, 483n36.

sidippus: poems on similar subjects should be adjacent to each other; poems that best match the subject heading should be placed nearest to it; poems of similar themes should be grouped together even if they belong to different subgenres; the Ptolemies should be given due honor.[7]

SUGGESTED ORDER FOR READING

Constructing a hypothetical model for Callimachus' book of epigrams based on these characteristics and principles of organization is an instructive exercise. Following is a tentative outline of what such a model could look like.

Prologue and Epideictica

Epigram 1 would serve as an excellent programmatic prologue for a book of epigrams, as Gutzwiller argues.[8] Here a stranger asks Pittacus, one of the Seven Wise Men, whether he should marry a bride who is superior to him or one who is more modest. The answer comes by indirection as the inquirer observes some children at play and understands their chant as an oracle directing him to choose the modest bride. This is a reference to the first *Iamb*, in which each of the Seven Wise Men, including

---

[7] These principles are defined and illustrated by N. Krevans, "The Editor's Toolbox: Strategies for Selection and Presentation in the Milan Epigram Papyrus," in *The New Posidippus: A Hellenistic Poetry Book*, ed. Kathryn Gutzwiller (Oxford: Oxford University Press, 2005), 81–96.

[8] Gutzwiller 1998, 224–26.

Pittacus, declines the gift of Bathycles' golden cup, which Thales finally dedicates to Apollo, the sponsor of Callimachus' literary program in *Aetia* 1 and *Hymn* 2. Also like *Aetia* 1 and *Iamb* 1, *Epigram* 1 seems to promote Callimachus' literary preferences for the small, childlike, and riddling. It is the longest epigram by far, and like many other prologues, it is addressed to a named individual.

Keeping poems on similar topics together, the programmatic opener would be followed by the seven epigrams on named poets and poetry, ending with *Epigram* 7, which praises Theaetetus, who took the "pristine path," with a clear reference to Apollo's advice to the poet in the *Aetia* Prologue (*Aet.* 1.25–28). The first section, then, would contain epideictic poems focused on literary figures that engage with Callimachus' literary program and link to the *Aetia* and *Iambi*. An attractive order of reading would be: *Epigram* 1 (Pittacus and the virtue of modesty); *Epigram* 27 (praise for Aratus who imitates Hesiod's theme and style); *Epigram* 6 (on Creophylus; an epic poet whose work is mistaken for Homer's); *Epigram* 48 (on Simos, a "small" tragedian); *Epigram* 29 (where a tragedian aims at a brief announcement of victory); *Epigram* 49 (on the absurd victory mask of Agoranax, a comic poet); *Epigram* 59 (where a tragedian, presents himself as an anti-Orestes); and *Epigram* 7 (praise for Theaetetus, a tragedian who took the "pristine path").

Dedications

Among the *anathematica* are epigrams for Arsinoe II (*Epig.* 5) and Berenice II (*Epig.* 51). These could be arranged first and last in this group following the structure of the *Aetia* (the first two books originally for Arsinoe, the last two for Berenice). *Epigram* 5 for Arsinoe is longer than a typical Callimachean epigram and clearly a dedication, while Berenice's drifts away from that form following the principle observed in Posidippus and Callimachus' *Iambi.* This section also includes three successive poems for Cretans (keeping similar subjects together), the last of which begins a series of three dedicatory poems to deities (Serapis, Aphrodite, and Demeter), all with unusual meters. This arrangement is inspired by the *Iambi*, where poems in stichic choliambic meters (*Ia.* 1–4) are followed by a series of metrical experiments, ending in a traditional choliambic trimeter. Also in this group are the five consecutive dedications lifted from the *Palatine Anthology* (*Epig.* 53–57). An attractive order of reading would be: *Epigram* 5 (dedication to Arsinoe II); *Epigram* 62 (Cretan dedication to Artemis); *Epigram* 34 (Cretan dedication to Heracles); *Epigram* 37 (Cretan dedication to Serapis); *Epigram* 38 (Simon dedicates tools of her trade to Aphrodite); *Epigram* 39 (Egyptian Timodemus dedicates a tithe to Demeter); *Epigram* 33 (Phileratis dedicates an image to Artemis); *Epigram* 24 (Aeëtion sets up a "small" statue of a foot soldier); *Epigram* 50 ("Little one" sets up a memorial to his nurse); *Epigrams* 53–57 (run in *Anth. Pal.* beginning with a dedication to Eileithyia for easy childbirth);[9] and, finally, *Epigram* 51 (dedication of Berenice's statue).

[9] Discussion of the arrangement of these poems in Gutzwiller 1998, 190–93.

Sympotic Poems

This section has its own programmatic opener, the Cyclops poem (*Epig.* 46), addressed to the physician Philippus of Cos. With its Doric dialect it is widely and correctly understood as an homage to Theocritus, especially his eleventh *Idyll*. This poem, too, is longer than most of Callimachus' epigrams and introduces the theme of music as a cure for the disease of love. Music and love are both defining elements of the symposium, here combined with wit and literary references. Its medical terminology is picked up in a second epigram (*Epig.* 43), where a stranger exhibits his love wound at a banquet; in a third (*Epig.* 52), an *eromenos* is called Theocritus; and in the fourth, the poet pronounces on both love and poetry (*Epig.* 28, "I hate cyclic epic," etc.). The section concludes with poems about the mortal perils of excessive drinking and love: on Menecrates of Aenus who died from drink (*Epig.* 61); on Erasixenus, the deep drinker (*Epig.* 36); and Cleonicus of Thessaly, whose corpselike appearance is caused by gazing at the beauty of Euxitheus (*Epig.* 30). These form a suitable transition to the epitaphs that follow. An attractive order of reading would be: *Epigram* 46 (the wisdom of the Cyclops); *Epigram* 43 (a symposiast wounded by love); *Epigram* 52 (Theocritus as *eromenos*); *Epigram* 28 (on wondering lovers and bad literature); *Epigram* 32 (poverty in poetry and love); *Epigram* 41 (a soul divided by love); *Epigram* 42 (a virtuous comast); *Epigram* 63 (a *paraclausithyron*); *Epigram* 44 (love as hidden fire); *Epigram* 45 (a lover's patience is rewarded); *Epigram* 25 (a girl is deserted for a boy); *Epigram* 29 (toast to a boy in unmixed wine); *Epigram* 61 (death by overdrinking);

Epigram 36 (unmixed wine takes off Erasixenus); and
Epigram 30 (love makes Euxitheus a corpse).

Epitaphs

These could begin with Callimachus' own fictitious epi-
taph: "You are walking beside the tomb of a son of Battus
who knew song well, and over wine how to laugh at the
right moments" (*Epig.* 35). Although unlike other openers
this is a short poem, it would be equally at home in the
previous section and so forms a neat transition between
the two. Here Callimachus is armed against the miseries
of love as described in the sympotica by adopting the Cy-
clops' remedies (*Epig.* 46). Also, this poem has a close
relationship to the epitaph of the poet's father (*Epig.* 21).
The latter poem comes at the end of the run of epitaphs
that Gutzwiller has characterized as the concluding nine
of Callimachus' whole collection. If we accept its final two
verses (which, it should be noted, Pfeiffer and Gow re-
ject), the poem circles back to the *Aetia* Prologue (*Aet.*
1.37–38) and becomes the poet's *sphragis*. This point is
supported by *Epigram* 13, which makes another direct
reference to the first *Iamb*. Here Charidas reports from
Hades that a great ox can be purchased for a small coin,
precisely repeating the message of Hipponax (*Ia.* 191.2).
An attractive order of reading for this section would be:
Epigram 35 (the poet's self-epitaph); *Epigram* 2 (for the
poet Heraclitus); *Epigram* 40 (for a retired priestess);
Epigram 16 (for sweet, talkative Crethis); *Epigram* 11 (for
a short Cretan); *Epigram* 9 (for virtuous Saon); *Epigram*
26 (for a virtuous woman of small means); *Epigram* 18 (a
merchant's cenotaph); *Epigram* 17 (another cenotaph);

Epigram 58 (a third cenotaph); *Epigram* 47 (on Eudemus' saltbox, which saved him from storms of debt); *Epigram* 4 (Timon the misanthrope speaks from Hades); *Epigram* 3 (another pronouncement from Timon); *Epigram* 23 (suicide of Cleombrotus after reading the *Phaedo*); *Epigram* 19 (Philippus buries his son); nine consecutive epigrams in the *Palatine Anthology* beginning with *Epigram* 20 (Cyrenean family loses both son and daughter); *Epigram* 22 (Astacides, the new Daphnis, is snatched by nymphs); *Epigram* 14 (sudden death of Charmis); *Epigram* 10 (wise Timarchus' debunks myths of the underworld); *Epigram* 12 (request to announce the death of Critias in Cyzicus); *Epigram* 15 (Timonoe unrecognizable on her tomb); *Epigram* 60 (for Cimon of Elis); *Epigram* 13 (Charidas confirms information on underworld in *Iamb* 1); *Epigram* 21 (epitaph for the poet's father repeating claims of the Muses' favor from the *Aetia* Prologue).

Reading Callimachus' epigrams in this way does not re-create his lost book, which is impossible. But it does reveal some of its important characteristics that are not obvious in the editions of either Pfeiffer or Gow and Page. It especially demonstrates how close the epigrams are structurally and conceptually to the poet's other principal works. Although some epigrams may have been written and circulated before their collection in a book, and some even may have been commissioned to adorn real tombs, once they were included in the book they became elements in an artistic creation. Reading them in the order suggested above shows that they are not random little gems, but integral parts of an organic whole like the *Aitia* and *Iambi*, which they frequently recall.

SIGLA

These abbreviations follow Gow-Page (1965), augmented with information in Cameron (1993).

P   *Anthologiae Palatinae* (Heidelb. Cod. Gr. 23 + Paris Suppl. Gr. 384)

   P^a (pp. 1–452) written by scribe A
   P^b (pp. 453–706) written by scribes B1, B2, and B3
   J   copyist of the rest, lemmatist and commentator
   C   corrector of Books 1–9

Pl   *Anthologiae Planudeae* (Ven. Marc. 481)
   Pl^a (ff. 2–76)
   Pl^b (ff. 81v–100)

Syllogae Minores

Syll. E   Sylloge Euphemiana (Paris. Gr. 2720; Laur. 57. 29, Paris. Gr. 1773, Vat. Gr. 1943)
Syll. $\Sigma\pi$ Sylloge $\Sigma\pi$ (written in AP)
Syll. S   Sylloge S (Paris. Suppl. Gr. 352, Paris. Gr. 1630)
App. B.-V.   Appendix Barberino-Vaticana (Vat. Gr. 240, Vat. Barb. Gr. 123, Paris. Suppl. Gr. 1199)

Apographa Codicis P.

Ap. B.   Apographon cod. Buheriani (J. Bouhier, 1673–1746)

Ap. G.   Apographon Guietianum (F. Guyet, 1575–
          1655)
Ap. L.   Apographon Lipsiense (J. Gruter 1560–
          1627)
Ap. R.   Apographon Ruhnkenianum (D. Ruhnken
          1723–1798)

BIBLIOGRAPHY

EARLY EDITIONS OF THE
GREEK ANTHOLOGY

Lascaris, Janus, ed. *Anthologia Graeca Planudea*. Florence: de Alopa, 1494.

Estienne, Henri, ed. *Florilegium diversorum epigrammatum veterum*. Geneva: Stephanus, 1566.

Reiske, Johann Jacob, ed. *Anthologiae Graecae a Constantino Cephala conditae libri tres*. Leipzig: Gleditsch, 1754.

Brunck, Richard F. Ph., ed. *Analecta veterum poetarum Graecorum*. 3 vols. Strasbourg: Argentorati, 1772–1776.

Jacobs, Friedrich C. W., ed. *Anthologia Graeca sive poetarum graecorum lusus ex recensione Brunkii*. Leipzig: Dyck, 1794–1814.

———, ed. *Anthologia Graeca ad fidem codici olim Palatini nunc Parisini ex apographo Gothano edita*. 3 vols. Leipzig: Dyck, 1813–1817.

Graefe, Christian F., ed. *Meleagri Gadareni Epigrammata. Tamquam specimen novae recensionis Anthologiae graecae cum observationibus criticis*. Leipzig: Vogel, 1811.

Meineke, August, ed. *Delectus poetarum Anthologiae Graecae*. Berlin: Enslin, 1842.

Hecker, Alfons. *Commentatio critica de Anthologia Graeca.* Leiden: Luchtmans, 1843.

Dübner, Friedrich, ed. *Epigrammatum Anthologia Palatina: cum Planudeis.* Paris: Firmin-Didot, 1864–1888.

Kaibel, G., ed. *Epigrammata graeca ex lapidis collecta.* Berlin: Reimer, 1878.

MODERN EDITIONS OF THE *GREEK ANTHOLOGY* AND THE *EPIGRAMS* OF CALLIMACHUS EXCLUDING EDITIONS OF HIS COLLECTED WORKS

Beckby, Hermann, ed. and trans. *Anthologia Graeca.* 4 vols. 2nd ed. Munich: Heimeran, 1967–1968.

Coco, Luigi, ed. *Callimaco: Epigrammi.* Manduria: Lacaita, 1988.

Gow, Arthur S. F., and Denys L. Page, eds. and comm. *The Greek Anthology: Hellenistic Epigrams.* Cambridge: Cambridge University Press, 1965.

Page, Denys L., ed. *Epigrammata Graeca.* Oxford: Clarendon Press, 1975.

Paton, William R., ed. and trans. *The Greek Anthology.* 5 vols. Loeb Classical Library. Cambridge: Harvard University Press, 1969. Vol. 1 revised by Michael A. Tueller, 2014.

Stadtmueller, Hugo, ed. *Anthologia Graeca Epigrammatum Palatina cum Planudea.* Leipzig: Teubner, vol. 1 (AP i–vi) 1894; vol. ii.1 (AP vii) 1899; vol. iii.1 (AP ix.1–563) 1906.

Waltz, Pierre, et al., eds. *Anthologie grecque.* 13 vols. Paris: Les Belles Lettres, 1928–1994.

Zanetto, Giuseppe, trans., and Paola Ferrari, intro. and comm. *Callimaco: Epigrammi*. Milan: Mondadori, 2000.

CRITICAL STUDIES

Acosta-Hughes, Benjamin. "Aesthetics and Recall: Callimachus Frs. 226–9 Pf. Reconsidered." *The Classical Quarterly* 53 (2003): 478–89.

Argentieri, Lorenzo. "Meleager and Philip as Epigram Collectors." In *Brill's Companion to Hellenistic Epigram*, edited by Peter Bing and John Bruss, 145–64. Leiden: Brill, 2007.

Bing, Peter. "Ergänzungsspiel in the Epigrams of Callimachus." *Antike und Abendland* 41 (1995): 115–31.

Bing, Peter, and Jon Steffen Bruss, eds. *Brill's Companion to Hellenistic Epigram*. Leiden: Brill, 2007.

Cameron, Alan. "The Garlands of Meleager and Philip." *Greek, Roman and Byzantine Studies* 9 (1968): 323–49.

———. *The Greek Anthology: From Meleager to Planudes*. Oxford: Clarendon Press, 1993.

Dihle, Albrecht, ed. *L'Épigramme grecque*. Entretiens sur l'Antiquité, t. 14. Vandoeuvres-Genève: Fondation Hardt, 1967.

Faraone, Christopher. "Callimachus Epigram 29.5–6 (Gow-Page)." *ZPE* 63 (1986): 53–56.

Giangrande, Guiseppe. "Three Alexandrian Epigrams. APl 167, Callimachus, Epigram 5 (Pf.), AP 12,91." In *Papers of the Liverpool Latin Seminar* 1976, edited by Francis Cairns, 253–70. Liverpool: School of Classics University of Liverpool, 1977.

Gutzwiller, Kathryn J. *Poetic Garlands: Hellenistic Epi-*

grams in Context. Berkeley and Los Angeles: University of California Press, 1998.

———, ed. *The New Posidippus: A Hellenistic Poetry Book*. Oxford: Oxford University Press, 2005.

Harder, Annette, R. F. Regtuit, and G. C. Wakker, eds. *Hellenistic Epigrams*. Leuven: Peeters, 2002.

Livrea, Enrico. "Due epigrammi Callimachei." *Prometheus* 15 (1989): 199–206.

______. "Tre epigrammi funerari Callimachei." *Hermes* 118 (1990): 314–24.

______. "From Pittacus to Byzantium: The History of a Callimachean Epigram." *CQ* 45 (1995): 474–80.

Meyer, Doris. *Inszeniertes Lesevergnügen, das inschrifliche Epigramm und seine Rezeption bei Kallimachos*. Stuttgart: Steiner, 2005.

Preisendanz, Karl. *Anthologia Palatina: codex palatinus et codex parisinus phototypice* editi i–ii. Leiden: Sijthoff, 1911.

Prioux, Évelyne. *Regards Alexandrins: Histoire et théorie des arts dans l'épigramme hellénistique*. Leuven: Peeters, 2007.

Radinger, Carl. *Meleagros von Gadara: Eine literargeschichtliche Skizze*. Innsbruck: Wagner, 1895. Reprinted in *The Greek Anthology* II, edited by Sonya L. Tarán. New York: Garland, 1987.

Reitzenstein, Richard. *Epigramm und Skolion: Ein Beitrag zur Geschichte der alexandrinischen Dichtung*. Giessen: Ricker, 1893.

Tueller, Michael A. *Look Who's Talking: Innovations in Voice and Identity in Hellenistic Epigram*. Leuven: Peeters, 2008.

Wifstrand, Albert. *Studien zur griechischen Anthologie*. PhD diss. Lund, 1926. Reprinted in *The Greek Anthology* I, edited by Sonya L. Tarán. New York: Garland, 1987.

Zedel, J. C. F. "Callimachi epigrammata duo emendate." *Bibliotheca critica* 2.1 (1780): 112–13.

EPIGRAMMATA

1 (54 G.-P.) *Anth. Pal.* 7.89; Diog. Laert. 1.79; *Suda* α 4305; *Suda* β 236

Ξεῖνος Ἀταρνείτης τις ἀνείρετο[1] Πιττακὸν οὕτω
  τὸν Μυτιληναῖον, παῖδα τὸν Ὑρράδιον·[2]
"ἄττα γέρον, δοιός με καλεῖ γάμος· ἡ μία μὲν δή
  νύμφη καὶ πλούτῳ καὶ γενεῇ κατ' ἐμέ,
5 ἡ δ' ἑτέρη προβέβηκε. τί λώιον; εἰ δ ἄγε σύμ μοι[3]
  βούλευσον, ποτέρην εἰς ὑμέναιον ἄγω."
εἶπεν· ὁ δὲ σκίπωνα γεροντικὸν ὅπλον ἀείρας·
  "ἠνίδε κεῖνοί σοι πᾶν ἐρέουσιν ἔπος."
οἱ δ' ἄρ ὑπὸ πληγῆσι θοὰς βέμβικας[4] ἔχοντες
10 ἔστρεφον εὐρείῃ[5] παῖδες ἐνὶ τριόδῳ.
"κείνων ἔρχεο," φησί, "μετ ἴχνια."[6] χὠ μὲν ἐπέστη
  πλησίον· οἱ δ ἔλεγον· "τὴν[7] κατὰ σαυτὸν ἔλα."

----

  [1] ἀνείρετο P: ἀνήρετο Pl, Diog. Laert.
  [2] Ὑρράδιον P: -ου CPl, Diog. Laert.   [3] σύμ μοι CSuda α
4305: σύν μοι P, Diog. Laert.: μοι σύ Pl   [4] βέμβικας CPl,
Diog. Laert.: βέμβεκας P: βέμβηκας *Suda* β 236
  [5] εὐρείῃ CPl, Diog. Laert., *Suda*: εὐρείην P
  [6] ἴχνια CPl, Diog. Laert.: ἴχνεσι P
  [7] τὴν CPl, Diog. Laert.: τὸν P

EPIGRAMS

1 (54 G.-P.) *Palatine Anthology*; Diogenes Laertius; *Suda*

Some stranger from Atarneus[1] inquired in this way of Pittacus,[2] son of Hyrras, the Mytilenean,[3] "Old dear, two marriages invite me. One girl is equal to me in both wealth and family; [5] the other is superior. Which is better? Please tell me which of the two I should take into matrimony." So he said. And the other pointed his walking stick, the old man's weapon:[4] "See there! They will tell you everything." These were boys spinning their swift tops[5] with whips [10] in a wide three-way intersection. "Follow their tracks," he said. The other stood nearer. The boys were saying, "Drive along your own course."[6] When he heard

---

[1] A city in Asia Minor on the mainland opposite Lesbos. It was associated with Aristotle, who wrote a poem honoring its ruler Hermias (Diog. Laert. 5.3–4; Ath. 15.696a–d). [2] One of the Seven Wise Men, whose advice was sought in Callimachus, *Iamb* 1 (*Dieg.* 6.15–16). [3] Mytilene was the principal city on Lesbos. [4] An ironic reference to Pittacus' early life as a warrior (Diog. Laert. 1.74; *Suda* π 1659). [5] A reference to a problematic passage in Homer (*Il.* 14.413), in which Hector whirls around like a top struck by blows. [6] The phrase is a proverb. A version in the *Suda* (χ 478) says that it was variously attributed to the Oracle at Delphi and other wise men. Here the meaning is studiously ambiguous: it could mean "strike your own top" or "drive along your own path."

CALLIMACHUS

ταῦτ ἀίων ὁ ξεῖνος ἐφείσατο μείζονος οἴκου
δράξασθαι, παίδων κληδόνα συνθέμενος.
15 τὴν δ ὀλίγην ὡς κεῖνος ἐς οἰκίον ἤγετο⁸ νύμφην,
οὕτω καὶ σύ, Δίων,⁹ τὴν κατὰ σαυτὸν ἔλα.

⁸ οἰκίον ἤγετο Diog. Laert.: οἶκον ἐπήγετο PPl
⁹ σύ Δίων Diog. Laert., Pf G.-P.: σύ γ᾽ ἰὼν PPl

2 (34 G.-P.) *Anth. Pal.* 7.80; Diog. Laert. 9.17 (Γεγόνασι
δ᾽ Ἡράκλειτοι πέντε . . . τρίτος ἐλεγαίας ποιητὴς
Ἁλικαρνασσεύς, εἰς ὃν Καλλίμαχος πεποίηκεν οὕτως);
2–5, *Suda* λ 309

Εἶπέ τις, Ἡράκλειτε, τεὸν μόρον, ἐς δέ με¹ δάκρυ
ἤγαγεν· ἐμνήσθην δ᾽ ὁσσάκις ἀμφότεροι
ἥλιον ἐν λέσχῃ² κατεδύσαμεν.³ ἀλλὰ σὺ μέν που,
ξεῖν᾽ Ἁλικαρνησεῦ, τετράπαλαι σποδιή,
5 αἱ δὲ τεαὶ ζώουσιν ἀηδόνες, ἧσιν ὁ πάντων
ἁρπακτὴς Ἀίδης οὐκ ἐπὶ χεῖρα βαλεῖ.

¹ δέ με C: δ᾽ ἐμὲ Diog. Laert.   ² ἥλιον ἐν λέσχῃ P,
Suda: ἡέλιον ἐν λέσχῃ Pl, Diog. Laert.: ἡέλιον λέσχῃ coni.
Bentley   ³ κατεδύσαμεν PPl: κατελύσαμεν Diog. Laert.

this, the stranger gave up grasping at the greater household, since he understood the children's oracle. [15] And as that man led home the modest bride, so you too, Dion,[7] drive along your own course.

[7] Dion is otherwise unknown, but he may be a poet to whom Callimachus is giving advice on the virtues of a modest literary style using metaphoric language from the *Aetia* Prologue. See Livrea 1995, 480. Other poets named in epigrams are Heraclitus (*Epig.* 2), Theaetetus (*Epig.* 7), and Aratus (*Epig.* 27). A variant in the principal manuscripts directs the poet's advice to "you," the reader.

2 (34 G.-P.) *Palatine Anthology*; Diogenes Laertius (There were five Heraclituses . . . the third was the elegiac poet from Halicarnassus, about whom Callimachus wrote in the following way); *Suda*

Someone told me, Heraclitus,[1] of your death, and brought me to tears. I recalled how often the two of us in conversation put the sun to bed. Perhaps, my friend from Halicarnassus, you have been dust for a long time, [5] but your nightingales[2] live on. Even Hades, the one who seizes all, does not lay a hand on them.

[1] Only one epigram of Heraclitus remains (*Anth. Pal.* 7.465), an epitaph for Aretemias of Cnidus, who died after giving birth to twins; one she left for her husband and the other she took with her. It, too, is addressed to a *xenos*, though there of a passing stranger.   [2] Possibly a metaphor for poetry generally (e.g., *Anth. Pal.* 9.184.9), or the title of a collection of Heraclitus' poems.

CALLIMACHUS

3 (52 G.-P.) *Anth. Pal.* 7.318 [J], εἰς τὸν αὐτὸν Τίμωνα;
Anth. Plan. [B], sine nom.

Μὴ χαίρειν εἴπῃς με, κακὸν κάρα,[1] ἀλλὰ πάρελθε·
   ἶσον ἐμοὶ χαίρειν ἐστὶ τὸ μὴ σὲ γελᾶν.[2]

[1] κάρα Pl: κέαρ P   [2] γελᾶν PPl: πελᾶν Graefe

4 (51 G.-P.) *Anth. Pal.* 7.317; *Anth. Plan.*

Τίμων (οὐ γὰρ ἔτ᾽ ἐσσί), τί τοι, σκότος ἢ φάος,[1]
   ἐχθρόν;
   "τὸ σκότος· ὑμέων[2] γὰρ πλείονες εἰν Ἀΐδῃ."

[1] σκότος ἢ φάος P: φάος ἢ σκότος Pl   [2] ὑμέων Pl:
ὑμείων P

5 (14 G.-P.) Ath. 7.318b; *Et. Mag.* 664.49; om. *Anth. Pal.*,
Anth. Plan.

Κόγχος ἐγώ, Ζεφυρῖτι, παλαίτερος·[1] ἀλλὰ σὺ νῦν
   με,[2]
Κύπρι, Σεληναίης ἄνθεμα πρῶτον ἔχεις,

[1] παλαίτερος Ath.: παλαίτερον Bentley: πάλαι τέρας
Schneider, Pfeiffer
[2] με Musurus: μοι Ath.

EPIGRAMS

3 (52 G.-P.) *Palatine Anthology* [J], Against the Same Timon; *Planudean Anthology* [B], Anonymous

Do not say "cheers"[1] to me, evil one,[2] but pass on by. For me, cheerful means no laughter from you.[3]

[1] The Greek *chairein* is alternatively a greeting, a farewell, and an expression of delight. [2] A form of address borrowed from tragedy (e.g., Eur. *Hipp.* 651). [3] Possibly a reference to another Timon, Timon of Phlius, whose poem, the *Silloi*, takes place in the underworld, where Timon sees and lampoons various dead philosophers. See Dee Clayman, *Timon of Phlius* (Berlin: De Gruyter, 2009), 75–142.

4 (51 G.-P.) *Palatine Anthology*; *Planudean Anthology*

Timon[1] (for you are no longer), which is hateful to you, darkness or light? "The darkness. There are more of you[2] in Hades."

[1] The Athenian misanthrope (Ar. *Av.* 1549, *Lys.* 808–20; Lucian, *Timon*). [2] The dead (Leon. Tar. *Anth. Pal.* 7.731; Crinag. *Anth. Pal.* 11.42).

5 (14 G.-P.) Athenaeus, *The Learned Banqueters*; *Etymologicum Magnum*; missing in *Palatine Anthology* and *Planudean Anthology*

I am a shell, Lady of Zephyrium,[1] a very ancient one. But you now have me, Cypris,[2] the first dedication of Selenaea,

[1] Arsinoe II is assimilated to Aphrodite, for whom a temple was built on Cape Zephyrium near Alexandria by Callicrates, the navarch of her husband, Ptolemy II Philadelphus.
[2] Aphrodite.

ναυτίλον³ ὃς πελάγεσσιν ἐπέπλεον, εἰ μὲν ἀῆται,
τείνας οἰκείων λαῖφος ἀπὸ προτόνων,
5 εἰ δὲ Γαληναίη, λιπαρὴ θεός, οὖλος ἐρέσσων
ποσσὶν ἄνω σπέρχω·⁴ ἔργῳ τοὔνομα συμφέρεται,
ἔστ᾽ ἔπεσον παρὰ θῖνας Ἰουλίδας, ὄφρα γένωμαι
σοὶ τὸ περίσκεπτον παίγνιον, Ἀρσινόη,⁵
μηδέ μοι ἐν θαλάμῃσιν ἔθ᾽ ὡς πάρος (εἰμὶ γὰρ
ἄπνους)
10 τίκτηται νοτερῆς ᾤεον ἀλκυόνος.⁶
Κλεινίου ἀλλὰ θυγατρὶ δίδου χάριν· οἶδε γὰρ ἐσθλά
ῥέζειν καὶ Σμύρνης ἐστὶν ἀπ᾽ Αἰολίδος.

³ ναυτίλον Ath.: ναυτίλος Kaibel   ⁴ ἄνω σπέρχω
Giangrande: ἰν᾽ ὤσπ Ath.en.   ⁵ Ἀρσινόη Et.M.: Ἀρσι-
νόης Ath.   ⁶ τίκτηται νοτερῆς ᾤεον ἀλκυόνος corr.
Bentley: τίκτει τ᾽ αἰνοτερῆς ᾤεον ἀλκυόνης Ath.

6 (55 G.-P.) Strabo 14.638; Sext. Emp. *Math*. 1.48; Eust.
331.5; Schol. ad Dion. Thrax (pp. 160.12, 163.36, 448.3
Hilgard)

Τοῦ Σαμίου¹ πόνος εἰμὶ δόμῳ ποτὲ θεῖον ἀοιδόν²
δεξαμένου, κλείω³ δ᾽ Εὔρυτον ὅσσ᾽ ἔπαθεν,
καὶ ξανθὴν Ἰόλειαν, Ὁμήρειον δὲ καλεῦμαι
γράμμα· Κρεωφύλῳ, Ζεῦ φίλε, τοῦτο μέγα.

¹ τοῦ σαμίου Strabo: κρεωφύλου SE, Schol. ad Dion.
Thrax   ² θεῖον ἀοιδόν SE, Schol. ad Dion. Thrax: θεῖον ὅμη-
ρον Strabo   ³ κλείω SE, Schol. ad Dion. Thrax: καίω Strabo

¹ Creophylus, a poet whom the *Suda* (κ 2376) locates on Sa-

a nautilus,[3] who sailed the seas. If there is wind, I stretch
the sail on my own forestays, [5] and if there is Calm,[4] the
gentle goddess, I sail ahead, rowing swiftly with my feet—
my name suits my work—until I fell by the shores of Iulis,[5]
so that I could be a much admired toy for you, Arsinoe.
Nor in my chambers as before (for I am airtight) [10] will
the sea-dwelling halcyon lay its egg. But give favor to the
daughter of Clinias, for she knows how to act nobly and is
from Aeolian Smyrna.[6]

[3] The description of the nautilus that follows is similar to Ar-
istotle's (*Hist. an.* 622b5).   [4] Galene, a Nereid (Hes. *Theog.*
244) whose name means "calm."   [5] A city on the island of
Ceos where there was a Ptolemaic naval base.   [6] Greek city
in western Anatolia. Aeolian Smyrna, the original settlement, was
an important trading center, but a new Smyrna was founded
nearby in the fourth century BC.

6 (55 G.-P.) Strabo, *Geography*; Sextus Empiricus, *Against
the Professors*; Eustathius; Scholia to Dionysius Thrax

I am the work of the Samian,[1] who once received the di-
vine singer[2] in his home, and I celebrate the sufferings of
Eurytus[3] and yellow-haired Ioleia, but I am called the
writing of Homer. For Creophylus, dear Zeus, this is a
great thing.

mos or Chios: "some say he was Homer's son-in-law, his daugh-
ter's husband; others say he was only a friend of Homer, and that
in return for his hospitality he received from him the poem *The
Capture of Oechalia*."   [2] Homer (Ar. *Ran.* 1034; Pl. *Phd.*
95a).   [3] King of Oechalia in Thessaly (Hom. *Il.* 2.730), who
offered to marry his daughter Iole to whoever defeated him in
archery (Hes. fr. 26.31–33 M.-W.). When Heracles succeeded,
Eurytus refused to honor his pledge. So Heracles killed him,
carried off his daughter, and destroyed the city.

7 (57 G.-P.) *Anth. Pal.* 9.565

Ἦλθε Θεαίτητος καθαρὴν ὁδόν. εἰ δ᾽ ἐπὶ κισσόν[1]
  τὸν τεὸν οὐχ αὕτη, Βάκχε, κέλευθος ἄγει,
ἄλλων μὲν κήρυκες ἐπὶ βραχὺν οὔνομα καιρόν
  φθέγξονται, κείνου δ᾽ Ἑλλὰς ἀεὶ σοφίην.[2]

[1] ἐπὶ κισσὸν Pl: κισσοῦ P   [2] σοφίην Demetr.: σοφίαν
PPl

8 (58 G.-P.) *Anth. Pal.* 9.566; *Anth. Plan.*

Μικρή τις, Διόνυσε, καλὰ πρήσσοντι ποιητῇ
  ῥῆσις· ὁ μὲν "νικῶ" φησὶ τὸ μακρότατον,
ᾧ[1] δὲ σὺ μὴ πνεύσῃς ἐνδέξιος, ἤν τις ἔρηται
  "πῶς ἔβαλες;" φησί· "σκληρὰ τὰ γιγνόμενα."
5 τῷ μερμηρίξαντι τὰ μὴ ἔνδικα[2] τοῦτο γένοιτο
  τοὔπος· ἐμοὶ δ᾽, ὦναξ, ἡ βραχυσυλλαβίη.

[1] ᾧ P: ὡς δὲ Pl   [2] μὴ ἔνδικα Pf.: μηνδικα P

9 (41 G.-P.) *Anth. Pal.* 7.451; *Anth. Plan.*

Τᾷδε[1] Σάων ὁ Δίκωνος Ἀκάνθιος[2] ἱερὸν ὕπνον
  κοιμᾶται· θνάσκειν[3] μὴ λέγε τοὺς ἀγαθούς.

[1] τᾷδε Boiss.: τῇδε PPl   [2] ὁ Ἀκάνθιος P: ὁ om. Pl
[3] θνάσκειν P: θνήσκειν Pl

EPIGRAMS

7 (57 G.-P.) *Palatine Anthology*

Theaetetus[1] took the pristine path.[2] If this path does not lead to your ivy wreath, Bacchus,[3] the heralds will cry out the names of others for a brief time, but Hellas will proclaim his skill forever.

[1] A poet whose dramas are lost, but six of his epigrams are preserved (G.-P. vol. 1, 182–83).   [2] A literary trope for originality akin to Callimachus' "untrodden ways" (*Aet.* 1.27–28).

[3] Ivy crowns were awarded to winners at the Greater Dionysia in Athens, suggesting that Theaetetus was not successful there.

8 (58 G.-P.) *Palatine Anthology*; *Planudean Anthology*

For the successful poet, Dionysus, the statement is brief: "I won," he says at most. But if someone asks of one whom you did not favor, "How was your luck?",[1] he says, "Things are tough." [5] Let this be the utterance of the one who broods on injustice; for me, Lord,[2] succinctness!

[1] Literally, "How did you throw?" as in a dice game.
[2] Dionysus.

9 (41 G.-P.) *Palatine Anthology*; *Planudean Anthology*

Here Saon son of Dicon[1] of Acanthus[2] sleeps the holy sleep. Do not say that the good die.

[1] The names of neither father nor son are otherwise known and could be allegorical: Saon (Savior or Safekeeper) and Dicon (the Just).   [2] Gow-Page identify at least four Greek cities called Acanthus, the most prominent on Chalcidice.

10 (33 G.-P.) *Anth. Pal.* 7.520; *Anth. Plan.*

Ἦν δίζῃ Τίμαρχον ἐν Ἄϊδος, ὄφρα πύθηαι
ἤ τι περὶ ψυχῆς ἢ πάλι πῶς ἔσεαι,[1]
δίζεσθαι φυλῆς Πτολεμαΐδος υἱέα πατρός
Παυσανίου· δήεις δ᾽ αὐτὸν ἐν εὐσεβέων.

[1] ἔσεαι P: ἔσεται Pl

11 (35 G.-P.) *Anth. Pal.* 7.447; *Anth. Plan.*

Σύντομος ἦν ὁ ξεῖνος, ὃ καὶ στίχος οὐ μακρὰ
λέξων[1]
"Θῆρις Ἀρισταίου Κρής" ἐπ᾽[2] ἐμοὶ δολιχός.

[1] λέξων C: λέξω PPl   [2] ἐπ᾽ P: ὑπ᾽ Pl

12 (43 G.-P.) *Anth. Pal.* 7.521; *Anth. Plan.*

Κύζικον ἢν ἔλθῃς,[1] ὀλίγος πόνος Ἱππακὸν εὑρεῖν
καὶ Διδύμην· ἀφανὴς οὔτι γὰρ ἡ γενεή.
καί σφιν ἀνιηρὸν μὲν ἐρεῖς ἔπος, ἔμπα δὲ λέξαι[2]
τοῦθ᾽, ὅτι τὸν κείνων ὧδ᾽ ἐπέχω[3] Κριτίην.[4]

[1] ἔλθῃς Pl: ἐθέλῃς P   [2] λέξαι P: λέξον Pl
[3] ὧδ᾽ ἐπέχω C in marg.: ἔχω P: υἱὸν ἔχω Pl
[4] Κριτίην P: Κριτίαν Pl

10 (33 G.-P.) *Palatine Anthology*; *Planudean Anthology*

If you look for Timarchus[1] in Hades, in order to learn something about the soul or how it will be for you hereafter, seek the son of his father Pausanius of the Ptolemaic tribe;[2] you will find him where the righteous are.

[1] Perhaps Timarchus of Alexandria (whose philosophical lineage includes Crates the Cynic), or some other philosopher who wrote a treatise *On Souls* that discussed the rewards of the righteous after death.   [2] There were Ptolemaic tribes named for Philadelphus both at Alexandria (*Vit. Ap. Rhod.*) and at Athens (Paus. 1.5.5).

11 (35 G.-P.) *Palatine Anthology*; *Planudean Anthology*

The stranger was short, nor will his inscription be long: "Theris son of Aristaeus, Cretan." But for me it counts as lengthy.

12 (43 G.-P.) *Palatine Anthology*; *Planudean Anthology*

If you ever go to Cyzicus,[1] it is little effort to find Hippacus and Didyme, for the family is hardly obscure. And to them you will deliver painful news, but nevertheless tell them this: that I hold their son Critias here.

[1] Greek city on the south coast of the Sea of Marmara.

13 (31 G.-P.) *Anth. Pal.* 7.524; *Anth. Plan.*

Ἦ ῥ᾽ ὑπὸ σοὶ Χαρίδας ἀναπαύεται; "εἰ τὸν Ἀρίμμα
    τοῦ Κυρηναίου παῖδα λέγεις, ὑπ᾽ ἐμοί."
ὦ Χαρίδα, τί τὰ νέρθε; "πολὺ[1] σκότος." αἱ δ᾽ ἄνοδοι
    τί;
"ψεῦδος." ὁ δὲ Πλούτων; "μῦθος." ἀπωλόμεθα.
5 "οὗτος ἐμὸς λόγος ὕμμιν ἀληθινός· εἰ δὲ τὸν ἡδύν
    βούλει, Πελλαίου βοῦς μέγας εἰν Ἀΐδῃ."[2]

¹ πολύ Pl: πολυς P   ² εἰν Ἀΐδῃ P: εἰς Ἀΐδην Pl

14 (44 G.-P.) *Anth. Pal.* 7.519; *Anth. Plan.*

Δαίμονα τίς δ᾽ εὖ οἶδε τὸν αὔριον; ἁνίκα[1] καὶ σέ,
    Χάρμι, τὸν ὀφθαλμοῖς χθιζὸν ἐν ἁμετέροις[2]
τᾷ ἑτέρᾳ[3] κλαύσαντες ἐθάπτομεν· οὐδὲν ἐκείνου
    εἶδε πατὴρ Διοφῶν χρῆμ᾽ ἀνιαρότερον.[4]

¹ ἁνίκα P: ἡνίκα Pl   ² ἁμετέροις P: ἡμετέροις Pl
³ τᾷ ἑτέρᾳ P: τῇ ἑτέρῃ Pl   ⁴ ἀνιαρότερον Suda, Jacobs:
ἀνιηρότερον PPl

15 (40 G.-P.) *Anth. Pal.* 7.522; *Anth. Plan.*

"Τιμονόη."[1] τίς δ᾽ ἐσσί; μὰ δαίμονας, οὔ σ᾽ ἂν
    ἐπέγνων,
εἰ μὴ Τιμοθέου πατρὸς ἐπῆν ὄνομα
στήλῃ καὶ Μήθυμνα, τεὴ πόλις. ἦ μέγα φημί
    χῆρον ἀνιᾶσθαι σὸν πόσιν Εὐθυμένη.

¹ Τιμονόη Pl: Τιμονίη P

410

EPIGRAMS

13 (31 G.-P.) *Palatine Anthology*; *Planudean Anthology*

Say, does Charidas lie beneath you? "If you mean the son of Arimmas of Cyrene, [he is] underneath me." O Charidas, how goes it down there? "Much darkness." The roads back up? "A lie." And Pluto? "A myth." We are done for! [5] "This story of mine is true. But if you want to hear something pleasant, in Hades a great ox can be had for a penny."[1]

 [1] The same witticism introduces Callimachus' first *Iamb* (*Ia*. 191.1–2).

14 (44 G.-P.) *Palatine Anthology*; *Planudean Anthology*

Who can be sure of tomorrow's fortune, when even you, Charmis,[1] whom we saw with our own eyes yesterday, we buried, distraught, today. Your father Diophon[2] has seen nothing more painful than this.

 [1] Possibly a real name, but also "Joy."   [2] Possibly a real name, but also "the Lost One."

15 (40 G.-P.) *Palatine Anthology*; *Planudean Anthology*

"Timonoe." Who are you? By the gods, I would not have recognized you if the name of your father Timotheus were not on the gravestone, and Methymna,[1] your city. I daresay your widowed husband Euthymenes grieved greatly.

 [1] Cities on Lesbos and also in western Crete.

411

CALLIMACHUS

16 (37 G.-P.) *Anth. Pal.* 7.459; *Anth. Plan.*

Κρηθίδα τὴν πολύμυθον, ἐπισταμένην καλὰ παίζειν,
  δίζηνται[1] Σαμίων[2] πολλάκι θυγατέρες,
ἡδίστην[3] συνέριθον, ἀεὶ λάλον· ἡ δ' ἀποβρίζει
  ἐνθάδε τὸν πάσαις ὕπνον ὀφειλόμενον.

[1] δίζηνται P: δίζονται Pl   [2] σαμίων CPl: σαμίην P
[3] ἡδίστην corr. Meineke: ἡδίσταν PPl

17 (45 G.-P.) *Anth. Pal.* 7.271; *Anth. Plan.*; *Et. Mag.*
643.46; alii

Ὤφελε μηδ' ἐγένοντο θοαὶ νέες· οὐ γὰρ ἂν ἡμεῖς
  παῖδα Διοκλείδεω[1] Σώπολιν ἐστένομεν.
νῦν δ' ὁ μὲν εἰν ἁλί που φέρεται νέκυς, ἀντὶ δ'
    ἐκείνου
οὔνομα καὶ κενεὸν σῆμα[2] παρερχόμεθα.

[1] Διοκλείδεω Pf.: Διοκλείδου PPl
[2] σῆμα Brunck: σᾶμα PPl

18 (38 G.-P.) *Anth. Pal.* 7.272; *Anth. Plan.*

Νάξιος οὐκ ἐπὶ γῆς ἔθανεν[1] Λύκος, ἀλλ' ἐνὶ πόντῳ
  ναῦν ἅμα καὶ ψυχὴν εἶδεν ἀπολλυμένην,
ἔμπορος Αἰγίνηθεν ὅτ' ἔπλεε·[2] χὠ μὲν ἐν ὑγρῇ
  νεκρός, ἐγὼ δ' ἄλλως οὔνομα τύμβος ἔχων
5 κηρύσσω πανάληθες ἔπος τόδε· "φεῦγε θαλάσσῃ
  συμμίσγειν Ἐρίφων, ναυτίλε, δυομένων."[3]

412

16 (37 G.-P.) *Palatine Anthology*; *Planudean Anthology*

The daughters of the Samians often sought out gossipy Crethis, who knew how to be a fine playmate, their sweetest workmate, always chattering. But she sleeps here the sleep that comes due for them all.

17 (45 G.-P.) *Palatine Anthology*; *Planudean Anthology*; *Etymologicum Magnum*; others

Would that swift ships had never even existed. We would not be lamenting Sopolis, son of Dioclides. But now his body tosses somewhere at sea, and instead we pass by his name and empty tomb.

18 (38 G.-P.) *Palatine Anthology*; *Planudean Anthology*

Lycus the Naxian did not perish on land, but in the sea. He saw his life lost together with the ship, sailing as a merchant from Aegina. He is in the wet sea as a corpse, while I, the tomb bearing only his name, [5] will announce this saying all too true: "avoid spending time at sea, sailor, when the Kids[1] are setting."

---

[1] A constellation whose setting in winter is associated with storms at sea (Arat. *Phaen.* 158–59).

---

[1] ἔθανεν Pl: θάνεν P   [2] ἔπλεε Pl: ἔπλεεν P
[3] δυομένων CPl: δυσμένων P

19 (46 G.-P.) *Anth. Pal.* 7.453; *Anth. Plan.*

Δωδεκέτη[1] τὸν παῖδα πατὴρ ἀπέθηκε Φίλιππος
ἐνθάδε, τὴν πολλὴν ἐλπίδα, Νικοτέλην.

[1] Δωδεκέτη PPl: Δωδεκέτην C

20 (32 G.-P.) *Anth. Pal.* 7.517; *Anth. Plan.*

Ἠῷοι Μελάνιππον ἐθάπτομεν, ἠελίου δέ
    δυομένου Βασιλὼ κάτθανε παρθενική
αὐτοχερί· ζώειν γὰρ ἀδελφεὸν ἐν πυρὶ θεῖσα
    οὐκ ἔτλη. δίδυμον δ᾽ οἶκος ἐσεῖδε κακόν
5 πατρὸς Ἀριστίπποιο, κατήφησεν δὲ Κυρήνη
    πᾶσα τὸν εὔτεκνον[1] χῆρον ἰδοῦσα δόμον.

[1] εὔτεκνον C: εὔτακτον P: εὐτέκνων Pl

21 (29 G.-P.) *Anth. Pal.* 7.525; *Anth. Plan.*; Schol. ad Hes. *Theog.* 81

Ὅστις ἐμὸν παρὰ σῆμα φέρεις πόδα, Καλλιμάχου
    με
ἴσθι Κυρηναίου παῖδά τε καὶ γενέτην.
εἰδείης[1] δ᾽ ἄμφω κεν· ὁ μέν ποτε[2] πατρίδος ὅπλων
    ἦρξεν, ὁ δ᾽ ἤεισεν[3] κρέσσονα[4] βασκανίης.

[1] εἰδείης Pl: ἠδείης P
[2] ποτε Pl: κοτέν P: κοτε Jacobs
[3] ἤεισεν P: ἤεισε Pl   [4] κρέσσονα P: κρείσσονα Pl

EPIGRAMS

19 (46 G.-P.) *Palatine Anthology*; *Planudean Anthology*

The father Philippus[1] buries his twelve-year-old son here, his great hope, Nicoteles.[2]

[1] A common name, but also "Horse Lover."
[2] A common name, but also "Headed for Victory."

20 (32 G.-P.) *Palatine Anthology*; *Planudean Anthology*

At dawn we were burying Melanippus,[1] but as the sun set the maiden Basilo perished by her own hand. After placing her brother in the fire, she could not bear to live. [5] The house of their father Aristippus saw a double tragedy, and all Cyrene was dumb with grief at the sight of that house of excellent children bereft.

[1] The names of Melanippus and Aristippus in line 5 are both attested on Cyrenean coins: *Num. Chron.* 1936 201 pl. 13.15 (ca. 325 BC); *Brit. Mus. Cat. Cyrenaica* 108 284a pl. 25.16 (ca. 300 BC).

21 (29 G.-P.) *Palatine Anthology*; *Planudean Anthology*; Scholia to Hesiod, *Theogony*

Whoever passes by my tomb, know that I am the son and father of Callimachus of Cyrene. You must know them both. One commanded the arms of his country,[1] the other sang songs mightier than envy [5] till the end of his days.

[1] The names of Callimachus' male relatives and their military and civil titles are recorded in Cyrenean inscriptions. See Laronde 1987, 110–13, 118; Cameron 1995, 7–8.

5   ἄχρι βίου·[5] Μοῦσαι γὰρ ὅσους ἴδον ὄμματι παῖδας
    μὴ λοξῷ[6] πολιοὺς οὐκ ἀπέθεντο φίλους[7]

[5] ἄχρι βίου Faraone huc transposuit e v. 6: οὐ νέμεσις PPl
[6] μὴ λοξῷ Schol. ad Hes. *Theog*. 82: ἄχρι βίου PPl
[7] 5–6 Μοῦσαι . . . φίλους = *Aet*. 1.37–38; secl. Pf.

22 (36 G.-P.) *Anth. Pal*. 7.518; *Anth. Plan*.

Ἀστακίδην τὸν Κρῆτα τὸν αἰπόλον ἥρπασε Νύμφη
    ἐξ ὄρεος, καὶ νῦν ἱερὸς Ἀστακίδης.
οὐκέτι[1] Δικταίῃσιν ὑπὸ δρυσίν, οὐκέτι Δάφνιν
    ποιμένες, Ἀστακίδην δ᾽ αἰὲν ἀεισόμεθα.

[1] οὐκέτι Salmasius: οὔκει P: οἰκεῖ Pl

23 (53 G.-P.) *Anth. Pal*. 7.471; *Anth. Plan*. [B], sine nom.;
Sext. Emp. *Math*. 1.48; Schol. ad Dion. Thrax (pp. 3.22,
160.15 Hilgard)

Εἴπας[1] "Ἥλιε χαῖρε"[2] Κλεόμβροτος ὠμβρακιώτης[3]
    ἥλατ᾽ ἀφ᾽ ὑψηλοῦ τείχεος εἰς Ἀΐδην,[4]
ἄξιον οὐδὲν ἰδὼν[5] θανάτου κακόν,[6] ἀλλὰ[7] Πλάτωνος
    ἓν τὸ[8] περὶ ψυχῆς γράμμ᾽ ἀναλεξάμενος.

[1] εἴπας sscr. P: πὼν Pl   [2] χαῖρε PPl: φαεινὲ ante Κλ.,
om. aut εἴπας aut χαῖρε, Schol. ad Dion. Thrax   [3] ὠμβρα-
κιώτης CPl: ὠμβρακιώτας P   [4] Ἀΐδην cett.: Ἀΐδαν P
[5] οὐδὲν ἰδὼν P: οὔτι παθὼν Schol. ad Dion. Thrax
[6] θανάτου κακόν P: θανάτου τέλος Sext. Emp.
[7] ἀλλὰ Πλάτωνος Pl: ἢ τὸ Πλάτωνος P
[8] ἓν τὸ Pl Sext. Emp.: ἓν τῷ P

Those on whom the Muses cast a favorable eye as children
they do not reject as friends when their hair is gray.[2]

[2] Lines 5–6 also appear in the *Aetia* Prologue (*Aet.* 1.37–38).
Both Pfeiffer and Gow-Page read them as a later interpolation,
though the sense of the lines suits both locations, and this would
not be the only example of Callimachus quoting himself in the
Epigrams and elsewhere.

22 (36 G.-P.) *Palatine Anthology*; *Planudean Anthology*

A nymph snatched Astacides,[1] the Cretan goatherd from
the mountain, and Astacides is now among the blessed. No
longer under the Dictean[2] oaks, no longer[3] will we shep-
herds sing of Daphnis,[4] but always of Astacides.

[1] Astacides (not found elsewhere) is a patronymic familiar
from Theocritus' seventh *Idyll*, where they serve as nicknames
for poets in a bucolic setting.   [2] Mt. Dicte in Crete, one of
the alleged birthplaces of Zeus (*Hymn* 1.4).
[3] An example of anaphora, which is associated with bucolic
poetry and used frequently in Theocritus' *Idylls*.
[4] Goatherd and principal bucolic hero (Theoc. *Id.* 1).

23 (53 G.-P.) *Palatine Anthology*; *Planudean Anthology*
[B], Anonymous; Sextus Empiricus, *Against the Profes-
sors*; Scholia to Dionysius Thrax

After he said, "Farewell Sun," Cleombrotus[1] of Ambracia[2]
leaped from a high wall into Hades. He had seen no evil
worthy of death, but he had read Plato's book *On the Soul*.[3]

[1] Possibly the student of Socrates who was in Aegina at the
time of his teacher's death (Pl. *Phd.* 59c).   [2] A city in Epirus
in northwestern Greece.   [3] An alternative name for the
Phaedo, which argues that the soul is immortal but rejects suicide.

CALLIMACHUS

24 (60 G.-P.) *Anth. Pal.* 9.336; *Anth. Plan.*

Ἥρως Αἰετίωνος¹ ἐπίσταθμος² Ἀμφιπολίτεω
ἵδρυμαι μικρῷ μικρὸς ἐπὶ προθύρῳ
λοξὸν ὄφιν καὶ μοῦνον ἔχων ξίφος· ἀνέρι δ᾽ Ἱππεῖ³
θυμωθεὶς πεζὸν κἀμὲ παρῳκίσατο.

¹ Ἠετίωνος Pl: ἠιετίωνος P
² ἐπίσταθμος P: ἐπὶ σταθμὸν Pl
³ ἀνέρι δ᾽ Ἱππεῖ Jacobs: ἀνδρι ἱπείωι P: ἀνδρὶ δὲ ἱππεῖ Pl

25 (11 G.-P.) *Anth. Pal.* 5.6; *Anth. Plan.*; Stob. 3.28.9; *Suda* υ 108

Ὤμοσε Καλλίγνωτος¹ Ἰωνίδι μήποτ᾽ ἐκείνης²
ἕξειν μήτε φίλον κρέσσονα³ μήτε φίλην.
ὤμοσεν· ἀλλὰ λέγουσιν ἀληθέα τοὺς ἐν ἔρωτι
ὅρκους μὴ δύνειν οὔατ᾽ ἐς ἀθανάτων.
5 νῦν δ᾽ ὁ μὲν ἀρσενικῷ⁴ θέρεται πυρί, τῆς δὲ
ταλαίνης
νύμφης ὡς Μεγαρέων οὐ λόγος οὐδ᾽ ἀριθμός.

¹ Καλλίγνωτος Pl: Καλλίγνωστος P   ² μήποτ᾽ ἐκείνης
P: μήποτε κείνης Pl   ³ κρέσσονα P: κρείσσονα Pl
⁴ ἀρσενικῷ C: ἄλλης δὴ Pl

418

24 (60 G.-P.) *Palatine Anthology*; *Planudean Anthology*

A hero quartered on Aeëtion of Amphipolis,[1] I am set up small on a small porch, outfitted with only a coiled snake and a sword. Being enraged at a Horseman,[2] he set me up as a foot soldier.[3]

[1] A city in northern Macedonia.   [2] The words here translated "at a Horseman" may be an intrusive gloss; some editors adopt the variant "at Epeius," the man who built the Trojan horse.   [3] The implication seems to be that a hero fully represented would be on horseback.

25 (11 G.-P.) *Palatine Anthology*; *Planudean Anthology*; Stobaeus; *Suda*

Callignotus swore to Ionis that he would never hold another, male or female, dearer than her. He swore. But it's true what they say, that lovers' vows do not reach the ears of the immortals. [5] Now he is afire for a boy, and as for the poor girl, as the oracle said of the Megarians, there is no account or reckoning.[1]

[1] The *Suda* cites this epigram in a discussion of an oracle given to the Megarians (or the Aegeans of Achaea) when they asked at Delphi who were the best of the Greeks and were told that they were neither third, nor fourth, nor twelfth, but of no account or reckoning.

26 (47 G.-P.) *Anth. Pal.* 7.460; *Anth. Plan.*

Εἶχον ἀπὸ σμικρῶν ὀλίγον βίον οὔτε τι δεινόν
  ῥέζων οὔτ᾽ ἀδικέων[1] οὐδένα. Γαῖα φίλη,
Μικύλος[2] εἴ τι πονηρὸν ἐπήνεσα, μήτε σὺ κούφη
  γίνεο[3] μήτ᾽ ἄλλοι δαίμονες οἵ μ᾽ ἔχετε.[4]

¹ ἀδικέων Meineke: ἀδικῶν PPl   ² Μικύλος Pl: Μεικύ-
λος P   ³ γίνεο P: γίγνεο Pl   ⁴ μ᾽ ἔχετε CPl: μέτεχε P

27 (56 G.-P.) *Anth. Pal.* 9.507; [Ach. Tat.] *Vit. Arat.* 5

Ἡσιόδου τό τ᾽[1] ἄεισμα καὶ ὁ τρόπος· οὐ τὸν ἀοιδόν[2]
  ἔσχατον, ἀλλ᾽ ὀκνέω μὴ τὸ μελιχρότατον
τῶν ἐπέων ὁ Σολεὺς ἀπεμάξατο· χαίρετε λεπταί
  ῥήσιες, Ἀρήτου σύμβολον[3] ἀγρυπνίης.[4]

¹ τό τ᾽ Blomfield: τὸ δ᾽ P [Ach. Tat.]   ² ἀοιδὸν P [Ach.
Tat.].: ἀοιδῶν Scaliger   ³ σύμβολον Ruhnken: σύντονος
P: σύγγονος [Ach. Tat.]   ⁴ ἀγρυπνίης [Ach. Tat.].: ἀγρυ-
πνίη P

28 (2 G.-P.) *Anth. Pal.* 12.43

Ἐχθαίρω τὸ ποίημα τὸ κυκλικόν, οὐδὲ κελεύθῳ
  χαίρω, τίς πολλοὺς ὧδε καὶ ὧδε φέρει·
μισέω[1] καὶ περίφοιτον ἐρώμενον, οὐδ᾽[2] ἀπὸ κρήνης
  πίνω· σικχαίνω[3] πάντα τὰ δημόσια.
5 Λυσανίη, σὺ δὲ ναίχι καλὸς καλός–ἀλλὰ πρὶν εἰπεῖν
  τοῦτο σαφῶς Ἠχώ, φησί τις· "ἄλλος ἔχει."

¹ μισέω Brunck: μισῶ Pl   ² οὐδ᾽ Meineke: οὔτ᾽ P
³ σικχαίνω Brunck: σικχάνω P

26 (47 G.-P.) *Palatine Anthology*; *Planudean Anthology*

I led a modest life with small means, doing nothing wrong or being unjust to anyone. Dear Earth, if I, Micylus,[1] ever approved anything wicked, do not rest lightly on me, nor should you other gods[2] who hold me.

[1] A real name (Diod. Sic. 19.88.5), but here probably meant to reflect its root, which means "small."

[2] The other chthonic deities (Aesch. *Pers.* 640).

27 (56 G.-P.) *Palatine Anthology*; Pseudo-Achilles Tatius, *Life of Aratus*

The theme and style is Hesiod's; not in every detail, but I do not doubt but that the man from Soli imitated the most honeyed of his verses. Hail subtle discourses, proof of Aratus'[1] late nights.

[1] Aratus of Soli, a contemporary of Callimachus whose astronomical poem, the *Phaenomena*, was widely admired.

28 (2 G.-P.) *Palatine Anthology*

I hate cyclic epic, nor do I delight in any road that carries crowds here and there. I detest a roving lover, and I do not drink from just any fountain. I loathe everything public. [5] Lysanias, you are beautiful, yes, beautiful. But before Echo can repeat this clearly, someone says, "Another holds him."[1]

[1] "Yes, beautiful" (*naichi kalos*) is approximately echoed in reverse by "Another holds him" (*allos echei*).

CALLIMACHUS

29 (5 G.-P.) *Anth. Pal.* 12.51; *Anth. Plan.*, sine nom. et
solum vv. 3-4; Schol. ad Theoc. *Id.* 2.150–53b

Ἔγχει καὶ πάλιν εἰπὲ "Διοκλέος"·¹ οὐδ' Ἀχελῷος
  κείνου² τῶν ἱερῶν αἰσθάνεται³ κυάθων.
καλὸς ὁ παῖς, Ἀχελῷε, λίην καλός, εἰ δέ τις οὐχί
  φησίν—ἐπισταίμην μοῦνος ἐγὼ τὰ καλά.

¹ Διοκλέος Schol. ad Theoc. *Id.* Cod. K: Διοκλέους cett.
Schol. ad codd.: Διόκλεες P   ² κείνου P: ἐκείνου Schol. ad
Theoc. *Id.* K   ³ αἰσθάνεται P: αἰσθάνεσθαι Schol. ad Theoc.
Id. K

30 (12 G.-P.) *Anth. Pal.* 12.71

Θεσσαλικὲ Κλεόνικε τάλαν τάλαν, οὐ μὰ τὸν ὀξύν
  ἥλιον, οὔ σ'¹ ἔγνων·² σχέτλιε, ποῦ γέγονας;
ὀστέα σοι καὶ μοῦνον ἔτι τρίχες· ἦ ῥά σε δαίμων
  οὑμὸς ἔχει, χαλεπῇ δ' ἤντεο θευμορίῃ;
5 ἔγνων· Εὐξίθεός σε³ συνήρπασε, καὶ σὺ γὰρ ἐλθών
  τὸν καλόν, ὦ μόχθηρ', ἔβλεπες ἀμφοτέροις.

¹ οὔ σ' Ernesti: οὐκ P   ² ἔγνων apogr.: ἔγνω P
³ σε apogr.: με P

31 (1 G.-P.) *Anth. Pal.* 12.102

Ὠγρευτής, Ἐπίκυδες, ἐν οὔρεσι πάντα λαγωόν
  διφᾷ καὶ πάσης ἴχνια δορκαλίδος
στίβῃ¹ καὶ νιφετῷ κεχρημένος· ἢν δέ τις εἴπῃ
  "τῆ,² τόδε βέβληται θηρίον," οὐκ ἔλαβεν.

EPIGRAMS

29 (5 G.-P.) *Palatine Anthology*; *Planudean Anthology*, Anonymous and only vv. 3-4; Scholia to Theocritus, *Idylls*

Pour again and say "to Diocles." Achelous[1] does not feel his sacred ladles in that toast. The boy is beautiful, Achelous, very beautiful, and if anyone denies it, may I alone get to know his charms.

[1] A river in Aetolia, the longest in Greece, and the name of its patron deity. It became synonymous with water itself (Eur. *Bacch.* 625), which is not mixed with wine in a lover's toast (Schol. ad Theoc. *Id.* 2.150–53b).

30 (12 G.-P.) *Palatine Anthology*

Cleonicus from Thessaly, alas, alas by the bright sun, I did not recognize you. Poor fellow, where have you been? You are only bones and hair. Has my evil demon taken hold of you?[1] Have you met with a grievous dispensation? [5] I knew it. Euxitheus has carried you away. Poor fellow, you went and looked at that beauty with both eyes.

[1] Eros.

31 (1 G.-P.) *Palatine Anthology*

That hunter Epicydes searches for every hare and the tracks of every deer, assailed by hoar frost and snow. But

---

[1] στίβῃ Fabri: στείβῃ P   [2] τῇ Brunck: τηι P

5 χοὖμὸς[3] ἔρως τοιόσδε· τὰ μὲν φεύγοντα διώκειν
οἶδε, τὰ δ' ἐν μέσσῳ[4] κείμενα παρπέταται.[5]

[3] χοὖμὸς P: οὑμὸς P[b]   [4] μέσσῳ P: μέσῳ P[a]
[5] παρπέταται P: προφέρεται P[b]

32 (7 G.-P.) *Anth. Pal.* 12.148

Οἶδ' ὅτι μευ[1] πλούτου κενεαὶ χέρες· ἀλλά, Μένιππε,
μὴ λέγε πρὸς Χαρίτων τοὐμὸν ὄνειρον ἐμοί.
ἀλγέω τὴν διὰ παντὸς ἔπος τόδε πικρὸν ἀκούων·
ναὶ φίλε, τῶν[2] παρὰ σεῦ[3] τοῦτ' ἀνεραστότατον.

[1] μευ Pf.: μου P   [2] τῶν apogr.: τὸν P
[3] σεῦ Pf.: σοῦ P

33 (21 G.-P.) *Anth. Pal.* 6.347

Ἄρτεμι, τὶν[1] τόδ' ἄγαλμα Φιληρατὶς εἴσατο τῇδε·
ἀλλὰ[2] σὺ μὲν δέξαι, πότνια, τὴν δὲ σάω.[3]

[1] τὶν apogr.: τὴν P   [2] ἀλλὰ C: ἀιλα P   [3] σάω corr.
Fabri: σάου P

34 (22 G.-P.) *Anth. Pal.* 6.351

Τίν με, λεοντάγχ' ὦνα[1] συοκτόνε, φήγινον ὄζον
θῆκε—"τίς;" Ἀρχῖνος. "ποῖος;" ὁ Κρήης.
"δέχομαι."

[1] λεοντάγχ' ὦνα Lobeck: λεονταγχωνε P

424

if someone says, "Hey, this beast is shot," he does not take it. [5] My passion is like this: it knows how to pursue what flees, but what lies at hand, it flies past.

32 (7 G.-P.) *Palatine Anthology*

I know that my hands are empty of wealth, Menippus,[1] but by the Graces, don't tell me my own dream. I suffer continuously hearing this bitter line. Yes, dear, of the things I hear from you this is the most unloverlike.

[1] The name of a Cynic satirist contemporary with Callimachus. He is probably not addressed here, but in combination with the oath "by the Graces," the name suggests a literary context. Cynics made a show of their poverty, which Callimachus uses to effect in *Iamb* 1 (*Ia.* 193.29–30).

33 (21 G.-P.) *Palatine Anthology*

Artemis, here Phileratis set up this image for you. But you accept it, Lady, and keep her safe.

34 (22 G.-P.) *Palatine Anthology*

To you lord, lion-strangler, boar-slayer,[1] he dedicated me, an oak branch. "Who?" Archinus. "Which one?" The Cretan. "I accept."

[1] Epithets of Heracles, whose slaying of the Nemean lion (*Aet.* 54–60j) and Erymanthian boar (Paus. 8.24.5) were two of his traditional labors.

35 (30 G.-P.) *Anth. Pal.* 7.415

Βαττιάδεω παρὰ σῆμα φέρεις πόδας εὖ μὲν ἀοιδήν
εἰδότος, εὖ δ᾽ οἴνῳ καίρια συγγελάσαι.

36 (62 G.-P.) *Anth. Pal.* 7.454; *Ath.* 10.436e

Τὸν[1] βαθὺν οἰνοπότην Ἐρασίξενον ἡ δὶς ἐφεξῆς
ἀκρήτου προποθεῖσ᾽[2] ᾤχετ᾽ ἔχουσα κύλιξ.

[1] τὸν C: οὐ P, Ath.   [2] προποθεῖσ C: φανερῶς Ath.

37 (17 G.-P.) *Anth. Pal.* 13.7 (Καλλιμάχου κωμικὸν τε-
τράμετρον); *P.Oxy.* 220 col. X, 6; om. *Anth. Plan.*

Ὁ Λύκτιος Μενίτας[1]
τὰ τόξα ταῦτ᾽ ἐπειπών
ἔθηκε· "τῇ, κέρας τοι
δίδωμι καὶ φαρέτραν,[2]
5 Σάραπι· τοὺς δ᾽ ὀϊστούς
ἔχουσιν Ἑσπερῖται."

[1] Μενίτας P: Μενείτης *P.Oxy.* 220 col. X, 6   [2] φαρέτραν
Gow: φαρέτρην P

---

[1] Lyctus, a city in Crete well known for its archers, who were
often employed as mercenaries (Paus. 4.19.4).   [2] Otherwise
unknown.   [3] A Greco-Egyptian deity who combined traits
of Osirus and Apis with Zeus and Hades. His worship was widely
promoted by the Ptolemies. See Fraser 1972, vol. 1, 246–76.

35 (30 G.-P.) *Palatine Anthology*

You are walking beside the tomb of a son of Battus[1] who knew song well, and over wine how to laugh at the right moments.

[1] The founder and first king of Cyrene (Hdt. 4.150–58), Callimachus' home city. The reference here is to the poet, who may be identifying himself as Cyrenean or suggesting that his aristocratic forebears were connected to the first kings. See the General Introduction on Callimachus' family. The name itself was no longer in use in Callimachus' time.

36 (62 G.-P.) *Palatine Anthology*; Athenaeus, *The Learned Banqueters*

The cup of unmixed wine, drained twice in a row, has taken off with Erasixenus, the deep imbiber.

37 (17 G.-P.) *Palatine Anthology* (a comic tetrameter of Callimachus); Oxyrhynchus papyrus; missing in *Planudean Anthology*

The Lyctian[1] Menitas[2] dedicated this bow, saying, "Here! I give to you a bow and quiver, [5] Sarapis.[3] The Hesperitae[4] have the arrows."[5]

[4] The inhabitants of Euhesperides (mod. Benghazi) on the coast of Libya. During the reign of Ptolemy III, it was refounded and renamed Berenice in honor of the king's wife, Berenice II, a patron of Callimachus and fellow Cyrenean. [5] It is not possible to date the battle precisely, but the dedication to Serapis guarantees a Ptolemaic context. The refoundation of Euhesperides may have met with local resistance easily put down by Ptolemy. For a likely date, see Laronde 1987, 396, and Fraser 1972, vol. 1, 582 for an earlier one.

38 (20 G.-P.) *Anth. Pal.* 13.24 (ἐπὶ τῇ τοῦ προάγοντος τετραμέτρου ἐσχάτῃ διποδίᾳ ἑνδεκασύλλαβον); om. *Anth. Plan.*

Τὰ δῶρα τἀφροδίτῃ[1]
Σῖμον ἡ[2] περίφοιτος, εἰκόν' αὐτῆς[3]
  ἔθηκε τήν τε μίτρην
ἡ μαστούς[4] ἐφίλησε †τόν τε πᾶνα[5]
  . . . .[6]
6   καὶ τοὺς αὐτοὺς ὁρῇς[7] τάλαινα θύρσους†.[8]

[1] τἀφροδίτῃ Blomfield: τῇ Ἀφροδίτη P   [2] Σῖμον ἡ
Wilamowitz: Σειμονη P   [3] αὐτῆς Salmasius: αὐτη P
[4] ἡ μαστούς Fabri: ἡμᾶς τοὺς P   [5] πᾶνα P: πανὸν
Schneider   [6] lacunam stat. Bentley   [7] ὁρῇς corr. Livrea:
ὁρῇ P   [8] θύρσους Bentley: θάρσους P

39 (19 G.-P.) *Anth. Pal.* 13.25 (ἐπὶ διπλασιασθείσῃ τῇ διποδίᾳ ἐπῳδὸς τετράμετρος πλεονάζων μιᾷ συλλαβῇ τοῦ ἑξαμέτρου); Heph. *Poet.* 55.15c; om. *Anth. Plan.*

Δήμητρι τῇ Πυλαίῃ,
  τῇ[1] τοῦτον οὐκ Πελασγῶν[2]
Ἀκρίσιος τὸν νηὸν ἐδείματο, ταῦθ' ὁ Ναυκρατίτης
  καὶ τῇ κάτω θυγατρί
5   τὰ δῶρα Τιμόδημος
εἵσατο τῶν κερδέων δεκατεύματα· καὶ γὰρ εὔξαθ'
  οὕτως.

[1] τῇ Heph: omit P
[2] οὐκ Πελασγῶν Heph.: ουκεπελασγων P

38 (20 G.-P.) *Palatine Anthology* 13.24 (a hendecasyllable after the final dipody of the preceding tetrameter);[1] missing in *Planudean Anthology*

These gifts for Aphrodite were dedicated by Simon, who gets around: an image of herself, the girdle that kissed her breasts, and a torch . . . and wands of ivy,[2] which you see, poor wretch.

[1] The lemmatist's description of the meter seems to refer to the preceding poem in *Palatine Anthology* (Asclep. 33 G.-P.), an iambic catalectic ending with the dimeter used here. See G.-P. vol. 2, 177.   [2] Accoutrements of Dionysiac ritual.

39 (19 G.-P.) *Palatine Anthology* 13.25 (a double dipody, the epode being a tetrameter which is longer by one syllable than the hexameter); Hephaestion, *On Poetry*; missing in *Planudean Anthology*

To Demeter of the Gate, for whom Acrisius (not one of the Pelasgians)[1] built this shrine,[2] and to her daughter below-ground[3] [5] Timodemus of Naucratis[4] dedicated one-tenth of his profits, for so he had vowed.

[1] Not a descendant of Pelasgus, but of Abas of Argos. Acrisius founded the Amphictyonic councils at Thermopylae and later at Delphi (Schol. ad Eur. *Or.* 1087; Strabo 9.3.7).   [2] The shrine, located in Thermopylae, where the Amphictyonic council met (Strabo 9.3.7).   [3] Persephone, the daughter of Demeter, who was abducted by Hades (Eur. *Alc.* 851–52).   [4] A city in the Nile delta where the pharaoh Amasis II allowed Greek merchants to settle in the sixth century BC (Hdt. 2.154).

40 (48 G.-P.) *Anth. Pal.* 7.728 [C], (ἐπὶ τῷ αὐτῷ τετρα-
μέτρῳ ἐνδεκασύλλαβον); om. *Anth. Plan.*

Ἱερέη Δήμητρος ἐγώ ποτε καὶ πάλιν[1] Καβείρων,
    ὦνερ, καὶ μετέπειτα Δινδυμήνης[2]
ἡ γρηῢς γενόμην, ἡ νῦν κόνις ηνο . . .
    πολλῶν προστασίη νέων γυναικῶν.
5 καί μοι τέκν᾽ ἐγένοντο δύ᾽ ἄρσενα, κἠπέμυσ᾽
        ἐκείνων[3]
    εὐγήρως ἐνὶ χερσίν· ἕρπε χαίρων.

    [1] πάλιν apogr. Buher.: πάλι P   [2] Δινδυμήνης Brunck:
Δινδυμίνης P   [3] κἠπέμυσ᾽ ἐκείνων P: κἠπέμυσα κείνων
Pfeiffer

41 (4 G.-P.) *Anth. Pal.* 12.73; Choerob. *In Heph.* 226.12
Cons

Ἥμισύ μευ[1] ψυχῆς ἔτι[2] τὸ πνέον, ἥμισυ δ᾽ οὐκ οἶδ᾽[3]
    εἴτ᾽ Ἔρος[4] εἴτ᾽ Ἀΐδης ἥρπασε, πλὴν ἀφανές.[5]
ἦ ῥά τιν᾽ ἐς παίδων πάλιν ᾤχετο; καὶ μὲν ἀπεῖπον
    πολλάκι· "τὴν δρῆστιν μὴ ὑποδέχεσθε[6] νέοι."
5 †ὀυκισυνιφησον· ἐκεῖσε γὰρ ἡ λιθόλευστος
    κείνη καὶ δύσερως οἶδ᾽ ὅτι που στρέφεται.

    [1] μευ P: μοι Choerob.   [2] ἔτι P: ἐπὶ Choerob. [K], ἐστὶ [U]
    [3] Elisio unica (Choerob. *In Heph.* 226.13 Cons)   [4] ἔρος
Choer.: ἔρις P   [5] ἥρπασε, πλὴν ἀφανές P: ἥρπασεν ἐκ
μερόπων Choerob.: μετώπων Choerob. [K]   [6] ὑποδέχεσθε
Hecker: μὴὑπεχεσθε P: μή νυ δέχεσθε Page

EPIGRAMS

40 (48 G.-P.) *Palatine Anthology* 7.728 [C], (in the same tetrameter followed by a hendecasyllable); missing in *Planudean Anthology*

A priestess of Demeter I was once, and then in turn of the Cabeiri,[1] sir, and afterward of Dindymene.[2] I became an old woman, who now am dust [...] the mentor of many young women. [5] And two male children were born to me, and I closed my eyes in their arms at a ripe old age. Passerby, farewell.

[1] The Great Gods, Cabeiri or Cabiri, were worshipped in mystery cults at Lemnos and Samothrace (Hdt. 2.51), where they were said to protect seamen (Ap. Rhod. 1.915–18; Diod. Sic. 4.43.1–2). Arsinoe II built a rotunda at Samothrace (*OGIS* 15 = *IG* XII, 8.227) and sought refuge there from her second husband, Ptolemy Ceraunus (Just. *Epit.* 24.3.1–10). [2] Cybele named here for a cult place in Phrygia (Steph. Byz. δ 84 Billerbeck s.v.).

41 (4 G.-P.) *Palatine Anthology*; Choeroboscus, *On Hephaestion*

Half of my soul still breathes, the other half, I do not know whether Eros or Hades has snatched away, except that she is nowhere to be seen. Has she gone after one of the boys again? Yet I often warned them, "Young men, do not receive a runaway!" [5] [. . .] for out there somewhere I know she is getting around, that lovesick one worthy of stoning.

431

42 (8 G.-P.) *Anth. Pal.* 12.118; Plut. *Mor.* 455b (*De cohibenda ira.* 5), sine nom.; *Sylloge Crameriana* (Par.Gr. suppl. 352, Anec. Par. vol. 4, p. 384)

Εἰ μὲν ἑκών, Ἀρχῖν᾽,[1] ἐπεκώμασα, μυρία μέμφου,
   εἰ δ᾽ ἄκων ἥκω, τὴν προπέτειαν ἔα.[2]
Ἄκρητος καὶ Ἔρως μ᾽ ἠνάγκασαν,[3] ὧν ὁ μὲν αὐτῶν
   εἷλκεν, ὁ δ᾽ οὐκ εἴα τὴν προπέτειαν ἐᾶν.[4]
5 ἐλθὼν δ᾽ οὐκ ἐβόησα, τίς ἢ τίνος, ἀλλ᾽ ἐφίλησα[5]
   τὴν φλιήν·[6] εἰ τοῦτ᾽ ἔστ᾽ ἀδίκημ᾽, ἀδικέω.

[1] Ἀρχῖν᾽ Bentley: ἄρχειν P   [2] ἔα inscr. et cod. Cram.:
ὅρα P   [3] μ᾽ ἠνάγκασαν Meineke: με ἀνάγκασεν P
[4] τὴν προπέτειαν ἐᾶν Dressel: τὴν βίαν ὅσσην ὅρα Syll. S:
σώφρονα θυμὸν ἔχειν P   [5] ἐφίλησα P: ἐφύλαξα Syll. S
[6] φλιήν Plut.: φιλίην Syll. S: ἰαρήν P

43 (13 G.-P.) *Anth. Pal.* 12.134; 3–4 Ath. 15.669d; 6 *Epimer. Hom.* (vol. 2, p. 743 Dyck)

Ἕλκος ἔχων ὁ ξεῖνος ἐλάνθανεν· ὡς ἀνιηρόν
   πνεῦμα διὰ στηθέων (εἶδες;) ἀνηγάγετο,
τὸ τρίτον ἡνίκ᾽[1] ἔπινε, τὰ δὲ ῥόδα φυλλοβολεῦντα
   τὠνδρὸς ἀπὸ στεφάνων[2] πάντ᾽ ἐγένοντο χαμαί·
5 ὤπτηται μέγα δή τι·[3] μὰ δαίμονας οὐκ ἀπὸ ῥυσμοῦ
   εἰκάζω, φωρὸς δ᾽ ἴχνια φὼρ ἔμαθον.[4]

[1] ἡνίκ᾽ Scaliger: ηγκεπινε P   [2] στεφάνων Ath.: στο-
μάτων P   [3] ὤπτηται μέγα δή τι Bentley: ὤπτημαι μεγα-
λητί P   [4] ἔμαθον P: ἔμαθε *Ep. Hom.* (vol. 2, p. 743 Dyck)

42 (8 G.-P.) *Palatine Anthology*; Plutarch, *On the Control of Anger*, unattributed; *Sylloge Crameriana*

If willingly, Archinus, I serenaded you, blame me a thousand times over. But if I came unwilling, overlook my recklessness. Neat wine and love compelled me. Of these, one drew me on, the other did not let the rashness stop. [5] When I arrived, I did not shout out my name or parentage, but I kissed the doorpost. If this is wrong, I plead guilty.

43 (13 G.-P.) *Palatine Anthology*; Athenaeus, *The Learned Banqueters*; *Epimerismi Homerici*

We did not notice that our guest had a wound. How painfully he drew breath through his chest—did you see?—when he drank the third cup,[1] and the roses shedding their leaves from his garlands lay all on the ground. [5] He was really fried. By the gods, I am not guessing at random: a thief myself, I know the tracks of a thief.

[1] The third toast to Zeus the Savior.

44 (9 G.-P.) *Anth. Pal.* 12.139

Ἔστι τι ναὶ τὸν Πᾶνα κεκρυμμένον, ἔστι τι ταύτῃ
   ναὶ μὰ Διώνυσον¹ πῦρ ὑπὸ τῇ σποδιῇ.
οὐ θαρσέω· μὴ δή με περίπλεκε· πολλάκι λήθει
   τοῖχον ὑποτρώγων ἡσύχιος ποταμός.
5 τῷ καὶ νῦν δείδοικα, Μενέξενε, μή με παρεισδύς
   †οὗτος οσειγαρνησ†² εἰς τὸν ἔρωτα βάλῃ.³

   ¹ Διώνυσον Brunck: Διόνυσον P   ² ουτοσοσειγαρνης
P: ὁ σιγέρπης Bentley   ³ βάλῃ Heinsius: βάλλῃ P

45 (10 G.-P.) *Anth. Pal.* 12.149; Schol. ad *Od.* 21.292;
P.Oxy. 221 col. XV, 33

"Ληφθήσει, περίφευγε,¹ Μενέκρατες" εἶπα Πανήμου
   εἰκάδι καὶ Λῴου τῇ τίνι; τῇ δεκάτῃ
ἦλθεν ὁ βοῦς ὑπ᾽ ἄροτρον ἑκούσιος. εὖ γ᾽, ἐμὸς
      Ἑρμῆς,²
εὖ γ᾽, ἐμός· οὐ παρὰ τὰς εἴκοσι μεμφόμεθα.

   ¹ περίφευγε P: περίφοιτε Bentley   ² Ἑρμῆς Brunck:
Ἑρμᾶς P

44 (9 G.-P.) *Palatine Anthology*

There is something hidden—yes, by Pan—there is something here—yes by Dionysus—a fire under these ashes. I am not bold. Do not involve me. Often a quiet river, unnoticed, eats away at a wall. [5] So now I am afraid, Menexenus, that this flatterer (?) will slip in and cast me into love.

45 (10 G.-P.) *Palatine Anthology*; Scholia to Homer, *Odyssey*; Oxyrhynchus papyrus

"You will be caught, Menecrates, flee as you may!" I said on the twentieth of Panemus,[1] and on Loeus the what? On the tenth, the ox came under the plow of his own free will. Well done my Hermes, well done. I do not have a problem with twenty days.[2]

[1] The ninth month of the Macedonian calendar. It is followed by Loeus.   [2] Each lunar month had thirty days, so Loeus, the tenth, is twenty days after Panemus, the twentieth. This is the interval of time between the narrator's meeting Menecrates, who resisted him, and the youth's capitulation.

46 (3 G.-P.) *Anth. Pal.* 12.150; Schol. ad Theoc. *Id.* 11.1;
4, Clem. Alex. *Strom.* 687 P; 9, *Et. Mag.* 168.4

Ὡς ἀγαθὰν[1] Πολύφαμος ἀνεύρατο τὰν ἐπαοιδάν[2]
τὠραμένῳ· ναὶ Γᾶν,[3] οὐκ ἀμαθὴς[4] ὁ Κύκλωψ·
αἱ Μοῖσαι τὸν ἔρωτα κατισχναίνοντι, Φίλιππε·
ἦ πανακὲς[5] πάντων φάρμακον ἁ σοφία.
5   τοῦτο,[6] δοκέω, χἀ λιμὸς ἔχει μόνον ἐς τὰ πονηρά
τὠγαθόν· ἐκκόπτει τὰν φιλόπαιδα νόσον.
ἔσθ' ἁμὶν †χ' ἀκαστας† ἀφειδέα ποττὸν[7] Ἔρωτα
τοῦτ' εἶπαι·[8] "κείρευ τὰ πτερά, παιδάριον,
οὐδ' ὅσον[9] ἀττάραγόν τυ δεδοίκαμες·[10] αἱ γὰρ ἐπῳδαί
10   οἴκοι[11] τῶ χαλεπῶ τραύματος ἀμφότεραι."

[1] ἀγαθὰν P: ἀγαθός Schol. ad Theoc. *Id.*   [2] ἐπαοιδάν
P: τὰν ἀοιδάν Schol. ad Theoc. *Id.*   [3] τὠραμένῳ van Eldick,
ναὶ Γᾶν Hecker: τωρραμενωναιγαν P   [4] οὐκ ἀμαθὴς Eldick:
οὐ καθῆμᾶς P   [5] ἦ πανακὲς Bentley: ηπανὲς P: ἡ πανακὴς
Clem. Alex.   [6] τοῦτο Salmasius: τοῦ P   [7] ποττὸν Brunck:
πρὸς τὸν P   [8] εἶπαι Kaibel: ιπαι P   [9] οὐδ' ὅσον P:
οὐδὲ σὸν Et. Gen.: οὐδὲ τὸν Et. Mag.   [10] τυ δεδοίκαμες
Bentley: τοι δέδοικα Et. Gen.: τι δέδοικεν P, Et. Mag.
[11] οἴκοι Ernesti: οἴκω P

47 (28 G.-P.) *Anth. Pal.* 6.301; Suda ε 2082

Τὴν ἁλίην[1] Εὔδημος, ἐφ' ἧς ἅλα λιτὸν[2] ἐπέσθων
χειμῶνας μεγάλους ἐξέφυγεν δανέων,[3]
θῆκε θεοῖς Σαμόθρῃξι[4] λέγων ὅτι τήνδε κατ' εὐχήν,
ὦ λαοί, σωθεὶς ἐξ ἁλὸς ὧδ' ἔθετο.

[1] ἁλίην P: ἁλίη Suda   [2] λιτὸν P: λυτὸν Suda

46 (3 G.-P.) *Palatine Anthology*; Scholia to Theocritus, *Idylls*; Clement of Alexandria, *Stromata*; *Etymologicum Magnum*

How fine a charm Polyphemus[1] discovered for someone in love. Yes, by the Earth, the Cyclops was not ignorant. The Muses shrink down the swollen wound of love, Philippus.[2] Indeed, the poet's skill is the drug that cures everything. [5] This, I think, and hunger are the only remedies against oppression. It eradicates the disease of loving boys. To merciless Eros I say this, "Have your wings clipped, little boy; we fear you not a bit. [10] Both cures for your grievous wound are in the house."

[1] The Cyclops who cures his unrequited love for Galatea with song in Theocritus' eleventh *Idyll*. Callimachus' use of the Doric dialect here suggests that he had this poem in mind.   [2] Possibly Philippus of Cos, a physician friend of the poet. The medical language that follows supports the identification, as does Theocritus' addressee in *Id*. 11, Nicias, who is also a physician (Gow, *Theocritus*, vol. 2 [Cambridge: Cambridge University Press, 1950], 208).

47 (28 G.-P.) *Palatine Anthology*; *Suda*

The saltbox on which Eudemus escaped great storms of debt by eating cheap salt, he dedicated to the gods of Samothrace[1] saying, "O people, I dedicate this box here according to my vow, saved from the sea."

[1] The Cabeiri or Cabiri, who watched over sailors (cf. *Epig.* 40 above, with note).

---

3 δανέων omit *Suda*
4 Σαμόθρηξι Wilamowitz: Σαμόθραξι P

48 (26 G.-P.) *Anth. Pal.* 6.310; Ap. Dysc. 2.493.3

Εὐμαθίην ἠτεῖτο διδοὺς[1] ἐμὲ Σῖμος[2] ὁ Μίκκου
    ταῖς Μούσαις· αἱ δὲ Γλαῦκος[3] ὅκως ἔδοσαν
ἀντ᾽ ὀλίγου μέγα δῶρον. ἐγὼ δ᾽ ἀνὰ τῆδε[4] κεχηνώς
    κεῖμαι τοῦ Σαμίου διπλόον ὁ τραγικός
5 παιδαρίων Διόνυσος ἐπήκοος· οἱ δὲ λέγουσιν
    "ἱερὸς ὁ πλόκαμος," τοὐμὸν ὄνειαρ ἐμοί.

[1] διδοὺς Ap. Dysc.: δίδου P   [2] Σῖμος P: Σημὸς C
[3] Γλαῦκος Bentley: γλεῦκος P   [4] τῆδε Brunck: τῆνδε P

49 (27 G.-P.) *Anth. Pal.* 6.311

Τῆς Ἀγοράνακτός με λέγε, ξένε,[1] κωμικὸν ὄντως
    ἀγκεῖσθαι νίκης μάρτυρα τοῦ Ῥοδίου
Πάμφιλον, οὐκ ἐν ἔρωτι δεδαγμένον,[2] ἥμισυ δ᾽ ὀπτῇ[3]
    ἰσχάδι καὶ λύχνοις Ἴσιδος εἰδόμενον.

[1] ξένε C: ξεῖνε P   [2] δεδαγμένον P: δεδαγμένον Bentley,
Pfeiffer   [3] ὀπτῇ Meineke: ὄπται P

48 (26 G.-P.) *Palatine Anthology*; Apollonius Dyscolus

Simus,[1] the son of Miccus,[2] dedicated me[3] to the Muses and asked for easy learning. And they, like Glaucus,[4] gave a great gift for a small one. I am dedicated here, gaping twice as wide as the Samian,[5] [5] the tragic Dionysus, listening to children as they recite my own dream, "Sacred is the lock,"[6] back to me.[7]

[1] The "snub-nosed," or "monkey-faced," but also a real name. A comic Simus appears in *Iamb* 4 (*Dieg.* 7.3).   [2] The "small one."   [3] Apparently a mask of Dionysus set up in a schoolroom.   [4] The Trojan hero who got a poor bargain when he exchanged his golden armor for Diomedes' armor of bronze (Hom. *Il.* 6.234–36).   [5] Samos was the site of the cult of the "Gaping Dionysus." The origin of the cult name is unknown (G.-P. vol. 2, 182), but the mask here is yawning from boredom.

[6] A quotation of Eur. *Bacch.* 494, where Dionysus warns Pentheus not to cut his long hair. The mask of Dionysus listens as the children recite Euripides' play.   [7] The god knows exactly what he said in the tragedy.

49 (27 G.-P.) *Palatine Anthology*

Stranger, say that I[1] am set up as a literally comic witness of the victory of Agoranax of Rhodes: I, Pamphilus,[2] burned not in love, but looking like a half-baked fig and some smoky lamps of Isis.

[1] A comic mask is speaking.   [2] Characters with this name appear frequently in comedy.

CALLIMACHUS

50 (49 G.-P.) *Anth. Pal.* 7.458

Τὴν Φρυγίην Αἴσχρην, ἀγαθὸν γάλα, πᾶσιν[1] ἐν
    ἐσθλοῖς
Μίκκος καὶ ζωὴν οὖσαν ἐγηροκόμει
καὶ φθιμένην ἀνέθηκεν, ἐπεσσομένοισιν[2] ὁρᾶσθαι.
    ἡ γρηῢς[3] μαστῶν ὡς ἀπέχει χάριτας.

    [1] πᾶσιν Bentley: παισὶν P   [2] ἐπεσσομένοισιν C: ἐπεσ-
συμένοισιν P   [3] ὡς inter γρηῢς et μαστῶν C

51 (15 G.-P.) *Anth. Pal.* 5.146

Τέσσαρες αἱ Χάριτες· ποτὶ γὰρ μία ταῖς τρισὶ
    κείναις[1]
ἄρτι ποτεπλάσθη κῆτι μύροισι νοτεῖ.
εὐαίων ἐν πᾶσιν ἀρίζηλος[2] Βερενίκα,
    ἇς ἄτερ οὐδ᾽ αὐταὶ ταὶ Χάριτες Χάριτες.

    [1] κείναις P: τήναις Wilamowitz, Pfeiffer   [2] ἀρίζηλος P:
ἀρίζαλος Brunck, Wilamowitz, G.-P.

52 (6 G.-P.) *Anth. Pal.* 12.230

Τὸν τὸ καλὸν μελανεῦντα Θεόκριτον, εἰ μὲν ἔμ᾽
    ἔχθει,[1]
τετράκι μισοίης, εἰ δὲ φιλεῖ, φιλέοις,
ναίχι πρὸς εὐχαίτεω Γανυμήδεος, οὐράνιε Ζεῦ·
    καὶ σύ ποτ᾽[2] ἠράσθης—οὐκέτι μακρὰ λέγω.

    [1] ἔχθει apogr. Voss.: οχθεῖ P   [2] σύ ποτ᾽ apogr. Oxon.:
σύποθ᾽ C

EPIGRAMS

50 (49 G.-P.) *Palatine Anthology*

While she was alive Miccus cherished Phrygian Aeschra, his excellent nurse, with all good things; and now that she is gone, he puts this up for future generations to see. In this way, the old woman receives thanks in full for her breasts.

51 (15 G.-P.) *Palatine Anthology*

Four are the Graces: in addition to those three, one has just been cast and is still damp with myrrh. Fortunate Berenice,[1] conspicuous among all, without whom the Graces themselves are not Graces.

[1] Berenice II, wife of Ptolemy III Euergetes and patron of Callimachus. See Dee L. Clayman, "Callimachus' Doric Graces (15 G.-P. = *Palatine Anthology* 5.146)," in *Dialect, Diction and Style in Greek Literary and Inscribed Epigram*, ed. E. Sistakou and A. Rengakos (Berlin: de Gruyter, 2016), 23–35.

52 (6 G.-P.) *Palatine Anthology*

Theocritus,[1] whose cheeks are growing dark beautifully: if he hates me, you should despise him four times as much; but if he loves me, you should love him. Yes, by Ganymede,[2] whose hair is lovely, O Uranian Zeus, even you once loved—I say no more.

[1] Possibly the poet, an older contemporary of Callimachus, though the name is common. Proof of this is alleged to be found in line 4 (a verbal echo of Theoc. *Id.* 8.59), but Theocritus' eighth *Idyll* is now considered to be spurious; see Gow 1950, vol. 2, 170–71, 180. If so, the author of that poem may be alluding to this epigram.   [2] A Trojan youth abducted by the gods to be Zeus' wine steward (Hom. *Il.* 20.232–35).

CALLIMACHUS

53 (23 G.-P.) *Anth. Pal.* 6.146 et iteratum post 6.274

Καὶ πάλιν, Εἰλείθυια,[1] Λυκαινίδος ἐλθὲ καλεύσης[2]
  εὔλοχος[3] ὠδίνων ὧδε σὺν εὐτοκίῃ·[4]
ὡς τόδε[5] νῦν μέν, ἄνασσα, κόρης ὕπερ, ἀντὶ δὲ
    παιδός
  ὕστερον εὐώδης ἄλλο τι νηὸς ἔχοι.

  [1] Εἰλείθυια Pᵃ: Εἰλήθυια P 146 et 274   [2] καλεύσης P
146: καλούσης P 274   [3] εὔλοχος PᵇCᵃ: εὔλεχος Pᵃ
  [4] εὐτοκίῃ P 146: εὐτυχίῃ P 274   [5] ὡς τόδε P 274: ὥστοι
P 146

54 (24 G.-P.) *Anth. Pal.* 6.147; *Suda* α 3105

Τὸ χρέος ὡς[1] ἀπέχεις, Ἀσκληπιέ, τὸ πρὸ[2] γυναικός
  Δημοδίκης Ἀκέσων ὤφελεν εὐξάμενος,[3]
γιγνώσκειν· ἢν δ' ἄρα λάθῃ καί †μιν[4] ἀπαιτῇς,[5]
  φησὶ παρέξεσθαι μαρτυρίην ὁ πίναξ.

  [1] ὡς omit *Suda*   [2] πρό C: πρὸς P *Suda*   [3] εὐξάμε-
νος C: αὐξόμενος P   [4] καί μιν P: καὶ δίς μιν Stadtmueller:
πάλι καί μιν Mair   [5] ἀπαιτῇς apogr.: ἀσπαιτῇς P

55 (16 G.-P.) *Anth. Pal.* 6.148; *Suda* μ 1418

Τῷ με Κανωπίτᾳ Καλλίστιον εἴκοσι μύξαις
  πλούσιον ἁ[1] Κριτίου λύχνον[2] ἔθηκε θεῷ,
εὐξαμένα περὶ παιδὸς Ἀπελλίδος· ἐς δ' ἐμὰ φέγγη
  ἀθρήσας φάσεις·[3] "Ἕσπερε, πῶς ἔπεσες;"

  [1] ἁ Meineke: ἡ C, *Suda*   [2] λύχνον C: λύχνιον P, *Suda*
  [3] φάσεις Wilamowitz: φήσεις P, *Suda*

442

EPIGRAMS

53 (23 G.-P.) *Palatine Anthology*

Eileithyia,[1] protector of birth, come again as Lycaenis is calling, bringing an easy birth for her pains. Just as now, Queen, your sacred shrine has an offering for a girl, later, may it have something else for a boy.

[1] Goddess of birth (Hom. *Il.* 11.270, 16.187, 19.103).

54 (24 G.-P.) *Palatine Anthology*; *Suda*

Asclepius,[1] recognize the debt that Aceson promised after he made a vow for his wife Demodice as paid in full, but if you should forget and ask for it again, this tablet says that it will furnish testimony.

[1] A god of healing (cf. Pind. *Pyth.* 3).

55 (16 G.-P.) *Palatine Anthology*; *Suda*

Callistion, wife of Critias, dedicated me, a lamp embellished with twenty nozzles, to the Canopian[1] god after making a vow for her daughter, Apellis. When you have looked at my lights, you will say, "Hesperus,[2] how you have fallen!"

[1] Serapis, who had an important temple in Canopus near Alexandria. See Fraser 1972, vol. 1, 256–58. [2] The Evening Star, bringer of light (Hom. *Il.* 22.317).

56 (25 G.-P.) *Anth. Pal.* 6.149

Φησὶν ὅ με στήσας Εὐαίνετος (οὐ γὰρ ἔγωγε
   γιγνώσκω) νίκης ἀντί με τῆς ἰδίης
ἀγκεῖσθαι χάλκειον[1] ἀλέκτορα Τυνδαρίδῃσι·
   πιστεύω Φαίδρου παιδὶ Φιλοξενίδεω.

[1] χάλκειον C: χαλκείων P

57 (18 G.-P.) *Anth. Pal.* 6.150

Ἰναχίης ἕστηκεν ἐν Ἴσιδος ἡ Θαλέω παῖς
   Αἰσχυλὶς Εἰρήνης μητρὸς ὑποσχεσίῃ.

58 (50 G.-P.) *Anth. Pal.* 7.277

Τίς, ξένος ὦ ναυηγέ; Λεόντιχος ἐνθάδε νεκρόν
   εὗρεν[1] ἐπ' αἰγιαλοῦ,[2] χῶσε δὲ[3] τῷδε τάφῳ
δακρύσας ἐπίκηρον ἐὸν βίον· οὐδὲ γὰρ αὐτός
   ἥσυχον, αἰθυίῃ[4] δ' ἶσα θαλασσοπορεῖ.

[1] εὗρεν P: εὗρέ μ' Agar, G.-P.   [2] αἰγιαλοῦ Hecker:
αἰγιαλούς A   [3] χῶσε δὲ C: χώσετε P   [4] αἰθυίῃ C:
αἰθύη P

56 (25 G.-P.) *Palatine Anthology*

The one who set me up, Euaenetus, says (for I myself do not know) that he dedicated me, a bronze cock, to the Tyndaridae[1] in return for my own victory. I believe the son of Phaedrus, grandson of Philoxenus.

[1] The Dioscuri, twin sons of Zeus and Leda. They were not cockfighters, but competed in other sports, Castor the horseman and Polydeuces the boxer (Hom. *Il.* 3.236–38).

57 (18 G.-P.) *Palatine Anthology*

The child of Thales, Aeschylis, stands in the shrine of Isis,[1] daughter of Inachus,[2] on the vow of her mother Eirene.

[1] Egyptian goddess of fertility promoted by the Ptolemies.
[2] The father of Io, who was pursued by Hera to Egypt. Io and Isis are often conflated (e.g., Hdt. 2.41).

58 (50 G.-P.) *Palatine Anthology*

Who are you, O shipwrecked stranger? Leontichus found me on the shore, a corpse, and covered me with a tomb, having wept for his own hazardous life. For he himself ranges over the sea not peacefully like a gull.

CALLIMACHUS

59 (59 G.-P.) *Anth. Pal.* 11.362

Εὐδαίμων ὅτι τἆλλα[1] μανεὶς ὠρχαῖος Ὀρέστας,
    Λεύκαρε, τὰν λίαν[2] οὐκ ἐμάνη μανίαν,[3]
οὐδ᾽ ἔλαβ᾽ ἐξέτασιν τῷ Φωκέος ἅτις ἐλέγχει
    τὸν φίλον· ἀλλ᾽ αἱ χ᾽ ἓν[4] δρᾶμ᾽ ἐδίδαξε μόνον,
5 ἢ τάχα κα[5] τὸν ἑταῖρον ἀπώλεσε· τοῦτο ποήσας
    κἠγὼ[6] τοὺς πολλούς[7] οὐκέτ᾽ ἔχω Πυλάδας.

[1] τἆλλα Ernesti: ταλα P   [2] λίαν Maas, Pfeiffer: ἀμάν
Schneider: μαν P   [3] μανίαν Ernesti: μανίην P
    [4] αἱ χ᾽ ἓν P: αἱ χῆν Davies   [5] κα Meineke: καὶ P
    [6] κἠγὼ Meineke: κἀγὼ P   [7] τούς πολλούς P: τὼς πολ-
λὼς Wilamowitz

60 (39 G.-P.) *Anth. Pal.* 7.523

Οἵτινες Ἀλείοιο[1] παρέρπετε σᾶμα[2] Κίμωνος,
    ἴστε τὸν Ἱππαίου παῖδα παρερχόμενοι.

[1] Ἀλείοιο Salm.: ἀλίοιο P   [2] σᾶμα Heringa: σῆμα P

61 (42 G.-P.) *Anth. Pal.* 7.725

Αἴνιε, καὶ σὺ γὰρ ὧδε, Μενέκρατες, οὐκ ἐπὶ πουλύ[1]
    ἦσθα, τί σε, ξείνων λῷστε[2], κατειργάσατο;
ἦ ῥα τὸ καὶ Κένταυρον; "ὅ μοι πεπρωμένος ὕπνος
    ἦλθεν, ὁ δὲ τλήμων οἶνος ἔχει πρόφασιν."

[1] οὐκ ἐπὶ πουλύ Zedel: οὐκέτι πουλύς P   [2] λῷστε Zedel:
ὥστε P

59 (59 G.-P.) *Palatine Anthology*

Happy was Orestes[1] of yesteryear, because mad in other respects, Leucare,[2] he was not mad with excessive madness, nor did he apply the test to the Phocian[3] that would prove his friendship. But if Orestes had produced just one drama, [5] he surely would have lost his companion when he had done it. I myself no longer have many friends like Pylades.

[1] Son of Clytemnestra and Agamemnon, brother of Electra, who murdered his mother after she had killed his father on his return from Troy. Afterward he was terrorized by the Erinyes until he was acquitted by the court of the Areopagus. His story is told in Aeschylus' *Oresteia* and Euripides' *Orestes*.

[2] Unknown, but possibly an Alexandrian dramatist.

[3] Pylades, Orestes' close friend, who was from the city of Phocis.

60 (39 G.-P.) *Palatine Anthology*

All you who pass the tomb of Cimon of Elis know that you are passing the son of Hippaeus.

61 (42 G.-P.) *Palatine Anthology*

Menecrates of Aenus,[1] you were not here for long. O best of friends, what did you in? Was it what did in the Centaur too?[2] "The fated sleep came to me, but miserable wine was the cause."

[1] City in Thrace, featured in *Iamb* 7 (*Ia*. 197.1).

[2] The Centaurs were notorious drunks (Hom. *Od*. 21.295–97).

CALLIMACHUS

62 (61 G.-P.) *Anth. Pal.* 6.121; *Anth. Plan.* [A], (ἄδηλον);
Suda κ 2317

Κυνθιάδες,[1] θαρσεῖτε, τὰ γὰρ τοῦ Κρητὸς Ἐχέμμα[2]
  κεῖται ἐν Ὀρτυγίῃ τόξα παρ' Ἀρτέμιδι,
οἷς ὑμέων ἐκένωσεν ὄρος μέγα, νῦν δὲ πέπαυται,
  αἶγες, ἐπεὶ σπονδὰς ἡ θεὸς εἰργάσατο.

[1] Κυνθιάδες *Suda*: κυνθίδες PPl
[2] Ἐχέμμα PPl: Ἐχέμμου C

63 (63 G.-P.) *Anth. Pal.* 5.23; *Anth. Plan.* [A], (τοῦ αὐτοῦ
[Ῥουφίνου])

Οὕτως ὑπνώσαις,[1] Κωνώπιον, ὡς ἐμὲ ποιεῖς
  κοιμᾶσθαι ψυχροῖς τοῖσδε παρὰ προθύροις.
οὕτως ὑπνώσαις, ἀδικωτάτη, ὡς τὸν ἐραστήν
  κοιμίζεις, ἐλέου δ' οὐδ' ὄναρ ἠντίασα.[2]
5 γείτονες οἰκτείρουσι, σὺ δ' οὐδ' ὄναρ· ἡ πολιὴ δέ
  αὐτίκ' ἀναμνήσει ταῦτά σε πάντα κόμη.

[1] ὑπνώσαις CPl: ὑπνήσαις P   [2] ἠντίασα Boiss.: ἠντία-
σας PPl

448

EPIGRAMS

62 (61 G.-P.) *Palatine Anthology*; *Planudean Anthology* [A], (authorship unclear); *Suda*

Cynthian[1] goats, buck up, for the bow of Cretan Echemmas is lying in Ortygia[2] at the temple of Artemis. With it he emptied the great mountain of you. But now he has ceased, since the goddess has arranged a truce.

[1] Cynthus, a hill on Delos known for its goats (*Hymn* 2.61).
[2] Old name of Delos (*Hymn* 2.59).

63 (63 G.-P.) *Palatine Anthology*; *Planudean Anthology* [A], (by the same [Rufinus])

So may you sleep, Conopion, as you make me sleep by this cold porch. So may you sleep, unfairest one, as you put to sleep your lover, who not even in my dreams has received pity. [5] The neighbors pity me, but you, not even in my dreams. Presently gray hair will remind you of all this.

CALLIMACHUS

FRAGMENTA EPIGRAMMATUM

1 (393 Pf.; 64 G.-P.)

a Diog. Laert. 2.111; Schol. ad Dion. Thrax (vol. 3, p. 192 Hilgard)

αὐτὸς ὁ Μῶμος
ἔγραφεν ἐν τοίχοις, "Ὁ Κρόνος ἐστὶ σοφός."

b Sext. Emp. *Math*. 1.309 (ἐπιγραμμάτιον . . . καθάπερ καὶ τὸ ὑπὸ Καλλιμάχου εἰς Διόδωρον τὸν Κρόνον συγγραφέν)

ἠνίδε καὶ[1] κόρακες τεγέων ἔπι "Κοῖα συνῆπται;"
κρώζουσιν καὶ "Κῶς αὖθι γενησόμεθα;"

[1] καὶ Fabricius: κου SE

2 (394 Pf.; 65 G.-P.)

a Ath. 7.284c

ἱερος δέ τοι, ἱερὸς ὕκης.

b Ath. 7.327a

θεὸς δέ οἱ ἱερὸς ὕκης.

FRAGMENTARY EPIGRAMS

1 (393 Pf.: 64 G.-P.)

a Diogenes Laertius; Scholia to Dionysius Thrax

Blame himself
wrote on the walls, "Cronus[1] is wise."

[1] The nickname of the Megaric philosopher Diodorus of Iasus, a contemporary of the poet's. It may mean "blockhead," as in Aristophanes (*Vesp.* 1480), or refer to Homer's "crooked-counseling" Cronus (*Il.* 2.205).

b Sextus Empiricus, *Against the Professors* (A casual epigram . . . just as was written by Callimachus against Diodorus Cronus)

See there even the crows on the roofs caw, "What conclusion follows?" and "How will we be again?"[1]

[1] The crows' comments refer to Diodorus' philosophical theory.

2 (394 Pf.; 65 G.-P.)

a Athenaeus, *The Learned Banqueters*

Sacred, the sacred fish[1]

[1] An unidentifiable fish called *hykēs*.

b Athenaeus, *The Learned Banqueters*

It is a god to him, the sacred fish.

CALLIMACHUS

3 (395 Pf.; 66 G.-P.) Steph. Byz. δ 140 Billerbeck s.v. Δύμη

Δύμη· πόλις Ἀχαίας ἐσχάτη πρὸς δύσιν ὅθεν καὶ Καλλίμαχος ἐν ἐπιγράμμασιν

εἰς Δύμην ἀπιόντα τὴν Ἀχαι[

4 (396 Pf.) Schol. ad Ov. *Ib*. 591

comicus ut liquidis periit dum nabat in undis: Menander comicus Atheniensis dum in Piraeeo portu nataret, submersus est, de quo nobilissimae a Graecis editae traduntur elegiae et a Callimacho epigramma.

5 (397 Pf.) Eustr. in Arist. *Eth. Nic.* 6.7.2 (*Comm. in Arist. Gr.* vol. 20, p. 320.38 Heylbut)

παράγει . . . εἰς μαρτυρίαν . . . καί τινα ποίησιν Μαργίτην ὀνομαζομένην Ὁμήρου. μνημονεύει δ᾽ αὐτῆς οὐ μόνον αὐτὸς Ἀριστοτέλης ἐν τῷ πρώτῳ Περὶ ποιητικῆς, ἀλλὰ καὶ Ἀρχίλοχος καὶ Κρατῖνος καὶ Καλλίμαχος ἐν τῷ ἐπιγράμματι καὶ μαρτυροῦσιν εἶναι Ὁμήρου τὸ ποίημα.

3 (395 Pf.; 66 G.-P.) Stephanus of Byzantium

Dume: an Achaean city in the far west, from which Callimachus says in his epigrams,

> going toward Dyme, the Achaean city

4 (396 Pf.) Scholia to Ovid, *Ibis*

as a comic poet perished while he was swimming in the watery waves: Menander, the Athenian comic poet, was drowned while he was swimming in the port of Piraeus, which the best known elegies produced by the Greeks recount, also an epigram by Callimachus.

5 (397 Pf.) Eustratius on Aristotle, *Nicomachean Ethics*

He introduces . . . as evidence . . . even a poem of Homer titled *Margites*. Aristotle not only mentions it himself in the first book of his *Poetics* (1448b30), but even Archilochus (fr. 303 West) and Cratinus (fr. 368 K.-A.) and Callimachus in an epigram, even they testify that the poem was written by Homer.

CALLIMACHUS

6 (398 Pf.; 67 G.-P.) *Vit. Dion. Per.* (Καλλίμαχος ἐν τοῖς ἐπιγράμμασι); Schol. ad Dionys. Per. 3 (Καλλίμαχος)

    Λύδη καὶ παχὺ γράμμα καὶ οὐ τορόν

7 (399 Pf.; 68 G.-P.) *Anth. Pal.* 13.9 (Καλλιμάχου πεντά-μετρον Βακχικόν ἔστι δὲ οὐ τέλειον τὸ ἐπίγραμμα); Hephaest. 19.1 Cons.; Schol. ad Heph. 271.12 sine nom.; om. *Anth. Plan.*

ἔρχεται πολὺς μὲν Αἰγαῖον διατμήξας¹ ἀπ᾽ οἰνηρῆς
    Χίου
ἀμφορεύς, πολὺς δὲ Λεσβίης² ἄωτον νέκταρ
    οἰνάνθης ἄγων.

  ¹ διατμήξας P: διανήξας Heph. et Schol. ad
  ² Λεσβίης Bentley: Λεσβίην P

6 (398 Pf.; 67 G.-P.) *Life of Dionysius Periegetes* (Callimachus in his *Epigrams*); Scholia to Dionysius Periegetes (Callimachus)

the *Lyde*,[1] a thick book and unclear

[1] An elegiac poem by Antimachus of Colophon (4th c. BC), praised by the epigrammatists Asclepiades (32 G.-P. = *Anth. Pal.* 9.63) and Posipippus (140 AB = 9 G.-P. = *Anth. Pal.* 12.168). They were consequently identified by the Florentine Scholia on the *Aetia* Prologue as Telchines, a name Callimachus gave to his literary rivals. In matters of style, "thick" is the opposite of Callimachus' "slender," and "unclear" contrasts with his preference for "pure."

7 (399 Pf.; 68 G.-P.) *Palatine Anthology* (the Bacchic [trochaic: corr. Bentley] pentameter by Callimachus is acatalectic); Hephaestion, anonymously; missing in the *Planudean Anthology*

Many jars come from wine-rich Chios, cleaving the Aegean, and many bringing nectar, the flower of Lesbian vines.

CALLIMACHUS

8 (400 Pf.; 69 G.-P.) *Anth. Pal.* 13.10 (τοῦ αὐτοῦ [Καλλι-
μάχου] τετράμετρον ἑκκαίδεκα συλλαβῶν, οὐδὲ τοῦ-
τον τέλειον); om. *Anth. Plan.*

ἁ ναῦς ἃ τὸ μόνον¹ φέγγος ἐμὶν² τὸ γλυκὺ τᾶς
   ζόας³
ἅρπαξας, ποτί τε ζανὸς⁴ ἱκνεῦμαι λιμενοσκόπω

¹ μόνον Bentley: μον P   ² ἐμὶν Bentley: εμειν P
³ ζόας Bentley: ζωᾶς P   ⁴ ζανὸς Bentley: Ζηνὸς P

9 (401 Pf.; 70 G.-P.) Heph. 64.4 Cons. sine nom.; id. 58.20
(τὸ Καλλιμάχειον τοῦτο ποιημάτιον)

Ἡ παῖς ἡ κατάκλειστος
τὴν οἵ φασι τεκόντες
εὐναίους ὀαρισμούς
ἔχθειν¹ ἶσον ὀλέθρῳ

¹ ἔχθειν Scaliger: ἔχειν Heph.

10 (402 Pf.) Caes. Bass. (*Gramm. Lat.* vol. 6, p. 255 Keil)

ithyphallicum metrum saepe recipit hunc tribrachum, ut
etiam apud Menandrum in *Phasmate* et apud Callima-
chum in epigrammatibus ostendi potest.